ROY SCHEIDER

To my husband, John Kachmar,
without whose love, support and help
this book would not have been possible

ROY SCHEIDER

A Film Biography

DIANE C. KACHMAR

McFarland & Company, Inc., Publishers
Jefferson, North Carolina, and London

The present work is a reprint of the illustrated case bound edition of Roy Scheider: A Film Biography, *first published in 2002 by McFarland.*

LIBRARY OF CONGRESS CATALOGUING-IN-PUBLICATION DATA

Kachmar, Diane C.
Roy Scheider : a film biography / Diane C. Kachmar.
Filmography p. cm.
Includes bibliographical references and index.

ISBN 978-0-7864-4059-7
softcover : 50# alkaline paper ∞

1. Scheider, Roy. 2. Motion picture actors and actresses—United States—Biography. I. Title.
PN2287.S332K33 2009
791.43'028'092—dc21 2002001092

British Library cataloguing data are available

Front cover: Roy Scheider as Sam Stoneman in *Sheila Levine Is Dead and Living in New York*, 1974 (Paramount Pictures)

Manufactured in the United States of America

McFarland & Company, Inc., Publishers
Box 611, Jefferson, North Carolina 28640
www.mcfarlandpub.com

Contents

Acknowledgments

I want to thank the director of libraries at Florida Atlantic University, Dr. William Miller, the assistant director for technical services, Janice Donahue and the assistant director for systems, Elaine Hyman, for giving me the support and resources to complete this book.

I would also thank my library colleagues for their encouragement and aid in my research, in particular, Rita Pellen, associate director of libraries; Ken Frankel, head of interlibrary loan; Dawn Smith, head of reference; Roberto Ferrari, head of circulation/CPM; Teresa Abaid, Maria Berenbaum, Linda Wiler, Anthony Verdesca, Dr. Helen Laurence, Karen Heinich, Dee Cael, David Pena, Margy Bullock, George Spozarsky, Joe DiLiddo, Amy Kornblau, Holly Hargett, Bill Armstrong, Robert Yunk, Fran Dilgen, Cathy Chesla, Julia Phillips, and Kenneth Kuby.

I wish to acknowledge my father and mother, Dan and Eleanor Farnsworth, my brother, Steve Farnsworth, and his wife, Sue, and my sister Nancy Cohen, who have always encouraged me in my writing. This project would not have come to fruition without Ed Erazo, Dr. Linda Golian, Nancy Wynen, John Seery, Katrina Larkin, Betsy Miller, Sandra Ballasch, Isabell Klein, Laurel Miller, Ellen Purdy, Jorge Fernandez, Sabine Biermann, Madeline F. Matz, and Ann Kenne.

Preface

This project began six years ago when a fellow librarian, Betsy Miller, asked me to find some interviews on Roy Scheider and send them to her. I found seven interviews in a quick search and duly forwarded them. I added more cites to the file as I found them and after three years I had 14 pages. I showed this file to another librarian, Angelica Carpenter, and she remarked that I had a book there. When McFarland and Company offered me the opportunity to write this book, I accepted the challenge.

Roy Scheider has made 50 films to date and has been a major film star for three decades, since his first film in 1964. Seven of Scheider's films are considered classics: *Klute, The French Connection, The Seven Ups, Jaws, Marathon Man, All That Jazz* and *Blue Thunder*. *Jaws* was the first movie to make $100 million at the box office. Twenty-five years later, the film remained on *Variety*'s Top 100 box office list. *Jaws* and *The French Connection* were included in the American Film Institute's Top 100 Films of the last 100 years in 1998. They were numbers 2 and 8, respectively, on the institute's June 2001 list of the 100 Most Thrilling Films ever made. These two films, along with *All That Jazz* and *Marathon Man,* were part of the "100 Years of Oscar's Favorite Movie Moments" tribute at the 71st Academy Awards ceremony in March 1999. The 20th anniversary of *All That Jazz* was December of 1999. The 25th Anniversary of *Jaws* was celebrated in June of 2000. September 2001 marked *The French Connection*'s 30th anniversary. Some firsts in Scheider's career include the inaugural made-for-cable film, *Tiger Town* (1983), one of the films shown on the first HBO Original Film Weekend, *Someone Has to Shoot the Picture* (1990), and the first film released over the Internet, *The Definite Maybe* (1999).

It is not always easy to find the real person under the "image" that Hollywood projects onto the big screen. As you turn these pages, I hope you will learn about Roy Scheider, not only as a movie star, but as a person with deep passions about life, his craft and the world around him.

Diane Kachmar
West Palm Beach, FL
Spring 2002

— 1 —

Early Influences

Roy Richard Scheider was born in East Orange, New Jersey, on November 10, 1932, to Anna S. (Crosson) and Roy Bernhard Scheider. His younger brother, Glenn, was described by Roy as "the sweet one. The good one. The athlete. I was the bad one. The black sheep." Roy's mother said, "I don't know where you come from. You're just not a Scheider."

The Scheiders were German immigrants. Roy's father was a third generation American. "He was Prussian all right. Strict! He ruled with an iron fist—often in motion."[1] "His word was *law*. If you didn't listen, you got a hard whack." His mother, on the other hand, "was *very* loving, almost femininely manipulative—she used soft words to keep my dad and me from ever really battling it out."[2]

The name Scheider is derived from the German verb *scheiden,* meaning to separate precious metals by chemical, electrolytical, or gravimetric means, like gold from lesser ores and silver from silver and lead ores. The profession dates back to the Middle Ages and was done predominantly in northern Germany.

Roy Bernhard Scheider worked as an auto mechanic and a part-time driving instructor. Later, he owned a gas station and garage. Anna was Irish. She left the Catholic church when it refused to grant her permission to marry a non-Catholic. Roy's father was a German Protestant, "a foreman in a Newark garage. She was ... working for the phone company. She got furious when they didn't think the man she loved was good enough. They got married at the Little Church around the Corner—the ... actor's church."[3] Whatever his parents' religious problems were, Roy solved his own early on. "Am I religious? No, I was brought up in a Protestant, churchgoing family, but then—without any action either way on the part of my parents—I just quit going to church. I just stopped believing. I don't feel a need for more belief."[4]

Roy was tested early in his life. At six years of age he was diagnosed with rheumatic fever: "When I was a kid, the treatment was bed rest, all the joints wrapped in cotton and you had to stay like that until your temperature went down." Roy's first attack lasted a year, and he was not diagnosed as free of the disease until he was 17, by which time, his lack of physical activity had made Roy "the fattest kid in school."[5] "When I was in grammar school and high school, I was short and fat, the last guy chosen on every team. That's a pain in the ass, always being last."[6] Roy attended the Chancellor Avenue grammar school in Irvington, New Jersey.[7] "When I was eight, I began working [at my father's gas station] on the weekends. I was driving cars around that place when I was 11 and I was making more pocket money than my friends. But what I ... wanted to do was go swimming with all the other kids."[8]

The rheumatic fever returned two more times, when Roy was 10 and 15. Roy has spoken many times about being a fat adolescent and hating himself because he weighed 190 pounds from his enforced bed rest. His mother, Anna, was his nurse and because of the fever's threat to his heart, Roy was watched very closely. Anna also liked to clean, so she kept his bedroom spotless. His bed was always made, even when he was lying in it. This practice left Roy unable to abide cluttered surroundings or sloppy piles of magazines or clothes lying around. The fever attacks lasted as long as 11 months at a time. Roy went to school in between, but his activities were restricted. Scheider had to be in bed at 7:00 P.M. and he wasn't allowed to run, ever. Roy was given permission to go to the movies, however, because there he could sit: "Every Saturday I went to the matinee in Irvington and my parents always took me along on Thursday, their night out at the movies. I sat in the front row, eating popcorn, with my feet propped up on the brass rail and my eyes glued on the screen. I dreamed and the movies took me to the South Seas, to all the places I wanted to go."[9]

His favorite actor was Spencer Tracy. Other movie stars who were role models for him were James Cagney, Lana Turner, Madeleine Carroll, and Tyrone Power. Those long hours of being bedridden had one benefit. They gave Scheider his "actor's imagination."[10] "My fantasy world was extraordinary. There was nothing I couldn't do. But in the real world I didn't do anything. I didn't ride a bicycle until I was 16."[11]

In August 1999, in a speech at the inaugural Hayground Circle scholarship benefit, Roy told the audience how important reading was to him during his enforced periods of bed rest: "While my parents were not readers, they brought me books. I escaped into those books and they helped me keep my sanity. If I hadn't been a reader, I would have gone crazy. The only escape was in books and in my imagination."[12] Writers were his heroes. Scheider read anything: comic books, junk, books from the library, books from relative and friends. He found Melville, Hemingway, and Fitzgerald in his late teens. "Books were [my] refuge when [I] was sick. Book buying [remains a] great joy."[13] He knew he had a fate, a destiny, and that he would survive the fever. He didn't know if he was going to be president or a writer or a lawyer, but he wasn't going to stay in that bed. There were places to go, and Roy wanted to see them all.

His family moved during Scheider's childhood from Orange, New Jersey, to nearby Livingston. They then moved to Maplewood, New Jersey, where Roy graduated from Columbia High School in 1950.[14] "At 17, [Roy] was finally pronounced cured and ... was given carte blanche to live a normal life. He went out and [did] all the things he had never been able to do. Swimming, playing baseball, boxing and dating girls."[15]

Scheider spent the first couple of months after graduation at the Jersey shore, running on the sand and letting the waves pound him to lose weight. When he came home, his father introduced him to a middleweight fighter, who took him to the YMHA and taught Roy how to box. Classed as a welterweight at 140 pounds, he was fairly fast and had a good left. Entered into the 1951 Jersey Diamond Gloves Tourney, Roy won his first match. He was knocked out in his second bout, and his nose was broken. Later in life, this injury was repaired with plastic surgery, which removed damaged cartilage, but he insisted the surgeon not change the shape of his nose and leave the bump. That bump marks him as a man who has struggled and survived and is as central to his movie-star persona as Barbra Streisand's and Robert DeNiro's noses are to theirs. On the molding of his now famous-visage, Roy said, "It was broken twice ... when I was a baby and I fell against a curb and then again when I was 17. I was boxing."[16]

Losing weight was crucial as a young adult: "I never went to high school dances or football games. I remained an outsider until I lost thirty pounds."[17] Scheider acted in his high school's production of Mary Robert Rinehart's *The Bat* and found a girlfriend: "We dated every Saturday. We'd go to a movie ... the soda shop, and then neck in the car until one or two in the morning—she didn't go all the way. But I ... sure as hell was tryin'."[18]

Roy Scheider's outspoken, stubborn father, Roy Bernhard Scheider, was a major influence in his life. Scheider had a difficult relationship with his dad for many years. He wanted his father's love and approval and felt strongly that he never got it. Scheider described his father as a man who could not say "I love you" easily and who would only say nice things about his son to other people. As the eldest son, with all of the burdens of expectation, Roy wanted to please his father, but never felt he did. Scheider's father passed away in the late 1970s after suffering two strokes. His mother, Anna, died in the 1980s.

To Roy, his father was full of contradictions. His dad hated everyone who was African-American, Catholic, Jewish, or Communist. Yet he married a Catholic, was friendly to the Jews who owned stores beside his service station, and went to an African-American dentist. The elder Scheider also employed African-Americans at his gas station. Yet Roy's father thought nothing of using derogatory epithets in front of his children. The first time Scheider saw Archie Bunker on television, Roy didn't find him at all amusing. He was with his father all over again.

Scheider credits Arthur Miller with finally helping him understand his contrary father. After Roy saw *Death of a Salesman*, there was no way he could ever see his father the same way again. The movie made his father a human being. After that, Scheider knew his father loved him more than he had ever imagined. Until then, Roy had only thought of him as a guy who told him what to do all the time, an ogre he had to deal with every day. This understanding, however, did nothing to alleviate Scheider's problem. He continued to feel shut out and unloved. Roy Senior considered himself an authority on everything. The only form of communication available to his son was argument. His father expressed love by arguing, fighting, and screaming. "My father ... was a strict disciplinarian. He ... beat the hell out of me. My biggest crime was ... disagreeing with him. I realized [as an adolescent] that [what] my father [told me] was not particularly true. I [took] the abuse in order to ... let him know he wasn't fooling me. My mother ... never [stood up for me]."[19]

"I learned from my father ... to be very critical. If I'm not careful, I'm very destructive."[20] "To this day, if I read an editorial or a piece in the paper that particularly supports a position I've always held, my first impulse is to cut it out, or call [my father] up, but of course, he's not here anymore."[21] Roy's father was openly derisive of his son's interest in books and movies. Law was going to be young Roy's career, whether he wanted it or not. It was enough that his father told him to do it.

Another major influence in Roy Scheider's young adult life was an African-American employee at his father's gas station, Friend Avery. In 1997, Roy Scheider named Avery as his first mentor in an original program he produced to raise the money to build the Hayground multicultural alternative school. After Avery's death in 1998, Roy endowed a scholarship in his name at Hayground and planted a tree there in his memory.[22] During the mentor program, Scheider described Avery as "the man who provided a sense of joy and support that ... he never found in his own father." Roy recalled how he was able, in return, to give Avery the affection he could not show his father. This early relationship "helped validate me."[23] Another idol of Scheider's youth was Willie Mays, the baseball player. What drew Roy was Willie's love of the game and how Mays played, not only with grace, but with joy. Fred Astaire was someone else Roy admired, mostly because Astaire danced with the same joy and grace Mays had on the baseball diamond.

Scheider enjoyed driving into New York City with his buddies. At 16 and 17, they would take someone's father's car—any one that was available—to go hear black musicians play jazz in the nightclubs. Scheider became a lifelong fan of jazz music. One boyhood friend remembered they drove "a blue Packard." When asked if he liked jazz music, the man replied, "We liked beer."[24] Scheider dreamed of living in New York after he finished college, as either a lawyer or a writer.

With his childhood illness behind him, his weight problem overcome, and a high school diploma in hand, Roy was ready to fulfill his parents' dream of sending their firstborn to college. They had all scrimped and saved for years for the money. Roy had worked several jobs, when he could, beginning with helping out at his father's garage.

Roy enrolled at Rutgers University and took the bus from Maplewood each day. He didn't particularly like living at home or the bus ride, but he persevered, joining the drama club and doing radio.[25] Roy made the college wrestling team. "I was the best of two 148 pound wrestlers on a half-baked team. I'd wrestle the [other] guy every week to see who would [compete against] the rival school. I knew I could beat him [but] I wasn't [that] good, either." Then there was the match with a blind African-American wrestler from CCNY that Scheider lost. "Fastest pin in America!"[26]

Roy met some students from Franklin and Marshall College in Lancaster, Pennsylvania. In his sophomore year, Scheider transferred to the liberal arts school. His second month there, he saw a performance of *Billy Budd*. Roy immediately signed up for the drama group as one of his extracurricular activities and was cast in the next production of the Green Room Club, *Knight of the Burning Pestle*.[27] He won the role of Humphrey, the comic suitor, in this musical comedy. His listing in the program stated that *Knight* was his Franklin and Marshall debut and named *The Bat*—his high school play—as his only theatrical credit to date.[28] This was the genesis of Roy R. Scheider, stage actor. "[In] *Coriolanus* ... I played an eighty-year-old senator. I liked the atmosphere. I liked being there at night. I found a home."[29]

Scheider credited Green Room with changing his life, saying he was more happy during the three hours they rehearsed every evening than he was anyplace else. "I was spending more time in the theater than ... any other place—including the bars. I really liked it, and I felt that people ... liked me doing it. [They were] good roles, mostly comedies. Like Ensign Pulver in *Mr. Roberts*, parts nobody dreams I would ... play now."[30] When he read the letter at the end of *Mr. Roberts*, Roy felt the power of his performance. He had the whole audience in the palm of his hand. That was the moment Scheider knew he had to be an actor.

"I had found a base ... that gave me a great deal of satisfaction and a lot of self-enjoyment and strangely enough, a kind of security that allowed ... my personality to improve and expand in all other directions. Acting for me was such a healthy thing ... it was a good thing."[31] Working in the Green Room Club productions brought Scheider under the influence of Darrell Larsen, the director of the theater at Franklin and Marshall. Larsen was a burly, chain-smoking man, built like Orson Welles. He found an apt pupil in Roy. Another college influence was Richard Gehman, a successful magazine writer of the 1950s and 1960s, who was then married to Estelle Parsons. Gehman and Parsons both encouraged Scheider in 1954 when Gehman wrote the play notes for the Green Room Club programs.

Darrell Larsen was a member of the Theater Guild during the Depression and worked as an actor and reader. When jobs became scarce in New York City, Larsen took an assistant professorship at Franklin and Marshall. The college liked him so much they built him a theater. Scheider described Larsen as someone right out of *The Man Who Came to Dinner*. In fact, he always thought Larsen looked like Alexander Woolcott: a big guy with a cigarette holder, who had ashes spilling down his chest and tended to be drunk all the time. Larsen was multisexual, a decadent-looking theater person who was also pragmatic and practical. "He was a curious blend of very well-read academic [and] wonderful theater teacher with a heart always in New York, so he'd go see every damn show every season, so he knew what was going on. His head wasn't buried in academic stuff."[32]

By his junior year, Scheider was vying for lead roles in the club, and in his senior year he played them. Roy Scheider appeared in nine Green Room Club productions in his two and a half years at Franklin and Marshall College. He performed in *Knight of the Burning Pestle* (Humphrey), March 5–14, 1953; *Stalag 17* (Reed), May 7–16, 1953; *The Tragedy of Coriolanus* (Sicinius Velutus), November 11–21, 1953; *The Good Fellow* (Jim Helton), March 5–15, 1954; *Mister Roberts* (Ensign Pulver), May 5–15, 1954; *Darkness at Noon* (Ivanoff), November 15–20, 1954; *Philoctetes* (Odysseus) and *The Tragedy of Tragedies* (King Arthur), March 9–19, 1955; and *My Three Angels* (Joseph), May 11–21, 1955.[33] Scheider also joined the Psi Kappa Psi fraternity, and continued wrestling.[34] He enrolled in the Air Force's ROTC program to stay out of the Korean War. Two years in a row he won the Theresa Helburn–John Baker Opdycke Acting Award.

A New York Theater Guild luminary, Theresa Helburn had endowed the acting award for the Green Room Club in 1954. John Opdycke was a successful writer of grammar books. The award paid for Scheider to come to New York, see three plays, and then visit backstage with the actors to learn the mechanics of the production. Roy tied with classmate Dick Orkin for this honor in 1954, for two years of work, and then won again in 1955. Scheider enjoyed his trips to New York immensely. He quickly became a favorite of Helburn. "I was brought to her apartment in New York, where she would serve these awful martinis."[35]

By the time Roy graduated with his pre-law B.A. in history in June 1955, he was a veteran Green Room Club performer. Scheider became president of the Green Room Club his senior year.[36] His last Green Room program listing noted,

"[Roy] has [been] in every play since the winter of 1953 ... in a wide range of styles both classic and modern and [has] been tremendously effective in all of them. He is one of the most talented actors we have ever had."[37] "One of the pleasures in regularly attending [Green Room plays] is watching the development of our student actors. [Consider] Roy Scheider. His ... talent was obvious ... [and] the development and control of that talent [was] fascinating ... to watch. With each performance he became more deft ... assured [and] more completely the character."[38]

"All my [acting] training was extracurricular, but I did learn a lot about movement and developing a character in three years. It wasn't so much that I wanted to be an actor. I realized in my senior year ... I was an actor. I had found a place that felt comfortable."[39] Roy decided to make acting his life's vocation. He believed his notices. "I didn't even say I want to be an actor—I had a feeling I was an actor."[40] "While [my parents] were proud of my theatrical accomplishments," he remembers, "they suggested that I forget acting and become a rich lawyer. I know I would have been a rich, *unhappy* lawyer."[41] Roy broke the news to his parents in a hotel room in Lancaster, Pennsylvania, the night before graduation. He told them he wasn't going on to law school. Scheider relates that there was a long silence, and then his father told him he was a "damn fool."[42] "He was aghast," Scheider remembers.[43] "My father practically disowned me when I announced I was going to be an actor—not a lawyer. He had worked hard putting me through college and he thought I [shouldn't] give up law."[44]

Roy had talked with his mentor, Darrell Larsen. Larsen wasn't that encouraging, telling Scheider (who is 5 foot 10) that he wasn't exceptionally tall, handsome, or leading man material, but that he thought Scheider could make a living acting. Later, Roy definitely felt he had made the right choice, claiming that except at the very beginning of his career, he was never out of work. He could play anything, young or old, Irish, Spanish, or Jewish. He was never limited in range by what he looked like. Acting was pure adventure, his way of living life on the sword's edge. There was only one obstacle left to Roy's newfound ambition. In 1955, the Air Force ROTC program called in the three-year service debt that Scheider owed.

— 2 —

Delayed Ambition

His career path now set, Roy appeared on two New York TV shows, the "US Steel Hour" under the auspices of the Theater Guild[1] and "Studio One" on CBS.[2] Roy also did summer stock at the Pocono Playhouse,[3] before the Air Force called him in to repay his service debt.

Details of Scheider's Air Force career are sketchy. Roy wasn't crazy about being drafted for the Korean War and getting shot at, so he had joined the ROTC in college to stay out of it. After college he owed Uncle Sam three years. Roy made first lieutenant during his time in the Air Force, but washed out of flight school after six weeks in Lackland, Texas, because he couldn't master the math needed to do navigation at night. He became an air traffic controller and was transferred to Oregon. Roy also served in North Dakota. Scheider managed to keep acting, if only in Air Force training films,[4] but freely admitted he wasn't officer material. He recalled that during one inspection, checking to see if the beds were made correctly, it was pointed out to him that he wasn't wearing his lieutenant's bars.

While in Oregon, Scheider became active in the local community theater. One night, at a party for the theater, he met a married surgical nurse. Phyllis worked at the University of Oregon Hospital. Her former married name has never been mentioned. Her marriage was already in trouble and her relationship with Scheider ended it. When Phyllis was granted her divorce, Roy married her and adopted her two boys. Scheider received his discharge in 1959, but remained in the Air Force reserve. He gathered up his new family, put them in a Volkswagen, and returned to New Jersey, where they settled in an apartment in East Orange. She got a job right away and he didn't, which was partly the reason their marriage didn't last. Roy was positive he could get acting work in New York, but it was slow going. He didn't know anyone and his saturnine face did not lend itself to the leading man parts he desired. Roy had never done any stage work in New York, so no one wanted to hire him.

He had planned to ask Theresa Helburn for a job initially, but she died a few months before his discharge.[5] "When I was in the Air Force, I used to get letters from [Helburn] saying things like, 'I know it rains a lot up there, be sure and wear your rubbers'—like from my mother! I thought, hell, when I get back to New York, I'll walk right into the Theatre Guild, and I'll be on Broadway in two weeks. Well, she died."[6]

Roy did odd jobs to earn money. He worked as a building superintendent/janitor.[7] His prolonged lack of success as an actor strained the marriage. He couldn't support them, and his wife's job was what they lived on. Scheider claimed he did love Phyllis, but he didn't love her enough to sacrifice his acting career. So Roy gave her all the money he had and the car and told her the marriage was over. "I [wanted] to be an actor, but I had no idea ... what it [would] take. After three years, the drive to be an actor overpowered [being] a husband and a father. I ... killed it. That's the one thing I can't forget. I [had] a responsibility. I didn't fulfill it."[8] Phyllis granted his divorce, moved back to Oregon, and refused to speak to him after that. Roy persevered, finding acting work wherever he could. He spent at least part of the summer of 1959 "as a member of the resident company of the Legion Star Playhouse of Ephrata."[9] This was a playhouse in Pennsylvania, about 10 miles northeast of Franklin and Marshall College. In 1960, Roy returned to Franklin and Marshall to star in a student production of *Richard III*. The new Green Room Club director cast him as the lead. Edward Brubaker was a former faculty advisor who had appeared in several plays with Scheider when Roy was a student at Franklin and Marshall, including *Knight of the Burning Pestle*, *Coriolanus*, and *Mister Roberts*.[10]

It may have been "the winter of his discontent," but after two years of struggling to make a name for himself, Roy Scheider's acting fortune was about to change. *Richard III* opened in the middle of a snowstorm on March 3, 1960. Roy received a rave review from Sam Taylor in the local paper: "Scheider ... came up with the most malevolent, scheming and cunning character to chill and thrill a local audience. With terrifying accuracy, he pinpointed the faults and strengths of the ... deformed Duke [and] succeeded ... in engendering a real hate, [and] a scornful sympathy. Great [inadequately describes] his performance."[11]

Word spread and the last five performances of the run played to standing room only, making the play a financial as well as an artistic smash.[12] Unbeknown to Roy, that first night there was an actor in the audience named Dennis King. "King ... was moved to send a telegram to ... *The New York Times*. 'A brilliant performance by an unknown actor in the title kept me in my seat until the end. The young man has a tremendous gift. His name is Ray Schneider [*sic*].'"[13]

Scheider said, "This English actor [King] in a touring company came to see it and came back raving about it was the best *Richard III* he ever saw. He wrote a letter to Sam Zolotow, who was doing the theater column for *The New York Times*. Sam Zolotow printed the whole goddam letter. Joe Papp read it, called me up in New Jersey and had me come over to audition [at the old Central Plaza]. I did my *Richard III* and wound up playing Mercutio. That was my first professional job in New York. My understudy was James Earl Jones."[14]

Roy was not cast in the Central Park festival, but was hired for another troupe that spent from February to May 1961 doing *Romeo and Juliet* in the high schools of New York as part of a city grant. He was proud to be in the first show Papp took on a tour all over the city. Henry Hewes wrote, "During the early part of 1961, Mr. Papp staged a production of

Romeo and Juliet in some of the city's high schools. Paul Roebling's vulnerably romantic Romeo and Kathleen Widdoes' petite and noble Juliet drew applause for their deaths, which the students explained as being their appreciation of the fact that unlike movies or TV, the theater allowed things to end unhappily as they do in life. And Roy Schneider's [*sic*] Mercutio was so amusing that the youngsters laughed even at his dying speeches. But what pleased them the most was Juliet's father's anguish at her 'death' after being so strict the previous scene."[15] Roy's last name would continue to be misspelled in print (as above) throughout his long career.

Howard Taubman went to a performance at the Charles Evans Hughes High School: "There were roars of laughter when ... the nurse whacked Mercutio with her fan and when Mercutio and Benvolio hunted Romeo in the night ... but these reactions ... were not nearly as impressive as the silence for Mercutio's Queen Mab speech. Roy Scheider is a lively Mercutio."[16] The cast included James Earl Jones as Gregory and the Apothecary. Roy's billing indicated he was not yet a member of Actor's Equity.

In the summer of 1961, Roy got his second job. Kenneth Barrow chronicled, "Early in 1961, Lawrence Langner was asked by the State Department to organize a theater company for a tour abroad. Langner asked Helen (Hayes) if she would care to recreate her Mrs. Antrobus in *The Skin of Our Teeth*. The only drawback was she would also have to play Amanda in *The Glass Menagerie*. Langner was adamant that this was the program of plays which best projected the view of American life and theater they wished to convey and which fitted with the third play, *The Miracle Worker*, which was also to be toured. So Helen played her least favorite role in thirty different countries in Europe, Asia, and South America in 1961."[17]

The tour was in two parts with a break in between, and Scheider worked hard to get hired: At that time, the Theatre Guild had just had a very successful tour in Europe with Helen Hayes and Mary Martin in *Skin of Our Teeth*. Now they were planning a tour of South America. Lawrence Langner, Theresa Helburn's partner, was holding auditions and I couldn't get any place. One day I went storming into his office and said, "You mean to tell me that, if Theresa Helburn was alive, the two-time winner of the Theresa Helburn award couldn't get a goddam job?" They handed me the tiny part of the telegraph boy in *Skin of Our Teeth*, made me stage manager and understudy for about twelve parts and I was off on a three-month tour.[18] The tour lasted from August 7 to October 28, 1961.[19]

Helen Hayes recalled, "We set off on the second part of our tour, in Central America and Mexico. Our last stop was Mexico City, where we opened at the Bellas Artes, the Palace of Fine Arts. We were all weary after that tour, but any one of us would have happily done it again. It was an exhilarating experience. Our shows were treated as cultural events by the host countries. Audiences seemed to appreciate our plays, and if they didn't always understand everything, they could at least follow the action."[20]

Scheider went all over the country for the next few years. He could not get work in New York if they didn't know who he was, so Roy went wherever he could play the biggest and most difficult parts. He appeared at the Boston Arts Festival, then worked at the Shakespeare Festival in Stratford, Connecticut, the McCarter Theater in Princeton, New Jersey, and the Arena Stage in Washington, D.C. "I wasn't interested in starting off with small roles in the New York theater. An actor learns more from a large part in a stock company than he does in a small part on Broadway."[21] "When I started out in 1960, I was able to get work in repertory because of my face."

His sharp features were said to resemble those of a Renaissance prince. "I could play Italians, Turks, almost anything, so I could [do] all three plays—during a repertory season."[22] "[I played in] almost every repertory company up and down the East Coast. De Classics, nuttin' but the classics. Ben Jonson, Moliere, Shakespeare."[23] Two other plays Scheider mentioned doing during this time were *Kiss Me, Kate* and *The Gazebo*.[24] I could not find any mention of Roy's work at the Boston Arts Festival, but there were reviews of some of the other plays he did in 1962.

"*The Duchess of Malfi* ... opened ... the season ... [at McCarter] as the first play of the winter-spring drama series in March of 1962 [and the series] ran for seven weeks." Howard Taubman observed, "Roy R. Scheider makes Ferdinand properly demonic." The other three plays were *Merchant of Venice, The Alchemist,* and *Knight of the Burning Pestle*.[25]

This project was similar to the New York high school tour the previous year. The mission was to provide professional-caliber performances for drama students to study, make living theater available to the community at large, and put on matinees for the students in the schools. Some of these schoolchildren were bused in from as far away as Cape May. This was Scheider's second time doing *Knight of the Burning Pestle.* His billing as Roy R. Scheider made this his first performance as a member of Actor's Equity. Scheider used this form of his name for all of his stage work during this period and in two films.

Roy's stint at the American Shakespeare Festival at Stratford, Connecticut, lasted from June 12 to September 16, 1962. Henry Hewes wrote, "[The festival] ... suffered chronicle [*sic*] complaints as it attempted to stage *Richard II* and *Henry IV, Part 1.* Luckily, Helen Hayes and Maurice Evans, offering excerpts from Shakespeare, proved a great enough drawing card to save the season financially."[26] Arthur Gelb reviewed both plays. He did not care for *Richard II* and was scathing in his remarks about star Richard Basehart and the production in general, with the exception of Philip Bosco's Bolingbroke. Gelb concluded that the production was "a not-very-near miss."[27] Roy R. Scheider, playing Sir Henry Green,[28] was spared his wrath by not being mentioned.

The following night, Gelb was more effusive about *Henry IV*, praising several performers by name, except for Hal Holbrook as Hotspur. Roy's notice mentioned the engaging love scene with Mortimer (attractively played by Roy R. Scheider) and his shy wife (played with delicacy by Anne Fielding)."[29] Gelb took notice of Scheider again in a third review: "It is gratifying ... to find actors like James Ray,... James Valentine, Roy R. Scheider and Richard Waring in the ... company. But their assured performances only make others in the troupe look worse."[30]

Stratford quickly became important in Roy's personal life. He met a young actress in the supporting company of footmen and ladies named Cynthia Eddenfield Bebout. It was not love at first sight. Roy had been with the festival all summer, and Cynthia joined in midseason, as an understudy for the female leads. She knew a lot about Shakespeare and immediately struck up friendships with everybody except him; he thought she seemed a little tough and unapproachable. So he crossed her off his list of desirable bed partners for the season.

A few weeks later, Scheider was in the local pub where everyone went for a drink after the show. Cynthia was in a booth with a guy and Roy was standing at the bar. He happened to notice she was looking at him. They exchanged glances. He looked away and when he looked back, she was still looking at him. Then Cynthia picked up her beer and poured it over the head of the guy she was with. He stormed out. Roy left the bar, walked over to her table, and demanded, "What did you do that for?" She replied, "To get you to come over here." He said, "You're kidding!" She answered, "You're here, aren't you?" So he sat down and, as he was fond of saying later, never got up.

Cynthia had seen him play Shakespeare the year before, in Joseph Papp's *Romeo and Juliet*, but did not remember it until three years after they were married. During that summer, "she took Roy up to Ontario to see how the Bard should really be done."[31] One other event of note took place: "I received my [Air Force] reserve captaincy in the dressing room of the Shakespeare Festival in Stratford, Connecticut. And everyone fell on the floor."[32]

Cynthia was cast as a lady-in-waiting. Her costume had a long train and every night another actress would deliberately step on her train. Bebout spoke to the other actress about it, with no result. So she asked Roy what to do. He said, warn her one more time and if she steps on the train again, tell her you'll punch her right in the mouth. Cynthia was surprised by the advice and her only reservation was that the other actress was larger than she was. Roy's solution was to give Cynthia 15 minutes of boxing lessons. That night, after her warning, it happened again. Bebout marched to the dressing room after the end of the play and whacked the actress right in the mouth. Later, in the pub, this same girl, not having learned anything, laughed at Cynthia again, and this time she was thoroughly punched out! Roy laughed hysterically at this, very pleased that Cynthia was not afraid to take care of herself.

Roy's next job brought him to Washington, D.C., to do plays with the resident Arena Stage Acting Company, which included Rene Auberjonois, Alan Oppenheimer, and Robert Prosky. The Arena Stage presented seven productions for 28 performances each during the 1962-63 season. *Once in a Lifetime* by George S. Kaufman and Moss Hart was staged beginning October 23. It is the only play of this season that listed Roy Scheider as a cast member, even though he appeared in three others. Henry Hewes recorded, "Artistically, the season was not a satisfying one for the Arena, where flat and unexciting performances were more the rule than the exception."[33] *Once in a Lifetime* was the only play reviewed in the *New York Times*.[34] Howard Taubman's review was favorable, but Roy was not mentioned in it. Scheider appeared in four of the first five plays and left in March before the last three plays were staged.[35] Roy's other roles were "Mosca in *Volpone*, The Ad Man in *12 Angry Men*, and an IRA Officer in *The Hostage*."[36]

After seven months of living together, Cynthia had enough of that arrangement and Roy agreed to get married. Marriage wasn't exactly what Scheider had in mind. He enjoyed the gypsy life of a stage performer and didn't want family tying him down. "I never wanted roots."[37] But Cynthia Bebout became the second Mrs. Scheider on November 8, 1962.[38] "I gave Cynthia a South American woolly monkey for a wedding present."[39] They kept the monkey as a pet until their baby daughter was born in 1964.

Del Tenney persuaded Scheider, while he was still working at the Arena, to come to Connecticut and costar in a low-budget Victorian horror film called *The Curse of the Living Corpse* with a cast that included Candace Hilligoss. The budget was so small that when asked about the movie much later in his career, Roy jokingly remarked that the film "was made for $1.50."[40] Scheider received second billing. "That was the first film I ever did. I ... thought: 'What a great way to learn how to be on a film.' I did that picture for $3.50 up at the estate of the architect [Gutzon

The Curse of the Living Corpse **(1964, 20th Century–Fox). The funeral march to the crypt. Philip: Roy R. Scheider; Hugh: Robert Milli; James Benson: Hugh Franklin; Robert: Dino Narizzano; Mother: Helen Waren; Deborah: Candace Hilligoss; Vivian: Margot Hartman; Seth: J. Frank Lucas. Three uncredited extras.**

Borglum] who did Mount Rushmore. It was great fun!"[41]

"It [was made in] three weeks. I played the heavy. I killed ... eight people. I wanted to learn [my] craft [by working] in as many things as [I] possibly [could]."[42] Roy played Philip Sinclair. The basics of the simple plot are that the old master of the house has died and unless the terms of his will are specifically carried out, he will return from the grave to take revenge. No one really believes the threat, until members of the family start dying.

Scheider has dual roles in this film: a visible one as Philip, the weak, consumptive, alcoholic second son, who is no good for anything but drink, and a concealed one as "the living corpse" of his father come back to life. Roy was hidden by a large black hat and cape, with a muffler wrapped around his face. Only his eyes showed, so the movie audience wouldn't know he was the murderer until the end of the movie. Scheider played both parts extremely well. Philip was a pathetic, whining wimp who no one believed would murder anyone. Scheider gave "the corpse" a very physical menace as he stalked and killed without mercy. Roy's performance brings Basil Rathbone to mind with his deadly sword cane and sweeping cloak.

Scheider wrote a one-page essay entitled "Starring in a Horror" about his experience:

> When they started this film, they went to the film library in New York, picked out all the titles of horror films that had made big money and from this list put together the three most popular words—"corpse," "living," and "curse." First they wrote the title,

> then they wrote the script. Anyway, as an actor who'd never done a movie, I couldn't pass it up. Not only that, but the script was the most outrageous thing I'd ever read in my life. I played the drunken-sot-weakling-brother. I got the opportunity to ... wear an outfit that looked like something out of *The Shadow*; move around the house for an entire hour and a half with the audience unaware I was the villain. At the end, when I'm found out, there is a tremendous battle in a quicksand bog, and I sink in it, and die. Every fantasy, every dream, every kind of horror story I ever imagined as a young man, I got to act out in one movie. This film has become a minor classic in that it plays on network television, in almost every major American city, on Halloween, usually about two o'clock in the morning. I've had friends call me up from San Francisco, New Orleans, Mexico City and say, "Oh, Roy, what I'm watching on my TV set! It's just terrific. And look how young you look, how strange!" This turkey has haunted me for fifteen years.[43]

Curse was released on a double bill in 1964 at the Paramount Theatre in New York City as the B picture to *The Horror of Party Beach*. Eugene Archer wrote, "[The] supposed corpse kills several members of his family. The most curious aspect ... is why after the first few homicides, the rest of the victims linger ... waiting for the worst. Audiences lured into the theater may ask themselves the same thing."[44]

The body count is impressive. The mother is burned alive in her bed. The brother is dragged to death by a horse. The maid's decapitated head is served for breakfast on a platter. The family groom is stabbed through the throat by Philip's sword cane. Philip's unfaithful wife, Vivian, is strangled and left floating in her bathtub. Philip dies in the quicksand bog, trying to drag his nephew Robert's wife into it. Deborah is rescued by Robert.

For publicity, Tenney persuaded Richard Burton and Elizabeth Taylor to attend the New York premiere as a joke. Audiences were also asked to sign fright releases before being allowed to watch the movie.[45] Some online reviews for this movie were done years after the fact, part of the cult following that Del Tenney's films have generated since their release.

Bad Movie Report stated:

> [*Curse*] serves as sort of a bridge between all the Reading of the Will in the Old Dark House movies of the 1930s to the body count movies of the 1980s, with its surprisingly intense, if fleeting, low-gore effects. The sense of period is well-maintained throughout, and if the dialogue gets a little florid, well ... chances are people really didn't talk like that in 1892, but they *should* have. The acting is also universally good. Scheider, though at an embryonic stage [in] his onscreen career, is rock solid, Milli and Franklin went on to do a lot of soap opera and TV work. Overall, [*Curse*] is a good, competent (if formulaic) little horror film, with only the occasional piece of less-than-sterling camera work ruining the mood. It's a shame that of all Tenney's films, this one is the hardest to find.[46]

The Astounding B Monster noted that *Curse* was shown in Disney theme park restaurants and later purchased by the Sci Fi channel (according to Del Tenney). Sci Fi aired the film on Halloween in 1993. This website had an interview with Tenney and offered its own critique:

> Del Tenney's limited but lasting body of cult film work is worth recounting as much for its economic ingenuity as for any intrinsic merit. With budgets pared to the bone, he delivered a handful of thrillers that are vividly recalled by those who saw them at an impressible [*sic*] age. Tenney turned [Borglum's] Connecticut spread into an admirably ambient Victorian setting. Detailing the varied and grizzly [*sic*] deaths of several members of a vindictive New England clan, the film's graphic chills are handily exploited by a young Roy Scheider (his screen debut) and Candace (*Carnival of Souls*) Hilligoss.[47]

The Curse of the Living Corpse. **A cloaked Philip strangles Vivian. Philip: Roy R. Scheider; Vivian: Margot Hartman.**

The poster art is lurid, mid–1960s, drive-in fare. "From Out of the Grave Stalks the Creature that Undrapes the Passions of the Living," it says, but curiously does not have credits. A female, not the dead father, is shown rising out of the coffin. The double-bill poster had the same art and inserted a smaller picture of the villain pulling on his victim. Scheider is on the poster, but you don't know it's him until you see the film. The woman on the poster looks like Margot Hartman, who played Vivian Sinclair and who was, according to both websites, Mrs. Del Tenney.

The film was released on video in the mid–1990s but is no longer available. Scheider's credit reads Roy R. Sheider on all the publicity for this film. *Curse* is notable for several first-time placements of biographical elements from Scheider's own life into his films. Philip is a sickly, asthmatic child confined to his bed, like Roy was with his rheumatic fever. Philip is abused by his father and is also a lawyer, the first of many Scheider would play on screen and television. Philip also drinks to blot out his pain, a recurring characteristic of many future Scheider characters.

— 3 —

Off Broadway

In 1964, Roy Scheider was hired for the only recorded performance during this stage of his career that wasn't off Broadway. The play was *The Chinese Prime Minister* at the Royale Theater. Henry Hewes wrote, "The amazing Enid Bagnold seems to have lost none of her delightful wit in *The Chinese Prime Minister*. Her thesis that old age should be—as it once was for elder Chinese statesmen—the best and most rewarding time of life was stated and restated in verbal summations and observations tied to the life of a 70-year-old leading lady. The talk was beautiful. However, the play was elliptical and failed to involve its audience in the decisions its characters were so wisely making."[1] Scheider was the understudy for the roles of Oliver and Tarver—the lead character's two sons, respectively played by Peter Donat and Douglas Watson.[2] Roy moved up to assume the role of Tarver in March, the last month of the run, when Watson left the cast. The play ran for 108 performances from January 2 to April 4, 1964. Scheider was listed in the *1963–64 Theatre World* entry for this play as "Roy Schneider."[3] Tarver was described by Howard Taubman in the opening night review as "the busy" son, as opposed to "the quiet" son, in his critique of Watson's performance.[4]

Roy and Cynthia Scheider's first child, a daughter, was born in 1964. They named her Maximillia, Roy said, because "it sounded pretty with Scheider. Maximillia was born prematurely with a mysterious blockage in her intestine. She spent the first eight months of her life in Bellevue Hospital, undergoing operations."[5] "When we were about to have our baby ... I said to Cynthia, 'What the hell can you put in front of Scheider?' My name, Roy, doesn't ... balance out in front of [an] obviously mid–European name so I said, 'If it's a girl we can call her Maximillia and if it's a boy we can call him the same thing.'"[6]

Roy's next role was in *The Alchemist* at the Gate Theatre, which ran for 46 performances from September 14 to October 24, 1964.[7] Roy had previously done this play with his costar, John Heffernan, at the McCarter Theatre in Princeton, New Jersey, in 1962. Howard Taubman said, "It is not too late to save the day. Some of the raucous bellowing can be subdued and some of the obvious bits ... could be toned down or eliminated. There are delightfully foolish and amusing things in ... Mr. Heffernan's and Mr. Scheider's performances."[8] This was the last play recorded where Scheider appeared with his wife, Cynthia. Scheider "hated wearing tights" in Elizabethan-era plays. The problem was that "the audience could see your knees knocking and there was nothing you could do about it. After you got warmed up, got your first laugh or reaction, then it was okay. You got your second wind and you were off. But those first few moments were torture."[9] A 30-minute excerpt ran on the CBS Sunday morning program "Camera Three" during the run of this play with a plug to go see the rest, now playing at the Gate Theatre. Scheider would work on CBS television shows based in New York for several years. This program was released in 1997 by the Creative Arts Television Archive.

Roy returned to the stage at Lincoln Center in *Tartuffe*, which began January 14 and played until May 22, 1965.[10] The *New York Times* review on January 15 does not mention him.[11] Scheider played two roles, Clerk and Sergeant, for 74 performances.[12] The play was directed by Roy's second theater mentor, Harold Clurman.

Roy was a series regular on the CBS soap opera "Love of Life" in 1965. Bonnie Bedelia, a cast member that year, remembered their time together: "He was gorgeous, and I had a big crush on him."[13] Nothing came of this attraction because Bedelia was 16 years old, and because Roy was married. This is also the first time that Roy costarred with Tony Lo Bianco. Scheider played Jonas Falk.[14] "I did 'Love of Life' for nine months. What a disaster," Scheider recalled.[15]

Roy quickly discovered soap operas were not for him. He liked the money and the exposure it gave him, but he hated the serial format. He ended up reading all of his dialogue off the idiot board and the teleprompter, unable to memorize his lines, because the story never progressed. He also was a guest star on the CBS show "The Defenders." Roy was billed too low to receive credit in *TV Guide* for this episode, his second cinematic brush with the law.

His work at Lincoln Center earned Roy his second opportunity to go on the road with the U.S. State Department's cultural exchange program. The National Repertory Theater, once again starring Helen Hayes and directed by Harold Clurman, put together another set of theater classics for an overseas tour which lasted two months.[16]

"In late 1965, [Helen Hayes] went on a Far Eastern Tour for the State Department, spending two months in Japan, Korea and the Philippines. Most of the time she was rehearsing and playing in scenes with actor-soldiers in army camps."[17] Scheider played the roles of a Nazi major in Arthur Miller's *Incident in Vichy,* staged in Los Angeles, and Jamie Tyrone in Eugene O'Neill's *Long Day's Journey into Night*, in Tokyo.[18] Clurman described his "demonstration" production of the O'Neill play in his autobiography.[19] Scheider spoke about his casting as the young Tyrone in a 1989 PBS documentary on Harold Clurman. Roy helped produce this video tribute to his mentor. Harold Clurman died in September 1980.[20] Roy valued his friendship with Clurman, a giant of the American theater. In the documentary Scheider said that "even in a chance meeting on the street, Harold always encouraged him in his art" and that he "always left their conversations feeling a foot taller."[21]

Roy told a story about the 1965 tour:

> Clurman stopped me in mid-read and said my interpretation of the younger Tyrone was boring him, i.e., he had seen it done that way

too many times. I didn't care to be taken to task in front of the entire company and then dismissed, so feeling like a horse's ass, I stayed up half the night, restaging the part. The next morning I positively floored Clurman with my new interpretation. When Harold expected me to sit down, I stood up. I turned the whole thing around, only to find out Clurman was trying to make a point about casting good performers, who could do what I did, even when it wasn't necessary. I received a nice round of applause for my effort.[22]

In the interview, it's readily apparent Roy did not like being called "boring." Scheider adored Clurman. He considered him one of the most knowledgeable all-around theater people he had ever met. Roy enjoyed Harold's childlike enthusiasm for the theater. Clurman told him to read every script—play or movie—six or seven times. Harold was of the opinion that most directors don't know anything about the theater, so it is up to the actor to have at least four options of his own to play the scenes. This way, if the director agrees, the actor is in luck, and if the director doesn't know what he is doing—which is usually the case—at least the actor is not left high and dry.

After his return to New York, Scheider appeared on the NBC series "Hallmark Hall of Fame" in the episode "Lamp at Midnight." He played the nephew of the pope and voted in the minority not to prosecute Galileo for heresy.[23] The television production was based on the 1965 stage play by Beryl Stavis. This program was released on videotape in 1983 as part of the George Schaefer Showcase Theatre Collection. Scheider was then hired for another CBS soap opera, "Search for Tomorrow." He played Dr. Wheeler.[24]

In early 1966, Roy was cast in a new play by John Arden, *Serjeant Musgrave's Dance*. The *Year's Best Plays* cited the work as "a moody expression of pacifism set in Victorian days to let it speak for itself without contemporary bias. The play is paced like a dead march, as it moves slowly toward its climax with John Colicos as the 'serjeant' who brings home a rotting corpse to show the complacent citizenry what war *is*. Its slowness in coming to the point weakened the very suspense for which it strove so carefully, but it was a powerful play nonetheless."[25] "A 19th Century British Army 'Serjeant' deserts with a few of his men and brings home the decaying corpse of a soldier killed in action to display it to the citizenry ... to horrify the folks back home with the realities of the wars in the colonies."[26]

John Arden wrote, "This is not a nihilistic [or] ... a symbolic play. Nor does it advocate bloody revolution. I ... write about ... violence. The sympathies ... are so clearly with [Musgrave] and then turn against ... his intended remedy. A study ... of the women [and] Private Attercliff should ... remove any doubts where the 'moral' ... lies."[27] Dustin Hoffman auditioned to be a member of the cast. Scheider claimed Hoffman was fired because he couldn't do the north country accent the character required after two weeks of rehearsals, even though his performance of the role was brilliant. The play opened March 8, 1966.[28] This is the longest running play of Scheider's 12-year career on stage in New York with 135 performances.[29]

"John Colicos ... is not completely successful as Musgrave. He has bearing and Scottish iron and fanatic zeal ... but in the high emotional moments, [it is more] strenuous externals, rather than internal agony. Leigh Wharton is effective as [a] soldier.... Roy R. Scheider is less effective as the third."[30] Stanley Kauffman received several letters protesting this less-than-enthusiastic review. He devoted a whole column to defend his right to think John Arden was overrated on March 20, 1966.[31]

Roy Scheider achieved another milestone with his first *Theater World* directory listing. It was a flattering picture, with his name spelled correctly. *Theater World* recognized the Broadway play *The Chinese Prime Minister* first, then listed two off-Broadway performances, *The Alchemist* and *Serjeant Musgrave's Dance.* Roy submitted his birth year as 1935 to *Theater World,* and the correct date of 1932 is rarely printed after that.[32] Roy did another version of *Incident at Vichy* in June 1966 at the Playhouse in the Park in Philadelphia. The play starred Jean Pierre Aumont and was directed by Milton Katselas. Scheider had third billing.

Roy's next job took him back to New Jersey. "Olney Theater will have done three new plays in the last three summers when it introduces Hugh Leonard's *Stephen D.* in July [1966], under the direction of James Waring."[33] This version with George Grizzard in the lead role was not very successful, although it's noted that the audiences liked Roy. Stanley Kauffman singled out four of the actors for praise in his review. Kaufmann wrote on August 5, 1966, "Roy R. Scheider has the jauntiness of a mocking, serious student."[34]

In the fall of 1966, Roy went to Buffalo, New York, and did *Cyrano De Bergerac* at the Studio Arena Theater from October 6 to October 29. He played Christian, the tongue-tied young soldier, to Aina Neimela's Roxanne, but was not listed as a member of the company for that season.[35]

After this, Roy bombed in New Haven, as he would candidly refer to it years later. The play was *What Do You Really Know about Your Husband?*" at the Schubert Theatre in New Haven, Connecticut; it opened on March 9 and closed on March 11, 1967. Roy played the son of a feuding older couple.[36]

Roy was hired for his third soap opera, "The Secret Storm," on CBS, and made the first issue of *Who's Who in Daytime TV.* Scheider's biographical paragraph mentioned Broadway, his work in repertory theater, films, and TV, and his two overseas acting tours.[37] He was also a guest star on the CBS summer replacement TV series "Coronet Blue." His episode aired July 24, 1967. *Stephen D.* was rewritten and recast with actor Stephen Joyce for off-Broadway. Roy happily quit "The Secret Storm," where he played Bob Hill,[38] to return in an upgrade of his earlier role, from a fellow student to best friend.

Scheider won an Obie Award in 1968 for his crowd-pleasing Cranly in the distinguished performances category.[39] The revamped *Stephen D.* ran for 68 performances from September 24 to November 12, 1967, at the East 74th Street Theater.[40] Clive Barnes liked the idea and the words, but thought the staging left something to be desired: "Roy R. Scheider cut a real character out [of] Stephen's best friend, Cranly—this was excellently done."[41] Walter Kerr filed an additional review on October 8, 1967: "[Stephen D., the lead] confides ... that he is ready to leave Ireland. The friend [Scheider] is surprised, disturbed, sorry ... he hesitantly inquires [if] Joyce [will] miss some ... he's leaving behind, particularly his best pal. Joyce replies ... 'what best pal?' Roy R. Scheider and Stephen Joyce are both superb."[42] Reporting on Scheider's Obie award, the *New York Times* listed him last and as "Roy R. Schneider."[43] *The Village Voice,* the sponsoring newspaper, did spell his last name correctly.

Despite his rave reviews and award, Roy still could not get any respect from his father. When he'd come home to New Jersey, his father would ask how he was doing with all the "fagolas" over in "Greenwich." It didn't matter that it was good theater. His dad attended the plays and even enjoyed some of them, but he still thought his son should be going to night school and studying law, as a backup.

Roy had landed two very small speaking parts in films. *Star!* opened on October 22, 1968, at the Rivoli Theatre and *Paper Lion* opened on October 23, 1968, at the Victoria Theatre.[44] The role in *Paper Lion* is the better part. Roy plays another writer for *Sports Illustrated* who bets Plimpton's editor (David Doyle) $1,000 that Plimpton won't make it one quarter as a pro quarterback: "He's gonna get killed."[45] Roy has a total of five lines.

Scheider's part as a summer stock theater director in *Star!* is even smaller. He is heard more than seen and wears heavy black eyeglasses that obscure most of his face, but Roy does have three lines of dialogue with the film's star, Julie Andrews. Scheider received no credit for either role and therefore is not mentioned in any reviews of these films.

Variety called *Paper Lion* "an amiable fiction."[46] The two reviews in the *New York Times* are polar opposites. Dave Anderson said, "The pro football devotee is extended a rare privilege. Do not spurn it."[47] Renata Adler noted, "There is something about reporter-centered journalism [referring to Plimpton's popular series of articles in *Sports Illustrated* about a sportswriter trying to be a pro baseball pitcher, quarterback, or boxer] that doesn't translate to the screen intact."[48] Adler didn't like *Star!* either. "People who like old-style musicals should get their money's worth. So should people who like Julie Andrews. But people who liked Gertrude Lawrence [the "star" of the title] had better stick with their record collections and memories."[49]

Star! was a major disappointment for 20th Century–Fox, which was trying to repeat the huge success of *The Sound of Music*, with the same star and director and Michael Kidd's famed choreography, only this movie was roundly panned. Most critics thought Andrews was all wrong for the part and that the movie was tedious, overblown, and way too long. A shorter version of the film was released later, called *Those Were the Happy Times. Star!* did little more than herald the demise of the big-budget screen musical.

Roy guest starred on the ABC series "N.Y.P.D." on February 6, 1968, playing a lawyer who wants to use a police brutality case as a media event to advance his election campaign. In the end, Scheider's character clears the cop of the false charges.

For Roy, the big event of 1968 was a theater strike. He was the leader of the American Actor's Committee and instigated a strike that caused Broadway to go dark for a week. Scheider recalled the strike as the most passionate period of his life, a time when sleep was unimportant and the destruction of his own stage career didn't matter.

Broadway producers were bringing shows from London and using the English casts without hiring any Americans. American actors were not allowed to work in England. When they arrived, the immigration officer took their passport and stamped it "Actor—No Work." Scheider wouldn't let the producers perpetuate the double standard. He won, the strike ended, and Roy's stage career continued, in between other work.

On December 30, 1968, Roy's fourth soap opera, "Hidden Faces," began as an experiment. It was canceled after six months at the end of June 1969 because of low ratings.[50] NBC had commissioned the mystery crime series as counterprogramming to "the homespun 'As the World Turns.' The show's lead ... lawyer Arthur Adams ... was defending Katherine Logan, a surgeon ... accused of killing a patient. [During] the trial, he falls in love with her." Cast members included Stephen Joyce, Tony Lo Bianco, and a very young Linda Blair.[51] Once again Scheider was involved with the law.

Roy said he had a part in *Nobody Hears a Broken Drum* in March 1969, but was not credited in the 1969–70 *Theater World* listing.[52] This play closed after six performances.[53] Roy was not mentioned in the *New York Times* review of this play.

In the spring of 1969, Roy was chosen as the lead in a Lincoln Center production. Otis Guernsey wrote, "Finally, there was the powerful drama by John Ford Noonan, *The Year Boston Won the Pennant*, using the baseball world and a baseball hero to symbolize Everyman as a wounded hero, ringed round with hostility and crippled little by little in mind and body until he is ripe for the kill ... one of the best offerings of the off–Broadway year, tightly directed by Tim Ward and grimly acted by Roy R. Scheider, who resembles George C. Scott in both appearance and ability."[54] The play had seven previews and ran for 38 performances. This comparison to Scott dogged Scheider his entire stage career. Roy said, "I'd walk in and the director would say, What are we going to do with this guy—is he a cousin or a brother or something?"[55]

Harry Gilroy declared, "Roy R. Scheider plays the pitcher, with the ... physical hardiness and ego [needed] ... on the mound [to] fire a baseball past ... big league hitters. When it comes to ... what is really going on ... Mr. Noonan has not given him the words. Mr. Scheider gives a powerful performance."[56] The play was staged from May 22 to June 22, 1969. A second review on June 8, 1969, urged readers to catch *Pennant* while it was still playing: "Roy Scheider plays Sykowski so well ... we do not resent the truths he is keeping from us, do not demand to know what it means to have an arm arbitrarily gone. Sykowski will explain nothing. He preserves as much of himself as he can."[57] This was the last recorded appearance of Scheider as a cast member at Lincoln Center.

Roy was cast as a regular on the CBS soap opera "Where the Heart Is" in 1969.[58] None of the published histories of this particular daytime drama tell what role Scheider played that first year or give the name of his character. Set in Norcross, Connecticut, the show chronicled "the conflicts, tensions, and drives" of the Hathaways.[59] Mary Ann Copeland stated, "This innovative serial challenged its audience by taking it through unfamiliar territory. Women constantly found themselves pregnant by men they didn't love but were physically attracted to."[60]

Scheider's next film, *Stiletto,* was released in August 1969. Roy had ninth billing. This is the first film where his credit reads Roy Scheider, as he apparently had earned his Screen Actors Guild (SAG) card. Scheider also told SAG he was born in 1935. Roy plays Bennett, a Mafia lawyer. His clients, the three mobsters on trial, are released. The reviews of *Stiletto* do not mention Scheider. Howard Thompson said in the *New York Times*, "*Stiletto*, the latest Mafia melodrama, has no point and absolutely no merit."[61] A review in *Time* also panned the film. *Variety* found it "a confusing, but often-fast-paced Mafia yarn."[62] Scheider's absence from the reviews is not surprising, but he is listed in the credits of the *Variety* review.

The next film Roy Scheider appeared in was *Loving*, released in New York on March 4, 1970. Scheider is billed 25th and plays an advertising associate in the same office as George Segal. Scheider has two scenes and in them he comes across as far more in control and competent in his handling of the pending Lepridon account than Segal's character, which is the recurring theme of the film.

Pauline Kael did not mention Scheider. She liked the film and applauded director Irving Kershner's control and understanding, along with the acting of George Segal and Eva Marie Saint: "An unusual movie—compassionate but unsentimental. It looks at the failures of middle-class life without despising the people; it

Loving (1969, Columbia Pictures). Brooks and his assistant Skip show his bid to Lepridon. Brooks: George Segal; Skip: Roy Scheider; Lepridon: Sterling Hayden.

understands that they already despise themselves. [The director] shows the lives of mediocre people for what they are, but he never allows us to feel superior to them."[63]

James Monaco said, "George Segal and Eva Marie Saint come close to providing the ultimate image of the suburban couple."[64] Roger Greenspun noted it was not perfect, but he did say, "It is a fine and gratifying film. *Loving* is a wholly New York movie ... and like the best New York movies, it is strong on reality. There is nobody in the strong supporting cast that I would want to fault."[65] Roy received more publicity and notice in this film than any previous part, as his main scene was chosen to be a black-and-white publicity still and a color lobby card.

Jerry Schatzberg cast his film *Puzzle of a Downfall Child* with several actors from the current stage company of Lincoln Center, including Roy, who received fifth billing as Mark. *Puzzle* had a long, contentious release, finally opening in New York on February 7, 1971.[66] Faye Dunaway considers the film her best work:

> It had an incredible script. It was the story of a model who has been all her life trying to get out of the business and then hated it when she was out. She spent her whole life waiting for the moment when she could get out and live a normal life. She could live by the sea, she could paint pictures, she could read, and she says in the film, "I hate it, I just hate it." You can't spend a life trying to get to a moment that you think that you are going to be happy, you have to be happy in a life and that was the great tragedy of this woman.[67]

Filming took place in and around New York City, at Mecox Beach in

Puzzle of a Downfall Child. **(1970, Universal). Lou Andreas and Mark have a talk. Lou Andreas Sand: Faye Dunaway; Mark: Roy Scheider.**

Bridgehampton, the Plaza Hotel, Central Park, Welfare Island, and Flushing Airport. The cast includes Barry Primus, an original member of the Lincoln Center Repertory Company. A series of flashbacks serves as the structure for a talkative rumination over the model's life. Faye believed that the blame for the ultimate confusion about the film could be laid at the door of Universal Studios: "They had completely no faith and they recut a lot of it. It does sometimes happen. They cut it and misconstrued it and did not lift a finger to sell it. It was not understood [to be] in anyway commercial and I don't think they were right but we'll never know."[68]

Dunaway continued, "In October of 1969, I returned to New York to begin filming [*Puzzle*] with Jerry. Relationships between directors and actresses are tricky enough, but here we are former lovers, once engaged to be married.... the weeks we spent working on *Puzzle* were a little like tap dancing on eggshells."[69] The film was based on the real life of Anne St. Marie, a 1950s model. Schatzberg had photographed her during his time as a fashion photographer and had always wanted to tell her story.[70] A premiere party was held for *Puzzle* in Los Angeles in December 1970. Faye Dunaway said, "Paul Newman [one of the producers] and Joanne Woodward were throwing a party for me at the Directors Guild to celebrate. The party turned out to be a big success."[71]

Pauline Kael does not mention Scheider in her scathing review: "The title is enough to warn one this is going to be literary in the worst way."[72] Kael then took the scriptwriter, Carole Eastman, and the star, Faye Dunaway, apart. Roger Greenspun said, "[This film] despite some lapses

Puzzle of a Downfall Child. **Lou, Mark, and Dr. Galba in a car. Lou Andreas Sand: Faye Dunaway; Mark: Roy Scheider; Dr. Galba: Barry Morse.**

and many excesses, is quite good. Faye Dunaway creates a character of such lovely, tentative lucidity ... [that it is] worth the whole movie. Other people are also fine (especially ... Roy Scheider as a smooth New York business success who manages ... to be sympathetic)."[73] This review is a milestone. Scheider's name is spelled correctly in both the review and the credits.

Jay Cocks thought it was the most overblown, pretentious film he'd seen in a long time and laid the blame equally on Dunaway, Schatzberg, and Eastman.[74] Allan Hunter wrote, "*Puzzle* ... did drop dead at the box-office, but it still rates as an 'A' success for Faye ... [who said], 'I have the greatest respect for Jerry as a director. I always like to work with people I know and like. Movies should be made with devotion and respect.' There are stylish touches of direction and obvious glimmerings of the fashion photographer's art. Jerry Schatzberg felt, 'It's a high quality picture. We've all worked hard on it, and no one has worked harder than Faye.'"[75] Dunaway reiterated in 1995, "*Puzzle* was never a big financial success, but it was very well regarded by many in the industry. [It] remains one of my favorite films."[76] *Puzzle* received a better reception overseas. The French loved it. At one point in 1972, Scheider had four films playing there at the same time: *The French Connection*, *Puzzle of a Downfall Child*, *Klute*, and *The French Conspiracy*.

Roy Scheider has stated that he had more than 80 stage roles,[77] but not all have been recorded for posterity. Roy's final off-Broadway appearance of this period was in June 1970 in a European import called *The Nuns*. This parable in two acts has three men hiding from the slave revolution in 1791 in a cave and posing as nuns.

It opened on June 1, 1970, and closed that same night.[78] Clive Barnes tried to be kind, but he could see no reason why this play was staged, even if it *was* a hit in Europe: "[It was an] ... evening [that] ... by its sheer ineptitude [may] become [one of the] treasured reminiscences held in dear horror." Barnes singled out Scheider for his only praise: "Roy R. Scheider was by far the best ... [with] a cigar-champing snarl that ... set him aside—he wears his habit with a difference—he is ... an actor who deserves much better."[79] As for holding the night in "dear horror," Joe Allen, the famous Broadway restaurant owner, mentioned *The Nuns* when replying to a question about Scheider's theater experiences on "This Is Your Life." Pat Sajak didn't quite understand Allen's answer, but Scheider certainly did, informing Sajak that "it opened and closed in one night."[80]

— 4 —

1971: Break-Out Year

After 12 years of increasingly better parts on the stages of East Coast theaters and with six minor movie roles to his credit, Roy Scheider had an October to remember in 1971, when *The French Connection* premiered in New York to critical acclaim. Scheider's previous film, *Klute*, released in July, also had received good notices. By April 1972, the two movies had won six Academy Awards between them. Scheider's professional acting career changed radically as these two motion pictures made him a movie star. Roy Scheider received an Oscar nomination for best supporting actor in *The French Connection*, and the publicity associated with the annual Oscar races finally brought him to national attention.

Most of the publicity that *Klute* received centered on Jane Fonda and was split between her acting and her antiwar activism. The reviews either praised or condemned director Alan Pakula's style and vision, when they were understood, or concentrated on Donald Sutherland, the title character. Sutherland said, "[It] was a film where the director had a specific idea, which I didn't particularly understand, nor was I particularly interested in. I fought with Alan Pakula a lot, there were a lot of things in *Klute* that didn't make any sense in terms of movies."[1]

Neither Roy Scheider nor his character, Frank Ligourin, were mentioned in the film's reviews, despite fourth billing for Scheider. Roy was featured in the theatrical trailer, but the scene was shown out of context and Scheider was not identified by his character's name. When Fonda did mention his character's name, Scheider was not in the scene. The film reviews of this period were short and mostly done in groups for several films with the same theme. In *Klute's* case, it was movies about prostitutes. These multiple reviews were then run under supposedly witty titles like "Five Queasy Pieces."

Scheider plays Fonda's brutal ex-pimp and former husband, who hasn't quite been banished from her life. Bree, Jane Fonda's call-girl character, alternately leaves and returns to Ligourin, a tough, coarse little man, who swears that his "ladies" freely seek his protection, despite the fact that

***Klute* (1971, Warner Brothers). Frankie gets tough with Bree in the Sanctuary (a disco). Frank Ligourin: Roy R. Scheider; Bree Daniels: Jane Fonda.**

Scheider's best scene in the film centers on Klute as he watches Frankie and Bree together in the disco. Frankie cruelly dominates Bree, but she stays with him until Ligourin gives her the drugs she wants. Roy did not have sufficient screen time to work in any biographical details, but this scene established a type of character he would play again in later films.

This Oscar-winning movie—Fonda won best actress—helped advance Scheider's career, despite his lack of notices in the reviews. I did find one review that mentioned Roy specifically, in the *Hollywood Reporter*: "Pakula has directed the supporting cast in such a way that everyone is strong but clearly supportive. Roy R. Scheider, who was shown to advantage in *Puzzle of a Downfall Child,* is fine as Fonda's ex–old man and pimp."[4]

one of them is violently murdered during the course of the film and Bree is threatened and almost killed. Frankie is a cruel, uncaring, possessive addict. His breezy dismissal of his ex-girls to John Klute is chilling. When asked about Jane McKenna, he says without remorse about his former "family" member, "She's gone, man. A suicide." Specifically asked about the other ex-girl, Arlyn Page, he doesn't care: "She's useless, a junkie."[2] Ligourin has no idea where Page is and shows little concern that his ex-wife, Bree, is being stalked by a killer.

In a film where the characters talk constantly and too much to hide their demons, Ligourin has little to say. Instead, he reveals his character's cruelty through stance and attitude. When John Klute attempts to extort information by threatening his arrest for being an addict, Ligourin goes toe to toe with the detective, despite the height and weight difference between the two men. The pimp informs Klute that he is "an out-of-town, know nothing private investigator" and tells him that he is "in better with the cops" than Klute could ever be.[3]

After Scheider became famous, more commentary on his *Klute* role was published. Nicholas Thomas acknowledged Ligourin as an important counterfoil to Sutherland's innocent character. "Roy played Jane Fonda's pimp, Frank, a necessarily small, seedy character from whose lips syrupy wooing and brutal epithets flow with equal credibility."[5] James Monaco wrote, "*Klute* remains one of the most important films of the seventies. A film whose significance multiplies every year we get further away from it."[6]

Scheider acknowledges the film's importance to his movie career: "I was working off–Broadway and [director Alan Pakula] hired me for my first [major] film role."[7] Billed as Roy R. Scheider, *Klute* would be the last film where Scheider used his middle initial. Roy enjoyed working with Jane Fonda. She was a total profes-

***Klute*. Frankie and his girls in the Sanctuary. Frank Ligourin: Roy R. Scheider; Bree Daniels: Jane Fonda; Trina: Rita Gam. Three uncredited extras.**

sional, who showed up on time and knew her work. Jane was able to improvise when needed and was willing to do anything necessary to make the movie better, including wandering the streets with him to observe real pimps and hookers at work. Scheider liked her passion for the project. They both wanted their characters to be realistic. "I did a lot of little things ... [including] *Paper Lions* [*sic*] and I played a summer stock director in *Star!* with Julie Andrews. The first part that got me anywhere was the pimp in *Klute* with Jane Fonda."[8]

There is some interesting casting in *Klute*. Jane Fonda and Donald Sutherland were lovers during the filming. One of the supporting players is Jean Stapleton, better known as Edith Bunker on "All in the Family." The film almost reunited Scheider with Robert Milli, who had played his brother in *The Curse of the Living Corpse*. Milli's picture is shown as the missing Tom Gruneman, the man John Klute is searching for. *Klute* was the first honoree of the New York Independent Film Project's Winstar Classic Tribute. IFP executive director Michelle Byrd said, "One of the things we are hoping to do with [this tribute] is to use it as a launch pad for more screenings and discussion of classic films."[9]

In between the release of *Klute* and before he hit it big in *The French Connection*, Roy was cast in the new "Cannon" TV detective series as a greedy lawyer villain in the episode "No Pockets in a Shroud." He plans to bilk a deceased Howard Hughes–type millionaire's heirs out of their money. The segment aired six weeks after the release of *The French Connection* on November 23, 1971, as the 10th episode of the first season.

The French Connection was screened at two New York theaters on October 7, 1971. Roy's six years of anonymity in films and television had finally ended. Scheider was cast before Gene Hackman. The first man hired to play Doyle had been Jimmy Breslin. In early rehearsals, Breslin was good at the action shots, but he couldn't say the dialogue convincingly. Director William Friedkin explained, "There were only two problems that I found trying to work [Breslin] into the part. One, he was the worst actor I ever saw in my life, and two, he had never driven a car. He couldn't drive."[10] As the film's climax depended on a knuckle-biting chase scene where the Doyle character pursues a subway train in a car he has commandeered, an actor who could drive had to be found to replace Breslin.

Friedkin told Robert Emery, "By that time I had cast Roy Scheider in the part of Buddy Russo, so I got Scheider and Breslin improvising for three weeks. We would go through ... the story and try to improvise dialogue.... On Monday Breslin would be brilliant and terrific. On Tuesday, he would forget what he did on Monday. Come Wednesday, he couldn't even remember what he was doing there. Come Thursday he might be drunk or not show up at all on Friday."[11]

Friedkin considered five other actors, including Jackie Gleason and Paul Newman, before going with Gene Hackman, his seventh choice. The director finally selected Hackman because 20th Century–Fox Studios was pressuring him to begin filming.[12] "Phil D'Antoni came to me and said, 'If we don't do it with Gene, we're not gonna have a picture, it's all gonna go away.' So I spent the weekend and thought it over and decided to go with Gene, partly by default. Almost every other actor [besides Scheider] that got in that picture, including Fernando Rey [Friedkin wanted Francisco Rabal, but casting mixed up the names], got into the film by default or mistake."[13]

Jeff Burkhart wrote, "*The French Connection* was an edge of your seat thriller with the greatest chase sequence ever filmed. It made a star out of Gene Hackman, who till then was still thought of as a supporting actor. It gave an enormous push to Roy Scheider's career."[14]

Roy considered *The French Connection* his big break. It was the role that made him an international star. Roy claimed he got the part by accident and because he kept showing up. There was a Broadway audition for a play with an English director. One stipulation was that every person in the play had to be six feet tall. Roy went anyway and stood in the rain for an hour, until it was his turn. His reading was interrupted twice by the director, asking if he were six feet tall. Roy assured him he was—in shoes.

The director was unconvinced and finally had a six-foot-tall staffer stand next to Scheider. Roy wasn't tall enough, and the director dismissed him. Scheider threw his script into the audience and started yelling that if James Cagney, Marlon Brando, or Laurence Olivier came to audition for him, none of them would get the job, because none of them were six feet tall! Roy told the director to take his six feet and shove them and walked out. Scheider didn't know that Bob Weiner, who was casting for Friedkin and Philip D'Antoni was there. After seeing this tirade, Weiner went back, convinced he had found the perfect Lieutenant Russo.

Friedkin sent Scheider and Hackman out on actual drug raids with their real-life counterparts, Eddie Egan and Sonny Grosso. They went up to Harlem and busted into shooting galleries. They were never the first ones through the door, but they were the fifth and sixth, without guns and scared. Scheider saw burners heating up the drugs, addicts with needles stuck in their arms, and a man lying dead from an overdose. They would watch all that, listen to the cops talk, and then go back to the car to write it all down for their improvisations of the conversations between them.

They wanted to make their dialogue as realistic as possible. Roy noticed that no one liked Egan very much, but everyone liked Grosso. One night he asked Grosso about Egan. And Grosso replied that, if he didn't like Eddie Egan, who would? Scheider considered that revelation the center of his character and from then on he knew exactly how to play his role.

"This was by far the most complex and difficult character I've ever played. It's suggested by a real policeman [Sonny Grosso], who found himself involved in a series of the most extraordinary circumstances. There is a great deal of surface action, but much inner reality to project. We spent over three months on New York locations during the winter, and neither snow, nor rain, nor sleet, nor head cold, nor union problems, nor anything else could keep us from our appointed rounds. It was a rugged, exhausting experience, but I think we've caught something special."[15] "I knew *French Connection* was one of the best cop films ever made because we really broke our backs to make it authentic. We didn't pull any punches in those scenes where we slapped people around. It was practically a documentary."[16]

There was not much chance for Scheider to insert biographical elements into this film, but he does order bourbon, his drink of choice, in the bar scene where Popeye first notices Sal and Angie Boca. Scheider's clothes reflect his own distinct style and are composed of items the audience will see on him again.

The French Connection raised Scheider's recognition factor tenfold. He was mentioned by name in four reviews of the film and received third billing. *Variety* took notice first on October 4, 1971: "Gene Hackman and Roy Scheider are very believable as two hard-nosed narcotics officers who, by accident, stumble on what turned out to be the biggest narcotics haul to date."[17]

Andrew Sarris mentioned Scheider twice: "The acting in *The French Connection* deserves special commendation for preserving the dignities and the idiosyncrasies of characterization in a context of almost total alienation. The rightness of all the casting extends beyond ability ... carried to ... 'archetypage': Hackman and Scheider as every pair of detectives."[18]

On November 1, *Time* ran a photograph of the real-life cops, Eddie Egan and Sonny Grosso, with its review. Jay Cocks wrote, "Gene Hackman plays Popeye Doyle, who likes to ogle girls in boots, break heads and bust blacks. Roy Scheider is his dogged, if only slightly less compulsive, assistant."[19] A still from the film, with Scheider prominently featured but not named, was printed in *Life* magazine on November 5, 1971, in a review of five other cop films released at the same time.[20]

Scheider's final notice came in Richard Schickel's *Life* review, on November 19: "I want to stress, along with the quality of Hackman's performance ... the vision of the city ... director William Friedkin gives us ... the ... god-awful, biting cold of ... midwinter—the way it seeps into the bones of Hackman and his partner (well played by Roy Scheider)."[21] Scheider's most prominent publicity was his third *Life* appearance on April 7, 1972. Roy was identified by name under his picture in a large two-page spread of the current Oscar nominees.[22]

Three other benchmarks of Roy's newfound notoriety were a *Mad* magazine parody of the film, "What's the Connection," and a mention of Roy's Oscar nomination in two soap magazines. *Daytime TV* noted he was no longer on "Where the Heart Is" but neglected to mention that he left the soap opera in 1969.[23] *TV from Dusk to Dawn* featured Roy in its "Catching Up with..." column in November 1972 and said he had been Bob Hill in "The Secret Storm."[24] They also neglected to note that this role was played in 1967.

The attention he received surprised

***The French Connection* (20th Century–Fox, 1971). A street bust of car thieves. Russo: Roy Scheider; Doyle: Gene Hackman; Mulderig: Bill Hickman. Two uncredited cops and three uncredited suspects.**

Roy. He was suddenly a movie actor. The fame excited him and the money was welcome, too, after many years of struggling to make ends meet on his stage salaries. Roy's daughter, Maximillia, told a story on "This Is Your Life," when the host Pat Sajak asked if there were tough times when she was little: "It was hard to keep $400.00 in the bank. My Dad used to say, 'I can either make money or be an actor.' He chose [acting] and we supported him."[25]

Scheider never planned to be a movie star—or a movie actor at all. His goal was to become a working actor in the theater.

His movie career ended up being dessert. Scheider had a powerful, naive belief in himself. He kept showing up and sticking his face in there, beating them down, showing up for the humiliation of being turned down time after time. Roy knew that he was special and sooner or later the casting people would recognize his talent. "I think I screamed at Julie Andrews in *Star!* ... I never thought [about a film career].... It ... evolved ... with *Klute* ... and [then as] Gene Hackman's sidekick ... I ... won a supporting actor nomination."[26] Scheider never thought his career would shift to film and he wasn't ready for it. Having never considered movies intellectual, he always thought he'd have to go back to the theater to find challenging material. Roy admitted that occasionally there was a film of great intelligence, but felt they were few and far between. Intelligence quotients notwithstanding, the screen claimed Scheider after these two films. It would be nine years before he made it back to Broadway.

Michael Shedlin wrote, "*The French Connection* remains a triumph of American commercialism. Opening in two theaters in New York on October 7, 1971, it grossed $302,648 in 19 days. By November 24, it [was atop] *Variety*'s weekly box office list [at] 6 million. Fox estimates the eventual worldwide revenue at 30 million."[27] "Final box office for *The French Connection* was 38.3 million, which was a huge return in the days before 100 million dollar movies. The motion picture grossed 26.3 million, domestically, with another 12 million in overseas sales. The film then sold to television for another two million dollars."[28]

Emanuel Levy stated, "The importance of *The French Connection* could not be overestimated, with the Oscar legitimizing its status as the best 'cop and caper' film of the decade."[29] James Monaco said, "Gene Hackman and Roy Scheider waded into the tough-guy cop roles with gusto. The film set a style for visceral excitement that has lasted ever since."[30] *The French Connection* has remained one of Scheider's most popular films. The documentary-style story and the realistic portrayal of working police officers earned this motion picture a reputation as the best "street" film to come out of that neorealistic period. In 1998, *The French Connection* was named number 71 of the 100 greatest films of the last hundred years by the American Film Institute. In 2001, the film was a subject on the "History vs. Hollywood" series on the History Channel and was named number 8 on the American Film Institute's list of the 100 Most Thrilling Films of the last 100 years.

Nicholas Thomas said, "As Buddy Russo ... [Roy Scheider] was the ideal, play it by the book offset to Hackman's obsessive Doyle."[31] Russo kept Doyle grounded and did not allow Popeye's obsession with Frog One to ruin their case. Russo fearlessly placed himself between the outraged Doyle and his intended victims. He pushed Popeye back as hard as Doyle pressed the suspects. Russo was Doyle's conscience and protector, even when Popeye didn't appreciate his partner's intervention. When Russo told Doyle to cool down, Popeye knew he'd better do it. They kidded each other as only two partners can. Nothing about Doyle phased Russo, even when Buddy came to take his partner to work one morning only to find Popeye handcuffed to the bed by the young, nubile, female bicycle rider Doyle had picked up the night before. Pragmatically, Buddy found the cuff keys and unlocked his partner so they could continue work on their drug case.

David Zinman explored the genesis of these all-too-human characters: "Popeye is not entirely fiction. He and his sidekick Buddy Russo (Roy Scheider) are based on two New York City detectives who got to be the terror of the narcotics underworld.

***The French Connection*. Doyle roughs up a suspect while Russo ends up on the ground. Doyle: Gene Hackman; Russo: Roy Scheider; Simonson: Eddie Egan. The other two cops and the suspect are uncredited.**

Eddie Egan and Sonny Grosso started with roundups of street junkies. They were nicknamed the Seven-Up Kids because those they arrested usually wound up with seven year sentences."[32] Roy would make a second film with producer Phil D'Antoni and Sonny Grosso in 1973, called *The Seven Ups.*

Peter Lev wrote:

> *The French Connection* is a very efficient, suspense-creating machine of a movie. It relies heavily on visuals to present the rhythm and feel of criminal activity and police investigation. Fast moving scenes are thrown at the [audience] without exposition [and] like detectives, we must somehow integrate them into ... the narrative. By making the [audience] work ... [the film] adds a modernist twist to a traditional genre.
>
> [The movie] carefully avoids making a political statement. Charnier [is] a corrupt French businessman and therefore not included in the stresses and strains of American sociopolitical life. Charnier is bringing in heroin, which is assumed to be a bad thing. To a large extent, the film's morality recalls the most traditional of westerns—we are for the white hats (the cops) and against the black hats (the crooks). The drama ... arises ... from how the white hats win out.[33]

Director Friedkin summed up the success of *The French Connection:* "[Hackman] had tremendous desire. He wanted every moment of every take to be the best he could do. It was also true of Roy Scheider. Fortunately, we all found each other at a moment we all had that desire."[34] Producer/screenwriter Walon Green—who would later work with Scheider and Friedkin on *Sorcerer*—stated, "*French Connection* was the first cop movie I ever saw where the cops acted like cops and didn't act like Hollywood people playing cops."[35]

Riding with Egan and Grosso gave Roy more reality than he wanted. Sonny Grosso had a local New York TV show called "Cop Talk." Roy was a guest in 1971.

> We would go in and bust a bar as you see in the film. We would shake them down and have everyone throw their stuff on the bar. It would take half an hour to clean the place out and then when it was over, one of the cops would come walking out and show Gene and me all the pistols that had been thrown up over the phone booths in the back of the bar. That means these guys were armed when we walked in. I remember telling my wife these stories and she was not happy.[36]

Scheider related more stories to Gordon Hunt in the series "Starring the Actors," sponsored by the American Film Institute and released by Worldvision video in 1985. Scheider stated that his costar, Hackman, found the research experience equally daunting. "We used to go out with New York cops on busts ... absorbing the atmosphere ... the way they talked and held themselves. We'd be stepping over addicts in ... filth. Gene said, 'This is [making] me sick.' I'm a big city guy, but it was making Gene crazy."[37]

For all its purported realism, *The French Connection* was still Hollywood movie fiction. The scene in which Doyle accidently kills FBI agent Mulderig, thinking he's Frog One, never happened. Eddie Egan did not shoot FBI agent Frank Wells. The mug shots at the end of the film are also false. In reality, all the principals arrested received longer jail sentences. Frog One did not escape: "Jean Jehan was caught in France, whose government refused to agree to his extradition to America."[38]

Grosso and Egan were reassigned, but much later in their respective careers and not because they had broken this case. Ironically, all of the pushers who are rounded up and arrested in the barroom bust in the film are off-duty New York cops. Thomas Rand, the location manager, said, "That was all cops in that bar scene. It was shot down at Roy's bar. It ain't there no more. We had to use nonunion help like that. We couldn't find any rugged-looking black guys that were in the Screen Actors Guild. There just weren't any at the time."[39] "The highly praised chase scene in the film was mandated by producer D'Antoni, who wanted a replication of a similar chase that had worked well in his earlier film, *Bullitt,* in 1968."[40]

Some of the problems Phil D'Antoni encountered during the making of *The French Connection* were described by Michael Druxman:

> D'Antoni had bought the Robin Moore book while it was still in manuscript form. After his success with *Bullitt*, Phil had no trouble selling the property to National General. They liked the idea, but took a lot of convincing to accept Friedkin as the director. Then, because of too many unsuccessful pictures, National General had some financial difficulties and could not give D'Antoni the budget he needed (2.5 million). D'Antoni explained this was the times as much as bad management.
>
> The public's tastes were changing and the studios struggled to find a product they would go see. Several studios had lost big money on splashy musicals like *Hello, Dolly* and were looking for the next low-budget *Easy Rider*. Discouraged, D'Antoni took the project back in turnaround, dropped his option and went on to another project. In 1970, 20th Century–Fox had some box-office hits and asked D'Antoni to resubmit. This time, the producer got the budget he needed and the film was green-lighted. D'Antoni and Friedkin spent 86 days riding around with Egan and Grosso to get the details of the film right.[41]

The Hollywood film community loved Friedkin's new "realism" and anointed him a wunderkind. Nominated for ten Oscars, *The French Connection* won five, including one for Friedkin as best director and one for Hackman as best actor. "The film also won Best Picture, Best Film Editing and Best Screenplay, for a script by Ernest Tidyman that Friedkin didn't like and claimed he didn't use."[42] The best supporting actor award went to veteran actor Ben Johnson for *The Last Picture Show*.[43] "1972 was the first of three Academy Award ceremony appearances for Scheider. He presented awards at Oscar ceremonies in 1976 and 1977."[44] Nominated for best actor in 1980, for 1979's *All That Jazz*, Scheider did not attend the ceremony.

Roy may have the final comment on the lasting effect of his role as Buddy Russo in *The French Connection*. In 1992, Scheider told Lynn Snowden, "I would never [need] a cab if I took all the rides ... offered me by the [New York] police! It's very nice."[45]

By the spring of 1972, Roy had become the movie star he had never planned to be, but his next acting offer was for a spy television series on ABC. The appeal for Scheider was that the episodes would be totally filmed in Europe. The series was called "Assignment: Munich."

— 5 —

Rocky Road to Stardom

The year 1972 began with a new play taped for the local New York PBS station, WNET. *To Be Young, Gifted and Black* was based on the plays of Lorraine Hansberry, the late African-American playwright who wrote *Raisin in the Sun*. The program was adapted from the stage play by Robert Nemiroff and the "NET Playhouse" performance offered excerpts from all of her plays. Scheider had several roles, but Roy's delivery of a drunken sunrise soliloquy from *The Sign in Sidney Brustein's Window* was his showcase piece. The program aired for the first time on January 22, 1972, on New York public television. It later aired nationally as a "Theatre in America" presentation on PBS in May 1974. An excerpt from *Les Blancs* was included in the 1988 video *Lorraine Hansberry: The Black Experience in the Creation of Drama*. The entire "NET Playhouse" performance was released by Monterey Home Video on February 4, 1997.

Roy was finished with his next project by the time this play aired. He had been offered a sizable sum of money by MGM to do an espionage TV series called "Assignment: Munich," with the understanding that it would be shot entirely in Europe. He had dreams of making *The Third Man*, working with Europe's finest actors and directors, and he couldn't understand why everyone else knew that after they had their pilot, they'd bring the whole thing back to Hollywood and only do a few cover shots in Europe. Halfway through the pilot, the studio told Roy exactly that. This was not what Roy thought he had signed up for and the last thing he wanted to do, so he called his lawyer to find a way out of his series commitment. The lawyer found a technicality. Roy had never signed a deal memo for the series. Roy wasn't going to do a Hollywood-style action/adventure/cop TV series, no matter how much he was being paid, so he got on a plane and came home. The studio sued him for breach of contract. The lawsuit was in the courts for three years. Eventually, the studio won and Roy had to pay $165,000. Even though he lost, Scheider felt he was better for not having done the series, which ran for a year and was canceled.

"Assignment: Munich" (1972, MGM Television/ABC). Portrait of Jake Webster. Publicity still.

Roy had other, more pressing concerns at home. "When [Maximillia] was eight, there was a recurrence [of the intestinal blockage that had caused her to be hospitalized as an infant and] more surgery."[1] This time his daughter's medical problem was corrected for good.

In February 1972, he received an Oscar nomination for his role in *The French Connection*. Scheider had become an actor to escape his upbringing, playing other people to avoid the parts of himself he didn't like. Roy had made a decent living on the off-Broadway stage and was beginning to have a film career, but he didn't have the recognition from the person he wanted it from the most, his father. Phil D'Antoni phoned Roy to tell him he had been nominated for an Oscar as best supporting actor. Scheider immediately called his parents in New Jersey. His mother came on the line. Anna thought it was wonderful. Roy heard her yell into another part of the house to tell his father, then she came back and continued the conversation. Afterward, Scheider walked around his apartment, trying to figure out what was bothering him about the call. Finally, it hit him. His father hadn't come to the phone. Why hadn't he? Roy knew why—his father was a man who didn't do things like that. He didn't throw compliments around. With an Oscar nomination, the whole world was recognizing Scheider's ability—everyone except his father. Roy recalled how this hurt him and added that his father didn't phone and commiserate when he didn't win the Oscar, either.

The "Assignment: Munich" pilot aired three weeks later on April 30, 1972, as an ABC world premiere movie. At that time it was announced as a fall series with a name change to "Assignment: Vienna." The *Boston Globe* wrote, "America's answer to James Bond will make his debut tonight (Sunday). Roy Scheider ... Gene Hackman's companion in *The French Connection* ... is a hard knuckles [*sic*] American agent [in] Munich ... tracking down a fortune in gold, battling a gang of thieves and outwitting an unknown adversary."[2]

The ABC press further described the project: "Harry Lange, the only man who knows where $5 million in gold is hidden, dies accidently the day after his release from prison. The suspense drama twists through the underworld of Munich as Webster [Roy Scheider] trails Lange's former partners. But one by one, they are brutally murdered ... and suddenly Webster realizes someone else is on the trail of the gold [and] Webster must do battle with an adversary he has never seen."[3]

Most of this information is wrong, including the program description. "Assignment: Munich" was a thinly rewritten version of *Charade*, the Cary Grant/Audrey Hepburn film. Robert Reed had the Walter Matthau role. Keenan Wynn had the George Kennedy role (without a hook),

"Assignment: Munich." Jake confers with Major Caldwell. Jake Webster: Roy Scheider; Major Caldwell: Richard Basehart. Publicity still.

The stolen loot was not gold, but had been changed from the rare postage stamps in *Charade* to diamonds. Jake had to find the diamonds for the major, while he kept an eye on the daughter. She was being threatened by her dead father's partners from the original heist gone bad. The three thieves were determined to find the money they were denied. They all end up dead by various means as in *Charade*. Major Caldwell confiscated the diamonds after Jake found where they had been hidden and saved the girl, only she went back to America without him. As in *Casablanca*, Webster said goodbye at the airport and watched as she boarded the plane. A German police inspector played by Werner Klemperer à la Claude Rains caused complications, but the good guys won. The one biographical note came when Jake called his newspaper buddy Mitch (Robert Reed) for information and they talked about the action to date in baseball metaphors. Scheider would continue to be cast in parts that required him to act like Humphrey Bogart or Cary Grant.

and so on down the cast. Lesley Ann Warren was the daughter, rather than the wife, of the dead gang member and played the Hepburn role, while Scheider's role, as an expatriate American (who was wanted for something in America) was closer to Humphrey Bogart in *Casablanca* than to Cary Grant's Treasury Agent. Jake Webster even owned an American cafe in Munich (his cover) called Jake's. He had a know-it-all German bartender instead of a piano player and a Major Caldwell (possibly CIA) he answered to. The major offered to clear Jake's name so he could return to America, after Webster did the job, of course.

Daytime TV magazine continued to track Scheider as a soap opera alumnus. He graduated from the "Where Are They Now?" to the "You Can See Them in the Movies" column. They ran his picture with the April air date six months after the pilot aired.[4] "'Assignment: Munich' became an ABC series in September 1972, as one of three revolving shows. The

***The French Conspiracy* (1973, Cine Globe). Lempereur arranges for Francois Darien to meet with crusading journalist Michael Howard. *Left to right:* Lempereur: Michel Bouquet; Francois Darien: Jean-Louis Trintignant; Michael Howard: Roy Scheider.**

producers replaced Scheider with Robert Conrad and renamed the series, 'Assignment: Vienna.' The TV show lasted one year with a time slot and format change mid-season."[5]

Scheider said, "The bad thing [about *The French Connection*] was, it was so good. I got inundated with cop scripts after that. It was the same role over and over. Everyone had a chase sequence, every scene was either set in a garage or a vacant lot or a warehouse with everyone getting gunned down. I hope actors will be offered something different [soon]. I know I don't want to do any more cop movies."[6]

Roy made two films with Jean-Louis Trintignant instead of the TV series. The first one, *The French Conspiracy*, is a "fictional retelling of the kidnaping of Moroccan leftist opposition leader, Mehdi Ben Barka" and was filmed in Spain.[7] The second film, *The Outside Man,* is "a sordid tale of betrayal among hit men within the Mafia" and was made in Los Angeles.[8] Roy claimed he was cast in *The French Conspiracy* because of the popularity of *The French Connection*.

Vincent Canby's first review of *The French Conspiracy* listed Scheider fourth in the credits but did not mention the actor: "[The film suffered] from a fatal mixture of reverence and foolishness," which Canby blamed partly on the director and mostly on the screenwriters. "The actors often look ridiculous."[9] Canby's second review called it "a botched attempt at the sort of movie Costa-Gavras has made into his own. [The screenwriters] have turned it into a hash that is sometimes unintentionally hilarious. It means to take its political point of view seriously, but the exposition is so complicated as to be unintelligible."[10] Molly Haskell was also confused and equally disenchanted: "Something happens to Trintignant, he gets killed. Something happens to the tape and ... I can't figure out what. An American crusading journalist (Roy Scheider) ... [is] part [of] it. There are no ... clues to the good guys, and the bad guys ... let the Americans take the ultimate rap."[11]

Daily Variety weighed in with: "Trintignant decides suddenly he must make up [for Volante's death] and tells all on a secret tape, but is killed by a supposed Yank CIA man, played with flair by Roy Scheider."[12] Pauline Kael said, "The method of this picture could stand as a textbook demonstration of how not to make a political movie."[13] Kael mentioned Scheider and figured out that he was a CIA agent, but she did not offer a critique of his role.

Not getting credit in this film was Scheider's lot. Colin Westerbeck devoted half of his review to what Scheider does in this movie, but never once mentioned the actor's name. "Offsetting ... Darien [Trin-

***The French Conspiracy.* Darien's incriminating taped confession is heard. *Left to right:* Michael Howard: Roy Scheider; Edith Lemoine: Jean Seberg; Vigneau: Bruno Cremer; Antoine Acconeti: Daniel Ivernel.**

tignant's character], *The French Conspiracy* has ... another journalist [who is]... undercover (C.I.A.). This ... character ... seems peripheral to events [and] ... later pops up unexpectedly to commit a crucial murder, calmly betray a friend and ... keep the conspiracy rolling. [He is] necessary because the conspiracy theories never quite manage to fit."[14] Known as *Plot* in Europe, the title change was the most logical thing to come out of this film. Margaret Tarratt declared, "*Plot*'s main strength seems to derive from the integrity of individual performances from the highly professional actors who at present enrich the French cinema.... As an exposure of corruption, the film lacks the impact ... expected from its subject matter and cast."[15] Roy was becoming famous in France with *The French Connection*, *Klute,* and even *Puzzle of a Downfall Child*, which the French adored. Scheider said that before *Jaws*, he would have been recognized in Paris faster than in Los Angeles. After *The French Connection*, they were comparing Roy to their own superstar, Jean-Paul Belmondo.

Scheider found the process of making *The French Conspiracy* amusing. He could not speak a word of French and was dubbed in afterward. Roy worked through the film by saying his line in English when the other actor stopped talking in French. He enjoyed working in Europe as the continent's different working rhythm fit his lifestyle much better. Scheider is a night owl. "The hours are different ... starting at 12 [noon] and going to eight, so that you at least have your mornings to yourself. I prefer those hours ... 'cause I'm not too sharp at 8 in the morning ... my head is still a bit foggy. By noon, I'm doing pretty good."[16]

Trintignant brought Roy the script of *The Outside Man.* His French costar thought it was a fine turnabout. Since

***The Outside Man* (1973, United Artists). Lucien gets the drop on Lenny. Lenny: Roy Scheider; Lucien Bellon: Jean-Louis Trintignant.**

Scheider had killed him in the previous film, it was now time for Jean-Louis to kill Roy. Scheider took the part because it was a chance to play an out-and-out heavy—his character was a hit man from Detroit. The film was released under the French titles *Un Homme est mort* and *Funerale à Los Angelos.*

Roy was working toward getting another American film. Many months before *The Exorcist* was filmed, William Friedkin had led Roy to believe he would play the part of Father Karras. Ultimately, he did not, and Scheider felt that one of the reasons was because William Peter Blatty (the screenwriter) and, perhaps, Friedkin himself felt he was too hard, too much the image of the tough detective. They wanted someone more dark, brooding, unsure, and confused. Roy had done a play by Jason Miller in 1969, *Nobody Hears a Broken Drum*, which closed after six performances. Roy had asked Harold Clurman to come and look at this play. Clurman saw it, liked it, and told Jason Miller that he wrote good characters, but he'd like to see him write something contemporary, something about his hometown. Jason Miller went out and wrote *That Championship Season*. As soon as they were ready to go in 1973, Jason offered Roy the part of the drunk in the story, but Scheider was off to Europe for *The French Conspiracy*, so he couldn't do it. Jason Miller had apparently noticed Scheider's ability for drunks.

William Friedkin then asked Roy to read *The Exorcist*, saying he thought he'd be perfect for it. One day months later, Scheider took Friedkin to see Jason Miller in a play. Friedkin and Miller got drunk about four nights later. Friedkin decided to cast Jason, who's dark, brooding, and Irish—just what he wanted for the film.

The Outside Man. **Lenny sights his man. Lenny: Roy Scheider.**

Scheider filmed *The Outside Man* and was duly killed by Jean-Louis Trintignant, his second on-screen death. Scheider plays Lenny, a hard-driving, gumchewing, hired killer. He chases Trintignant's character all over Los Angeles before Bellon finally gets the drop on him and kills him. Bellon was hired to make a hit on a Mafia don and then found himself running for his life after the man who hired Bellon ordered him killed, so the murder of the don couldn't be traced back. Trintignant kills Scheider and his employer and then dies trying to escape one last time.

The Outside Man is rare in that it is basically a French film, with a French crew, that was shot entirely in Los Angeles, with mostly American actors. *Variety* felt "that names like Roy Scheider and Angie Dickinson would definitely help" sell the film in America.[17] Scheider had third billing. An X-rated version of this film was screened in Los Angeles on June 27, 1998.[18]

Roy returned to New York and was cast by Phil D'Antoni in yet another film based on the exploits of real-life New York cop Sonny Grosso. Roy felt he owed a lot to Phil D'Antoni, that from the first day he walked into his office, D'Antoni had absolute and total faith in him. It was wonderful to have that kind of support. Principal photography on what the *Los Angeles Times* called "Phil D'Antoni's sequel to *The French Connection* began ... [the second week in January] in the Bronx."[19]

Phil D'Antoni talked about making *The Seven Ups:* "I first presented ... [the film] to ... [20th Century–Fox production chief] Elmo Williams, just after completion of ... *The French Connection.* When Fox expressed interest ... our conversation turned to ... directors. The more we discussed [it], the further apart we [were] until he suggested, I [was] the person."[20]

The French Connection also helped Cynthia Scheider change careers. She had begun to assist a few cutters working for Time-Life documentaries and had done three or four. With Roy's help, she got an editing job on *The French Connection*—as an assistant with no pay—in the cutting room. Jerry Greenburg (the editor) took a liking to her and she worked for him (with pay) on *Pelham One Two Three.* Scheider said, "When she edited *Seven Ups,* I found it rather disconcerting to find my wife telling me which of my scenes didn't work. Her approach to the material was so much different than mine. But she was right."[21] There is a Scheider family inside joke in this film. One of the villains, Moon, has a meeting. As he walks past a group of schoolchildren, the teacher asks one of them, "Maximillia, can you tell me?"[22] The camera, however, does not stay on the children long enough to determine if Scheider's daughter is there.

I did not notice anything else biographical in the film, but being the star allowed Scheider to dress in a style that movie

The Seven Ups **(1973, 20th Century-Fox). Buddy tracks Moon to the auto graveyard. Buddy Manucci: Roy Scheider.**

viewers would soon to come to recognize, complete with sweatshirts with the sleeves hacked off and leather jackets. Scheider felt that by the time an actor is 40, he should have some idea what looks good on him, and his wardrobe in this film does make Scheider stand out. Roy felt that he had found a style for himself, and he continued to choose the same kind of clothing to wear in his films as his career continued.

Philip D'Antoni shared a story about filming for 13 weeks in New York City. On location in midwinter, there were numerous logistical problems and merely moving equipment and a crew of 50 or 60 people around town was an enormous job. He was liable to attract a huge crowd in a minute, so D'Antoni often resorted to hidden cameras and a minimal street crew. There was one shot in downtown Brooklyn in which he used four cameras, two hidden in nearby vans, one atop a building, and one inside the window across the street. Phil walked the actors through the scene without having anyone notice them. But when he started filming, two policemen, who happened to be passing through the area, noticed the kidnapping. They rushed into the scene, but the two actors convinced them that they were police, too. So the real cops went into the street and held traffic while the actors continued their kidnapping. It turned out to be a perfect shot, so he kept it in the film. D'Antoni also let Scheider do a lot of his own stunt driving, although it gave him several bad moments worrying about losing his leading actor. Roy was a good driver, and he became a better one fast.

Scheider said about his first starring role, "I don't think of myself as part of the new breed," but identifies instead with actors like Gable, Tracy, and Bogart. "[I'm] a throwback [to] the kind of actor ... I saw [in] movies ... in the 40s and the 50s. These were ... men who ... never gave up. They always fought. Money never meant much to them, but surviving meant a great deal. They existed ... when an actor had to be a man."[23] Roy Scheider only accepts parts that portray men with strong characters, men who are like the rugged individuals he admires. "My idea of a leading man was a man who led. He set the tone, the pace, the style. And he was always the strongest. That's the way I like to act. I prefer playing the biggest part, the most challenging part, the most difficult part. I'm not a very

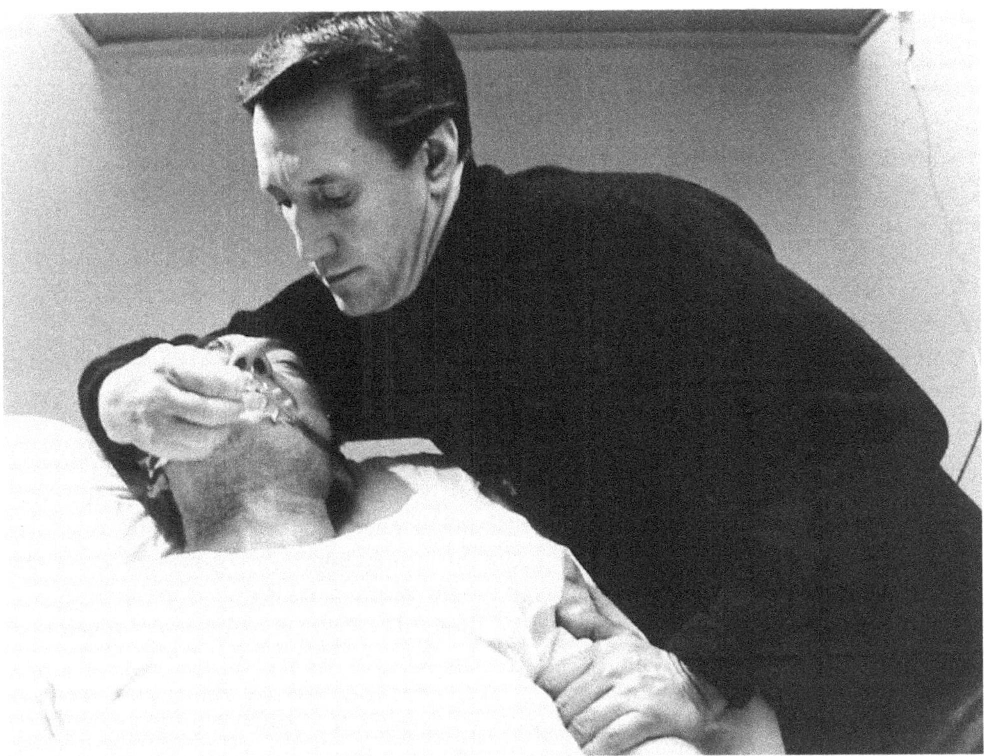

***The Seven Ups*. Buddy interrogates Carmine for the name of Ansel's killer. Buddy Manucci: Roy Scheider; Carmine Coltello: Lou Polan.**

good follower, but I'm a terrific leader." But that doesn't mean Roy has to be tough. Roy feels that if a character is successful, "I want him to be tough when he has to be, but I want people to see a human being first."[24] In a bit of real-life casting, one of the detectives, Mingo, is played by New York City detective Jerry Leon. Sonny Grosso was also a technical advisor on the film.[25]

The *Chicago Tribune* called *The Seven Ups* a sequel to *The French Connection*, noting, "There's going to be a sequel, as yet untitled, set in Paris, with Gene Hackman going there and teaming up with a gendarme, played by Jean-Paul Belmondo."[26] *French Connection II* was made and released in 1975, but Belmondo did not get the part. The idea of casting Belmondo as Hackman's partner was interesting, since he was the French actor everyone kept saying Roy Scheider resembled. Mary Campbell continued, "The movie [*Seven Ups*] is misleadingly titled ... [and is] ... the future adventures of ... Sonny Grosso—the real cop."[27]

Vincent Canby called *The Seven Ups* "a vicious, mechanical clumsy thriller." Roy Scheider is mentioned in the review but is not critiqued, except for Canby noting, "the film's characters have less individuality than performing bears."[28] Stuart Alexander said, "Buddy [played by Roy Scheider], achieves a convincing ambiguity ... whether he's ... clean ... or corrupt. Leader of *The Seven Ups*—he's cool and tough, and like Dirty Harry, not adverse to using ... unethical methods to achieve results. With a well-constructed plot and a good pace ... [it is] a reasonably entertaining police thriller."[29]

The *Independent Film Journal* wrote,

"A slick, but undistinguished action piece which unfortunately comes nowhere near the classy appeal of the earlier films. Roy Scheider has a good face and effectively carries his tough-guy role while not tempering it with too much range."[30] Roy Frumkes noted, "The acting is very capable, believable and stimulating."[31]

David Denby declared it "a pure genre film with hardly a single original or creative element ... remarkably efficient and well made and thus should satisfy connoisseurs. Cops, hoods, guns, chases ... shootouts ... and ... sadistic thug-cop (Roy Scheider) with no personal characteristics whatsoever. [The film] is perfect ... the perfection of nullity."[32]

Jay Cocks stated, "*The Seven Ups* are a squad of special cops. They are brutally efficient. Roy Scheider, the leader ... has just the right grave, anonymous face for the part, the right quality of eruptive violence. There are no heroes here."[33]

"This clumsy story of four brutal cops shares ... the ugly abrasiveness [of *The French Connection*] without ... its swift pacing or elegant editing" was the judgment of Paul D. Zimmerman. "Scheider doesn't have the weight or the presence to carry a movie by himself.... His sawed-off face [is] an emblem of implacability. D'Antoni prizes efficiency above feeling or morality."[34]

Later in the year, *The Seven Ups* and *The French Connection* were released as a double bill with the tag line "Back to Back, Chase to Chase." The chase is the one element that *The French Connection* is most remembered for. The movie was featured in an American Movies Classics documentary called "Hollywood behind the Badge," which aired in 1999.

After assaying Sonny Grosso a second time, Scheider was ready for a change of pace. He found it in *Sheila Levine Is Dead and Living in New York.* "I ... immediately [tried to] get out of the cop mold [after *The Seven Ups*]. I liked [*Sheila Levine*] because it reinforced my position as a leading man. I played a doctor, I didn't shoot anybody; I didn't muscle anybody. It was ... a light, romantic comedy." Rex Reed agreed: "A ... disaster for everyone but Scheider, who came out of it with a deluge of fan mail, a new leading man reputation and an elevated salary. Now if you want Roy Scheider, you gotta pay."[35]

Roy was playing his first romantic screen lead. After years of smacking people around and chasing them through warehouses, he felt it was nice to jump into bed with someone. It was his first seminude love scene. You believe it when Sam slides out of bed and away from Sheila. As Dr. Sam Stoneman, Roy has to show how a bastard bachelor can turn into a sweet, vulnerable guy, eager for marriage. In a key scene, torn between Sheila and her sexy roommate, Roy shows the right confusion. He goes for the undulating roommate, but his heart isn't in it.

Sheila Levine appealed to Scheider. He made the picture knowing that Jeannie Berlin was difficult to work with and that Sidney Furie was a sentimental director. The film had some marvelously funny scenes in it, but they were cut in favor of the soap opera. He saw the first edit; it still had some comedy in it, but the next time he saw the film, it had been cut to its romantic bones and he had become a cut-out himself—of a leading man. Scheider conceded that while his part had been minimized, at least he was capable of other things than kissing hubcaps and that he was effective in scenes with ladies. "The hardest thing ... was working with Jeannie Berlin. You don't do a picture with that one unless you have a personal stake in it. She's very disturbed and it was difficult for the director."[36]

"If I wasn't married today and the father of a ten-year-old girl ... I would be living my life much like the character I play in *Sheila Levine*." Sam Stoneman is a contemporary bachelor living in New York City and serving a doctor's residency at a large Manhattan hospital. He is available, cool, responsive, and attracted to modern women and their feelings.

***Sheila Levine Is Dead and Living in New York* (1974, Paramount Pictures). Portrait of Roy Scheider as Sam Stoneman.**

So is Roy Scheider. Scheider is chased by two women: Sheila herself and Sheila's swinging-single roommate. The actor with the tough-guy image was now playing his first romantic lead. "I'd rather be chased by girls than by automobiles. I actually live in New York where the [film] takes place. I have a strong feeling for the Sams and Sheilas [of] Manhattan. I come in contact with these people every day. I've had affairs, relationships and acquaintances with women as a caring man who relates to each interaction, and I think that's approaching the search for love in the utmost of universal terms." Director Sidney Furie was so impressed with Scheider's feel for the milieu of Sheila's story that Roy was encouraged to make suggestions regarding dialogue and to incorporate nuances from his own lifestyle to heighten the atmosphere.

"In *Sheila Levine* there is truly a modern concept of man-woman relationships being portrayed on the screen. The cliche of the bachelor about town has gone out the window. Sam relates to people and to Sheila in particular. He wants a steady relationship. It is Sheila who feels unworthy and backs away from an emotional commitment. It is only through Sam's care and concern that she is able to unwind and accept herself as a person worthy of love. Through Sam, she becomes liberated." Roy Scheider is Sam Stoneman; feeling so much of the character's "insides" has made it comfortable for the actor to bring the "insides" outside for the viewers to see and feel.[37]

Vincent Canby disliked the movie, saying, "Sheila has lost her wit. Watching Sheila shlep from one arbitrary disaster to another is not funny and it's not moving. It's also a total waste of talents of Miss Berlin and Roy Scheider, who plays the handsome, sensitive unmarried doctor."[38]

Rick Herrmann described the film as "pure Hollywood kitsch: Sheila Levine has found her man, Sam Stoneman has discovered the woman he loves ... and as the movie ends, there's nothing more to be said. Furie's sensitivity should be applauded."[39]

Scheider admitted that a story he tells in this film is autobiographical. Roy describes the first time he ever wanted to kiss a girl. He had been playing Spin the Bottle and to his delight, the bottle pointed straight at a girl he liked. He walked over, held out his arms, and she made a face and went, "Yecch." It took him a long time to get over that rejection. After that girl said "Yecch," he was always afraid. He didn't want to be the one who could get hurt, the

***Sheila Levine Is Dead and Living in New York*. Sam feeds Sheila some stew. Sam Stoneman: Roy Scheider; Sheila Levine: Jeannie Berlin.**

one someone could say yes or no to. It took him almost 40 years to have enough confidence in himself to get over that feeling. Other biographical elements that Scheider includes in this film are his love of cooking, when he comes in and takes over making dinner, using dancing as foreplay to having sex, and, as noted earlier, drinking bourbon to blot out his pain.

Molly Haskell liked the star: "But we shouldn't blame Roy Scheider for being a spectacularly compelling leading man. He exudes a quiet, sexy, old-fashioned, Shetland-sweater '50s kind of charm and makes the transition from semi-cad ... to committed lover with grace."[40] Stephen Farber didn't care for the film: "Director Sidney Furie expects us to root for Sheila and Sam ... [but] by the time Sam capitulates, he has [been] so insensitive that the 'happy ending' has a distinctly sour taste.... Some people may be seduced by the movie's synthetic romanticism.... she gets her Prince Charming."[41] Pauline Kael didn't care for the film either: "His extraordinarily passive doctor makes sheep's eyes at her while Kate leads him around by the nose. When he finally delivers his declaration of love ... a muscle twitches and you half expect the audience to burst into applause: at last, Scheider has done something."[42] Judith Crist claimed that the screenwriter, Kenny Solms, "has set the cause of women back some 40 years. Jeannie Berlin emerges as a dull klutz. Roy Scheider tries to be as dumb as his role, and almost succeeds."[43] James Monaco called it "execrable" and a "witless, nasty, humorless film."[44]

William Everson declared, "[If] the players are, in real life, reasonably intelligent and wide-awake, then ... the performances are masterly exhibitions of the 'method' technique. The hero (Roy Scheider) is a … throwback to the leading-men of French sex-dramas … his homely features … tentative smiles … indicate an inner sensitivity."[45] Gene Siskel liked the film, but did not mention Scheider's performance. "The welcome surprise of the movie is Roy Scheider," said Charles Champlin. "As the doctor in Sheila's life, he is both strong and sensitive and he has a remarkable soliloquy … which is a consummate piece of romantic acting. Scheider is a terrific discovery, perfectly cast."[46] *Variety* called it "a very appealing bittersweet romantic drama with comedy … right in step with the contemporary realization that swinging isn't everything. Jeannie Berlin's title performance is outstanding, and Roy Scheider's excellent performance as her reluctant lover is a major career milestone."[47]

Patricia Kearney was a little more timely in her review of *Sheila Levine* for *Daytime TV* magazine than she had been for "Assignment: Munich." In the May 1975 issue, Kearney ran a still from the film and noted, "It took about a year, but *Sheila Levine* … has finally been released. It's a good suspense story … and the star, Roy Scheider (ex–Bob Hill, 'The Secret Storm,' among other roles) has gotten good reviews."[48] These reviews, good or bad, would turn out not to matter because one month after *Sheila Levine* was released to theaters, *Jaws* came out. By August, Roy Scheider was one of the stars of the highest-grossing film ever made.

— 6 —

A Shark Eats a Boat

Much has been written about *Jaws*, the first film to make $100 million at the box office. *Jaws* is considered a classic by most standards. The film's 25th anniversary in June 2000 prompted yet another round of commentary, adding to the voluminous material already published. Everyone has an opinion on *Jaws*. Whether the film is classified as cinema or over-the-top entertainment, the movie remains one of the most popular films of all time. It was named number 48 in the American Film Institute's Top 100 Films of the last 100 years in 1998. A 25th anniversary DVD version of the film was released in July 2000 with 75 minutes of extra scenes and interviews culled from the 20th anniversary's laser disc. Sales of this DVD broke a record for DVDs and pushed the film's revenue even higher. It was rated the number 5 DVD reissue of 2000 by the website CDNOW and named number 47 in a list of the 50 most essential DVDs compiled by *Entertainment Weekly* during the week of January 19, 2001. Despite all of the multimillion-dollar megahits of the 1990s, *Jaws* remains on *Variety*'s annual list of top-grossing films.

George Perry wrote about the appeal of *Jaws*. "Almost every year there is one film that receives more media attention than any other, and word of mouth requires it to be seen by anybody who wants to stay in the social swim. Producers marvel at its grosses, the public clamour [*sic*] to go to it, the theatres accept special conditions, and for weeks it is a talking point; inspiring newspaper cartoons, comedians' wisecracks, and critics' in-depth analyses. In 1975, that film was *Jaws*."[1] *Boxoffice* magazine reported, "After its first five weeks of theatrical distribution, [*Jaws*] already ranks among the top ten most successful domestic film[s] of all time ... [and it] already has had a greater impact on the public consciousness than any motion picture in history, according to Universal."[2]

Robert Osborne added, "*Jaws* became the top moneymaking film attraction of all time in a scant 78 days [after its release in June 1975]. Impact-wise, it made sharks so scary that all summer—the beaches were deserted. Director Steven Spielberg originally wanted Jon Voight to play the young ichthyologist ... but Voight was unavailable. Spielberg then considered Joel Grey and briefly, Mark Spitz."[3] Richard Dreyfuss accepted the role of Hooper under protest as an actors' strike loomed.

Screenwriter Carl Gottlieb kept notes on the filming, which were published in paperback shortly after the film was released. *The Jaws Log* is the "official" version of what happened that summer on Martha's Vineyard. Gottlieb wrote, "The casting of Martin Brody was … important. He [was] … on screen … throughout the story, and his character was the most complex … as a man who lets others shape his decisions, even [when] those decisions cost people their lives; he would … discover his flaw, struggle to correct it, and emerge at the end … as a man who has faced … the demons inside him and conquered them while … subjecting himself to … physical danger. It was a very sought after part."[4]

David Brown, the coproducer, said, "Casting, to some extent was a group effort. Richard Dreyfuss applied … for Hooper. So did Joel Grey. Spielberg liked Dreyfuss. Dreyfuss then read the script and wanted to rework it. We all liked Roy Scheider, but Spielberg was slow to come around. Robert Shaw was my idea. We had tried to get Sterling Hayden."[5]

Carl Gottlieb theorized about why Charlton Heston passed: "Heston wanted very much to play Brody, but he had saved a 747 jetliner in *Airport '75* and he was going to save Los Angeles in *Earthquake* and it didn't seem right for him to be wasting his time with a little New England resort community."[6] Nigel Andrews noted, "Spielberg wanted Robert Duvall for Brody, but … Duvall … coveted Quint. Spielberg said no. Spielberg would later admit he was wrong."[7] Robert Shaw was not the first choice for Quint, but Sterling Hayden ended up having too many tax problems.

Roy Scheider told how he was hired for *Jaws* several times. He met Spielberg at agent Andrea Eastman's Christmas party. Steven was talking to writer Tracy Keenan Wynn about the logistical problems he was having, trying to shoot this movie Roy had never heard of, about a giant shark that comes out of the water and destroys a boat.

***Jaws* (1975, Universal). Portrait of Roy Scheider as Martin Brody.**

Spielberg recalled their conversation: "Roy Scheider came over [and said], 'You really look depressed.' 'I know. I'm having a horrible time casting this movie *Jaws*.' 'Well, tell me the story.' It [took] half an hour … at the end … [Roy said], 'I can play Brody.' [Steven replied], 'You know, you're right.'"[8] Nigel Andrews added, "Spielberg saw *The French Connection* and liked Scheider's ordinary-Joe quality."[9] Scheider told Andrews, "I was introduced to Steven Spielberg by … Tracy Keenan Wynn. They were talking about a huge shark … cracking a boat in half. I thought these guys were demented.… About two months after that I got a call from Steven Spielberg. I was the first main character cast in the movie."[10]

Spielberg called Scheider to read his

script with an eye toward him playing the cop. Roy credited Steven for scooping all of the good parts out of the book and tossing out the rest. Spielberg redid the characters so that they each had a passion that a movie audience could understand. Each guy was on the boat for a different reason. Spielberg understood that movies work off human conflict, not special effects. Scheider respected Steven from the start. And in the end, Spielberg's age was an advantage. Roy felt that a veteran director would have committed suicide because the mechanical shark didn't start working until shooting was nearly over.

Carl Gottlieb recorded, "So Roy Scheider, an early favorite of Steven, got the part and first billing. Brody was a welcome change ... and we worked long and hard to develop a rounded, deeper character."[11] Another version of the Christmas party story was included in Scheider's reminiscences on the *Jaws* 20th anniversary laser disc.

Nigel Andrews continued, "The actor's film-editor wife, Cynthia, was doubtful at first. 'We both were,' said Scheider. [Roy] came to see *Jaws* as something special. 'I didn't look on [it] as a horror film. I called it a survival story.' Spielberg may have also discerned that there are two Scheiders, one who casts wry abrasive glances at the unfolding mayhem and one who is in there intrepidly panicking."[12]

Gottlieb said, "Spielberg asked that Benchley's ... characters be made more sympathetic. Once the actors were chosen, the characters were ... altered to resemble the actors physically and socially. Brody became a New Yorker ... and ... the shark killer because [we needed] a hero who starts out weak and ends up strong."[13] Scheider brought his own sense of family to the part and some fear of the water, but there is little else biographical about Brody, except for wardrobe choices. The first of many appearances of Scheider in his underwear occurs in this film along with more sweatshirts with their sleeves hacked off.

"When ... they started to encourage me to make changes—wearing glasses, bumping into things, falling down—I was worried. I just had to realize ... I should come across as bumbling, dumb, ineffectual, and klutzy." Roy's frustrations went deep. He didn't get to act at all on most days—courtesy of a malfunctioning Bruce, in-camera yachts and so on—and was told to do less when he did. Spielberg said Brody was a borderline paranoid character and "a man who is paranoid never believes his own paranoia. A man who is paranoid never believes in himself." Scheider knew it meant that he should "keep doing less." There was method in the mental pressure Spielberg put on him. "A worried, emasculated-feeling actor would best convey a worried emasculated-feeling police chief."[14] Scheider said, "I resisted Steven at first.... I saw the wisdom of it when the whole film was cut together and I 'understood' the wisdom of it when we were shooting, but emotionally it was a whole different thing."[15]

Roy told Rex Reed, "It was hell, man. It started [as] a 78 day shoot ... budgeted at 3½ million. It [was] six months and 6 million before we finished. We were driven crazy by the logistics—bad weather, building permits ... we ... only [had] a week to film at any location. Steve Spielberg [was] only twenty-six, but he never lost his cool. Spielberg was a rock."[16]

Very little was said at the time, but in later years it came out that Robert Shaw drank too much on several occasions and bullied costar Richard Dreyfuss. Nigel Andrews shed some light on their feud:

> Spielberg dates the two men's falling out from the day the alcohol-prone Shaw poured himself a whiskey saying, "I would give anything to be able to just stop drinking." Dreyfuss said, "OK" and threw the drink out of the porthole. "He didn't forgive me for that,"

***Jaws*. Ellen tries to comfort Martin after the Kintner boy is killed. Chief Martin Brody: Roy Scheider; Ellen Brody: Lorraine Gary. Outtake or a recreated publicity still. Gary is holding a coffee mug, not a shot glass; there is no shot glass in Scheider's hand and he is wearing his police shirt, not the brown flannel shirt he wears in the film.**

> says Dreyfuss. Shaw went on to needle and provoke Dreyfuss almost every day that they worked together. He accused [Rick] of being a coward and offered him $1000 to climb the boat's 70-foot mast and then jump off into the ocean. Dreyfuss refused, so Shaw kept upping the offer until Spielberg intervened. On another day, Shaw aimed a fire hose at Dreyfuss, whereon the younger actor stalked off the set for the day saying, "That's it. I don't want to work with you anymore. Go fuck yourself."[17]

Scheider told Nancy Griffin, "Shaw ... [bullied] him all the time."[18]

Dreyfuss amused himself by dating any available women. *Duddy Kravitz* had just opened to excellent reviews, and apparently everyone on the island had seen *American Graffiti*. "When everybody began to lose their mind on the Martha's Vineyard location, Roy stayed cool. He was kind of a cheerleader for everyone else," said Spielberg.[19]

When sailboats on the horizon delayed filming or when the hydraulic shark refused to run, Scheider knew what to do. "While most ... sat around impatiently, Roy Scheider [settled] on the beach in his navy blue bikini ... and retouched his tan."[20] Scheider informed Rex Reed, "Martha's Vineyard is home to every big yacht and sailboat ... everyone comes there. So ... these regattas [were] going on constantly. Finally we decided [to] reshoot when regatta season was over. But the water was too choppy, with five foot waves. So we [went] into the harbor for close-ups and got hit with a northeaster for six days."[21]

Gottlieb's official explanation about the shark that refused to work was "nobody had ever built a working ... 25-foot great white shark that could swim, be photographed from all angles, and perform certain tricks, like biting a man in two, attacking a boat, [and] suffering strikes from harpoons and missiles."[22] Phillip Taylor added, "Instead of the original 52-day shooting schedule, the film took three times longer than that to complete because of the difficulties of shooting at sea and because of problems with the three 24-feet one-and-a-half ton mechanical sharks. The first Bruce sank on its first test and the second one exploded. For their part, the actors were conscious of a potential disaster since the film depended not on their skills, but upon the acting abilities of a cross-eyed mechanical monster whose jaws would not close properly."[23]

"It was like a wake," said director Brian DePalma, who was visiting the set at the time. "Bruce's eyes crossed, and his jaws wouldn't close right." As everyone stood around debating what to do with the prima donna shark, Richard Dreyfuss declared, "If any of us had any sense, we'd bail out now."[24]

Scheider described one of the shark problems: "The producers asked [the press] to please not dwell on the mechanical shark. So naturally, these reporters went down to the shed … took lots of photos, and wrote stories about [the shark]. It's amazing how many people … gave us this line of bull. They … wanted to expose … we were having difficulties with the shark."[25]

Time printed many details of the mechanical sharks. "They were … "made largely of plastic, [weighing] 1½ tons … [and they] cost about $150,000.00. Built for different purposes—one for left-to-right [filming] … another for right-to-left … a third for underwater scenes—each was … operated by hydraulic pistons and compressed air. The controls … were operated by 13 technicians using scuba."[26] John Culhane had more information about Bob Mattey's designs: "The platform sharks always presented a full side to the cameras. They could 'swim' for more than 60 feet by riding the track along specially greased rails. They could dive, surface and look at the camera, thanks to the pivot arm. They could also wave their tails, bite and chew. But for them to do all these things took a crew of fifteen shark operators."[27]

Roy related to Peter Biskind, "Because we had nothing to shoot, we had so much time that we became a little repertory company. You had a receptive director and three ambitious, inventive actors. So in a strange way, the inability of the shark to function was a bonus. We seized this occasion to elevate the material into marvelous scenes among these three guys."[28]

Scheider took credit for his famous reaction shot, where he sees the shark for the first time. He expresses horror in utter silence. Everyone in the theater screamed. To Roy that was the "as if" that worked for him. He pointed out that there was no shark in front of him when he did that shot, because it still wasn't working. Roy also wrote the line, "You're gonna need a bigger boat." On the 20th anniversary laser disc Scheider noted, "That line became part of the language, it came to identify anyone who was ever faced with an insurmountable problem."[29]

Scheider's wife and daughter came for a visit. Roy flew his daughter in from camp. "I always try to treat my daughter as a *person*. I don't distinguish between 'correct' male and female pastimes. She plays baseball, she roller skates … and she can be very feminine."[30]

Roy only cracked twice during all those frustrating months, and both incidents involved food. One was at a wrap party that Verna Fields hosted. Everyone knew how important the affair was to Fields and that only made it worse. By all accounts, Roy started the food fight. Carl Gottlieb explained, "Over dinner at the Kelly House, Roy, Steve, Rick, Dick, David and some others got into a furious food fight, splashing wine on each other, throwing mashed potatoes, getting a serious case of the sillies."[31]

Scheider admitted, "I … poured a plate of fruit cocktail … on [Spielberg's] head. That's when it started. Dreyfuss immediately … threw his wine in my face. I took a big wad of pate … and smeared it on Spielberg's coat. All hell broke loose. Ravioli went over Dreyfuss … fourteen people started throwing food. The cook and the staff loved it. The tourists … thought we were typical Hollywood riffraff."[32] In the 20th anniversary interview, Scheider described how they "waited and waited and waited for the shark to work, waited for the sailboats to clear the horizon and how all the months of being on the island were making everyone a little flaky. So one night, there was this tremendous buffet and I said to Ric Fields, 'Wouldn't it be funny if there was a food fight ... suppose someone started throwing food?'"

Spielberg picked up the tale: "Roy started it, he picked this gob of mashed potatoes and threw it in my face. Before I could pick up any food, Dreyfuss threw his dessert in Roy's face ... I mean, right in his face, the nose, the eyes, everything. Scheider then picked up two desserts and heaved them at Dreyfuss, who ducked, and they hit someone else." Spielberg said he "felt like Jimmy Cagney in *Mr. Roberts*, because he was the one who couldn't finish the picture so the crew could go home."

Scheider recalled, "A great melee, food flying everywhere. The kitchen staff came out and that was the most hilarious thing they had ever seen, but I don't think some of the townspeople found it so amusing. But it was a tremendous blowing off of steam."[33] Steven added, "I remember Roy and Rick, covered with food, diving into the pool to clean off and all this once yummy food rising to the surface like technicolor silk in the once turquoise pool. So I jumped in with them to get clean. This is what happens in the Navy when you don't get shore leave."[34]

Edith Blake explained, "Verna Fields decided late in the season that everyone in the movie had been so nice to her that she would have a dinner party ... and she chose [the] popular and proper buffet night." Blake spoke with a hostess at the Kelly House about the incident. Jean Protzman said, "[I] overheard Roy and Rick deciding to shock the stuffy proper people and shock them they did. How it started no one admits remembering. It was only a noisy kind of upheaval but things got out of hand and someone started throwing food." The next day Rick and Roy told Jean it was a shame; they felt that had anyone else behaved that badly he would have been thrown out but "because it was us, we got away with it."[35]

Protzman related another incident from her front row seat at the Kelly House. "One morning at breakfast Steve Spielberg, Rick Dreyfuss and Roy Scheider, full of gaiety, started clowning and singing and soon they were standing on their chairs for better delivery. The consensus of the diners seemed to be, 'Damn actors, can't stop acting, even at breakfast,' which the waitresses thought was unfair since the men were just full of such good spirits. Yet one wonders if the room had been empty."[36]

Roy's other blowup came over catered lunch on board the *Orca*. Carl Gottlieb wrote:

> So here comes Roy, a mad gleam in his eyes ... carrying this tray ... that is supposed to be lunch.... Roy ... threw the tray on the deck ... screamed at the A.D. ... shouted at Steven and ... unburdened himself of all the frustrations and observations ... for the last seven months. It ... took hours for Steven to calm him down and walk it off, which isn't easy on a small boat.
>
> Robert Shaw had his golf and his stories. Ricky Dreyfuss had his petulance and his love-life. Roy Scheider finally blew it over the food and special effects delays. The cabin boy picked up the mess, and the next day Roy was fine. No one was sorry to see the summer end.[37]

David Brown, ever the diplomat, said, "One of the most difficult things about *Jaws* was keeping the actors from developing 'island fever.' Roy Scheider threw a plate of food that displeased him to make a point about catering."[38]

Dreyfuss and Spielberg still have bad memories of shooting this film, but Scheider claims only to have fond ones: "I loved the ocean. I loved the outdoors. I thought if I was going to be stuck on a movie, this was the one to be stuck on."[39] Scheider continued, "I never made jokes about the shark. I never called the shark Bruce, ever."[40] The shark was named in honor of Spielberg's Beverly Hills lawyer, Bruce Ramer.

Probably the worst experiences Scheider had during the filming of *Jaws* were two unplanned sinkings of Quint's shark boat, the *Orca I. Orca II* was the specially built stunt boat rigged to sink on cue. *Orca I* was not supposed to sink, but like everything else that went wrong that summer, it did. The *Jaws* press book explained the differences between the two boats: "A Novi-type wooden swordfish fishing vessel was purchased and revamped with a flying bridge to double as *The Orca*, Quint's vintage fishing boat. A partial duplicate was later fashioned of fiberglass from a mold of the [first] ship's hull for scenes [when] *The Orca* sinks."[41]

Carl Gottlieb remembered the first unplanned sinking:

> The boat [was] rigged to tip by a complicated arrangement of underwater cables. The big moment, everything is triggered, and whoops! Here goes *Orca*! One of the eye bolts in the hull anchoring the boat pulls out, along with a big section of planking, leaving a table-sized hole in the hull. In minutes ... the boat is ... listing badly, tipping drunkenly. The superstructure is [top] heavy ... there [are] ... men and equipment ... on the flying bridge, and ... not much ballast in the hold. Someone shouted, "She's going over."
>
> [The cameramen] are trying to save the cameras, with priceless film inside. Rick and Robert jump into the ocean ... the rest of the crew ... right behind them. Roy Scheider is trapped in the cabin ... where he is supposed to be for ... the shot, only now he's *really* trapped ... but ... manages to fight his way clear. The boat capsizes and sinks, and the sea is full of swimming men, small boats maneuvering to effect rescues, and ... parts of tripods, slates, scripts, coffee cups, lights, [and] cameras.[42]

The cameras were recovered and the film saved by inventive thinking and a rush flight to the lab.

Scheider did not have to reach far into his personal life to find fear of the water. When asked about how he knew to play death as a method actor, Roy admitted, "The closest [I] ever came in [my] life [to a death experience] was a near-drowning."[43] He does not enlighten us when this incident occurred, but it doesn't sound like it happened on the set of *Jaws*.

"Scheider only got hurt once, when he cut open his toe ... closing down the film for three days until he could walk again."[44] "He injured his toe ... later it became so badly infected he was ordered off his feet.... Production was shut down for three days."[45]

Edith Blake added more detail to the first sinking:

> While *Sinking-Orca* was being constructed ... real *Orca* sank... as the three R's—Roy, Rick and Robert—were battling the shark ... trying to sink them. To simulate the effect *Orca* had been firmly anchored by her port eye bolts and two boats were jerking her from starboard, something ... had to give, and it was a port plank. Jonathan Filley [the drunk young man in the opening sequence where the shark eats the skinny-dipping girl], operating one of the launches ... was shooting the breeze with his father when someone bellowed, "Hurry up, we're sinking."
>
> They were also yelling at Roy Campbell on *White Foot* (the harbor tug) to come ... and haul them out ... with his crane, but with no result. *White Foot* didn't move. *Orca* was going down pretty fast and Jonathan Filley had just deposited a load of people from her to another boat when it occurred to him and Charlie Blair ... to beach her. Charlie quickly got a line on *Orca*'s bow and headed for shore. He made it within 15 feet whereupon Jonathan in a little Boston Whaler gave her [the] final push. It was not until 10:00

Jaws. Roy Scheider, Robert Shaw, and Steven Spielberg stand in water on the _Orca_ while three unidentified crew members work around them. Outtake.

P.M. that *Orca* was towed in, propped up on the ways, and Kenny Dietz was called in to salvage her water-soaked engine. They worked through the night and had her back on station for the shark to take apart in the morning.

This time *Orca* was supposed to catch fire after her engine exploded, only in true *Jaws* style, she really did catch fire. Special effects men had been pouring oil on the hot exhaust, sending up great pillows [*sic*] of smoke. This was fine until they poured on too much. As

> the smoke from the fake and eventually real fires piled into the sky, they were spotted by some irritatingly alert young pilot who reported a burning boat to the Coast Guard [which] gave all concerned a tongue lashing that no one heeded, as Barbara [the production secretary] said, "In a business where it costs $1000 a minute you can't stop for little things like burning boats." The honey wagon, with its Universal dressing rooms, the trucks and the Teamsters were the only visible evidence of *Jaws* in town during the day. But [at] last light ... the strange little fleet, running lights atwinkle, would trail into the harbor, carrying their exhausted illusion makers home. They'd be off again so early in the morning that most tourists weren't up to see them go.[46]

The second unplanned sinking was another close call for Scheider: "There was no time to work out these ... stunts. You ... pray. You don't know what the hell [will] happen ... the shark did split the boat in half. I was up to my shoulders in water and I got out of there like a torpedo. The fear just drove me out of the cabin like I had been shot. We got marvelous things on film at [the] expense of [many] people's necks. People ... got hurt.... there was nothing normal about making *Jaws*."[47]

Mik Cribben, who was visiting the set at the time, described the incident: "Just before 5:30 ... Steve Spielberg ... called 'Action.' The shark came down on the boat ... the boat [filled] up with ... water. I saw Roy Scheider dive into a mass of nail-filled pieces of wood ... and he did not come up for a very long time."[48]

Scheider tended to minimize the sinkings in his post–*Jaws* interviews, mostly done in the late 1990s. He talked instead about doing the prep for the stunt of crawling out of the sinking *Orca*—when it was supposed to sink. Scheider has volunteered the story several times about "how he and stunt coordinator, Ted Grossman, worked together putting knives and axes where Scheider could use them if he needed to."[49]

One recent recounting of this story by Scheider was in "The Directors" series on the Encore cable channel on June 7, 2000, when the series profiled Steven Spielberg. Scheider continued, "In *Jaws*, there were several times that the shark almost capsized the boat. The last thing I wanted to be ... was a stuntman. In one film [*The Seven Ups*] I've seen a stuntman accidentally hit a truck. People [don't] realize how many get killed and injured making movies."[50] "I did all my own stunt work, not because I wanted to.... We were working on a boat in tight spaces ... there was no way a stuntman [would not be] shown full face in the close-up."[51]

Scheider continued to be prudent long after his *Jaws* experiences: "I won't get certified as a diver, so I don't have to go down there, because a person could drown."[52] Other mishaps included Dreyfuss almost being imprisoned in his shark cage and two support boats colliding. Spielberg narrowly missed being smashed on impact in that crash. He also did a cameo as an Amity Point Life Station worker.

Carl Gottlieb also had a close call while filming. Originally, Meadows was supposed to be there when the wreck of Ben Gardner's boat was found. In an agonizing story session, Gottlieb conceded there was no reason for Meadows to be in the scene, and Steven insisted it would be spookier to play it at night with just Brody and Hooper. Before this decision, Gottlieb, Scheider, and Dreyfuss were sent out in a small Boston Whaler, *Fascinating Rhythm*, to film the scene as first scripted. The boat was quite overloaded, with the three principals, Freddy Zendar to run the boat, Steven the director, a cameraman, a camera operator, a sound recordist, a script supervisor, and a grip. In the hold were about 1,000 pounds of batteries to power the portable lighting.

They began to film various setups, the cameraman balancing the 40-pound

Panaflex camera on his shoulder and trying not to fall in every time the boat hit a wave. Rick Dreyfuss was pretending to drive. Roy Scheider was clinging to the aft transom, seasick. Gottlieb pretended to tie them up as they pulled alongside. Fred Zendar was below the gunwale, actually steering the boat and throttling the engine for Rick, who had never run a boat before. Except for Roy, they were all acting like crazy. He was seated next to barrels of real dead fish heads, which the prop man had obligingly placed on board as "chum," so he didn't have to act sick.

On the third take, Gottlieb leaned over, but the gap was too wide and he fell out of the boat into the icy water. Cut! Freddy Zendar saved Gottlieb's life by pulling the key out of the ignition, stopping the propellers. While Carl was treading water, Zendar scrambled to find the ladder to put over the side, so he could climb back into the boat. The ladder was put over and Gottlieb was pulled back aboard in record time by Zendar and Scheider. After some hot soup and a clothing change, they filmed the scene. Total lost time: one half hour.

Later in the afternoon, Steven directed them to head into the waves because there wasn't enough splashing. Fred shook his head, put them about, and during the next take, the cameraman goes "Oops" as a wave almost swept him over the side. The swell crashed over the bow and dropped 100 gallons of sea water onto the sound recorder, who took a wet earphone out of his head and commented, "That's a wrap for sound." Cold, drenched in spray, seasick, and thoroughly uncomfortable, the Boston Whaler crew headed back in with a $2,500 Nagra sound recorder shot.

Despite these setbacks, the film did finally get made. Roy recalled the first time he saw the film with the public: "They laughed and they screamed in all the right places, they did everything we hoped they would do."[53]

Robert Bookbinder assessed the results:

> Robert Shaw, Richard Dreyfuss, and Roy Scheider—all ... became major stars as a result of *Jaws*. It was the subject of one of the most extensive publicity campaigns in history, and to this day ... Universal freely admits they sold *Jaws* as an "event" first and a motion picture second. During the eight months prior to its release ... Richard D. Zanuck and David Brown ... Peter Benchley ... and Verna Fields embarked on a remarkable nationwide tour to promote ... "*Jaws*-consciousness." The ad campaign on radio and television was especially well devised. These ads became known for the at once catchy and chilling slogan, "None of men's fantasies of evil can compare with the reality of *Jaws*."

The film had a staggering promotional budget of over $2.5 million and began a trend that was later to become an integral part of future megahits, like *Star Wars*. To coincide with the picture's release, consumer products such as T-shirts, tote bags, and lunch boxes were marketed and sold by the millions, each featuring the familiar logo of the shark's head rising from the water. The poster "added greatly to the film's selling power, combining the two elements that never failed to attract customers—sex and violence. The poster consisted of a giant phallic shark's head rising toward a nude female swimmer."[54]

Scheider discussed with Gordon Hunt that "his own reaction of fear during the movie paralleled Brody's, and that yes, Scheider was the 'everyman' character in the film. And that his victory was the audience's victory." Scheider then asked Hunt, "Why is there always sadness in victory?" Hunt replied, "For something to win, something has to lose." "There are several reactions in that climactic scene, beyond the initial elation of having beaten the monster, and I could appreciate the effort that went into that loss."[55]

In 1998, Scheider taped commentary to be played during the commercial breaks of *Jaws* on Turner Network Television in 1998–99. Scheider, sitting in a lawn chair on a beach, told some anecdotes for TNT viewers. The clip where Brody gets slapped by the grieving widow Kintner was shown. "I remember that very well. The actress had no idea how to hit someone in the movies. Every time she slapped me, she really slapped me and it hurt like hell. She had no control. A couple of times I wanted to strangle her, but it was very effective."[56] Actress Lee Fierro said, "It took 17 takes and he stood there and let me do it. I heard later he had to go to a chiropractor."[57]

Scheider remembered "Spielberg on the camera barge, hat down over his head, waiting and waiting and waiting for the shark to work." Roy described how the sharks were made and that the saltwater took a terrible toll on the exposed pneumatics that controlled the sharks. Mattey and his effects team struggled to make the sharks work, day after day after day. The entire film was shot in the ocean, except for the closeup of Ben Gardner's decomposed head coming out of the boat, which was added after the first preview in Dallas, and was shot in editor Verna Field's swimming pool. Roy's last story was a discussion of his character and how Spielberg kept telling him, "no, no, no," every time he tried to strengthen Brody. Spielberg did not want anyone to think Brody had the remotest chance of killing the shark.[58] The clips aired mostly on the TNT Saturday night movie.

In a TNT "New Classics" version, aired during Super 70s movie week, Scheider related different tales. Roy revealed how they "all went out to sea that first day and promptly got seasick. By dint of chewing on crackers and experience, most everyone got 'sea legs' after a while. The problem was that when [I] went back to [my] hotel room to shower at night, [I] would continue to rock back and forth, back and forth and this went on for seven months."

The next story was about Ted Grossman briefing him for the sinking of the *Orca* (the planned one) and where the knife and the ax were. Scheider then remarked how "they left [me] all alone with the knowledge they had never sunk this particular boat before and they didn't know what was going to happen. [I] was not happy." Scheider's last new anecdote (after a repeat of the Brody-as-wimp story previously related) was about the screening and how "Dreyfuss didn't believe in the film. After the 'family' screening, Rick jumped up into his arms and starting screaming how wonderful the film was."[59] "We're great! We're sensational!" Dreyfuss kept shouting over and over again.[60] In a second TNT "New Classics" showing, also on the Saturday night movie, Scheider described how the film became a blockbuster, "skyrocketing all around the world. Everybody wanted to see this movie." He told how he met Spielberg (the Christmas party story) and how he thought the premise of the film "was loony." Scheider said there is a "universal fear of water. Anything you can't see into is frightening." Roy then teasingly declared, "Yes, I swim in the ocean, but I don't go out very far." Scheider lives on the beach. "I have good respect for the water. Since making this film, I swim looking over my shoulder a lot."[61] In July 1999, Roy was interviewed again. Scheider is aware he will best be remembered as Brody, a man who lives on an island, but is afraid of the water. Roy also took credit for his ending line "Smile, you son of a bitch!"[62]

John Culhane explained how the shark explosion was achieved:

> Special effects experts loaded a model shark's head with gallons of squid and red paint. A demolition expert from Woods Hole Oceanographic Institute set a dynamite

> charge. The head exploded, but in now-typical *Jaws* fashion, it did not shower enough "blood and guts" over the scene. The shark's head was now destroyed, but the other explosions could be simulated by using real compressed air to explode a dozen gallon tins of squid and red paint between the camera and actor Roy Scheider, and adding these gory showers to the shot of the shark's head blowing apart.[63]

Vincent Canby wrote, "If you think about *Jaws* for more than 45 seconds, [it's] nonsense, but it ... can be ... great ... fun if you like ... the wits scared out of you at irregular intervals.... [The actors] ... work very hard ... to be alive, and ... come across with wit and easy self-assurance."[64] Canby mentioned *Jaws* again in a lengthy review of *Rollerball* as "a much more entertaining and witty example of science fiction. The ... shocks and sharks [are] carefully calculated to scare ... you when you least expect it. Everyone involved ... [knew] exactly what this ... movie is meant to do. There's a bit of gore ... but it's Grand Guignol stuff."[65] Stephen Farber was less kind: "The shallowness of these characterizations are aggravated by sloppy acting. Because he exercises some restraint, Roy Scheider comes off best, Shaw bellows and blusters and Dreyfuss ... mugs coarsely and relies on a manic cackle that is becoming something of an irritating tic."[66]

Films Illustrated said, "Roy Scheider is particularly good as the landlubber police chief who has to overcome psychosomatic seasickness to take part in the expedition ... but [Shaw] makes too strident a bid for attention."[67] "Most of this, despite an intense performance by Scheider, is flat-brush melodrama,"[68] said Charles Champlin in the *Los Angeles Times*. There was also in the same section a huge two-page ad, which consisted of two posters with different tag lines and pictures of the three shark hunters with Brody's wife. Kenneth Turan liked the film: "One of the many joys of *Jaws* is the excellent acting which helps make the plot more plausible and thus more frightening. It is light years better than the average. Roy Schneider [*sic*] is properly baffled as the police chief."[69] William Pechter felt, " Though Roy Scheider's quietly understated performance provides a solid average-man Ishmael to anchor the audience's empathy and point of view, Robert Shaw's sub-Ahab ... is just sufficiently redolent of the smoked hamminess of a Robert Newton to leave me ... longing for the real thing."[70]

"The three men in a tub who go hunting the shark are played to varying levels of competence," Gene Siskel declared. "Because these actors have delivered strong performances in ... other films, I'm inclined to fault casting.... the lean, intense Scheider doesn't have the bearing of ... a police chief."[71] Susan Rice thought, "*Jaws* ... is good, clean, mindless Saturday matinee fare. It has no religious, moral, or philosophical pretensions.... [it] exists to make us scream with horrified pleasure ... it relies heavily on the menace of the unseen. It's got solid, visceral appeal that never, ever taxes the intellect."[72] Scheider, having put up with 23 years of critical analysis of the film said, "It's not an intellectual thriller, it's what it is. The fact that it was made so well elevated it to another level."[73] James Monaco stated, "Without Dreyfuss and Robert Shaw (and to a lesser extent), Roy Scheider, *Jaws* wouldn't have been the film it was."[74] In June 2001, the American Film Institute named *Jaws* the second most thrilling film ever made, right behind *Psycho*.

Scheider was more than ready to do his next project by the time he was done with *Jaws*. It was a film called *Lightstone*, a detective drama set in the 1940s. This movie never got made.

In early 1976, *Jaws* won a People's Choice Award, after being voted the

***Jaws*. Richard Zanuck (left), Roy Scheider, and David Brown at the People's Choice Awards with the award *Jaws* won. Publicity still.**

favorite movie of 1975. Richard Zanuck and David Brown collected their award, with Roy Scheider there to cheer them on. "*Jaws* snapped up the Movie of the Year award [at] the second annual People's Choice Awards ... Thursday, February 19, [1976] [held at] the [Santa Monica] Civic Auditorium."[75]

At the 1975 Oscars, held on April 10, 1976, Robert Shaw was asked to cohost and Roy Scheider was given an award to present. Neither had received an Oscar nomination, despite Universal's vigorous ad campaign in *Variety* to get nominations for all three lead actors earlier in the year. Robert Osborne described the ceremony: "Roy Scheider was up next [the fourth presenter of the night], joined by 21-year-old newcomer Margaux Hemingway [who wore] a red and white striped 'Betsy Ross' bicentennial dress and resembled a barber pole. [Osborne does not record Scheider's attire.] They announced the Best Sound Award, which was awarded to Roger Hoyt, Roger Heman, Earl Madery and John Carter for *Jaws*. Robert Shaw followed Walter Matthau as the second host of the night."[76] *Jaws* went home with three awards: best sound, editing (Verna Fields), and best score (John Williams).[77] *Jaws* was nominated for best picture, but did not win. Spielberg was not nominated for Best Director and that was considered a snub by some. Zanuck, Brown, Spielberg, and the cast may not have won Oscars, but they had their record-breaking box office receipts

"Dinah!" (20th Century–Fox, 1975). Roy Scheider on Dinah Shore's talk show. Roy Scheider, Ruth Buzzi, Dinah Shore, Melba Moore, and Marvin Hamlisch. Publicity still.

and their People's Choice award. Zanuck, Brown, and Spielberg also had their percentage, so they could cry all the way to the bank.[78]

Jaws became a global phenomenon. Scheider's next film for Universal would star him. Roy was in demand. He was everywhere in the last half of 1975, from the cover of *People* magazine to Dinah Shore's talk show.

— 7 —

Olivier and Beyond

After the overwhelming response to *Jaws*, Scheider took care selecting his next film project. It was not a role anyone expected him to accept, given his new stardom. Scheider wanted to do *Marathon Man* for the challenge: "With a thriller, so much of the plot is a Chinese puzzle. The task is not to give an audience too much information ... not to play an emotion [they are] not supposed to know as yet. We have to keep saying no. We don't want to tip that off."[1]

Many people in the industry were surprised when Roy took the third lead, but Scheider liked the part. He could see it had several layers. The film implied that Roy's character had a homosexual relationship with another agent, Commander Janeway, played by William Devane.

Preview magazine mentioned this relationship in its "Sneak Preview" of the film, but it was not widely publicized at the time.[2] Doc Levy was a double agent, who lied to his brother about what he did for a living, had run away from his father, and was a cold-blooded killer for hire. In addition to all of this, Roy had a wonderful death scene when Laurence Olivier murdered him.

Roy almost didn't get the part. The director, John Schlesinger, didn't think Dustin Hoffman and Scheider could be brothers because they didn't resemble each other. Schlesinger asked Scheider to test. Understandably angry at being asked to do this after agreeing to take a lesser part, Scheider nevertheless went in and improvised with Hoffman a scene of them meeting, where they shadowboxed and ended up embracing. Schlesinger liked it and Roy was hired.

During rehearsal, Olivier, Hoffman, and Scheider realized something was missing—a scene to cement the bond between the two brothers. They called the author, William Goldman, who said he couldn't write the kind of scene they were looking for and it would be more natural coming out of their own personal experiences. Scheider remembered his test, and they added it to the film. Roy did have his own life experience of being the older brother. Other biographical elements in this film include a push-up routine in his underwear in his hotel room, taking his brother out to dinner in a fancy restaurant, and filching one of the chocolates as he wraps the band-aid box of diamonds for delivery.

Scheider also rewrote some of his lines to better suit his part. This talent was called on by Sir Laurence Olivier. Roy told Gordon Hunt what is obviously *his* favorite story:

> We were running our lines in rehearsal and his timing was off. It was late, he was tired, he had recently been sick, but Olivier was gamely trying to say the lines as written, but he kept pausing and throwing off the pace. Finally Schlesinger said, "Sir Larry, is there a problem?" They tried to get rid of the pause, but it wasn't working.
>
> The next day Olivier came in with a yellow pad and asked me, "Roy, dear boy, do you think you could change a few lines for me? You see, I have to react to the operative word in the sentence." Scheider is all at once amused and extremely happy to help. "So I took a yellow piece of paper and moved all the key words he needed to react to from the end of the sentence—diamonds, brother, et al.—to the beginning of the sentence and he could run his lines without the pause and we got it.[3]

William Goldman, the screenwriter, was consulted on this line change during the same rehearsal and later wrote, "That moment—when the actor of the century asked me if I minded if he switched six words around—is the most memorable incident of my movie career. Olivier. Calling me 'Bill.' Asking *me* would I mind. That's high cotton."[4]

Goldman related another Scheider, Hoffman, and Olivier rehearsal story:

> Rehearsal. A mock set is prepared. Hoffman lies down, closes his eyes. Scheider mimes opening a door, bangs his foot down to indicate the closing of the door, and Hoffman springs awake, mimes getting the flashlight and says his Shanghai line. The rehearsal stops. Hoffman [tells] the director ... that he thinks it's wrong for his character to have a flashlight in his bed table. Schlesinger tells him we'll get to it later. Continue rehearsing. But Dustin Hoffman is very much a star and has to be dealt with. [Goldman details a long argument about the flashlight.] Through all this, silent and waiting, stands Scheider. And that is probably my strongest memory of the situation—it took an hour, by the way—Scheider, waiting quietly, a perfect gentleman throughout. In my opinion, [Hoffman] didn't want the flashlight because his fans would think him chicken ... but that is the kind of thing one dares not mention to the star.[5]

Roy Scheider publicity still from Scheider's publicist. It was given out sometime between 1975 and 1978.

Douglas Brode also mentioned Olivier's impatience with Hoffman's method: "As always, Hoffman wanted to understand everything about the character he was playing—in true method acting tradition—in order to become the man and thus get him right. A polished/technician craftsman like Olivier was a bit put off by that. 'Why must he go through all this Sturm and Drang?' he would ask people standing about him on set, waiting for Hoffman to get into

Marathon Man **(1976, Paramount Pictures). Portrait of Roy Scheider as Scylla.**

character so he could perform."[6] The most famous story of Hoffman's overzealous preparation had Dustin coming in to film after a long weekend and looking terrible. When asked, Hoffman admitted he had stayed up the entire weekend to "get into character" for being sleep deprived. Olivier thought that was ridiculous. When challenged by Hoffman as to how else he was going to do it, Sir Laurence's reply became instantly classic. "Acting?" Olivier asked quietly.

William Devane said, "I had never been on a picture with a director the caliber of John Schlesinger. It was important. I wanted ... Roy's part. Everybody turned down *Marathon Man*. Scheider told Schlesinger, 'Who the hell wants to see a picture like this?'"[7]

Gordon Hunt wanted to know, "What was it like slapping the world's greatest actor?" Scheider laughed. "Yes, while he was aware he was acting with Heathcliff and *Hamlet* and *Henry V* and *Richard III*, he couldn't let that get in the way, even though he was getting little jolts from things Olivier was doing while they were acting together. Roy overcame that by realizing in rehearsals that even 'the Great Olivier' had to stumble around like any rank amateur until he knew his character and where he was going and how he was going to get there."

Hunt asked about Roy's character's murder and how getting stabbed looked so painful the way Scheider played it. "It was 2:00 A.M.. Olivier did not have the strength to play the scene the way Schlesinger wanted, so I instructed Olivier to put his hand right in there." Scheider pointed to his crotch. Olivier was told to put that metal thing in his groin, and Roy would do the movement. And that's what they did.[8]

In an interview done when *Marathon Man* came out, Roy hardly talked about the film, despite the article's three prominent pictures from the movie. Scheider was more interested in stating how much he disliked Hollywood and "the film-and-how-to-be-in-it"competition. "The end result finds you maneuvering, manipulating and machinating [at] the Beverly Hills Hotel pool to ... push yourself into projects that may not even exist. I live ... in New York, where the Polo Lounge is 3000 miles away."[9]

Douglas Brode analyzed Scheider's character.

> *Marathon Man* whisks us around a complex triangle of characters whose lives are seemingly unrelated. Scylla (Roy Scheider) seems to be some kind of a spy,... Babe (Dustin Hoffman) is a Columbia graduate student, [and] Szell (Laurence Olivier), is the one-time boss of a Nazi concentration camp ... and has long since converted the fortune he amassed into diamonds which rest in a safety deposit box in New York. But a fatal automobile accident which, at first glance, has nothing to do with any of them, will quickly tie the three characters together in a tale of terror and torture.
>
> Szell must leave the safety of his hideaway ... [to] claim his fortune, putting him in

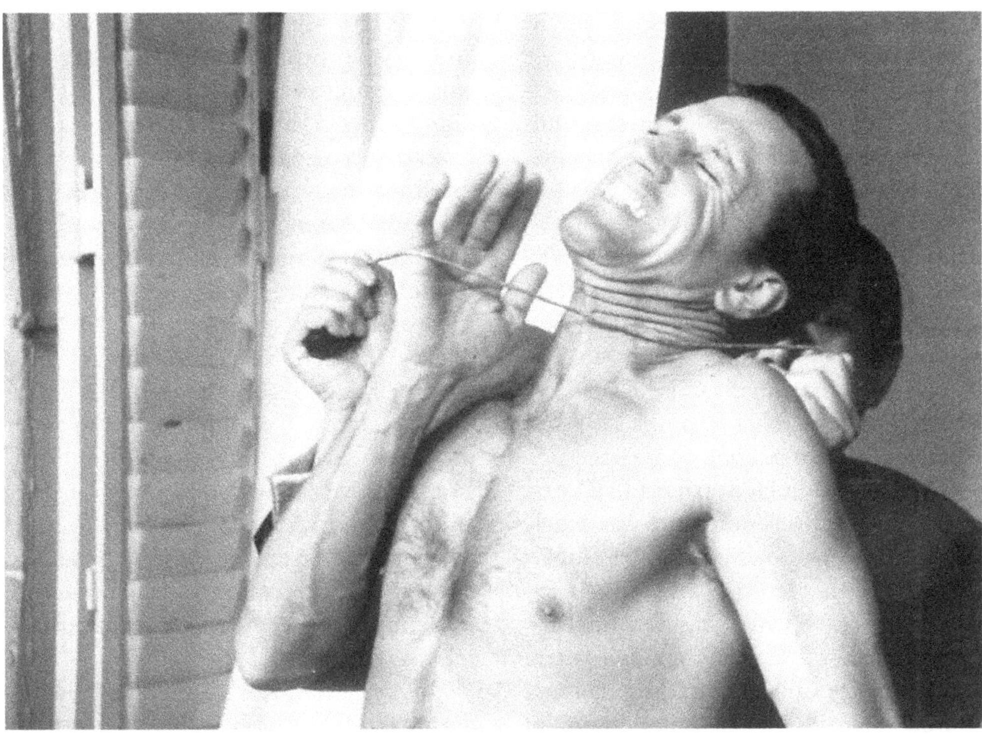

Marathon Man. **Scylla fights being strangled by Chen. Scylla: Roy Scheider; Chen: James Wing Woo.**

> conflict with Scylla and, after Scylla's death [Szell kills him], Babe [learns] his pleasant business[man] brother, Doc,... is actually an international agent known as Scylla. Scheider's role is clearly less defined than the other two, but eventually he comes to stand for the international intrigue shenanigans of the 1960s. At one point, Devane [a fellow agent] explains ... the special government agency, referred to only as the Division ... he and Scheider are members ... but much of what he says turns out to be pure fabrication.... viewers are not sure whether the two were working for any government at all.[10]

The *National Review* offered, "And if all the good guys are 'ethnics' in sweatshirts and turtlenecks, all the baddies are WASP–German–CIA–Nazi types in coat and tie. 'Doc' ... tries to play the Establishment game ... but can't really because he is Who He Is: ... he is stabbed by the enemy."[11] Vincent Canby mentioned Roy as part of a "super-secret CIA type organization" but he does not critique Scheider's performance. Canby calls the movie "a literally breathtaking nightmare, that turns out to be, within the film, absolutely true. It just wants to scare the hell out of you—and it does."[12]

Almost all of the other reviewers followed Canby's tack. The super-secret CIA organization is mentioned several times, and it is noted that its agents, in particular Scheider's and Devane's characters, are couriers for Szell, but with their own secret agenda. In the dozen reviews of the film, Scheider is mentioned about half the time and a few try to explain Doc's significance to the plot, but only two reviews say anything about Scheider's performance. *Variety* stated, "[The] film spends literally half its length getting ... basic plot pieces ... moving. By which time it's asking a lot if anybody still cares why Hoffman's brother (Roy Scheider) is a mysterious globetrotter.

As for performances ... Scheider has the warmth of a loan shark's collection agent."[13] The other mention came in *Saturday Review:* "Laurence Olivier ... brings soul-cringing credibility to evil. Roy Scheider as the brother, William Devane as his colleague, Marthe Keller as a lovely pawn ... are all brilliantly cast. *Marathon Man* [is] a potential neoclassic of the thriller genre."[14] James Monaco called it "the most elegant and extreme contribution to the genre."[15] In June 2001, the American Film Institute named the film number 50 of the 100 Most Thrilling Films made.

When Dustin Hoffman made *Wag the Dog* (1997) and his performance was widely recognized as parodying producer Robert Evans, a long-hidden "gag" reel from *Marathon Man* was shown to insiders on *Wag.* It "was made ... at Par[amount], where stars Laurence Olivier, Roy Scheider and Hoffman all did takeoff imitations ... of Evans." Evans says the reel is now "locked up," but he was "flattered that Hoffman was reviving his portrayal."[16]

The *York Daily Record* was of the opinion that "this movie did for dental visits what *Jaws* did for swimming."[17] *Marathon Man* is considered one of the better thrillers that came out in the 1970s. Lawrence Olivier won best supporting actor at the Golden Globes, and Roy obligingly picked up his award for him.[18]

With his movie career established, Scheider still had an issue he needed to resolve. Roy's father had already had two strokes and Scheider didn't want his father to die before they had it out over Roy Senior's unloving ways. One day, his wife, Cynthia, had enough of him complaining about the situation and sent Roy to New Jersey to settle the matter.

Scheider went to his parents' house, threw his mother out of the kitchen, and sat down with his father. He told his dad that he loved him and that everything Roy had done in his career was to please him, to make him happy, to make him love Roy, and to help him feel that Scheider was worth having as a son. It was not that Roy didn't know his own worth, but he wanted his father to say out loud to him, that he loved his son. Yes, he told his uncles, his aunts, and his mother, but Roy wanted to hear him say it, right here, right now. After several false starts, his father finally said the words. Roy hugged him and they both cried. After that, Roy said, it was amazing how their relationship changed. His father took an interest in what movie he was making, how Roy was investing his money, and how Cynthia was doing with her film editing. All of a sudden, they were friends. That day was a rite of passage for Scheider, like a ritual or ceremony that he needed to move into another phase of his life. All it took was a simple "I love you."

A year later, Roy's father died. Scheider was sad, but he had the comfort that they were at peace with each other. A year afterward, on Christmas Eve at his brother Glenn's house in New Jersey, Roy asked his mother if she knew what went on that day. His father had never told her anything, except that it was between him and Roy.

Scheider also admitted to problems in his marriage after *Jaws.* One day Roy and Cynthia put everything on the table—anything they had been unable to say to each other over the years—examined it and decided it simply wasn't important enough to cause them to separate or divorce.

From that time, there was nothing Roy and Cynthia did not say to each other. They even threw things, progressing from epithets to pillows to small ashtrays. That was within their rules. They had an understanding about Roy's occasional extramarital infidelities, that the affairs that happen during a period of separation are only filler until the two people who really count for each other are reunited. If they were together, an affair would be betrayal. Neither was overly enamored of marriage, but they did need something to commit to. Cynthia took a job as an editor on his next film, *Sorcerer*, and accompanied Roy on the location shoot to the Dominican Republic. "I asked Billy Friedkin if Cynthia could work on the picture as well. He was delighted. Naturally, she has to go over every frame of the film many times. Her first loyalty is to the director. It's her job to perpetuate the director's vision."[19] Cynthia would edit two more of Roy's films after *Sorcerer*.

Scheider and his wife may have fought and raged on that location, but having Cynthia there may have kept Scheider from strangling director William Friedkin. The shoot soon became an ordeal similar to what had happened to Francis Ford Coppola in the Philippines with *Apocalypse Now*. No one on *Sorcerer* had a heart attack during filming à la Martin Sheen, but several crew members probably came close.

Peter Biskind wrote:

> Friedkin was beginning pre-production on *Sorcerer*, his quixotic attempt to remake *The Wages of Fear*. *Sorcerer* was supposed to be a little 2.5 million in-between movie while he was waiting to launch his next big project, *The Devil's Triangle*, about the Bermuda Triangle, except that instead of planes and ships sinking to the bottom, he had the notion that they would go up into space. But Spielberg beat him to it with *Close Encounters*. Friedkin had always been competitive with Coppola. Coppola was going to the Philippines to shoot *Apocalypse Now*, [so] Friedkin would go to South America to shoot *Sorcerer*, an ambitious, pricey foray into the heart of darkness.[20]

The part that Scheider played was originally written for Steve McQueen. Thomas Clagett declared, "[McQueen] didn't want to leave the country for ten months. He'd just married Ali McGraw and there was no part for her in the film. [Walon] Green [the screenwriter] said they should have probably rewritten the part of Scanlon ... at that point because McQueen was ideal in a silent part like that."[21] Friedkin would not give McQueen the producer job he wanted for Ali McGraw, so she could come along, but he was willing to give Scheider's wife the film editor's job Roy requested. For whatever reason, McQueen turned down the role. "[Scheider] was absolutely wrong for that part," Friedkin told Clagett. "The biggest casting mistake I've ever to date made. I thought he did a damn good job, though. Most pictures don't need a star. *Sorcerer* needed stars, I'm afraid. These characters were written for people bigger than life. They required guys who bring with them the baggage an audience understands. McQueen, Clint Eastwood, Jack Nicholson. I went for months trying to get them, but none of these guys wanted to go [to the Dominican Republic]."

Clagett continued, "Most of the supporting actors, too, were not the first choice, [Friedkin admitted]. The only character in *Sorcerer* that was cast as I wanted him was Amidou. The rest ... were all fifth, sixth and seventh. Well, no, Francisco Rabal [Nilo, the Mexican assassin] was about second or third choice. But not Scheider and not Bruno Cremer, who played Manzon, the Frenchman. I liked Cremer, but the part needed Jean-Paul Belmondo or Leno Ventura.

"Scanlon looks and sounds reminiscent of Humphrey Bogart in *The Treasure of the Sierra Madre* with his battered hat, unshaven face and tough guy stance. It was exactly what Friedkin wanted, too, according to Walon Green, who said that Friedkin purposely molded Scheider's performance into Fred C. Dobbs. But watching Scheider strain and pull, one can see his nerves screeching with every snapping plank and swaying motion [of that bridge]. Scheider may have had to act, as Green

Sorcerer. **(1977, Paramount/Universal). Roy Scheider in full Bogart costume as Juan Dominguez.**

said, but with his gladiatorial visage, Scheider's Scanlon is believable, gutsy and most important, desperately human."[22]

There are not as many visible biographical elements in this film as in others since Friedkin wanted Bogart. Scanlon is from New Jersey, when he could have easily been a mobster from New York City, and at the end, his last desire is a dance.

Scheider's preparation for this role required some additional skills:

> Last Spring, on a deserted stretch of back road in Ventura County, California, Roy Scheider climbed behind the wheel of a clumsy ancient truck. He then performed a series of hazardous maneuvers, throttling the vehicle to top speed to take hairpin curves and slalom down steep grades. "I was rehearsing to stay alive," Scheider said with characteristic understatement.
>
> Scheider plays the most experienced driver of the four ... a one-time wheel man for a New Jersey mob. "When we got to the Dominican Republic, I appreciated all that practice back in the states. Billy's approach to *Sorcerer* ruled out rear-screen projection or trick photography. The actors, the vehicles and the terrain were too closely integrated into the composition of each shot. So what you see in the film is exactly what happened," Scheider explains. "When I take a mountain turn on two wheels, on a road with potholes the size of shell craters, that's the way it was. No one but Billy Friedkin could have persuaded me to take the insane chances I did. But when it was over and I looked at the rough footage I knew it was worth it. The next time I'm asked to write down my occupation ... I think I'll put down Billy Friedkin's driver.[23]

"The stuntmen complained ... the principals were doing all the stunts. The most dangerous scene ... was ... where we were driving over the rope suspension bridge in a horrible storm and we kept swaying back and forth. What the audience [saw] on the screen is what really happened."[24] Publicity for *Sorcerer* stated it took more than three years to bring the picture to the screen. Roy continued, "Some people thought I was crazy, going into the Dominican jungle with Billy Friedkin for the better part of a year, when I could have made maybe three pictures for three times the money during the same period."[25]

Peter Biskind chronicled:

> Friedkin's behavior made a difficult situation impossible. He was said to have fired scores of people during the course of the production, including Dave Salven, his long time line producer, and five production managers. "I was the only guy he couldn't fire, because I was the leading man," says Scheider. "I said

***Sorcerer*. Scheider walks away from the car crash, while three unnamed extras walk the other way out of the shot. Outtake.**

> to Billy, you have to stop firing these people because I'm tired of going to the airport and saying goodbye to them."
>
> Bud Smith, Friedkin's editor, [concurred]. "He fired the director of photography, Dick Bush ... and the whole camera crew left. He fired the head of the Teamsters, and all the Teamsters left. With all that rolling stock, there must have been thirty, forty Teamsters there, so we had to bring in a whole new crew."[26]

Roy added, "We were so far inland, we couldn't get an English-speaking station on the shortwave. Our only contact with the outside world [was] The *New York Times* by helicopter. The news was five days old, but we waited for it with our tongues hanging out."[27]

At first Scheider was willing to support the film, until Friedkin blamed the failure of the movie on him, saying, "But nobody gives a shit about Roy Scheider in that part. Scheider is an interesting second or third banana. But he is a not a star. I've told him that ... and it's not a secret."[28] It certainly wasn't after Friedkin's comments were published.

Friedkin then fled his bad reviews to live in France with his wife, actress Jeanne Moreau. Scheider admitted Friedkin was a smooth talker. He had talked Scheider into doing an entire movie without what Billy calls "sentiment" or "melodrama." They didn't need any heartfelt moments. Roy had gone to Friedkin when he was afraid the movie had lost track of where it was going. The director sat down and sweet-talked him into believing it would all work out. In the end, the movie didn't make sense.

Scheider stated that Friedkin was an extraordinarily gifted filmmaker, who told stories with pictures and shot beautifully. He was also bright, well-read, and well-rounded, but underneath there was a peculiar get-even philosophy. It made Friedkin angry, made him work out of distrust and paranoia, and made him run a movie set where everyone was on edge. Friedkin believed he got the best work out of people that way. Roy did not.

Friedkin said, "I wasn't prepared for my success or failure. I felt ... buffeted by fate without any control over [my] destiny. That's one of the themes of *Sorcerer*. No matter how much you struggle, you get blown up." Friedkin calls *Sorcerer* "the favorite of all the films that I've made. It's about revenge, vengeance, betrayal—this is how I feel about life.... life is filled with betrayal ... false promises ... fate is waiting around the corner to kick you in the ass."[29]

Scheider expressed some post-picture feelings to Gene Siskel in 1980: "I was most disappointed in ... *Sorcerer* given the time and energy that went into it. The director ... calls it 'his existential melodrama.' Well ... done technically ... there is [not] enough [in it] ... for ... audiences to [root] for its characters. That sort of thing is fatal."[30] Scheider has not worked with Friedkin since this debacle. Scheider will talk about the movie if asked, but was conspicuously absent from "The Directors" series program on Friedkin made for the Encore cable television channel in 1995, which included *The French Connection* and *Sorcerer*. Scheider is loyal, but he remembers when injustices are done to him. "Since I am a Scorpio, I have a very long tail and I don't forget. Sometimes I'd wait two, three years, but it doesn't go away."[31]

Peter Biskind commented:

> A week later, *Sorcerer* did follow *Star Wars* into [Mann's] Chinese [Theater]. Dark and relentless, especially compared to Lucas' upbeat space opera, it played to an empty house and was unceremoniously pulled to make room for the return of C3PO, et al. *Sorcerer* was a major disaster, grossing only a piddling 9 million worldwide. Friedkin was dumbstruck. He couldn't believe the public didn't like it. He could not believe the critics didn't like it. The picture is punctuated by some striking images, but it is self-consciously arty and pretentious. Fatally trapped between America and Europe, commerce and art, Friedkin had finally achieved the worst of both worlds, an American remake of a French classic that was too episodic, dark, and star challenged for a late 70's American audience that was very different from the audience that had flocked to *The French Connection*.[32]

James Monaco wrote, "Sorcerer is full of extraordinary shots ... but somehow technique overwhelms meaning and emotion."[33]

Vincent Canby was one of the few critics who liked *Sorcerer*. He felt the narrative structure fatally crippled the film, but still thought it was "a walnut movie—a good little melodrama surrounded by pulp. In the way he moves and looks, Mr. Scheider is the dominant note of reckless desperation."[34] Canby revisited the corpse of the movie on July 10, 1977: "[*Sorcerer*] has some extremely good performances by Roy Scheider and Bruno Cremer, among others, but it should have been much, much tighter, less cinematically grand. It [needs] almost any other title than *Sorcerer* ... [used] to associate it with [*The Exorcist*]."[35] This title is almost explained in the *Sorcerer* press book, and it's odd that Scheider offered the explanation, rather than Friedkin: "Billy noticed that all the trucks in that part of the world are painted with mysterious symbolic legends, signs to outwit the devil and ward off evil spirits. Milk truck drivers, banana drivers, all of the truckers have their rigs painted with these beautiful, grotesque symbols. One of the island's most gifted artisans was found and put to work. The symbols he painted were based on the names we had given the trucks ... *Lazarus* [and] *Sorcerer*."[36]

David Badder wrote, "Losing a quarter of its ... length cannot have helped, [the film] seems remarkably lacklustre [*sic*],... the overall mood ... is unsure, if not ... impenetrably obscure. Scheider's role was so underwritten ... to consist ... of 'meaningful' stares off camera and mournful grimaces ... a complete miscalculation."[37]

Kenneth Turan agreed: "While Friedkin [creates] elaborate backgrounds for his four drivers, we still don't care about them. We can see everything is there ... we can see the wheels turning, but nothing ever ignites. We ... are never made to feel, and in a film like this, feeling is everything."[38] James Monaco added, "*Sorcerer* may have not been worth the 23 million it cost to make, but it certainly did provide an interesting trip."[39]

Films Illustrated stated, "*Wages of Fear* [an alternate title for *Sorcerer*] is no exception to the general rule [of sequels], despite a reliable star (Roy Scheider) and a topnotch director (William Friedkin). In fact, if anything, it's somewhat below the usual par."[40]

The summer of 1977 was not the best time for Roy Scheider. He lost *The Deer Hunter*. He had spent a good deal of time with director Michael Cimino preparing for the part, but couldn't get out of a contract that committed him to *Jaws 2*, and the role went to Robert DeNiro. It may have been for the best. Michael Smith stated, "Two weeks into production, Roy got the finished script and disagreed with the ending. (Michael [Roy's character] goes back to Vietnam to find his buddy, Nick, only to watch him kill himself in the final Russian Roulette game.) Roy reasoned that this guy would not go halfway around the world to find his friend, only to have him kill himself. Well, the good old 'creative differences' reared their ugly head and Roy walked."[41]

A contractual obligation he hadn't fulfilled came back to haunt Scheider that summer when his "Assignment: Munich" lawsuit was finally settled. An October 16, 1975, *New York Times* article stated: "NYS Sup. Ct. Justice George Carney ruled that Roy Scheider ... must pay [MGM] 120,000 plus interest for three years, because he refused to make more episodes [of "Assignment Munich"]. MGM says it paid Scheider's replacement, Robert Conrad, $17,500 an episode because [of a] contract ... with ABC-TV."[42] *Modern Screen* printed the story in January 1976 and set the amount owed at 120,000.[43] Scheider appealed. "*Jaws* star Roy Scheider is readying ... for ... 'round four' in his long-running 'dispute' with MGM. 'For the first time ... the seven appellate judges will consider [if] I even had a contract. I contend I did not. It's been damaging to ... my career ... saying I owe ... 120,000.00.'"[44] The original judgment against Scheider was for $2.5 million. "Roy was still ordered to pay damages by the judge, because 'by custom' performers who make pilots go on making the series. This [decision cost him] $163,356.00." [After the interest was calculated].[45] "[I paid] 165,000.00, after losing a court battle, to get out of a television espionage series, [I] had agreed to do for Metro-Goldwyn-Mayer. All the money I made right up through *Jaws* went to pay that debt, but it was worth it."[46]

Universal used its contract to make Scheider reprise Brody and he was not happy about it. Roy was reluctant to repeat something he had already done: "[There is nothing] new to create here ... dammit! People will flock to ... see the shark ... not me."[47] Roy had tried to get out of *Jaws 2*. He pleaded insanity and went crazy in the Beverly Hills Hotel. His act was so convincing that Barry Diller, head of Paramount, where he was making *Sorcerer*, actually called to see if Roy was stable enough to do his picture. But nothing could get

***Jaws 2* (1978, Universal). Chief Brody gives Len Petersen a parking ticket. Chief Martin Brody: Roy Scheider; Len Petersen: Joseph Mascolo. This scene was cut from the video version.**

him out of *Jaws 2*. He was locked into his contract. So, Scheider finally agreed, did the job the best he could, and hoped the public would forgive him.

Why should they even do a sequel? The box office success of *Godfather II* and other sequel films made it inevitable. David Brown knew the pressure he and Richard Zanuck were under. The expectation was a bigger and better shark, and others would produce the film if they didn't. *Jaws 2* turned out to be the most expensive film that Universal had made up to that time (1978) and cost the studio almost $30 million.

Michael Smith said, "Although both [Steven] Spielberg and Richard Dreyfuss wanted to be part of the *Jaws* sequel, the delays in Alabama on *Close Encounters of the Third Kind* kept them both out of the production. Universal had already promised a June 16, 1978, opening to theater owners in 1977."[48]

That deadline kept Spielberg from directing, as he wanted a year to do preproduction if he took over the film after John Hancock was fired. Roy said, "[Spielberg] agreed to do it if they would give him five months to develop what he considered a worthwhile story.... They wouldn't give him that time. I was all for it but they didn't want to wait five extra months."[49] Scheider, knowing the contractual inevitability of his playing Brody again, stalled Universal and made *Marathon Man* and *Sorcerer* to put as much distance between the first and second *Jaws* as he could. He agreed to financial terms that quadrupled his base salary from the first *Jaws* film. Scheider also negotiated for points, a percentage of the film's net profits. Roy was paid very well for this film. He took his usual fee for a ten-week shooting schedule, which would have wrapped the film in July, plus a $35,000 bonus for each week past that the shooting schedule ran over.[50] The *Star* quoted, "$500,000.00 for 12 weeks work and 35,000.00 each additional week."[51] Scheider certainly learned from the first *Jaws,* as his points deal and overtime contract attest. He made enough money to buy a house in Beverly Hills after the movie, as filming lasted 32 weeks beyond the initial wrap date of July 1977.

Roy Loynd stated:

> After ... four years, [Brody] would [be] more secure in his job ... more relaxed, more confident, somewhat of a local hero. Scheider

Jaws 2. **The Brodys duck out of the condo grand opening party. Chief Martin Brody: Roy Scheider; Ellen Brody: Lorraine Gary; Sean Brody: Marc Gilpin.**

> explained, "In the first *Jaws*, the ... entire town ... knew there was a monster out there. This movie is different. Only the audience knows [about the shark]. Not even Brody is sure. I'll be doing my damnedest to play everything light enough so the character [says] to himself, 'Aaaaah, maybe I'm crazy,' or else I'll look like an ass. I have to see the shark ... and the surprise bag for the audience is what the shark is going to do."[52]

Scheider continued, "I will do the best damn job I can. You're not always handed the deck you want so you run with the deck you have. Brody loses his job over what Amity elders deem his shark paranoia. It would be a mistake to play that paranoia morosely or tragically. [My] task ... was to show that behavior through action and make it believable."[53]

One of the recurring biographical elements on display in this film was getting drunk to hide his pain. After Brody is fired, he comes home inebriated and sings "Hail to the Chief" to his deputy. Brody shows a certain fastidiousness and a penchant for hacked-up sweatshirts. He uses dancing as foreplay to romance his wife. Scheider also makes the point that he can't navigate, telling Hendricks to forget about starboard, larboard, and point.

Roy has a love/hate relationship with the press. Scheider dislikes interviews, almost as much as sequels, but sees them as necessary. It can be difficult dropping his pants in public, but given the choice he'd rather flash than be ignored. One of the crew he was close to was the unit publicist, Al Ebner. Ebner hired the daughter of former president Gerald Ford to shoot publicity pictures. Susan Ford had the run of the set and snapped dozens of pictures. Several ended up in Ray Loynd's *Jaws 2 Log*. One day she apparently tried to take one too many of the reluctant star. Susan told Rona Barrett, "Scheider was riding in one speedboat ... I was in another, shooting boat-to-boat. When Roy saw me taking pictures, he stood up, turned his back, and fiddled with [his] belt. Down came his trousers and he mooned me. I laughed so hard my lens fogged up."[54]

At the Navarre Beach, Florida, location there was what *People* magazine called "a disagreement on the set of *Jaws II* [*sic*] that led him to deck director Jeannot Szwarc in the middle of the meeting."[55] David Brown told the story in his autobiography:

> The director, Jeannot Szwarc, and Roy had it in for each other almost from the start. Roy's room was next to mine ... and too often he would slip a message under my door with derisive references to Jeannot. [Roy] went off to Martha's Vineyard to film a brief sequence and continued to complain by telegram. I thought about this war between our star and director and wired Scheider to meet me in my room ... immediately on his return. Szwarc was also invited. Verna Fields ... was visiting that day. I invited her. When they were all gathered in my room, I asked Scheider and Szwarc to say everything they had on their minds and settle their differences.
>
> Jeannot remarked to Scheider, "You have quite an ego." Scheider exclaimed, "*I* have an ego? Why, you son of a bitch!" He grabbed Szwarc and flung him against the wall. Szwarc was fifty pounds heavier but Roy was in great shape. They started wrestling. When they fell on the floor, I piled on top of them. Verna screamed, "Don't hurt his face!" She didn't mean me or Jeannot. Verna decided to enter the fray and [sit] on top of us. Verna was so heavy that we screamed for mercy and started to laugh uncontrollably as we disentangled ourselves. Once freed, I put a bottle of scotch on the table and poured enough in each glass to get us gloriously drunk. We then played the truth game. Scheider wanted more attention. There were 19 young children ... and they required intense [direction]. Roy wanted the same. "I need to be directed, too." Roy was thought of as someone who could take care of himself. From that time on, Jeannot directed Roy as carefully as the least professional actor ... and the war ... was over.[56]

Scheider stated once director Szwarc was aboard and shooting began in Florida, "Now things get interesting. Everyone starts pushing their weight around, their power around ... the electricity of tension. When [you're in] a creative period, whoever's juices are hottest will predominate. And without that you can't create. You need argument. Jeannot's and David's egos will get burned. And ... something better comes out of that struggle. My ego will get burned, too. It's ... a revolution. You need that struggle to do anything worthwhile."[57]

> Scheider's need to carve out a role in the give-and-take of combat, friendly or otherwise [was evident]. Two months into production ... Scheider blew up at an unsuspecting director Szwarc one afternoon in the midst of rehearsing a big scene in the Holiday Inn's vaulted indoor Holidome. 200 surprised extras [were the] audience and Scheider, waiting between camera "takes," suddenly lashed out at Szwarc for wasting time with the extras, taking too much time for technical matters, for ignoring the principal actors [Scheider's real complaint], and finally, the most stinging assault of all, for being a television director. Now the [creative] electricity [of tension], was alive in the air. David Brown, ever unflappable, called a break, the acrimony was patched up and, after 30 minutes, the cameras were peacefully rolling again.[58]

David Brown told another story from Navarre Beach:

> Practical jokes can defuse ... dangerous

tension during the deadly "mid stretch." On Roy Scheider's birthday [November 10] we decided nobody ... would mention it. Birthdays were usually noted and celebrated and Scheider knew that. As the shooting day wore on, he was at first puzzled and then furious. It finally became clear that he was going to be spending the evening alone in his room. Teddy Grossman [the stunt coordinator and Roy's stunt double], his closest friend, talked to Roy at the end of the day. "Teddy, are you doing anything tonight?" Teddy replied, "I do have a date." Roy snapped, "Jesus, I hoped you were free." Teddy then said, "My girlfriend knows a terrific girl, maybe I can get her to come." Roy's expression brightened. "Can you?" Roy was married, but the idea of a dinner date was appealing. Arrangements were made to meet in [a] remote café where a married movie star and his date were not likely to be noted by the local paparazzi. Meanwhile, the entire company prepared to dine at the same cafe. As they entered and spotted Roy at a secluded table, they roared, "Happy Birthday!" The party was on.[59]

For all of Brown's peacemaking, one annoyance to Szwarc didn't go away. Scheider had arrived with a deep tan and as the summer wore on and Scheider spent more and more time reading scripts on the beach, the tan got deeper. By early fall Roy's skin was too dark to match up with the other characters. Szwarc asked Scheider to cool it under the sun. Roy refused.

Scheider spoke about some of the equipment problems they had:

You are always contending with tides, surf and winds. We had to deal with jellyfish, sharks, waterspouts and hurricane warnings, too. If you are out there in a small boat or on a 20 foot square [camera] barge and there are waves ranging from six to ten feet, everyone and everything gets bounced around like a jellybean in a cement mixer. When you are filming on water, every boat in the picture has to be anchored in place ... so you spend four hours anchoring the 11 sailboats in position, and just when you are ready to shoot—the wind changes. The sails are all blowing the wrong direction and you have to start all over!... [Another constant battle was the unrelenting corrosive effect of saltwater.] "This ... took its toll ... on our special effects shark and its support equipment. Thousands of metal parts ... rusting away, freezing up or being eaten away. Even when the equipment was sitting on the beach, the corrosion continued, because the air was loaded with salt."[60]

"Bruce—as the original man-made menace was named, has been superseded by three even more lifelike sharks who perform better than their predecessors, and were nicknamed Bruce Two, Earl and Harold (after David Brown's Beverly Hills lawyer!)."[61] Another unforeseen problem was the aircraft carrier *Lexington* taking up the entire horizon when it came and went from its home base in Pensacola.[62]

On *Jaws 2* Scheider was alone as the star of the picture. Many of the crew felt he had staged his flare-up with Szwarc to make a classic grandstand play because it was the right place and time. Ray Loynd stated, "Scheider took a suite at the Holiday Inn ... where he could face the sea, and make sorties down to the sand [to read] scripts ... by his agent. He avoided ... the Saturday night wrap parties ... and found his closest companions [from the first film] ... set decorator Phil Abramson, stunt man Teddy Grossman and publicist Al Ebner, with whom he occasionally drove to distant Fort Walton for a seafood dinner."[63] Scheider did take care of the friends he had. "One night ... Scheider and some stuntmen found themselves facing an hour's wait. Then a waitress spotted [Roy] and asked for an autograph. Scheider smilingly agreed [if] ... the group could have a table. Word came back ... a table awaited if Scheider ... agreed to let the owner ... have his picture taken with the star in the kitchen ... a conspiratorial feast was enjoyed by all."[64] Ray Loynd concluded his chronicle of life on the set: "Scheider ... was also, in more philosophical moments, able to throw everything into unassailable perspective. 'Once you start taking yourself seriously,' he said, 'as a movie star or an actor, you're in trouble. Your mind begins to bend.'"[65] Scheider did not escape the shark unscathed. He slipped on the deck of the police launch and "suffered two cracked ribs after taking a nasty fall."[66] "He was helping some kids. But brave Roy is going on with the filming, taped and wearing a brace."[67]

The insatiable press continued to forage for stories. The *Star* tabloid talked to John Hancock after his firing (in August). Hancock blamed his departure on the mechanical shark. "It's been ... a year and a half and [the mechanical sharks] still can't swim or bite. You get a couple of shots and [the shark] breaks. I've ... been on the picture ... a year. That's more time than I ever intended to [spend doing] a shark picture."[68] The *Star* also held a "Write your Own Ending to *Jaws 2*" contest that ran all summer. The winner was printed in the October 18, 1977, issue.[69]

Not long after the film wrapped, one of the teenagers in the film was interviewed. "[David] Elliott (Larry Vaughan) [said], 'All of the Hancock footage was scrapped and ... a week's worth of cover shots in New England featuring Roy Scheider [were] used in the final print. The Florida locale was not ... ideal.'[70]

Principal location photography ended three days before Christmas 1977, on Shalimar Bay near Destin, Florida; the coastal town which served as Amity. The December weather was brutal. Ice formed on the clapper board and the actors had to put ice cubes in their mouths to prevent their breath from showing. Roy Scheider spent his final days on camera half in and half out of the water as he climbed over the huge cable in the final sequence at Cable Junction. The exhausted cast and crew winged home on December 23. In mid–January they would converge for the final time, with 13 of the teenage actors, for an exceptionally long five weeks of postproduction photography in Hollywood. The final camera rolled on the West Coast on February 18, 1978.

The publicity for *Jaws 2* began a month later with a stop at the Show-a-Rama exhibitors' convention in Kansas City on March 14, 1978. Joining star Roy Scheider and director Jeannot Szwarc were actress Lorraine Gary and producers David Brown and Richard Zanuck. "Each person stressed ... that *Jaws 2*, while still a sequel, can stand as a separate entity, a quality picture built on its own merits." Brown said, "We had to convince them that [it] was a Class A film ... [not made only] to exploit the ... first film."[71]

Scheider informed Leticia Kent, "'*Jaws II* [*sic*] is a contractual commitment. My plan is [to] ... arrange my career [to] work in ... small films. And I want to do ... one play every two years.' [Now rich], he's [left] his rent-controlled Upper West Side apartment ('I feel like a traitor') [for] the fashionable East Side."[72]

Roy also said, "If they said ... you [have] the choice of two million dollars or not to do it, I would not be here. I ... never [did] a part for money ... that includes the theater. You ... get up in the morning, look in the mirror, and feel a lot better."[73]

Peter Biskind observed, "Sequels were considered declassé. *Jaws 2* became the first example—followed quickly by the *Rockys*—of a practice that would fly in the face of all that the New Hollywood stood for."[74]

The *Star* ran a picture of Scheider, Dreyfuss, and Spielberg together at the Broadway premiere of Bob Fosse's *Dancin'* in early May 1978, with a caption describing them as "The Men from *Jaws*" even though two of them were working on *Close Encounters of the Third Kind.* [75]

Scheider was asked to present at the 32nd Annual Antoinette Perry (Tony) Awards on June 4, 1978. The program aired on CBS. Roy gave the award for outstanding performance by an actress in a featured role in a Broadway musical, right after two of the nominees performed an excerpt from *Ain't Misbehavin'*.[76]

In one of the odder publicity gimmicks, Szwarc and Scheider hosted a lunch for the press at Universal Studios on Friday, June 9. "The main dish served was shark meat a la Polette. The press was [given] a specially prepared *Jaws 2* cookbook subtitled, 'Turnabout is Fair Play,' with 14 recipes for ... shark. The ... special recipes, researched by the best Los Angeles restaurants, were not for ... the general public."[77]

Merchandising featured many more products and sponsors than for the first film. Roy Scheider was willing to do promotion, now that he had a piece of the action, and did. Some *Jaws 2* products included "Coca-Cola (plastic cups), Baker's bread (one trading card), Topps bubble gum (another trading card), a T-shirt and pants from Sears, Collegeville Halloween costumes, Bibb Company towels, beach pads, throw pillows and blankets, movie posters, a soundtrack album, a souvenir program, shark jaws, shark tooth necklaces, Ideal's *Jaws 2* game, coloring and activity books, comic doodles, a stuffed shark, a model kit of Brody's police truck and three paperbacks; Hank Searls' novelization, *The Jaws 2 Log* by Ray Loynd and Great Shark Stories."[78]

One of the last promotional interviews Roy did for the film was on "The Mike Douglas Show" on December 29, 1978. He showed two clips from *Jaws 2* and spoke briefly about the film. He discussed the sequel issue with Douglas and how he was "contracted" to do the sequel: "I can't imagine anyone else playing that part except me. I would be upset if I saw anyone else playing that part." Cohost Jerry Lewis added, "The audience wouldn't accept anyone else and whoever signed Roy was very smart."[79]

Molly Haskell wrote, "With *Jaws 2*, we are back on ... Amity, that Hollywood hybrid of Martha's Vineyard elitism and Fort Lauderdale juvenility. If *Jaws 2* [takes the] man-vs-shark story only half a step, at least it is not a clone. If ... you prefer violence fairly impersonal, [this film] ... is your poison."[80] The *New York Times* review is generic and does not critique performances except to state that Scheider's Brody came across as "worried and ill-tempered."[81]

Martin A. Jackson raved, "This is a neat and often captivating adventure film, with enough action to satisfy even the most jaded viewer. It is big, expensive, slick and quite nakedly a piece of popular entertainment that does its job well."[82]

Gordon Gow opined: "*Jaws 2* stands frequently in the doldrums, its drama blighted by a magnification of the incidental flaw in its predecessor: the shark is the most interesting. [At] least [there is] a basically genuine feel to Roy Scheider's ... lugubrious police chief Brody."[83]

Robert Bookbinder said:

> Confident of another success, Universal lavished *Jaws II* [*sic*] with a huge budget ... and an extensive publicity campaign that was, once again, heralded by a catchy slogan—Just when you thought it was safe to go into the water. However, the finished film ... never came close to the quality of the Spielberg original, and though it did well at the box office, it remains a rather stilted motion picture. Most of *Jaws II* simply does not work. The only time it really comes to life is when Scheider, Gary and Hamilton are on screen and—sad to say—the rest was pretty dreadful. Despite its faults, the performances in *Jaws II* are generally good, especially that of Roy Scheider, who didn't want to make the film and did so only to fulfill his contract.[84]

***Last Embrace* (1979, MGM-US). Harry and Ellie take the train to Princeton to talk to Professor Peabody. Harry Hannan: Roy Scheider; Ellie Fabian: Janet Margolin.**

"The final gross for *Jaws 2* was 102 million, making it the fifth highest grossing film of 1978."[85] The amount makes *Jaws 2* the second biggest moneymaker of Scheider's career, right behind the original *Jaws*. It stayed on the *Variety* list of top ten box office of all time for many years until it was supplanted by the multimillion-dollar films of the 1990s.

Roy Scheider was asked about being a sex symbol. "Once in a while, I catch myself standing in front of a mirror, combing my hair, wondering ... and then I take a good look at my face, this mug with the broken nose and its 30 degree warps, and I have a terrific time laughing [at the idea]."[86] "I'm not unaware [of my sex appeal] ... but I'd like to think I'm a sexy guy not only because I'm in the movies.... sooner or later the movie star, the 40-foot face disappears and then you are on your own. What you are able to maintain after that is really who you are. If I have any charisma or sexuality ... it's normal ... we all have it in our own way."[87]

Looking for a change from kids, sharks, and sequels, Roy Scheider's next feature was a Hitchcock-type thriller, *Last Embrace*, with then-neophyte director Jonathan Demme, who would later make *Silence of the Lambs*. Roy has worked with many younger or first-time directors, with decidedly mixed results. "With Demme signed on to helm, the filmmakers started to discuss how to people their movie with actors. No one involved can even remember anyone other than Roy Scheider who was ever considered for the starring role."[88]

David Scott declared, "He makes movies [if] ... the part is challenging, or ... he likes the people involved. 'Brody's more vulnerable, but Hannan becomes more [so]

Last Embrace. **Harry is stalked in the graveyard. Harry Hannan: Roy Scheider.**

as his situation becomes more dangerous. [Acting] provided [me] ... an opportunity to be vulnerable under make-believe circumstances. I can turn it on or off.'"[89]

As Scheider's character is having a nervous breakdown for most of the film, it is more difficult to identify biographical elements. There is an underwear scene. Harry also goes out and buys the necessary groceries to cook dinner, once his character gets over Ellie's invasion of his apartment. Ellie calls him "the Peacock," a term Scheider has used to describe himself. Cynthia Scheider has her first credited role as the sister of Hannan's department store contact, Adrian. She is introduced to Roy's character and has two lines.

Demme said, "I thought the story had potential to be a contemporary film noir and ... Roy Scheider could be the Humphrey Bogart of the seventies. The screenwriter, David Shaber, and I had a terrific time working together, and [with] one more draft ... we could have had something."[90]

Michael Bliss wrote,

> When a director with a distinctive style subjugates that style to another director's—the results can be disappointing. There is no way to speculate what *Last Embrace* would have been like if the script was ready before filming and if the film's star, Roy Scheider, had been more cooperative during production. As Demme recalled, "I was kind of wallowing in style ... a lot of energy went into style more than content." Roy Scheider has none of James Stewart's sophistication and wit. Janet Margolin is hardly the locus of passion Kim Novak was. Harry's fits—a spastic reaction in a lab and a sweaty, screaming awakening from a nightmare—seem like cliched examples of what it means to be disturbed. The scene in Demme's film is meant to explain Harry's guilt about his wife dying in an ambush meant for him and provide an explanation for the anxiety he is always feeling. Where in Hitchcock, the Gol Hadam

> linkage would only be a McGuffin ... in *Last Embrace* the idea is made to bear the impossible burden of unraveling the unbelievable actions ... in the film. Demme subsumes his stylistics to the most embarrassingly elemental of concepts.[91]

Roy was spotted at the *Manhattan* premiere in August 1979.[92] The magazine article written about the event plugged *Last Embrace.* The film was also included in a year-end *Playboy* article on "Sex in the Cinema." *Playboy* would write several articles on Scheider's films over the next five years. The film was released in May 1979. Roy appeared on the *Today* show on May 2 to talk about *Last Embrace* and his hopes for it. He also talked about his exercise routine.

Andrew Sarris said, "The biggest problem with *Last Embrace* is ... the letdown in ... [the] plot ... from vaguely institutional paranoia to a personal vendetta. Scheider and Margolin reenact a tortured odyssey ... equal parts of 40's neuroticism and 70's paranoia. I found myself curiously absorbed."[93]

Leigh Charlton declared, "*Last Embrace* recalls some classic Hitchcock. Fortunately, the film never dips into parody, although it is often intentionally funny. Hitchcock would approve. 'Some films are slices of life, mine are slices of cake,' the master once said. *Last Embrace* is a satisfying morsel."[94]

Rona Barrett added, "Demme has copied ... Alfred Hitchcock and he serves the Master well. Roy Scheider, ... with romantic fear [combines] his natural toughness with his sexy style. For all these plusses, [*sic*] *Embrace*'s whole is sadly less than its parts ... [The plot will send] synopsis writers to an early grave."[95]

The film was not a success. Everyone blamed the script. "I told Jonathan Demme [don't] let my girlfriend die at the end," Scheider says, implying that the movie died along with her. "Let her live, let me turn her in. Audiences ... will have me waiting 15 years for her to get out of jail."[96]

Last Embrace did not make Roy a romantic lead and that was a disappointment for him. He wanted to expand from playing cops and do something different, something risky with his career. Michael Musto wrote, "[He] carved his own niche as a tough guy with a core of vulnerability, a street-wise hero possessing an innate, almost inappropriate elegance. 'There [is] something about me that ... looks reliable,' [Scheider] says, looking reliable. 'Sometimes ... I want to break out ... and play something silly, stupid and wild.'"[97] Roy was finally given the opportunity to do that in *All That Jazz.*

— 8 —

Dancing for Fosse

"The project began as *Ending*, a story co-written by [Bob] Fosse and Robert Alan Aurthur. [Aurthur was terminally ill with lung cancer and died of a heart attack before the film was completed.] Basically, it was about a man who examines his life as it is ending."[1]

"There were problems getting the film launched and problems getting it finished. Paramount had the script first, but let it go to Columbia Pictures. Both companies were nervous about its commercial possibilities. Columbia, Fosse, Aurthur and executive producer Daniel Melnick could not agree on a budget. Richard Dreyfuss, the first actor set to play the lead, decided he was not right for the part and quit. Studio executives were less than enthusiastic about his replacement, Roy Scheider."[2]

"Scheider got the role of Joe Gideon partly because he can really sing and dance (he's done both on the stage) and partly because of his astonishing resemblance to Fosse."[3] Scheider convinced everyone involved he could look like a dancer. He felt very strongly, as an actor, that he could do anything.

Fosse said Dreyfuss was afraid of the dancing. Dreyfuss was used to working with directors who would give him more freedom to improvise than Fosse. Martin Gottfried wrote:

> The search for a new Joe Gideon took on the intensity of a manhunt. Daniel Melnick suggested Paul Newman. Sidney Lumet suggested Alan Alda or Gene Hackman. (Lumet had agreed to play Paddy Chayefsky in the picture, although the part was later cut.) Sam Cohn repeatedly recommended Roy Scheider. He arranged for Aurthur and Fosse to meet the actor in his office and they liked him on sight. ("A very nice man," Aurthur felt.) Scheider was eagerly and earnestly agreeable to whatever Fosse suggested, whether it was about the part or his working methods, although he was no more of a dancer than Richard Dreyfuss.
>
> Melnick felt Roy Scheider "wasn't charming enough." [Melnick] suggested George Segal. Agents had called offering Elliott Gould and Robert Blake. In the midst of the meeting Warren Beatty himself telephoned. They tossed more names in the hopper. Alan Bates (too British), Jack Lemmon (too old). Dan Melnick privately told Bob Aurthur, "Don't let Sam Cohn stampede you into Roy

Scheider. Jon Voight is reading it now." But after watching a special screening of *Coming Home* ... [Fosse] decided he would go with Scheider. Probably.

"Let's talk to Warren Beatty some more," Melnick pleaded.

"I forgot to tell you," Aurthur replied, "Warren said he would only play the part if Gideon doesn't die."

"Well, then," Melnick said, "[forget] that idea. God forbid we should make a commercial picture." Cohn urged Melnick to accept Scheider, and Fosse offered to work alone with the actor for a week before making the final decision.[4]

Fosse went off to select a cameraman, finally deciding on Guiseppe Rotunno, who had worked with Federico Fellini and had the necessary experience for all that Fosse had planned for the film. "Then [Fosse] went off to spend the week he had promised to work with Scheider. Even now, he wasn't sure about the actor coming across as a dancer. 'I think Roy can do it,' he told Melnick, 'but I'm not sure. I can't even take responsibility for telling you that I know he can do it, but I have a hunch he can.'"[5]

Kevin Boyd Grubb chronicled, "Other actors considered to replace [Dreyfuss] included Jack Nicholson and David Carradine. Finally, [Fosse] cast Roy Scheider. Scheider was not a dancer, but he had an athletic, wiry body and after he grew a goatee, bore more than a passing resemblance to the gaunt choreographer in black everyone knew as Bob Fosse."[6]

Roy went to be interviewed and they asked him what musical experience he'd had. Scheider replied, except for playing a gangster once in *Kiss Me Kate*, he had none. But he had done a lot of Restoration comedy and crumb-ball things like *The Gazebo* in his early stock days and college and knew he could draw on that experience.

Scheider further described his audition process: "I [told my agent], 'Tell Fosse to forget every movie he ever saw me in.'" For three hours a night for a week, Fosse and Roy read the part. Fosse said he didn't want to see Roy dance. "But as soon as we made our deal, he sent me straight to a dance mistress."[7]

***All That Jazz* (1979, 20th Century–Fox/Columbia). Joe sings goodbye to life. Joe Gideon: Roy Scheider.**

Roy didn't mind. Later he wrote, "So enthusiastic and electric was Mr. Fosse's choreography that his troupe and I would have danced through a brick wall if he asked us to … convinced that [we] will never look better."[8]

"Eventually, Bob said, 'Okay, we'll go. But I warn you. There will be bad days [on the film] and I will not smile and I will not be happy no matter what you do.' Roy observed, 'There were never bad days for me.'"[9] There were long, hard days doing dance routines with Ann Reinking and Ben Vereen, which weren't easy. They gave Scheider aches in muscles he didn't know he had, and he would come home exhausted.

"Bob and I got along well because we both have the same acting technique. It's called the Yugoslav total immersion into absolute make-believe reality. What it boils down to is: don't get caught acting. Bob demands great verisimilitude in his films."[10]

"As an actor I'd like … parts that expand … my talent. Gideon is a hell of a role. I shall sing, dance, and make love. My performance … will come as a total surprise. I should be doing … this … dangerous, challenging—and absolutely outrageous movie."[11]

Al Pacino was offered *Kramer vs. Kramer* before Scheider was, but Pacino turned down the role. Then Dreyfuss walked off *Jazz*. Bobby Benton, who wrote and directed *Kramer*, asked Roy to do it, but Stanley Jaffe, the producer, wanted Hoffman. Then Roy got *Jazz*. "There were very heavy doubts, but I wanted … a chance to prove I can be light, funny, romantic. Joe Gideon … is a combination of Fosse and myself. Flop sweat—that's what you get when you think you are bombing out. That's the real autobiographical link."[12]

When Scheider started, the most difficult thing for him as an actor was to convince himself he could portray a choreographer who tells all the top-flight dancers what to do. In the early stages, Bob would tell him about personal experiences help Roy to help Roy better relate to the character. But as the picture went on and Scheider gained confidence, Fosse gave him more freedom to use his own instincts. Roy drew the line, however, when asked if playing Joe Gideon would make him slow down, stating it was just an acting role and while he had his own workaholic symptoms, he was never quite as bad as Joe Gideon.

There are, however, some biographical elements in *Jazz*. As stated previously, Scheider was no stranger to affairs outside his marriage. Gideon's daughter is named Michelle, which could be a blend of Maximillia (Scheider's daughter) and Nicole (Fosse's daughter). The young actress cast (Liz Foldi) looks like Roy, which was interesting since both real-life daughters resemble their mothers. As it is Fosse's autobiographical film, Nicole was slipped into the film as a dancer warming up for tryouts. Furthermore, Scheider has no underwear under his hospital gown and moons the camera when the orderlies drag him out of the boiler room. Joe also accuses Kate of two-timing him with someone taller than himself.

The script for *Jazz* was outrageous, assaulting, highly melodramatic, very funny, stupid, silly, and vulgar. Roy knew it would be a wonderful movie. He also knew Bob Fosse would be lucky to get it made. It was a little reminiscent of the films *Catch 22* and *The Ruling Class*, but for the most part, it was unique. Scheider wondered who would give Fosse the money to do it.

Roy loved the witty, sardonic script—writ large on a broad canvas of a movie—and knew the role would give him a lot of opportunities he hadn't had in movies before:

> I had never had a heart attack, never choreographed a show ... so I [had] to find parallel situations in my life.... It has to come out of what I have experienced as a human being.
>
> While making the movie I had to think of the times I selfishly neglected my family or my daughter or a friend because I was so manically possessed with either the show I was in or the play or movie or whatever it was ... put those who are near and dear—a little in the background so we can get out there and do ... whatever this thing is that we are crazy about doing.[13] "Bob and I spent ... time ... reading the script together and talking about our lives. When you spend that much time with somebody, you absorb ... who ... and what they are and what they like and don't like."[14]

Rona Barrett stated, "Many predicted his failure, but Scheider, having brushed up on his dancing technique, made moviegoers believe he was the hard-driving, sex-and-death obsessed choreographer. 'I lost eight pounds and turned to skin and bones. I thought my legs would fall off."[15] Scheider revealed to Ron Gluckman, "It was [hard], physically and mentally ... [but] also the most satisfying. I'm not naturally a singer or dancer, so it required an extraordinary amount of work to prepare for the part. I worked daily with the dance master and mistress, learning the steps for each scene."[16]

"The dancing wasn't a problem—you attack each section simply as a job. I've been jogging every morning, not because I like it.... I need to get alive at that hour. [The movie is] about death, but [it is also] pro life. [To make] death ... as endlessly lovely as a woman!"[17]

Ann Reinking, who plays Kate, Gideon's mistress in the film, was asked if Roy was a quick study at dancing: "He was great. And we found out he was a good weight lifter and that [he] liked baseball a lot, so [he] did a lot of baseball slides. And [he was] lifting a lot of girls. [He was] great. A lot of the girls thought [he was] the best partner they ever had."[18]

Roy and Ann became friends, as they both became inexorably entwined and identified with Bob Fosse in their professional lives. In 1999, Scheider taught at the Broadway Theater Project, a three-week training program for theater performers from around the world, run by Reinking. The subject was Fosse and *All That Jazz*. Scheider told the students that he still considers *Jazz* his best film, not only because of the great direction, but because it's a fabulous role, a three-dimensional part that called on every aspect of his experience.

Reinking added that Scheider's research into playing Fosse sometimes yielded frightening results. She once began talking to a man on the set she was sure was Fosse, only to get a closer look and find out it was Scheider: "I marveled at [Roy's] incredible skills to duplicate and imprint another person's idiosyncrasies, especially in regard to Bob. He had it all: the stances, the way he talked to dancers, the cigarette hanging from his mouth."[19] Gwen Verdon recalled that her husband told her, "Roy moves and looks and acts the way I feel."[20]

One of the dancers in *All That Jazz*, Leland Schwantes, interviewed for a 1999 documentary on Fosse, agreed with that point: "It was spooky to see them standing together, dressed alike. Scheider had grown the same facial hair. He really got it. He became Fosse."[21]

Gordon Hunt asked, "What was it like playing Bob Fosse with him standing two feet from you?" Scheider replied, "I never played Fosse. I had to play me. I could act the outside surface of Fosse, but to be honest to the camera, the performance had to come out of my experience ... my pain and terror. In some of the hospital scenes, I asked Fosse what it was like to have a heart attack. He said it was like having a crushing weight on his chest. So

All That Jazz. **Joe Gideon with a pile of scripts.**

when it came my turn I had [a crew member] put his knee on my chest and bear down. You can't see him because of the camera angle, but I could feel it. Don't tell anyone I told you that."[22]

Roy's daughter, Maximillia, was interviewed during the making of *Jazz* in *Seventeen* magazine and commented on her father's work habits. "In some ways, my father and I are *The Odd Couple*. He's Felix Unger—a perfectionist in every way. And I'm Oscar Madison. I admire my father a lot," she says. "When he starts something, he finishes it."[23]

The film almost didn't get completed. It came down to the weekend of the long knives. Paramount wanted them to stop shooting, assemble what they had, and decide later if the film needed the remaining fantasy sequences. Producer Melnick struck a deal by offering to sell half the film to another studio. He put together 40 minutes of film, took it to Hollywood, and ran it for Alan Ladd, Jr., at 20th Century–Fox, who bought it. "A later coin toss decided how the film would be distributed, with Fox getting the domestic rights and Columbia the foreign rights."[24]

"The wrap party was held March 10, 1979, and a glamorous party it was, all dressed up at Tavern on the Green, the sprawling and beautiful Central Park restaurant. It was a giant affair ... crowded and noisy with hundreds of actors, technicians, executives and secretaries. Columbia Pictures and 20th Century–Fox had invited staff from both coasts."[25]

The New York theater community did not like *Jazz*, as it hit close to home and many felt they were being held up for ridicule. Martin Gottfried wrote, "In real life, Harold Prince took it personally. 'John Lithgow is wearing his glasses the way I do,' Prince noticed (propped above his brow), 'and he is rehearsing on a set like ours for *Pacific Overtures*.'"[26] This reaction amused Roy. He loved the conceit of Fosse choreographing a grand finale death scene to his life while he was still alive. Scheider explained that the jealousy and competition among theatrical people is what made their reaction to the film so violent. Certain composers and lyricists Fosse had worked with, especially John Kander and Fred Ebb, felt they were being parodied, even though most of the characters were composites and the film was generally cynical about everything.

"Even Fosse had to admit, 'I don't think I've ever seen a picture quite like this. Good or bad, if you like it or you don't like it, it is not a copy of anything. That I'm very proud of.'"[27] Ironically, Fosse *did* die of a heart attack. "He was walking to the theater for opening night of a revival of *Sweet Charity* in Washington, D.C., September 23, 1987."[28]

Art Sarno wrote, "*All That Jazz* is an autobiographical film, perhaps the most nakedly autobiographical movie ever made. It is a highly personal film, told with imagination, originality and unsparing honesty. Among the strongest features of the film was the Oscar nominated performance of Roy Scheider as the Fosse surrogate figure, Joe Gideon. Totally unlike anything he's done before, Scheider ... creates a character filled with nervous energy and seemingly motivated by the belief that to stop working or even slow down for a second is to risk failure."

"A startling change of pace, it is the most critically acclaimed role of Scheider's career, a fact that gives Scheider no small sense of triumph. What makes this all the more satisfying is that he wasn't even first choice for the part. For a long time, Scheider, thanks to his many macho screen roles, was stereotyped as a tough guy. *All That Jazz* might change his image, but that doesn't concern him."[29]

Scheider told Sarno, "The audience creates the image. You don't do anything. They lock onto you. You become a quantity they either enjoy seeing or they don't ... that shows up at the box office. I always knew I could make a living as an actor, but I never thought I'd get this far."[30] "That *All That Jazz* was a hit came as a surprise to everyone. Before the picture opened, director Steven Spielberg questioned ... Fosse's ending. 'He's not going to release the film with that ending, surely.' 'Yes, he is,' replied Scheider."[31]

"Destruction isn't the way to go ... [for] a guy who says, 'Hey, I want another chance.' An even bigger problem is the ending ... after two hours [with] a guy who finally decided life is worth living, he dies. Joe went too far. He made a mistake."[32]

Douglas Slater wrote, "Nowhere is this more clear than in Roy Scheider's brilliant performance. [Joe is] ... a selfish, egocentric, insincere sensualist ... charming and irresistible to the audience and those around him. His death is curiously moving ... how someone might appear to ... other people, in the face of dying."[33]

Jeffrey Wells opined "I found Fosse's ego and death tripping personally repulsive ... show tunes and body bags don't mix, no matter how you cut the cadaver. Roy Scheider handles ... a microphone and a two step as [well as] ... his acting, which is typically excellent."[34]

In the same issue of *Films in Review*, Rob Edelman commented, "Bob Fosse's *All That Jazz* is a mesmerizingly brilliant, though flawed film. Roy Scheider is primarily an actor in dramatic films ... yet this is the best role and performance of his career."[35] The magazine's capsule review stated, "At once breathtaking and irritating. Roy Scheider excels."[36]

Vincent Canby agreed: "With an actor of less weight and intensity, [the film] may have evaporated as we watched. Mr. Scheider [is] a presence to reckon with. With him, the film's ending becomes coolly comic. He's a defiant Don Giovanni who's beaten, not by the devil, but by a coronary occlusion."[37] Seven months later, Canby revisited the film: "The leap that Mr. Scheider's casting required of our imaginations, as well as of Mr. Scheider's talents, paid off in one of the year's most provocative performances ... that illuminated the psychic chaos within the character without calling undue attention to the decor of his razzle-dazzle existence."[38]

Frank Rich was not taken with the film: "Though Scheider is a wry, sensitive actor, he soon gets lost in the vulgar theatrics. So does the subject of death. [There are] closeups of open-heart surgery, but few insights into Gideon's soul. What Fosse regards as self-analysis often comes out as egomaniacal self-congratulation."[39]

Andrew Sarris was equally unimpressed: "*All That Jazz* is better danced, photographed and edited than it is written. Scheider strives heroically to imply more than is expressed ... but he seems to be swimming underwater ... in a part-talkie with loud music and effects ... fascinating ... as the first truly grown-up musical."[40] Jimmy Summers offered cautionary praise, while admitting the film is "a matter of personal taste. It's not your usual bright-lights-and-tap-shoes movie musical, but thank God, it's not. Dance is shown as ... beautiful, sensuous and exciting, but it's also ... hard, sweaty and exhausting work. Describing *All That Jazz* ... is difficult."[41]

Rex Reed offered, "A cross between Fellini and Pal Joey [a role Fosse played], a heel taking stock [of life] and finding himself knee deep in horse manure. Fosse [is] played with desperate energy and sweat soaked honesty by Roy Scheider. The result is unflinching ugliness, often embarrassing, sometimes brilliant, always cinematic, ultimately self-defeating."[42]

Tony Crawley wrote, "Roy Scheider surprises everyone—himself included—by singing and dancing a storm. 'Sure, it's based on Bob's life,' comments Roy, '...ultimately, a synthesis between Bob and me ... not quite all of him, not quite all of me, but both of us.'"[43] Judith Crist noted: "Fosse, via Scheider, paints so ruthless a self-portrait of a self-centered single-minded theater professional relying on sexual connections rather than human relations that, frankly my dear, we end up not giving a damn whether he lives—or dies. Scheider [is] first-rate."[44] *Boston* magazine said, "On a scale of one to Fellini's *8½*, this hyperventilating flick scores about a 2½. One of the [film's] less successful gimmicks is a series of conversations between ... Gideon and Death (Jessica Lange). About halfway through, one longs for Death to make a house call."[45]

Dan Rottenberg stated, "Bob Fosse attempts to bare the soul of a hotshot musical director. As he lies dying, [Gideon's] life passes before him in a succession of dance numbers. The death scene is longer than *La Traviata*'s, and is not as good."[46]

Gary Arnold was asked, "Seen *All That Jazz* yet?" He hadn't. "'[It's] a musical about a guy having a heart attack made by a guy without a heart.' It would be difficult to improve on that capsule review. [The film is] ... an acridly maudlin spectacle [of] Bob Fosse ... impersonated with harrowing authenticity by Roy Scheider."[47]

With these reviews, the film became a critical coup for Scheider and Fosse, even if it wasn't an immediate hit at the box office. Scheider revealed to John Mariani, "People ... say to me, 'Yours was the greatest performance I saw in my life.'"[48]

Martin Gottfried declared:

> Quite remarkably, *All That Jazz*, for the third Fosse movie in a row, was up for Best Picture and once again he was nominated for Best Director. Nominated [as well] were Roy Scheider for Best Actor, Fosse and Bob Aurthur for Best Original Screenplay, Guiseppe

> Rotunno for Cinematography, Albert Wolsky for Costume Design, Tony Walton and Philip Rosenberg for Art Direction, Alan Heim for Editing and Ralph Burns for Musical Score. That made a total of nine nominations, quite an achievement for a film that had been greeted with mixed reviews and only had been doing moderate business.[49]

The nominations were announced on February 26, 1980.[50]

In between his nomination and the awards ceremony, Roy addressed the 94th graduating class of the American Academy of Dramatic Arts on April 1, 1980, at the Music Box Theater. "You have to endure [in show business] because it's so full of disappointments and frustrations. If you have the courage to keep showing up, you can make it."[51]

Dustin Hoffman was favored to win best actor for *Kramer vs. Kramer*, and he did. "Roy Scheider was watching the show from Joe Allen's restaurant in New York." After his loss, "Roy Scheider was consoling his fifteen-year-old daughter, who began weeping. Newspaper photographers snapped Scheider as he comforted his child."[52] Bob Fosse tried to get Roy to go at the last minute, but Scheider knew Dustin had it all wrapped up. Roy was glad Hoffman won. He certainly deserved the Oscar, but perhaps not for that picture. If Hoffman couldn't win it for *The Graduate*, *Midnight Cowboy*, or *All the President's Men*, it was good he won it for *Kramer*.

Scheider told *Us* magazine right before the ceremony, "I'm human, so I like being rewarded. Getting an Oscar is [a reward from] your peers. I knew [the role] would give me a lot of opportunities I hadn't had in films before." Scheider was uneasy about competing with pal Hoffman. "It's like having a playoff between Cezanne and Picasso."[53] John Mariani asked Scheider if *Jazz* had given him aspirations to be a director, like Fosse. "No, I couldn't take it. It's just the most exhausting job in the world, from six in the morning until eleven at night, thinking of every element all day long."[54]

Season Pass wrote for the film's cable premiere:

> There isn't a dull moment in Bob Fosse's driving, dazzling, semi-autobiographical [film]. Fosse has always been a master showman and ... his latest movie doesn't disappoint. Roy Scheider, the excellent veteran actor who finally has a chance to reveal the full extent of his impressive range, plays Joe Gideon ... a workaholic who smokes incessantly and pumps himself up for each new day by taking ... Dexedrine. He is also a shameless womanizer. Gideon's life is one long death wish, and while his life reportedly parallels Fosse's in many ways, it is clear the director views his alter ego with more pity than admiration. Few viewers will leave *All That Jazz* without some strong feelings.[55]

The film remains a favorite and has many fans. In recent years, internet web reviews of the film have appeared. Carmel Degan wrote, "The music deepens rather than cheapens this extraordinary, dangerously breathless musical, often compared to Fellini's *8½*. Scheider has never been more commanding, he surely earned his Academy Award nomination. The film is the crowning achievement of Fosse's splendid career."[56]

Shortly after *Jazz* opened, Ann Reinking's roommate, a young actress named Brenda King, sighted Scheider while they were both out shopping. "They met in the aisle of Zitomer's, an East Side pharmacy. Brenda introduced herself as an admirer of his work. He thanked her, asked about Annie, chatted briefly and went on his way."[57] Ten years and two more introductions later, Brenda King would become the third Mrs. Scheider.

— 9 —

High-Flying Eighties

After filming *All That Jazz*, Roy did something he had wanted to do for a long time and went back to the stage. *Betrayal* had played in London's West End and this was the first version to be done by an American cast on Broadway. Roy signed for the smaller, more restrained role of Robert, the cuckolded husband. Blythe Danner played the adulterous wife. The best friend was Raul Julia. This play had a twist. The audience was told the ending first and then the play traced the adultery back through each scene to the beginning of the affair.

Betrayal premiered on January 5, 1980, became one of the hits of the season, and ran for six months. "[It] is Harold Pinter's first full length play ... [since] 1976 [and] *No Man's Land*."[1] It was also the first Pinter play to be a commercial success.[2] Roy was nominated for a Golden Globe, a British Academy Award (BAFTA), and an Oscar for *All That Jazz* during the play's run. Roy did not win anything he was nominated for, but *Jazz* did tie for the Palm D'or prize at Cannes in late March. It was doubtful Roy would make it to Cannes because of the play, but he managed.

Roy considered this Cannes experience one of the greatest times of his life. He had two days for the trip, a whirlwind flight out of New York on the Concorde to Orly in Paris. From there he took a Lear jet to Cannes. He arrived at the Carlton Hotel and the place was crawling with press. The next morning Roy did a press conference for *All That Jazz*, and in the evening there was a screening of the film. The audience went crazy. He was sitting in the balcony with Fosse, and the entire theater turned around and applauded them. Fosse was in shock. Roy had to lift him out of his chair to acknowledge the ovation.

Afterward, they went to a castle for a party. As they got out of the car and were walking up the crowded driveway, the lights went up on the parapet of the castle. The members of the local high school band, with trumpets and snare drums, stood up and played a march for them. It was fabulous.

Scheider had returned to Broadway partly because he felt he needed to do a play because of the guilt that many theatrically trained actors feel when they go on to movie careers. Theater was where they started, where they learned their craft, and they feel they owe something. Theater allows actors to wrestle with some interesting ideas, the kind not normally found in movies. In Harold Pinter's *Betrayal*, even though the role of Jerry was a wonderfully romantic part, Scheider felt the smaller part of Robert was more difficult and complex. He wanted a struggle and a challenge, something to sink his teeth into. Scheider knew how it looked to have his name listed third, to have people say: Oh, isn't that noble. He's a big movie star coming to Broadway to do a play, and he's taking third billing in the grand style of the theater. Actually, Roy believed it should be that way, and he was happy to do it.

Performing live was harder and more frightening than Scheider remembered, putting himself out there on the line. Every night that Roy made his entrance, his heart was pounding, his palms were sweating, and he thought he would faint. He handled his fears by realizing he was afraid he'd forget his lines and make a fool of himself. Scheider turned that fear around, shifted that energy into something positive, to get it working for him. Then he would be so good it would scare him. Another technique Scheider developed was to find someone in the audience whom he knew didn't like him or whom he didn't like. He would be *really* good that night. Also it worked when there were people out there he loved. And if he couldn't find anyone he loved or hated, he picked out a pretty face and said, this one's for her.

One night Roy's techniques were tested. Henry Kissinger had someone call. Kissinger wanted to see the play and sit in Scheider's house seats. Roy said no. Kissinger could pay his money and sit anywhere he wanted, but not in Roy's seats. Scheider didn't want to see him there or know when he was there, and he didn't want Kissinger coming backstage to his dressing room afterward.

It was satisfying for Roy to return as a star in an actual Broadway hit, something he had been unable to achieve in his earlier stage career, despite 12 years of trying. After Blythe Danner left the play and was replaced by Carole Lagerfeldt, Roy received first billing until the run ended.

Robert demonstrated almost all of the facets of those who have gone through marriages, romances, and adulterous romances. Scheider was the first of the three actors signed, even though Jerry was the leading man's role. The producers were surprised when Roy wanted to play Robert. The character got to Scheider as a guy who used humor and cynicism to conceal his real feelings. Roy identified with that. Here was a guy who hurts—who hurts a lot—and the thing that hurts him is that his wife is having an affair with his best friend. And because it is his best friend, he stifles it all. Robert spends 80 percent of his time hiding from what he feels. Scheider said, "I haven't met many men like him ... the kind of guy [who] says, 'Oh, by the way, so and so is having an affair with my wife,' and then moves on, changes the subject. He ... is a man ... in ... pain. He suffers inside."[3]

Scheider invited Harold Pinter and Antonia Fraser (on whose romantic relationship *Betrayal* was loosely based) to see *All That Jazz* with him. Pinter was skeptical and felt he wouldn't like the film, but he stayed with it. Even though Pinter thought the Angel of Death number was a silly conceit, he ended up being rather touched by Scheider's death in the film. Roy was flattered by this reaction.

Scheider knew there were plenty of opportunities for him to do plays if he had the desire. After spending 15 years doing every kind of play, from Molière and Shakespeare to Tennessee Williams and

Betrayal (1980, Trafalgar Theater). Jerry and Robert talk about Jerry's affair with Robert's wife. Robert: Roy Scheider; Jerry: Raul Julia.

Thornton Wilder, and working for low wages, he wasn't eager to run back to that life. An original play like *Betrayal* was different. Roy had read about the play in *Time* and bought the book. Then he called his agent and asked him to get a meeting with the director. They had lunch and the project was put together.

Michiko Kakutani interviewed Scheider two weeks into the run. "This withholding of feeling, this use of words to conceal rather than reveal ... emotion was ... difficult. The body and the words are shields to hide ... very violent passions." Scheider said, "In Pinter, you are feeling the emotions completely, but suppressing them."[4]

Harold Clurman reviewed *Betrayal* for The *Nation:* "The Americans evince more personal feeling. Roy Scheider is constrained (through direction) to be as English as possible; his scene at lunch with Jerry ... has a hurt and bitterness that brings dramatic vivacity and poignancy ... that was absent ... in London."[5]

Walter Kerr stated, "Mr. Scheider, jaw muscles tight and eyelids blinking rapidly as he overrides each new affront, pursues the Chinese box puzzles that surround him with a poisonous, unfaltering poise. Now rigid with rage, now trembling with indignation, he is content to bait, taunt, torment—by intimation."[6] Elliott Sirkin said, "In *Betrayal*, [Scheider] conveys a virile, highly controlled magnetism."[7]

The Fireside Theater book club wrote, "Each step of the way, Pinter reveals more ... about ... their triangular relationship. With dialogue that moves in curves ...

digressions ... wittily tangential allusions ... knowing flippancies ... things are ... almost never what people say they are."[8]

Robert Brustein revealed, "Scheider ... shows us why actors find Pinter so appealing. His face sharp as a knife, his eyes as hooded as a reptile's, his character as well pressed as his trousers, he manages ... to conceal more than he reveals, tantalizing us with ... subtext."[9]

The *New York Times* announced Scheider won the Delia Austrian Medal from the Drama League of New York on June 9, 1980, and was honored at their annual luncheon for the most distinguished performance on stage.[10] *Betrayal*'s run came to an end in June. Franklin and Marshall College bestowed honorary doctorates on both Scheider and his wife, Cynthia, and asked Roy to be the commencement speaker.[11]

Scheider was asked if he ever became impatient with the slow pace of film acting and scenes that are filmed out of sequence. Roy replied it wasn't as stimulating as disciplining himself for eight live performances a week. He also didn't have the personal control over his destiny that he did in the theater. Being bored while making movies is part of making movies and if one said it was boring, it ended up being twice as boring. If Roy completed filming his scenes by 3:00 P.M. and tomorrow they were shooting the end of the movie even though they only started making the film, he would go home and think through his part, plan it, chart it, and come in ready to do the work. Roy had no patience with people who get bored. The boredom is their own fault.

In eight short years, Scheider had carved a place among the New York actors who had become popular marquee names in the last decade. Scheider's battered features fit right in with the other unconventional leading men of that time, Al Pacino and Robert DeNiro. Peter Biskind wrote, "A lot of the energy that animated the New Hollywood came from New York; the 70's was the decade when New York swallowed Hollywood, when Hollywood was Gothamized."[12] Roy was included in a 1986 book, *New York Actors: Face to Face*. In 1985, on "Saturday Night Live," Scheider said the difference between New York and Los Angeles is that "in New York we know we are crazy."[13] He disliked Los Angeles because he couldn't go for an ice cream there without running into three directors, four producers, two writers, and six agents—all talking about their properties. Sometimes Roy only wanted to talk about ice cream.

In March 1980, Roy Scheider joined "an Actor's Equity rally to protest the proposed demolition of three of Broadway's oldest theaters for the 54 story Portman Hotel Complex." The event was also attended by Tony Randall, Lucie Arnaz, and Jose Ferrer.[14] Scheider (in sunglasses) was photographed, holding a protest sign. The picture was published in *People*.

Roy wrote a letter to the editor of the *New York Times* protesting the editing of the Woody Guthrie movie *Bound for Glory* shown on CBS television. Apparently to have enough time for commercials, CBS cut the songs in the film. Scheider asked if this was "the work of Pinkerton strike breakers and if CBS was going to show the Jesse Owens story, would they cut the film in the middle of the 100-yard dash?" The *New York Times* was amused enough to print the letter with the tag line "Shame, shame" on July 27, 1980.[15]

On April 4, 1981, Scheider helped out friend Werner Erhard's Hunger Project by narrating the slide show at the End World Hunger Benefit in Washington, D.C. Roy said, "I always thought hunger and starvation were supposed to be with us always, like death and taxes." The benefit expected to raise $30,000, with two-thirds of the funds earmarked for UNICEF and Africare and the rest going to Erhard's Hunger

Project. Scheider said his *Betrayal* costar Raul Julia got him involved. This was his second appearance for the group. Scheider had to interrupt the shooting of his new film to attend this charity event. "The film's called *Stab!* Meryl Streep is in it. It's ... an icebox movie. You get home, you open the icebox and you say, "Hey, wait a minute.'"[16]

Roy returned to the set of *Stab!* (eventually released as *Still of the Night*), which was being written and directed by Robert Benton. Roy plays psychiatrist Sam Rice. His patient, George Bynum, is murdered. Bynum had admitted to Rice he'd been having an affair with a coworker at the auction house. The woman in question, Brooke Reynolds, visits Rice at his office. She asks Sam to return Bynum's watch in order not to reveal the affair to his widow. Rice is attracted to the shy and extremely nervous Brooke, even after the police say she could be his patient's murderer and that Rice is next. Despite that danger, Sam falls in love with her. After many twists, turns, and more dead bodies, Rice clears her name and saves Brooke from the real murderer.

The film is a homage to Hitchcock with Streep playing the "cool blonde" à la Grace Kelly and Eva Marie Saint. Scheider has Cary Grant's role as a normally smart man over his head in a situation rapidly going out of control. Scheider's psychiatrist character falls in love with a woman he thinks is a murderer and who may murder him. The problem is, does he go to bed with her or take her to the local police station? The film isn't funny, but Scheider hoped the audience would care about the people in it.

Roy enjoyed working with Meryl Streep. He considered her a bright woman, well grounded in her craft with a superior talent. He liked that she worked hard, was dedicated, and didn't waste time on the set. It was a pleasure to work with people like that. The outside reputation of actors doesn't mean anything. The work situation

Still of the Night (1982, MGM-UA). Dr. Sam Rice pauses in the doorway.

is always the same. Meryl Streep had this enormous reputation, but Roy found her to be a terrific, bright, level-headed, honest, down-to-earth person. In turn, Streep enjoyed working with Scheider. Meryl told Elaine Dutka, "[Roy] has that special Cary Grant quality—adding an element of class to the circumstances."[17]

Scheider recollected:

Three or four years back, [Benton] was working on a script about a female Jack the Ripper. I had forgotten all about it until I got a call. The problem of believability has been compounded. The man is a psychiatrist ... who had years and years of training. He knows she spells trouble, but his passion keeps overruling his head.... that's what makes the part fascinating and fun for me. The audience sees the movie through my eyes. It was a special joy to work with Meryl Streep. At the same time I fall in love with her, [the audience] must fall in love with her, too.... If they react the way I do, it will be love at first sight.[18]

Nick Smurthwaite wrote:

Benton ... first had the idea of making *Still of the Night* back in the seventies, when he was sidetracked into making *The Late Show*, after that came *Kramer* and a lot of pressure. "It seemed to me I should go about as far away from *Kramer* as I could in my next film."

Sam Rice ... receives a visit from the woman, whom he feels he knows through his ex-patient's revelations, and is instantly attracted by her nervous allure. At the same time he feels she is unbalanced and possibly the murderer. Should he tell the police, who are hot on his heels, or should he try to establish her guilt (or innocence) for himself? It is a classic movie conundrum.

On paper, if not on celluloid, the teaming of Scheider and Streep looked like a winner. Despite his reputation for tough action films ... Scheider is a sensitive man who acts from the inside out. He spent years as a well-respected stage actor before breaking into movies, and he was given his first break by Joe Papp. (Something else he has in common with Streep is his agent, Sam Cohn.) The movie Benton seems to have drawn on the most for his story of spiraling obsession was Hitchcock's *Vertigo*. [Benton said], "We didn't set out to make a Hitchcock picture.... we were thinking more of the original *Cat People* and Fritz Lang's *Women in the Window*. Some people assume because Meryl is blonde ... there are point of view shots ... [and] an auction gallery that it's Hitchcockian.... this territory is so staked out by Hitchcock that there is nothing you can do that won't remind someone of him." Benton and his principal actors, Scheider and Streep, were actually more interested in the psychological aspects of the story. Scheider reconstructs therapy sessions [and] engages in dream interpretation. "I wrote that as a plot device because ultimately I wanted him to walk into that dream." The film's surreal climax ... is both scary and visually striking, deliberately shot in diffused style that evokes that eerie dream. *Still* ... provokes a kind of cerebral fear.

Still of the Night was not well received, either in the USA or Great Britain, although some critics admired the performances of Scheider and Streep, and the stylish camera work. The critics' general consensus was it was slow-moving, muddled, and implausible. Doubtless they were expecting more from the feted team of Benton and Streep. The mood of the movie is resolutely cool and the style uncluttered, with minimal use of incidental music and, surprisingly in a murder mystery, no gratuitous violence.[19]

Benton divulged, "Roy Scheider helps shape the psychiatrist he played. It's something [director Robert] Altman showed me."[20]

Eugene Pfaff wrote, "Benton had been working on the script periodically for four years, constantly changing the plot to make the film a true tribute to Hitchcock. Meryl enjoyed the opportunity to work with Benton again and continued to make plot changes and contribute to the revision of the script, as she had done in *Kramer vs. Kramer*."[21] "But the magic combination of

Still of the Night. **Sam attends his first Crispin's auction. Dr. Sam Rice: Roy Scheider; several uncredited auction attendees. The woman sitting next to Scheider is his second wife, Cynthia. Outtake.**

Benton-Streep did not work again. There were innumerable problems ... because of delays in filming schedules and constant script rewrites. The accumulation of problems on the set had their effect on Meryl and cast a pall over the entire cast and crew. Benton was so dissatisfied with the film that he decided to delay release indefinitely to do extensive editing."[22]

This film has some interesting biographical elements. Sam gives up a promising baseball career in the minor leagues to become a psychiatrist. He is still a fan, however, listening to the ballgames on the radio in between sessions with patients and displaying Yankee memorabilia—a cap, ball and glove—in his office. Sam is a native New Yorker and has no fear of Central Park at night, even after he is mugged and chastised by the police detective that he should have known better. Scheider was living in a Central Park West apartment at the time, so they were practically filming on his doorstep. Sam is a compulsive neat freak, always cleaning up after his patients and his mother. He is once again an unattached character, having recently been divorced, and is attracted to blondes. In the most blatant inside joke, Brooke takes Sam to an art auction and Rice sits down briefly next to a dark-haired woman. It is Roy's wife, Cynthia, in yet another instance of Scheider inserting his family into his films.

The auction was well researched by the director. "Benton ... asked Arnold Glimcher and Jeffrey Hoffeld of the Pace Gallery to play ... bidders. Tom Norton, [formerly with Sotheby's], was hired as a technical advisor [and] was asked to play the ... auctioneer. 'Norton knew ... how the auction master would act.' Benton wanted an auction house ... as authentic as possible."[23]

In March 1982, the Scheiders bought a winter home in Key West, Florida.[24] The house at 630 Dey Street dated back to 1884 and was a bit of landmark, even before it became the home of a movie star.[25] Roy had heard about Key West from Bob Fosse, who told him it was a wonderful, grungy place, with good weather all year round.

On June 12, 1982, Roy took part in an antinuclear march in New York City. His speech at the rally was not included in the 1984 documentary that chronicled this event, *In Our Hands*, but his on-street interview was. Scheider said, "I felt very good ... on Nuclear Disarmament Day. The atmosphere was terrific. I gave my half-minute harangue at the United Nations and I was very pleased to do it. We must get into the streets ... because the disarmament issue means our lives."[26]

Roy gave a long tribute to TV pioneer Edward R. Murrow at the 34th Emmy Awards, which aired on ABC on September 19, 1982. He was introduced by host John Forsythe as "an actor for all mediums," citing his early television and stage work. Reading from a five-page script, Scheider quoted Carl Sandburg, Shakespeare, and even Murrow himself, using several different voices and inflections. He even included a prop cigarette in the monologue, the cigarette being Murrow's trademark. The bulk of the tribute was about Murrow's fight to expose Senator Joseph McCarthy's anti–Communist, witch-hunting activities in the 1950s.[27]

Meryl Streep later admitted to Diana Maychick, "[*Still of the Night*] was a mistake, ... from the start I had [a]'who-the-hell-cares' attitude about the story. I did it because I love Benton and I wanted to work with him again. It was shot in New York so I just rolled out of bed to go to work. I was with my baby more than I had ever been. I didn't have to work every day."

Maychick wrote, "The main problem was a lack of rapport between Meryl and Scheider. Toward the end of filming, she admitted there was a lot of tension between them. It was partly the result of what they were asked to do in the script. Meryl was not only cast as the typical [Hitchcock] blonde icicle—[her] role [was] as artificial as polyester. Meryl had no reference point. The movie was set in a world of 100-dollar-an-hour shrinks, Chivas Regal and lead crystal, a world in which Meryl has had a hard time fitting in." Streep sums up the failure: "People who are smart just can't do something they think is popular just because it is selling now."[28]

Maychick continued her post mortem:

> The next film of an Oscar winner is often a box office bomb. This gloomy prediction held true when *Stab!* was released in December of 1982. Benton finally released the film under the new title *Still of the Night*. The critics universally panned it. [They] ... did not find the situation remotely believable with no rationale for Scheider and Meryl to fall in love. The suspense was dull and flat, with obvious red herrings that do not prevent the audience from guessing who the killer is halfway through the film. Most criticized was the contrived ending which placed Brooke, Sam and the killer together at the climax. The principal weakness was the hokey renditions of Hitchcock's classics, most notably *North by Northwest* and *Vertigo*; Benton had intended it to be a tribute to Hitchcock. He failed miserably in the eyes of the critics, who thought he was merely ripping off the master.[29]

David Ansen said, after listing everyone's earlier successes, that the film "announces itself as an A-list affair from the outset. One can only mourn the waste of talent. What possessed Benton to [do] this tired old script? Flirting with Hitchcock's ghost is a dangerous game. Benton ... hasn't concocted a story strong enough to stand on its own."[30]

Nick Smurthwaite said, "Its release was vastly overshadowed, on both sides of the Atlantic, by the opening of *Sophie's Choice*. This resulted in the unusual situation of the leading actress being acclaimed for one film and reviled for another. The irony was that Meryl in many ways found *Still of the Night* more challenging, intellectually at least, than *Sophie's Choice*."[31]

Vincent Canby called the film "clever but chilly in the way of something with a mechanical heart. Mr. Scheider, an excellent actor, is too intense—too serious, really to suggest the wildly romantic nature that the doctor discovers in himself. Mr. Benton's screenplay ... doesn't provide the room [for] such discoveries."[32]

Richard Schickel couldn't quite figure out why the film failed. He noted, with some weariness, "This year's (or should one say, this month's) Alfred Hitchcock pastiche is ... sober rather than ... raffish. Scheider is ... stalwart and workmanlike, but one longs for the goofy exasperation [of] Cary Grant. Scheider can play a loony tune ... if anyone bothers to ask him."[33]

Michael Wilmington felt that "the personality of ... Robert Benton is so far from Hitchcock's, more open and generous, the twists seem to get a new edge. Benton cannot really turn the vise, like DePalma, but he establishes a consistent tone of understated urban paranoia."[34]

Robert Asihina wrote, "Scheider overacts furiously ... but his good, or perhaps melodramatically intense, acting rarely overcomes the bad script. Streep is far too brittle to convey the allure ... Benton intended.... no one could breathe life into such a cartoon figure."[35]

Scot Haller wasn't thrilled: "Scheider and Streep are a bargain basement Cary Grant and Grace Kelly. Scheider's role is uninterestingly written. He's a real dolt. Scheider doesn't play Sam any smarter than the script makes him. Unfortunately, his nowhere man performance shackles Streep. [*Still of the Night*] is misguided to the end."[36]

Andrew Sarris blamed the casting and the script: "Roy Scheider ... the obsessed psychiatrist who is ... snared by the sheer ominousness of the Streep character, compounds the problem of casting with a performance of nervous intensity disproportionate to the meager amount of motivational information in the script ... too much is being left unsaid."[37] The *Film Journal* stated, "This is a major disappointment. Like most filmic tributes, it lacks a soul of its own. There are no weak spots in the acting, from Scheider to Streep to Tandy to Sommers—everyone is earnest and believable. But the script falls short."[38]

Lawrence O'Toole said, "*Still of the Night* is sharply shot, appealingly designed, intelligently crafted and features interesting actors. None [of] that matters ... the story is labored, contrived and ... preposterous. Streep and Scheider do not ignite the screen with erotic tension. They give real meaning to ... *Still of the Night*."[39] Bruce Williamson called the film "a romantic suspense drama with just enough intelligence and urgency to carry you to a fairly predictable climax. Roy Scheider and Meryl Streep do what they can, although their star turns somehow raise expectations that the movie never fulfills. I'd call [this film] a medium grade disappointment."[40]

People expected more: "It's disappointing ... that all they are doing is cribbing from Hitchcock. Benton approaches the master hat in hand, and [his] classy style is too cautious to generate much heat. Scheider is sterling throughout ... his scenes with his shrink mother, [Jessica Tandy],... suggest [the] movie that might have been."[41] Judith Crist said, "Scheider presents a saturnine mix, and Streep, in still another facet of her vast talents, epitomizes the uncertainties of a woman whose wounds are all interior. Together they present a fascinating study of suspenseful relationships in the solution of a murder mystery."[42]

The *Washingtonian* declared, "Robert Benton's new thriller is a little Hitchcock compendium with stylish scares and wry intelligence. The allusions become a bit distracting. Nevertheless, Scheider's gift for paranoia, Benton's crisp direction, and Nestor Almendro's [*sic*] cool, expressive lighting produce a sleek entertainment."[43] "Now it's Robert Benton's turn. He certainly has the style right. It's the movie's expert stylishness that qualifies it as homage and not plagiarism. Scheider and Streep are both excellent as usual and [are] performers Hitchcock would have cast had he had the chance," said Jimmy Summers.[44]

Scheider agreed with the critics that audiences don't like weakness. They want their leading men to be strong and they don't care if they are good or evil. They didn't like him in *Still of the Night* because the movie was too still and his character was too soft. "[Scheider] only hesitantly agrees that his role in [the film] was not his typical film character, but also adds that the harsh reviews were undeserved. [Audiences] ... were shocked at Scheider's mild mannered style."

The critics said, "Roy Scheider is so dull in this movie." Scheider defended himself with, "Hell, that was my character."[45] Scheider was also accused of giving away the ending of *Still of the Night* at a joint appearance with Meryl Steep at the LA Film Critics Awards, but cheerfully set the record straight by pointing out it was Streep who gave the plot information.[46]

The film Roy Scheider had wanted to do in 1981 was *The Verdict* (1982). Produced by Richard Zanuck and David Brown, Roy lobbied hard for the role of the drunk-on-the-skids ex-attorney, Frank Garvin, as it had Oscar written all over it. Brown and Zanuck wanted Robert Redford, if they could get him. They finally did not, but not for lack of trying, and the role went to Paul Newman, who received an Oscar nomination for it.[47] The failure to get this role and the poor performance of *Still of the Night* after Scheider's three-year layoff from film was most certainly a disappointment, but the 1982 Christmas season wasn't a total loss for Roy.

On December 28, Brenda King and Roy Scheider met again:

> Brenda returned to New York City with her friend Shirley MacLaine. The night after they arrived there was a gala Christmas dinner at Tavern on the Green, where Brenda met a lot of Shirley's old friends, including a writer named Noel Behn.
>
> Coincidentally, three nights later, Shirley and Brenda bumped into [Noel] again at Elaine's. He was sitting with Roy Scheider. [Noel Behn was one of Bob Fosse's friends.] "Brenda, hi, come on over, there's someone I'd like you to meet." As Noel began to introduce them, Brenda interrupted, "Oh, I know Roy, I've had a crush on him for years."
>
> Roy followed up with, "Of course, I know Brenda and the crush is mutual."
>
> "Does this mean we're engaged, Roy?" Brenda quipped.
>
> "Brenda," Roy said, looking her straight in the eye, "You keep forgetting. We've been married for years."
>
> Brenda said, "[I] turned bright red and beat a hasty retreat."[48]

However, the impression had been made and Scheider called her the next time business brought him to Los Angeles.

Nancy Cobb wrote, "For a year and a half, he and Brenda had an on-again-off-again [extramarital] relationship before Roy returned [to] his wife, determined to make it work. Ultimately, it did not."[49] Three years would pass before Roy and Brenda saw each other again.

Scheider stated in a 1980 *Playboy* interview that he and his wife had an understanding and had an open marriage. Roy now thinks twice about what he says for publication because he got in trouble for saying whatever was on his mind. He had thought that as long as he told the truth, he had nothing to worry about, only to discover he put himself in a bad light and hurt others.

Bob Fosse asked Roy to play Hugh Hefner in *Star 80*. The film chronicled the death of Dorothy Stratten, who was friends with Hefner. She was shot to death by her estranged husband, who then killed himself. Scheider wanted to work with Fosse again, as it was one of the happiest working relationships he had ever had, but he didn't want to do a cameo. It was not because the part was small, but because Roy believed a film can be spoiled by familiar faces cropping up in minor roles.

"Fosse had written a character into the script called Roy. He's … an assistant to Hefner, and … someone says to him, very sarcastically, 'Thanks a lot, Roy. Thanks for all your help' … because this guy … is … no help at all. [It was] Fosse's way of getting back."[50] Roy told Fosse, "I would love to do it for you … but … it doesn't sit well with me, and I don't think you need [my cameo].… you should get [a lesser-known] actor."[51]

Another *Jaws* movie was being filmed in 1982 and there was the usual speculation that Roy would come back as Brody. Desmond Ryan wrote, "Scheider blew up Bruce, the … shark in *Jaws* and electrocuted Bruce's successor, [Earl], in *Jaws 2*. [Roy] exhaled a cloud of cigarette smoke at the … thought of *Jaws 3* and laughed. 'Mephistopheles … couldn't talk me into … *Jaws 3*.' They knew better than to even ask."[52]

Roy did get the film he wanted in 1982, courtesy of John Badham. Badham wasn't the devil, but a hot young director, and even though it was another cop role, Scheider took it. He liked the script, convinced his agent, and happily went off to do *Blue Thunder* to ensure his unavailability for *Jaws 3-D*. When Scheider told his agent, Cohn said, no, you are not going back in uniform. Roy told him not to worry. It was only a flight suit. No badges.

Scheider hit it off almost immediately with John Badham. Badham reciprocated, saying that Roy was quite unlike most movie stars, who delight in making problems and seeing how long they can hold up a production because they believe their own press releases and have to act like children. Roy, however, was a remarkably mature person with tremendous patience and professionalism. Not that he was by any means a pushover; Roy was strong-minded and had definite opinions, but Scheider understood that the picture had to get done.

Badham said Scheider's contribution was that he gave Murphy some depth. Scheider had good humor and a world-weary quality, and his humanity came through on the screen. His gentle humor took the curse off wooden establishing scenes. "The work that Scheider [did] is as good as anything he's done, there's a lot of charm and humor, a lovely kind of quality he has."[53]

Randy Lofficier wrote, "Scheider plays a cop with a conscience fighting against other government powers to protect what he knows to be right. The moral stand is one reason why the actor accepted the part of Murphy." Scheider said, "This [movie] had such a strong political underbelly.… it was worth it."[54]

Scheider likened flying a helicopter to being at the top of a gyroscope. He became proficient at flying the chopper, even though there was always a stunt pilot on the other stick. Roy was allowed to take off, set the copter down, and play around with it. Scheider was prepped by pilot Jim Gavin, the second unit stunt-flying director. Gavin asked Roy if he was ready to do the take. Gavin flew the helicopter on the side and all over the place so quickly that Scheider swore at him. But they ended up being great shots for the film. The only time Roy was really nervous was when the camera ship flew close to his copter.

Scheider didn't want the blades hitting one another. Roy drew the line at being in the copter when it fell several feet, rolled over on its side, crumpled up, and spewed glass shards. He wouldn't do it then and now, when anyone urges him to do something foolish like that, he will tell them, if it's so easy, do it yourself.

John Badham added, "It turned out that Scheider was flying the helicopter most of the time, because along the way Jim Gavin was teaching him how to fly. I have film I shot myself ... of the first time Roy took the stick. He did a lot better than me. I was learning to fly, too, but he was much better than me. He was even taking off and landing."[55]

"When we got to the closeups ... Jim Gavin was flying the helicopter and Malcolm was simulating flying.... there was no room for me to go along. When I saw the dailies the next day ... [McDowell's] eyes were as big as saucers. 'Malcolm ... we can't [use] this. You look terrified.' So we [did] it a second time.... you see him looking very stern, but the minute Jim Gavin [said], 'Cut,' he would fall apart."[56] Scheider didn't mind flying as much as Malcolm McDowell did and was sympathetic. "McDowell would either throw up before we went up or throw up when we came down. He's the real hero."[57]

In the first draft of the script, Murphy's character was incredibly stoic; he didn't have too many laughs. Scheider pleaded with John Badham to let him and Danny Stern have some fun and improvise to make the film as light as possible. Badham encouraged this camaraderie, which made Scheider happy. Roy wanted his character to be human, more sympathetic, and not look like he had lockjaw. Daniel Stern, for his part, liked Scheider and said Roy was a regular guy, calm and cool under pressure, and he had absolutely no pretensions or ego. Even with all of his contributions, Scheider still wasn't happy with the finished film. He would have axed the Arco Tower scene as he felt it was out of character for Murphy to draw missile fire to it. Murphy should have picked a place that was obviously abandoned, where innocent people wouldn't be endangered. He would have also gotten rid of the scene where the helicopter came down on the cars. That was overkill.

Director Badham admitted to a budget of "22 million. They wouldn't let us take [Roy and Malcolm up in the helicopters] until we'd filmed every other part of the movie. And the last thing we did ... was their close-ups for the chase at the end. [There was] absolute insistence by the pilots [to work out] what we [did]."[58]

The American premiere of *Blue Thunder* was held on "the opening night of the Los Angeles Film Exposition Wednesday, April 13, 1983, at the Avco Center Cinema in Westwood, California. The premiere was a benefit for the Filmex Society."[59]

Mal Vincent reported: "All of the *Blue Thunder* hoopla was tied with the opening night of the Los Angeles Film Exposition, a festival dedicated to the internationality of movies. Traditionally, the opening night is given to an American film—*Blue Thunder*—this year. Following the film, the jewel bedecked crowd left for the Beverly Hilton Hotel for the annual Filmex Ball, complete with orchestra and dinner (with blue lightning bolts enmeshed in flowers as the centerpiece of each table). Each studio was assigned its own table.... it was Columbia and the *Blue Thunder* crowd who were the objects of the most scrutiny." On the morning after the big night, Roy Scheider spoke to Vincent. "That wasn't a typical audience last night. A lot of people [were] hoping it would be awful." Did he mind costarring with hardware? Roy laughed and said, "Well, this type of picture does require more than just acting. I don't suppose I will get [another] Oscar nomination."[60]

Roy didn't receive a nomination, but there was at least one critic who thought he should have: "You have to imagine the danger of the situation that's going on, because it's not really going on, is it? Working with an actor, you're getting a live response from the person in front of you, so it is much easier to work with people than it is to work with machines."[61]

The biographical elements in this film are not blatant. Scheider has a good rapport with the young actor who plays the son of his girlfriend, and he dresses in his typical style, but there is nothing beyond that. Scheider was enthusiastic about the project. He enjoyed attending a preview in New York, where the audience went wild, cheering and clapping. He had not seen that since *Jaws* and was glad that women seemed to like it, including his wife, Cynthia, who loved it. He was surprised because generally his wife loathed hardware movies.

To cap his sweet victory of having a hit movie in 1983 that was *not Jaws 3-D*, Johnny Carson, a skilled pilot, had *Blue Thunder* screened. Carson invited Scheider to come on "The Tonight Show." Scheider eagerly accepted. They had never met before. Roy was a little nervous but respectful. He plugged *Blue Thunder* and his upcoming NBC movie, "Prisoner Without a Name, Cell without a Number," which aired the following Sunday.

Vincent Canby was convinced the movie was a "succession of old-fashioned thrills, the kind that can be experienced in today's new fashioned pinball parlors."[62] Canby wrote about the action and the characters in a second review two days later, but he didn't say one word about Scheider's acting in the film.[63] *Los Angeles* magazine's notice read, "Fortunately, while *Blue Thunder* does have some curiously muddled moments, overall it's ... made to be watched from the edge of your seat. There is a lot of perverse wit in *Blue Thunder* ... most of the film belongs to Scheider."[64]

Stephanie von Buchau declared, "The nonstop action and breathtaking stunt flying may appeal to some, but the political implications of the plot are chopped to bits in all that whirring and whizzing."[65] "This preposterously entertaining rabble-rouser ... seems to proceed from a mind saturated with video games," stated Pat Dowell. "The casting is perfect: Roy Scheider plays the shaky hero haunted by memories of Vietnam; [Malcolm McDowell is] his nemesis, a gung-ho military pilot at the heart of the conspiracy."[66]

Dave Kehr felt the movie made its point: "Badham had the sense to cast ... familiar, accomplished character actors—Roy Scheider, Warren Oates ... Malcolm McDowell—who ... bring a sense of human eccentricity to bear against the cold, clean angles of the high-tech props and sets. Moral qualities in the film ... only ... increase its effectiveness."[67] "Judging by my absence of fingernails, I vote it the summer of John Badham. *Blue Thunder* is ... a super peeping tom helicopter. Scheider was ... great ... in *The French Connection* ... *Jaws* and *Jaws 2*. Since *All That Jazz* ... he has ... big screen charisma, owning said screen,"[68] wrote Richard Fuller.

Scott Haller called the film "a coup for the technocrats: the title role is played by a helicopter. *Blue Thunder* encourages hero worship of a machine. Scheider plays in effect the sidekick. [He] ... is to respond with awe and astonishment. [Murphy is] Dean Jones in *The Love Bug* as reimagined by Alexander Haig."[69]

Julian Petley said, "The film ... manages ... to have it both ways ... reveling in high-technology thrills while at the same time condemning the ... calculating callousness of the Complex. Ideologically schizoid ... the final aerial confrontation [is] a heart-stopping game of cat and mouse. Eat your hearts out, *Whirlybirds*!"[70]

***Blue Thunder* (1982, Columbia Pictures). Murphy is briefed on the computers by a female tech. Frank Murphy: Roy Scheider; Computer Tech: Zohra Lampert. This scene is not in the film.**

David Ansen felt, "Scheider makes a good hero, his lean and trim physiognomy perfectly at home in this mechanized, no-frills world, while his sardonic wit conveys his bruised iconoclasm."[71]

Robert Asihina wrote, "The co-star is Roy Scheider, who is locked in whisper mode throughout. He is one of those strong, silent, slightly wacko Vietnam vets with lots of guts and not much tolerance for his superiors."[72] *People*'s opinion was: "For a silly preposterously plotted film ... *Blue Thunder* is surprisingly absorbing ... a real popcorn movie. Saddled with most of the lifeless lines is Roy Scheider. Scheider could play this kind of part in his sleep—but instead he gives his all. When it works, wow."[73]

Guy Flatley loved it: "*Blue Thunder* is a knockout. Nerve-piercing, intelligent and sublimely entertaining, John Badham's brilliantly paced flick zooms ... to the top of the thriller class. In his juiciest role since JAWS [*sic*] Roy Scheider scores as a helicopter cop. You won't be sorry you went ... for the ride."[74]

A "making of" featurette ran on Nickelodeon on its "Movie Magazine" program hosted by Leonard Nimoy. The short contains two excerpts from an interview done on the set. Scheider talks about the reality of the plot, how all of the equipment used in the film existed at that time, and how they wanted to use it for crowd control at the upcoming 1984 Olympics. Scheider also mentioned that the public should be on guard that this technology is not used to invade their privacy. *People* reported that "ABC ordered a Gazelle helicopter for covering the 1984 Olympic games after seeing *Blue Thunder*."[75]

A publicity gimmick that didn't work

***Blue Thunder*. Murphy's ex-girlfriend pays him a visit. Frank Murphy: Roy Scheider; Kate: Candy Clark. This is a recreated publicity still; this scene is not in the film.**

was Roy Scheider's picture on the cover of the May *Esquire*, with only a caption plugging *Blue Thunder* and "Prisoner without a Name" on the inside cover. The readers, expecting an in depth interview inside, did not react well to "the new idea, which jokingly became known as 'the fiasco,' [which] ... was to put a pretty boy on the cover in much the same way *Cosmopolitan* puts a pretty girl on the cover."[76] Now *Esquire* will only feature someone on the cover who also has an article inside. Scheider's tendency to be first at something surfaced once again. *Blue Thunder* was released on DVD by Columbia Tristar Home Video in 1998.

A great believer in the rights of the individual and privacy, Scheider agreed to do a TV movie called "Prisoner without a Name, Cell without a Number" after a long session with the producer, Linda Yellen. Yellen was thrilled when he agreed to play Jacobo Timerman, especially since Scheider didn't know her work and she had to make her pitch for "Prisoner" in a marathon meeting. When the meeting ended, Roy was willing to take a chance with the fledgling producer, and the budget was set at $2.5 million.[77]

Yellen wanted a hero who had a classic, American, Gary Cooper quality of quiet strength. She received many comments on how different Roy looked from the real Timerman, a plump, baldish man, but Yellen saw a basic strength and machismo in both men. They had a certain gleam in their eyes that is true of all great men and were extremely charismatic. There was chemistry between Scheider and costar Liv Ullman as well as with Yellen. Linda noticed that women on the set were attracted to him. "We shot the movie in New York in January and February [of 1983] and began editing on Feb. 15. We've had a very tight schedule."[78]

"Prisoner without a Name, Cell without a Number" (1983, NBC). Roy Scheider and Liv Ullman pose with their real-life counterparts, Jacobo Timerman and his wife, Risha. Publicity still.

Castulo Guerra, who played Gabriel Vega, a fictionalized character based loosely on one of Timerman's employees at *La Opinion,* said, "Working with Scheider has been very important for me. He dominates the filming techniques. Besides, he's very accessible and shows an impressive camaraderie, which makes it very easy to work with him."[79]

Scheider talked about the project: "What we tried to do ... was show the substance and political importance of what happened. You can never be 100 percent accurate, because that's impossible. But you try [as] hard as you can and hope that the audience gets the impact, the relevance of the story."[80] Scheider is proud of the docudrama, having beat out Richard Burton and Edward Asner to play Timerman. "I don't normally do television ... but this particular project ... I felt was an important statement about human rights."[81]

> I don't do frivolous things that have nothing to say to people. I think it's a natural impulse for people to perform for each other, to explain what they are feeling about life.... It's why I continue to be an actor ... why I like my job ... because I can show people in transition or peril or in a critical situation, show people in change. I can get an audience to empathize with what I'm doing, which is the reason we all go to the theater or to the movies or television, to have [a] dramatic, cathartic experience that enriches us or makes us larger than we were before we went in.[82]

Scheider opened his home in Key West on March 4 and 5, 1983,[83] for " the last round of House and Garden Tours for this year's Old Island Festival Days."[84]

"On April 1, 1983, NBC pulled 'The Jacobo Timerman Story' from its early May schedule ... leading to speculation In Some Circles [*sic*] that [it] was too hot a potato to air." A spokesman for NBC said,

"Would that it was so." The official NBC line was that the two-hour docudrama "needed more post production work."[85]

Roy said to Chet Flippo, "I don't doubt there has been a lot of pressure on the network. This show does not speak well for ... Argentina's human rights policy. NBC, at one point, pulled the show. Now we're on, but they've scheduled us against 'Alexander Cohen's Parade of Stars.'"[86] This sacrifice scheduling against a special in effect guaranteed a smaller audience for the controversial drama.

In between the release of *Blue Thunder* and the airing of "Prisoner," Roy returned to New York to join "Colleen Dewhurst, Zoe Caldwell, Robert Whitehead, and Stella Adler and many other friends ... [who gathered] on May 15, [1983], at the Hunter Playhouse for an evening of reminiscences and to toast the first Harold Clurman professors."[87]

"Prisoner" finally aired on May 22, 1983. Jerry Buck wrote, "NBC wanted it reedited. [Linda Yellen said], 'I wanted to convey the passionate love affair that sustained [the Timermans].... the chemistry between Roy Scheider and Liv Ullman was magical.'[88] No stranger to controversy, Yellen had previously produced "Playing for Time" with Vanessa Redgrave. Scheider supported her decision, which did not make the writer of the script, Budd Schulberg, happy. Scheider explained, "It was basically a political document ... [and] people would be turning their knobs off in twenty minutes, because they would have been completely involved in the politics of Argentina, which they would not have understood. So the effort was made to slant the story to more of [what] Mr. Timerman went through personally ... to give the audience enough background ... in politics ... to understand what is going on."[89]

"I've never had the experience of being incarcerated for that amount of time. My performance was the result of hours talking to Mr. Timerman, trying to feel what it is like to be that alone and helpless. We all begin to think about the books and movies we've seen ... like *Papillon* ... and I said, when you were alone ... did any of that literature occur to [you]. Timerman said no, he never thought of *The Count of Monte Cristo*, never in any way saw himself in a romantic position at all."[90] It is interesting that the two biographical elements that Roy uses to illuminate Timerman's struggle are a fitness routine (sit-ups), while he is in prison to stay in shape, and that his idea of torture during house arrest is not having anything to read.

Stephanie Mansfield wrote, "A tedious, depressing drama salvaged only slightly by Roy Scheider's performance. Unfortunately, his moments of brilliance are all too brief. Still, fans of Scheider ... will find [him] doing his utmost to bring cinematic substance to the real-life drama. ['Prisoner' is] ... worth sitting through ... to see Scheider shine."[91]

Sandra Earley called the movie "ornamental and entertaining" and "predictable, cynical television. The book—and Timerman—deserved better. Scheider maneuvers sure-footedly within the shallow waters of the film."[92]

Scheider was asked about Timerman's reaction. Timerman "had seen it many times ... [and] it is disturbing every time he sees it ... [as] it could never be totally accurate to what he went through ... certain sections ... are very painful for him—he goes through a kind of sadness and joy realizing how much [his family] loved him and how much they sacrificed to get him out. He feels it generally reflects the truth."[93]

In June, Roy's daughter, Maximillia, married her college sweetheart Scott Connolly, whom she had been dating for a year and a half. Roy was pleased: "They did the square thing and got married. She goes

"Prisoner without a Name, Cell without a Number." The Argentine secret police torture Timerman. Jacobo Timerman: Roy Scheider; with uncredited extras.

back to being a junior next year and he goes back to being a senior."[94]

Scheider's last project in 1983 was for the Disney channel. He starred in the first made-for-cable movie, *Tiger Town*. Scheider wrote an article for *Playboy* about his experience. A producer friend, Susan Landau, called and asked Roy to go to Detroit for six days. He would work out with the baseball team for three days and shoot the movie for the other three. Baseball fan Scheider didn't need much persuading, even though the production could only afford to pay him scale.

Scheider went to FAO Schwartz, bought a bat and glove, and talked some kids in Central Park into practicing with him, since they had recently seen *Blue Thunder*. It reminded him of those long, lazy, summer twilights when his father spent hours trying to teach him to throw and catch a baseball. "Not up here, not down there, but right *here*—chest high," his father would bellow and threaten to go back into the house if Roy didn't straighten up his aim. Scheider bought Ted Williams' *The Science of Hitting* and read it. Roy hadn't played softball for three years, hardball for 20.

Scheider met Sparky Anderson, the manager, and was turned over to William "Gates" Brown, the batting coach, after spending a night in the batting cages practicing. Tiger pitcher Fahey agreed to pitch to Roy while Gates observed, delivering balls at half of the major league pitching speed. Scheider was too eager and had to learn to wait for pitches to come across his

Tiger Town **(1983, Disney Channel). Buddy Young slides into home plate to win the pennant. Buddy Young: Roy Scheider. The other ballplayers are uncredited.**

power zone. Roy did improve, but the practicing took a toll. Every time he missed a ball, he pulled his rib muscles. His regular workout of sit-ups and push-ups aggravated the soreness. That night Scheider observed a game against the Angels, with Gates counseling him on game strategy, while he observed dugout behavior.

One more day of practice yielded a hit to the outfield fence that Scheider was deliriously happy about, and that practice finished off Scheider's rib muscles. Filming began. Scheider's character had to look bad at the plate in the early sequences. Taking cut after cut and missing only heightened his pain, and they needed every minute in that stadium as they had the grandstands filled with Detroit fans who had volunteered to come out and be the crowd for not much more than lunch. For two days, Roy suffered. He was not skilled at running bases, which required him to run with his left leg dragging and his right leg slightly splayed to keep his balance. The muscles in his groin were stretched in ways he never expected. By the last day, he was verging on becoming a cripple.

Actors have this macabre sense that the closer they come to death, the better their performance is. Scheider's final headfirst slide into home plate brought a sigh of relief. Safe. The hero's welcome. The completion of the film. Roy staggered into the locker room exhausted, unable to turn his upper torso, legs bowed like a drunken cowboy. It would take him almost a month to recover. But Roy knew it was worth it: "When I saw the final product ... I really looked like a ballplayer. I had satisfied the director, the producer and ... myself. Thanks, Gates. I'll never forget that shot down the left field line, a boyhood dream come true."[95]

Scheider told *Time* that he had wanted

***Tiger Town*. Roy Scheider in Tiger uniform on the field with the director, Alan Shapiro. Publicity still.**

to portray a baseball player but never had the chance. "As a kid, I played sand-lot softball," he recalled. "Now here I am acting out a fantasy I've had since I was dreaming of ways to get out of New Jersey."[96] The project began filming on July 11, 1983.[97] "I want to do baseball the way you've never seen it before," said director Alan Shapiro. The story was based loosely on Al Kaline, the former Tigers star outfielder, and Detroit's world championship season of 1968.[98] *People* covered the event. "For [manager] Sparky Anderson ... breaking in a rookie [is] routine. This time ... instead of calling shots ... he was in them ... and the rookie was a star who wasn't kidding. 'Roy showed he was a professional by trying to learn ... about baseball before undertaking the role.'"[99] *Tiger Town* was shown with much hoopla on October 9, 1983, and its success spawned a whole new cable genre.

In publicity for the film, Roy said, "Like everything I do or don't do, it always rests with the script. I thought [*Tiger Town*] was charming, honest, inspiring, touching and sentimental in a very good way. Because I love baseball, I fell for it, hook, line and sinker."[100] "I play [someone] who feels he has only one chance to prove himself. My character is a guy who is down on himself; he's not performing ... the way he should. Something happens to him, and he moves to another place. That's exciting to watch."[101]

Tom Jory wrote, "It's ... all you might expect of a family film, heartwarming, hopeful, inspirational, slightly sentimental. Ultimately, Shapiro's hometown sensitivity is the difference between a mediocre film and a good one. The ballpark scenes [are] ... among the best ever made. *Tiger Town* is ... classy ... a good start."[102]

Tom Shales added, "This low key, but engaging [cable] movie about a strug-

Tiger Town. **Buddy watches the game from the dugout. Buddy Young: Roy Scheider.**

gling baseball team was better than the live-action features that Disney has made for theaters in recent years."[103] *Variety* said, "As Young, Roy Scheider plays with conviction."[104]

Ed Hayman of the *Detroit News* was equally impressed: "The story is told through the eyes of Alex. Thus we never really get to know Scheider's quietly desperate Billy Young [*sic*]. He remains a distant, heroic figure throughout, yet he never seems larger than life, and a real character emerges. This is taut, subtle work."[105]

Alan Shapiro, the director of *Tiger Town*, has several pages devoted to the film on his website, including a scan of one of the tickets they handed out to 5,000 Tiger fans to show up for the filming. It was called "Pennant Day at Tiger Stadium with Roy Scheider and Justin Henry" and "filming [took place] on Saturday, July 16, 1983."[106]

Roy was popular with the fans recruited to fill the stands. They surrounded him during the filming breaks, and he enjoyed the attention. Scheider accepts this adulation as part of his job, something he is supposed to handle. At home in New York City, Roy goes everywhere he wants to go. He does attract attention here and there, but he doesn't believe in hiding, going with entourages, or dodging places because he is afraid of being recognized.

Shapiro stated that the biggest problem he had filming was "Scheider's dark tan.... we had to surround him with black players because the white players would wash out" (from the lighting requirements).[107] Disney held an invitation-only special screening at its Burbank studios on October 13, 1983.[108] *Tiger Town* was well received and won the 1985 Cable Movie of the Year Award.[109]

Scheider was asked when he would do another film with Steven Spielberg. "Spielberg is an old pal and he keeps threatening to make another movie with me. Every time I see him he's got another project, but then he goes off and makes movies that he doesn't particularly need me for, but I keep telling him, 'Steven, when are we going to make that small movie, you know, about people?' I remind him of that all the time."[110]

Director Peter Hyams wanted Roy Scheider for *2010*, his sequel to *2001.* He told Arthur C. Clarke of his casting hopes in *The Odyssey File,* a book-length compilation of computer correspondence between Hyams and Clarke from September 16, 1983, to February 7, 1984, during preproduction of the film.[111] By Halloween Hyams had a trailer to show in the theaters.[112] Hyams wrote Clarke, "November 9: The casting seems to be going well. I will tell you who is going to play Floyd as soon as I know. There is an actor who I want. I am too superstitious to say his name now. For some reason or other ... every actor want[s] to be in this film."[113]

"November 14: I have signed Roy Scheider to play Floyd. This is not for publication … however it is official. I am thrilled. Roy is exactly the actor I had in mind. Our film has just taken a significant step forward."

Clarke replied on November 15: "Delighted to hear about RS. He's a magnificent and memorable actor—I was enormously impressed by *All That Jazz*." Hyams wrote back: "I told Roy Scheider of your happiness. He was thrilled. (He hasn't been yelled at by you yet.)"[114]

On November 21, the *2010* trailer began playing ahead of *Yentl*, to which Hyams wrote: "*Yentl* is a fine film … and is attracting large audiences … which is good for us. I received a number of reports over the weekend that the audiences went crackers over the trailers."[115]

Scheider does not appear in their correspondence again until December 5, when he came out to Los Angeles to visit Hyams, so they could get to know each other. Clarke sent: "RS: Welcome Aboard! You've already had two of the great lines in modern movies: 1) 'You're gonna need a bigger boat.' 2) 'I wonder if Kubrick ever gets depressed.' Hope we'll give you some more." Hyams replied the same day: "Roy was thrilled by your note. I showed him the sets and models today. I think he got a sense of how much effort is going into this silly enterprise."

Hyams added on December 6: "I spent most of the day with Roy. It's wonderful to hear him read some of the scenes out loud. He has that miraculous quality of making dialogue sound believable. He is a very bright man … and a very kind one. He was astounded that you had remembered the Kubrick line. He had forgotten it."[116] On December 9 Hyams told Clarke: "Roy is going home to New York this weekend. I couldn't have found a better actor for the role … or a nicer man to work with."[117] Scheider attended the *Scarface* premiere that weekend.[118]

Hyams does not mention Scheider again until January 17: "Roy Scheider has arrived. I am testing almost daily. Keep February 6th in your head. That is the date we begin in earnest."[119] Early on in this correspondence, Hyams, a Dodgers fan, tried to interest Clarke in baseball. Clarke, an excellent table tennis player, declined the offer.[120] No doubt, Hyams found Scheider much more receptive to talking about baseball.

Hyams told David Elliott, "My first priority is people, not machines. That's why I cast actors who can dominate the frame, like Roy Scheider, Lithgow and Mirren. Scheider … convinced me there was a real shark in *Jaws*. When Roy … said, 'We need a bigger boat,' I believed it."[121] Richard Hollis stated, "Hyams was convinced that the film was about characterisation [*sic*] more than hardware, and he peopled the film with people who argue, raise their voices and react more like the modern space traveller of recent space epics. Scheider … is perfect in the part of Dr. Floyd."[122]

Roy Scheider brought some of himself to the character of Floyd in his wardrobe choices and personality traits. After the Russian astronaut Max is lost, Floyd offers bourbon to the Russian captain after obviously imbibing himself to help his pain. Later on, when asked by Curnow what he misses most about Earth, Floyd says, hotdogs and mustard at Yankee Stadium and, by extension, baseball.

Scheider described *2010* to the press: "Peter Hyams has struck a good balance between hardware and people. He may have gone a bit too far at the end in his effort to make people understand, but … you should … err on the side of giving … too much rather than not enough explanation."[123]

Scheider told Gene Siskel, "I don't play [a guy] for whom … adventure is a piece of cake. He's … worried … about

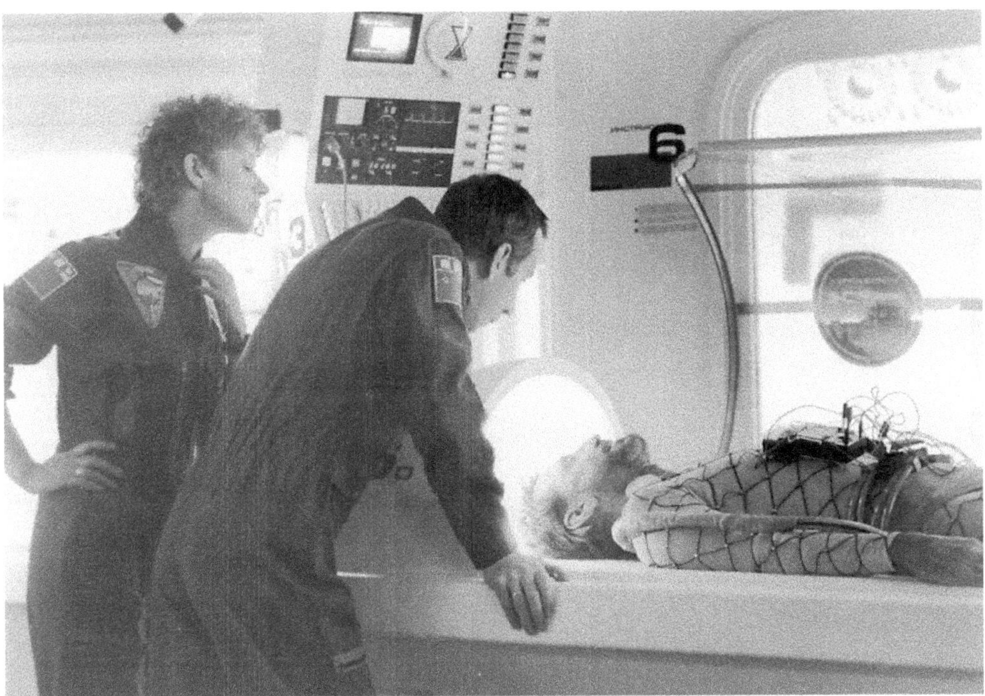

***2010: The Year We Make Contact* (1984, MGM-US). The Russian captain and doctor awaken Floyd two days early. Dr. Heywood Floyd: Roy Scheider; Captain Tanya Kirbuk: Helen Mirren; Dr. Vladimir Rudenko: Savely Kramarov.**

[his] family ... the ship and ... [himself]. This guy ... is afraid of failing, because he was responsible for sending the five astronauts up ... in *2001*. And he's afraid ... that there won't [be any family to come] back to."[124]

"I was Peter's first choice ... [he] had me in mind while he was writing the screenplay. I read the first 80 pages ... and ... was interested. He explained to me what he planned to do with the rest ... and I agreed to do it."[125] Roy didn't consider the film a sequel as "80 percent of the movie really hasn't got much to do with *2001*, [and it's] ... a much better story. I think the audience will have a better time. The film's plot will be much clearer. There's a story you can hook onto here."[126]

Elya Baskin, who plays Russian cosmonaut Max, said, "I've always admired Roy Scheider as a craftsman. He is a fantastic professional, he knows *exactly* what he wants. He is very equipped. I learned from him. When you work around somebody that good, it gives you a lot of confidence and inspiration."[127]

Arthur C. Clarke was brought to the set toward the end of filming. There were publicity shots taken of Hyams, Clarke, and Scheider. Clarke was given Scheider's silver crew jacket. Hyams snuck Clarke into the film in two places, as an inside joke. The first was a fake *Time* magazine in the hospital where Jessie Bowman lay comatose. Clarke and Stanley Kubrick are on the cover as the U.S. president and the Soviet premier, respectively, with the caption "War?" Clarke's other cameo is in the scene with Milson and Floyd in front of the White House. He is seated on a bench to the right of Milson, feeding the birds.

Clarke got an unexpected surprise that day. The filming had to stop by a certain

***2010: The Year We Make Contact*. Roy Scheider as Dr. Heywood Floyd.**

time as President Ronald Reagan's helicopter was flying over. Roy was not happy to be packed off like baggage. "I grabbed the still photographer and said, 'Just watch me.' When the helicopter flew over, I dropped my pants. The photographer got the picture and it ran in *The Washington Post*."[128] When Clarke was asked to comment, he said tactfully, "I was feeding pigeons [at the time] and didn't notice." They were specially trained pigeons brought in for the scene.

Neil McAleer, Clarke's biographer, wrote, "The slang word for the rumored gesture is mooning. The persistent rumor, officially denied by MGM's publicity department ... [was] that one of the lead actors made an impolite gesture with his body as President Reagan flew overhead preparing to land."[129]

The *Washington Post* wrote, "The MGM-UA crew had to stop filming as *Marine One* approached and Scheider, in a playful mood, jumped up and pretended to 'moon' the presidential party as the helicopter flew over. One eyewitness swore Scheider dropped his pants (revealing a black bikini)."[130] Jonathan A. Zimbert, an associate producer, demurred, saying it wasn't "mooning" in the classic sense. Roy bent over but didn't pull down his pants, he only pretended to. Zimbert pointed out that the White House roof is full of snipers, and they didn't want him to get shot, so they didn't let him do it. Both the freelance cameraman and an MGM still photographer apparently recorded the incident.

"CBS Morning News" producers, who were also there, declined to discuss what was on their tape as it is not their policy to discuss their outtakes. One CBS news source said that he heard secondhand that it was like a "quarter moon" at most. White House press aide Mike Weinberg said that, whatever happened, it was not seen by

Marine One passengers. Repeated attempts by the *Post* to contact Scheider failed.[131]

Clarke wasn't the only person to get a VIP tour of the set. Prince Andrew dropped by during his visit to Los Angeles in April 1984. *Newsweek* ran a photo of the prince with Roy. Scheider commented, "A likeable kind of guy."[132]

"Britain's Prince Andrew looked into the future, Hollywood style ... where he watched filming of the movie, *2010*. At one point he even directed a scene from the movie starring Roy Scheider."[133] "Roy Scheider escorted the prince around the set, [and] said Andrew 'was very personable. He's been doing this a long time. He's good at it.' At the studios, Scheider demonstrated how actors are filmed flying weightlessly through space. The British Olympic committee ... paid for [Andrew's] visit."[134]

In January 1984, Roy attended a fundraiser for the Committee for Concern in support of the Sandinistas at Michael Douglas's house, where he "gave readings and testimonies describing atrocities." Jacobo Timerman was also there.[135]

"Scheider says filming *Tiger Town* made him a Detroit Tigers fan, so he returned to Tiger Stadium to ... promote the [cable] movie's big-screen debut [in three Detroit theaters]. Scheider tossed out the first ball yesterday in the Tigers' 5–3 victory over ... Toronto. *Tiger Town* opens tonight."[136] The Tigers also won the World Series in 1984 and director Alan Shapiro said they gave him "prime seats to all the games."[137]

Scheider was in LA working on developing a romantic comedy film called *Everything's Jake*. Written by Anthony Palmer and slated to be directed by Peter Medak, the project never got out of the development stage.[138]

2010 was released on December 7, 1984. Vincent Canby wrote, "The cast is a good one. Mr. Scheider and Ms. Mirren, fine actors both, do exactly what's required of them, which mostly means being strong and stoic. [*2010*] is not a movie that is likely to attract or interest audiences not already hooked on the genre."[139]

Gillian MacKay opined, "Like its predecessor, *2010* has barely enough plot to make it around the block, let alone Jupiter. *2001* was a feast for the eye. In *2010* the once-novel special effects are stale and formulaic. The characters of ... Floyd and ... Bowman ... are as bland ... as before."[140] The *Washington Post* said, "*2010* assembles a talented cast, [then casts] them adrift. Scheider reprises his likeable no-nonsense briskness, but he can't save lines like 'We are only tenants of this world—we have been given a new lease—and a warning, by the landlord.' *2010* is a one-man-tour-de fizzle."[141]

The *Washington Times* called *2010* "a solidly entertaining if entirely conventional film ... marred only by its somewhat sappy ending. The skilled cast led by Roy Scheider ... brings ... a sense of realism unmatched by any science fiction film in recent memory."[142] Noah Ribischon observed to Bill Gates, "And the letters HAL are one removed from IBM." Gates replied, "Which they claim they weren't thinking of when they did it."[143]

Variety Weekly seemed to understand what happened best: "It's hard to accept ... with war between their countries imminent, the Soviet side would suddenly blindly follow Scheider, led by his ghosts. The audience ... [is] rushed along by too many Big Thoughts that aren't coming together in the monumentally important way Hyams hopes for."[144] The other reviews concentrated on the farfetched plot, or the lack of same, and whether Hyams had produced a sequel worthy of *2001*. Most thought Hyams did not, and they didn't like the ending.

Us magazine printed a blind gossip item on November 19, 1984, that stated, "[Scheider] has approximately one more year before a current situation totally dissolves."[145] After years of trying to work it out, the Scheiders had finally decided their marriage didn't work. Roy "entered into a property settlement in 1984 ... where he agreed to pay $100,000.00 per year,"[146] but Scheider's divorce from Cynthia Bebout would not be final until January 1989.

—10—

Choices and Changes

Publicity for *2010* carried over into 1985. In the syndicated "Making of *2010*" featurette that aired on cable, Scheider talked about the fish-out-of-water aspect of his character, how Floyd was a civilian who was thrust into being an astronaut. His character went up there to find out what had happened to his men and then had to deal with the political situation getting in the way. One of the themes of the film was teamwork. That appealed to him. Scheider was pleased everything they did in the film was conceivable—that we would have the necessary technology in 2010 to make the trip to Jupiter. His final comments centered around the monolith, what it represented, and how they deliberately did not define it, so the audience members could make up their own minds.[1]

Expectations were high, although many critics thought Hyams would never equal *2001*, no matter how many aspects of the film he was involved in. His four jobs on the film—writer, director, producer, and cinematographer—were a record at that time, according to *Variety*.[2]

Roy Scheider made an appearance on "Good Morning America" to plug *2010*. Joan Lunden liked the film, and Roy responded to her obvious enthusiasm. She introduced Scheider as "an earthy type" and noted that "*2010* was a change for him, playing a scientist caught between battling superpowers and the supernatural." Scheider talked about the teamwork concept and aspects that explore "the creation of life that almost gives the film a mystic feeling."

Joan said she "felt awe and the audience did, too." Encouraged, Roy replied that awe was close to what the audience was supposed to feel, even though he never felt that himself. The script had attracted him the first time he read it. He talked about "the journey of [my] character, what changes [Floyd] went through and [how] he was changed by the experience." When asked if it was hard to work with hardware, Roy allowed that he "needed to summon up more make-believe, but [I] could do it, even though it was more fun to work with people, rather than talking computers." His "bevy" of Russian emigre costars helped: "The fact they were real Russians and spoke Russian to each other, which I didn't understand, really helped with the notion that I was out in space on a Russian ship."

Lunden commented on his Everyman quality and his ability to do that kind of role. Scheider took it as a compliment: "If I'm touching or reaching those people on that level, then I'm doing my job, that's why I'm an actor." They spoke briefly about his invalid childhood and how he used his imagination to escape. Lunden's final comment was how family oriented the film was—no foul language, no nude scenes. Scheider admitted it was "squeaky clean," and he hoped people would enjoy the film for the message of peace it brought.[3]

Scheider appeared on "Saturday Night Live" on January 19, 1985, as the guest host. Roy's three skits were a good cop–bad cop routine (a take-off on *The French Connection)*, the scalping of Super Bowl tickets, and a tipsy Knicks fan who sings along with Penny Lane, Billy Crystal's drag queen character. Scheider's character was convinced that Penny was a woman and wanted a date. Roy's monologue was a story from a Knicks basketball game at Madison Square Garden. There should have been a plug for *2010*, but there wasn't.

Roy did the voiceover for a Volkswagen GTI commercial and Chuck Berry supplied the music, "No Particular Place to Go." The spots first aired during the "Ellis Island" miniseries.[4]

2010 was released on video in 1987 and on DVD in 1998. Owned by Ted Turner, the film frequently airs on his cable channels. On Scheider's birthday, November 10, 1998, Turner included birthday greetings to Roy during the commercial breaks of the film.

Roy began working on two new movie projects in early 1985. The first film was based on a book by Leonard Michaels, which Scheider had read and wanted to bring to the screen. The second was a long-awaited collaboration with director John Frankenheimer on an Elmore Leonard book they both wanted to film.

Roy Scheider loved the honesty of *The Men's Club*. He felt it would make a great film about how men feel about relationships. Scheider persuaded a diverse group of fine actors to join his club, including Frank Langella, Harvey Keitel, Richard Jordan, Treat Williams, David Dukes, and Craig Wasson. "I'll be a silent producer," he says, "I'm just starting to get into producing, which is a position I find attractive. There's a certain satisfaction in seeing a movie done that the audience likes."[5] Edited by his wife, Cynthia, it was the last movie they did together.[6]

Roy traveled to Las Vegas on April 15, 1985, for the Marvin Hagler and Tommy Hearns middleweight championship fight.[7] The next morning, on "Good Morning America," he discussed the fight with host David Hartman, who introduced Scheider as "a wonderful actor." Scheider said that he felt good, but he didn't think Hearns did. They talked about the glitz and glitter of Las Vegas. Hartman inquired, "Had you seen Hagler fight before?" "Oh, yes. I don't know what Hearns was doing, but Hagler was nonplused by it and stuck with him until he got over it and then moved in. Hagler stuck to his fight plan and it was over very quickly."

When Hartman mentioned Scheider's own boxing history, Roy said, "It was two bouts at the Diamond Glove Tourney in Elizabeth, New Jersey, and I really didn't like it. I had gone to the gym to lose weight. It was the trainer, Georgie Ward's, idea to make me a boxer and personally I had no aspirations to it as a career."

Hartman asked if he got emotionally involved in the fights and Scheider admitted that his "heart was going a mile a minute. The ring is small, you are surrounded by people who expect you to fight, there's no place to run. You have to do it."

Scheider admired the spirit that made them go in there and do it. Roy then mentioned that he was prepping *The Men's Club* and that "in October I am going to Venice to do Hemingway with Robert Altman." "Venice in the fall is a tough life," replied Hartman. Scheider laughed and agreed.[8]

Altman mentioned the project in an interview given April 1. Altman was "writing the screenplay ... has the backing from European interests, and he plans to start shooting in Venice next fall [1985], with Roy Scheider and maybe Julie Christie." Interviewer Steve Sonsky was skeptical. "Whether ... audiences will see [this], or [it] will meet the same fate as ... other 'lost' Altman efforts, remains to be seen."[9] Sonsky was right. This Hemingway adaption was never green-lighted.

In June 1985, Roy Scheider was honored by Columbia High School as the first of two inductees into the newly formed Columbia High School Hall of Fame. The idea was the brainchild of Student Council president Andrew Shue, who would go on to become an actor himself. "The CHS Hall of Fame honors graduates for their distinguished achievements in their chosen professions and personal endeavors. To be considered, the candidate had to be a role model for his classmates and today be dedicated to making a positive impact on society."[10]

Roy dubbed a voiceover narration track for *Mishima: A Life in Four Chapters*, a film about Yukio Mishima, the prolific Japanese writer who committed ritual suicide at the age of 45. The movie was in Japanese with subtitles. The English narration was added to help American audiences understand the film. Scheider read passages from Mishima's autobiography, explaining the different events of his life. Directed by Paul Schrader and produced by Francis Ford Coppola and George Lucas, this movie received considerable press coverage, mostly because of Schrader's reputation, but did not do well at the box office. Paul Attanasio said, "*Mishima* tries to make sense of both its subject's life and his work, and ends up illuminating neither. Part [is] stylized scenes, played on theater sets, which encapsulate three of Mishima's novels. The other ... (with a voiceover narration by Roy Scheider) flashes back to ... Mishima's life."[11] The film was released on video in 1986 and on DVD in 2001.

Roy was "rollicking at the Roseland, June 10, [for the 10-year] anniversary celebration [of] World Hunger, with Count Basie providing the music. Scheider [gave] a brief talk."[12] Roy continued his support of the project he had committed to eight years ago.

Scheider's impending divorce was mentioned a second time in *Rona Barrett's Gossip*. In November of 1985 the magazine printed, "He is in the middle of a personal crisis that would take [another] year to resolve."[13] In 1992, Brenda King said, "Roy was married at the time and going through a difficult period."[14] In December 1985, Roy attended the premiere of *Santa Claus: The Movie* with Cynthia. This film was directed by Jeannot Szwarc. *Jaws 2* alumnus Jeffrey Kramer and Roy's *2010* costar John Lithgow had roles in the film.

Roy narrated the PBS documentary "Follies: In Concert" on the "Great Performances" series on March 14, 1986.[15] He provided brief profiles of the performers, including Lee Remick, Elaine Stritch, Adolph Comden, and Betty Green, during scenes of the rehearsal. The program concluded with the actual performance.[16] "An unusual and entertaining documentary ... the creation of that historical evening of theater. New York's biggest theater event of 1985."[17]

"*The Men's Club* [is] a scorching and serious film about male consciousness raising. Scheider used his clout [and] the film [was] made for ... 2.5 million ... [after the] script had lain dormant ... for two years.

"Follies in Concert" (1986, PBS). Roy Scheider with star Lee Remick.

their hair, is so clammily sensitive that it will be lost on men. The lengthy whorehouse sequence ... isn't likely to be a hit with women. It's well acted—Roy Scheider, Harvey Keitel and Treat Williams [are] the least at sea."[20]

Bruce Williamson declared, "The Club's members ... end up on a violent food-and-booze orgy after a consciousness raising session ... then [go] off to a brothel. The rest ... is generally disastrous—clumsily orchestrated scenes ... that range from deadly dull to downright embarrassing. Only the casting director can claim a coup."[21] Laurie Stone thought the book was outdated in 1981 and in 1986 the movie was even more passé: "The men's dialogues are too well crafted to be credible; they are also too pointless to be worth hearing. The film ... applauds the men for being shamelessly mean ... what was retro in the past is still flourishing. Its mantra could be: Long live hatred of change."[22] Will Joyner wrote, "This film ... about ... upscale guys who attempt the male equivalent of a female support group, looks like an early run-through of a promising but problematic stage play. Scheider and Keitel in particular have a good feel for the blend of confession and confrontation."[23]

There are several biographical elements in *The Men's Club*. Cavanaugh—in Michaels's book—was a seven-foot basketball player, not a World Series–winning baseball player, although baseball references in a Scheider film are no surprise by now. There is a scene where Cavanaugh is

[Roy stated], 'The ... actors became a club. The purpose: to do a movie. The method: exchanging truths.'"[18] *The Men's Club* was released in September 1986.

Kris Turnquist wrote, "[It had] all the earmarks of a high-powered ... ham fest, [but] ... the movie is so inept it doesn't even make you angry. With material that's weak [and] direction that's impotent—Scheider throws himself into his shell-of-a-man role. [He] succeeds in being so creepy you wish [he'd] go away."[19] The film bewildered Janet Maislin: "The early part ... [where male] members let down

The Men's Club **(1986, Atlantic Entertainment). The members of the club. Philip: David Dukes; Solly Berliner: Harvey Keitel; Kramer: Richard Jordan; Cavanaugh: Roy Scheider; Terry: Treat Williams; Harold Canterbury: Frank Langella; Paul: Craig Wasson. Publicity still.**

reading in bed late at night while his wife sleeps. In another scene, he tells the club an anecdote about picking up a willing woman at the grocery store to have quick sex and ends with the amused observation that his wife has no idea what he will find when she sends him out grocery shopping. Scheider told *Redbook* that, when he was home, he did all of the grocery shopping and most of the cooking. Cavanaugh also makes another date for sex from a pay phone while out jogging.

Cynthia Scheider has the third (and last) of her on-camera cameos in this film, as a diner in the foreground at the Outdoor Café when Cavanaugh invites Phillip to come to the club meeting. This was her first full editing credit on one of her husband's films.

Box Office magazine listed the film as grossing $1.9 million from 500 theaters in its first 10 days of release.[24] Scheider blamed Atlantic Releasing for the film's poor box office claiming the marketing campaign was all wrong. They took an art film and released it wide. The film starred seven well-

***The Men's Club*. Cavanaugh and his wife at a party. Cavanaugh: Roy Scheider, Mrs. Cavanaugh: Helen Shaver. This scene is not in the film.**

known actors, so they put an unknown actress on the poster. The movie came and went quickly to scathing reviews.

Scheider became a spokesperson for Nikka Whiskey in Japan.[25] Roy was adamant about where he wanted his movie career to go: "I would love to play more comedy. I did in my theater career, and ... in stock and college. I was ... the character man, the clown. Something happened ... when I came to New York. I got ... [stuck playing] a lawyer ... a policeman or a gangster."[26] Roy understood that getting a comedy is easier said than done: "There are only a handful of actors who can get financing to do humor movies. It's the hardest kind of movie to get made.... this is disappointing ... because my ... theater background was comedy. But my introduction to ... movies was playing these serious, hard-nosed characters."[27] Scheider's next movie would star him as yet another hard-nosed character.

In *52 Pick-Up*, Harry Mitchell is a philandering husband caught in a blackmail crisis by an extramarital affair. John Frankenheimer said:

> While I was in England [filming *Holcroft Covenant*], I read Elmore Leonard's *52 Pick-Up*. I called my agent and asked him to find out if the movie rights were owned. He called me back and said they were owned by Menachem Golan and his partner Yoram Globus at Cannon. I said, "Oh, God, that's awful." [My agent assured me] that they started a whole new policy [of] hiring good people and they are going to up the budget. I said, "Call them and see if they want me to direct the picture." He called back and said that they did and that the terms were acceptable. Roy Scheider called me and said he loved Elmore Leonard's stuff and the character in *52 Pick-Up* particularly and he'd like to play him. Menachem agreed to hire him and as soon as Roy came aboard, he and I got together with [Elmore] Leonard and the three of us collaborated on making the script a

dramatization of the novel, which is essentially what we shot.[28]

In the syndicated cable featurette "The Making of *52 Pick-Up*" Scheider said, "Cannon had been wanting me to do a film for them for some time. They had another script, but I knew they had *52 Pick-Up*. I held out until they gave me that one."[29] Scheider's signing was announced on February 14, 1986, when it was noted that he had been honored at the 1986 ShoWest media convention in Las Vegas with a career achievement award.[30]

Frankenheimer continued, "I took the budget to Menachem. He said, 'It's a million dollars too high.' I knew he meant it because he told me exactly what he was going to pay Roy Scheider for the picture. [$1 million.] That's the way [Golan] does business. So Roy agreed to do it. So I said, 'We could make the movie here in Los Angeles [instead of Pittsburgh] for a million dollars less.' [Golan] said, 'Fine,' and that was it."[31]

> I was stuck with a script that wasn't what I wanted. Roy Scheider had contacted me about being in the picture. I always wanted to work with him. Menachem Golan said, "Fine, we'll hire him." After a week of negotiation, Roy was signed on. He had the same reaction to the script ... that it missed Leonard's book. I called [Leonard] and said, "I read *52 Pick-Up*, I love your dialogue, and we have a script that doesn't work." I sent [Leonard] the script, he read it, called me back and said, "I see what you mean." I said, "Why don't you and I, with Roy Scheider, ... write the dialogue?" He sent me pages, Roy and I went over them, changed them, always going back to the book. In about three weeks we had a good script based completely on [the] book.[32]

Scheider had been taking more of a hand in rewriting his scripts and was particularly proud of some scenes he put into *52 Pick-Up*. In one, he's hiding out in the garage, afraid to face his wife, putting new spark plugs into his Jaguar. She comes in to yell at him and says, "If you'd just been doing that, we wouldn't be in this mess." Roy took credit for the ending, a climactic showdown between himself and the criminal ringleader. Scheider concluded he was about 70 percent satisfied with the finished film.

52 Pick-Up (Cannon, 1986). **Alternate poster photo, the one Scheider wanted, without him holding the gun. Roy Scheider: Harry Mitchell; Ann-Margret: Barbara Mitchell.**

Kirk Honeycutt interviewed Roy Scheider about *52 Pick-Up* in 1992:

"[Roy] was very instrumental in shaping the script," Honeycutt told the audience.

Scheider replied, "The blowing up of the car was my idea."

"It was a briefcase in the book."

"That's right. I thought we needed something ... more dramatic ... something with the car. We wrote ... the business about [the villain] always playing and touching the car. So that when the phone call comes ... I plant the idea of throwing the car into the deal. Then you see [Mitchell] go to the garage, and he tampers with the car, and he produces that ending."

"It's interesting how you plant something in the first act and pay it off in the third act. Was there anything about the character itself that grabbed you?"

"Well, at the time, I was going through a rough relationship in my own life concerning an outside attraction, and some of that

***52 Pick-Up*. Harry Mitchell confesses to his wife that he's having an affair.**

was interesting. This movie took a lot of flak because of the murder scene of the young girl."

"[That scene] is tough."

"Unfortunately, the movie ... got very, very good reviews, but the scene of killing her was usually examined in the first paragraph. The moviegoer was so put off by the description of it that a lot of people thought the movie was about that kind of brutality. It's not. Perhaps, we should have had more screen time developing the difficult relationship between Ann-Margret and myself. It might have helped the picture."

"I think ... those scenes ... are there, especially the coffee table scene."

"It's a good scene. And I always felt we needed more of those."

"What is John like as a director?"

"He is very possessed with obsessions ... stories where people are obsessed. John ... [is] a bit of a martinet ... very demanding of his staff [and] crew. He expects his actors to be on time and be enthusiastic."

"John's films are very kinetic, too. Does he work closely with you, or does he let you go about your business?"

"The actors ... he chooses ... have ... qualities he wants. He encourages you to use those qualities ... bring [them] out ... to serve his picture and his story."

"What did you discover about this character?"

"[Mitchell] likes running his company. He's been in the Air Force. He's a fighter pilot, so he likes responsibility. Except for [his wife's] cooperation, he goes about without the police to solve the problem [facing] him. He's quiet. He's self-organized. He goes by his instincts."

"I know Cannon didn't really back [the film] the way they should have. But do you feel anything else might have hindered it from reaching an audience?" Honeycutt asked.

"No. But it's not a high concept movie, nor is it about any great world-shaking theme or philosophy. I don't think it's an important movie, [but I think] it's a good movie ... very exciting ... a good thriller, and it provides something to hold onto for an evening. It's a good piece of work by a good filmmaker."

"Would you have made the same choice?"

"Yes. I would have made it pretty much the same way. I would have [cut] ... some of the rough edges off the scene [where] the girl is killed, and I would have insisted on ... more ... romance."[33]

Scheider came back to the importance of the coffee table scene in his interview on the Encore documentary series "The Directors" about the films of John Frankenheimer. The other scene Scheider thought made the movie was the ending, where Harry Mitchell blows up Alan Raimy in his Jaguar with the ransom money. This was Scheider's idea, right down to the song played on the tape, "Stars and Stripes Forever."[34] Scheider added four biographical elements to this film. Aside from the fact that Scheider had extramarital affairs and was now getting a divorce, Harry Mitchell drives a Jaguar. Scheider owned a green Jaguar for many years. Mitchell was in the Air Force and was a fighter pilot, the career Scheider missed when he washed out of flight school. In the book, Harry works for an automobile manufacturer.

Mitchell is kidnapped (the second time) outside the Joe Allen Restaurant. Scheider's involvement with Joe Allen and his restaurants dated back to the late 1960s when Scheider would hang out in the New York restaurant and go to the same gym for workouts. When Allen was looking for investors to open a place in Paris, "he got six or seven actors out of the restaurant to invest ... and it was very successful. The next place was L.A., so I went in for a bit more ... then I went in on the one in London ... then I went in ... on the one in Toronto ... so I sort of have a piece of each one of them. I did it because he's a friend of mine ... those restaurants are really watering holes for people like us ... it's a hangout ... you can go all over the world and see the people that are in your industry ... and it's pleasant."[35]

Elmore Leonard said, "Frankenheimer sent me the script. He suggested a scene I might add. All I did was add commas where proper names are used in the dialogue, and spell all right with two words. The only thing I didn't like ... was the nudity—especially Vanity."[36]

Frankenheimer detailed the film's distribution deal:

> Yoram said, "We are spending two million dollars on the distribution of this picture." I said, "That's not enough. You can't get this picture out there for [that]." Cannon never previewed films for critics. I made them do that. In fact, I made a terrific mistake. I knew Sheila Benson at the [*LA*] *Times*. I guess the scenario was she didn't like the movie and didn't want to give me a bad review, so she assigned the review to another *Times* critic, who was not a regular film critic and who gave me the worst review I've ever had in my life. I got raves from everyone else. Menachem took double truck ads quoting all the great reviews and saying *52 Pick-Up* was the best reviewed film Cannon ever had. But they didn't know how to market the picture and never really spent any money publicizing the picture. The people who saw it loved it, but not enough people saw it. It's a very good movie ... should have been a hit, could have been a hit.[37] "There wasn't enough advertising, so consequently the picture did not do what we hoped it would do because the public didn't know about it. People who see this picture on video, go 'My God, what a fascinating movie!' They didn't know it had been in cinemas."[38]

52 Pick-Up opened on November 7, 1986, on 700 screens.[39] Roy Scheider appeared on the "Today" show. Bryant Gumbel asked about playing cops and whether or not Scheider thought he was typecast. Did he seek out those kinds of roles? Scheider replied, "Those sort of roles seem to find me and if I had my way, I'd do more of a variety of things." They talked about Harry Mitchell, his blue-collar roots, and the blackmail situation he found himself in. Gumbel observed that before they came on the air, Scheider was excited about his good reviews in the New York morning papers. Bryant was surprised Scheider wasn't more cynical. Roy replied, "I'm an actor. I want to be able to communicate with an audience—I like to think there's one out there. And if the reviews are good for the film, that's terrific."

Gumbel mentioned Scheider's rewriting of the script. Roy credited Frankenheimer "for giving him some leeway to make changes which need to be done in the transition from book to movie." Scheider assured Gumbel that "the master [Elmore Leonard] was consulted and gave his blessing." Bryant asked Roy if it was difficult to top himself, considering some of the things he had already done." Scheider replied, "Yeah, yeah, but that's the challenge. You don't try to do the easy stuff. You try to do the hard stuff. Translating this material into a good movie is not so easy." Scheider praised Frankenheimer, saying the director "provided a good freeway for the actors ... we got some very good performances." Gumbel agreed, "The good reviews were deserved."[40]

Two short featurettes publicized *52 Pick-Up*. The first one, on "Sneak Previews," basically only offered a synopsis of the plot through a montage of clips from the film and was produced by Media Home Entertainment. The second short included the actors and director Frankenheimer talking about their characters and the film. Roy said the film had "very interesting, subtle, intriguing shades of gray all over it, and that there were no lily white characters, including mine." Scheider also liked the dual meaning of the title. It "has all kind[s] of connotations, it has the connotation of the kid's card game, where you throw the 52 cards on the floor and say, pick them up, that's the game. There is also that kind of challenge, given to my character and to John Glover's character, as the two nemeses in the film, they both throw challenges at each other, so it has a lot of abstract meanings, besides the literal one—money." Scheider loved the ending, comparing it to "the shower scene in *Psycho*. The audience would identify with it on a visceral level and having once seen the film, they would never forget it."[41]

Janet Maislin liked this film, praising most everyone in the cast in one way or another: "Roy Scheider gives a leathery, tough guy performance as Mitchell, just right for these surroundings."[42] Ed Kelleher wrote, "*52 Pick-Up* ... is as pointless and irritating as the joke card game. The good news is that despite the picture's ricocheting style—nasty realism one minute, wacky comedy the next—and some uneven performances, it contains enough audience-grabbing moments to redeem itself."[43] J. Hoberman said, "Another fantasy of two worlds, a bit more robust in its sleaziness, John Frankenheimer's *52 Pick-Up* is the ultimate guilty husband movie. A cool cat with a silver jag, Scheider comes across as even more competent when compared to the clownish shake-down artists."[44]

Bruce Williamson named *52 Pick-Up* "the choicest thriller in aeons. Co-starring Roy Scheider and Ann-Margret ... in deep jeopardy with murderous blackmailers, this is a mean, lean ... ugly suspense drama. With nary a let up in nastiness, *52 Pick-Up*'s harrowing game of wits features ... a really knockout stint by John Glover."[45]

Rita Kemply recorded, "Director John Frankenheimer ... never misses a chance to exploit sex or violence in this taut, tacky, t&a adaptation ... set against a backdrop of cheap sex shops and strip joints, Frankenheimer is happy as a pig in a dumpster. Scheider is solid as the adventure capitalist."[46] Rob Salem was of the opinion: "There are some terrific cards in this deck—some real losers, too—spread all over the screen. With a competent cast of 'face cards' ... [including] leads Scheider and Ann-Margret ... [it] had the potential to be a first class thriller. Alas, it wasn't in the cards."[47] Bill Hagen stated, "Scheider, whose acting is like his appearance, very taut and wiry, no fat, delivers his customary solid work as Harry. With the talent involved ... it should have been much better, but never gets beyond mediocre."[48]

Roger Hurlburt wrote, "A well-crafted drama with a disturbing aftertaste. Scheider has garnered one of his very best roles and Ann-Margret is superb. Insane violence abruptly replaces a simple criminal plan. If films, like art, are ... considered reflections of the times they are created ... viewers be warned."[49] Bill Cosford also thought the film had merit: "*52 Pick-Up* ... is a straight ahead thriller. No tricks, no goofy stuff. Frankenheimer ... knows a good B-movie when he sees it. Frankenheimer has Roy Scheider and Ann-Margret as the good-but-not-innocent folk, which is nice casting. [They] are good choices because they don't interfere."[50]

Roy explained to Susan King, "I thought we were misinterpreted with that [murder]. That was not done to titillate an audience. It was to show the two guys that committed it were warped and sick. But the critics ... jumped on that incident."[51]

Roy lamented to Martin Burden that the baseball game in the film, where the first blackmail payment is made, caused a problem for the real Mets pitcher. "The bright [movie] lights bothered Dwight Gooden and the game was held up. I felt very badly about that. After the delay, Dwight lost his stuff and lost the game."[52] Scheider, ever the baseball fan, was able to insert his favorite sport into yet another movie. *52 Pick-Up* was released on video in March 1987.

Scheider was asked to appear in *Jaws: The Revenge*. "Roy Scheider ... is negotiating with Universal. [It will] ... be a cameo. The script ... calls for him to be eaten by the shark early in the action." Roy's press agent said, "Mr. Scheider has not agreed to be in the *Jaws* movie." Universal said, [We] don't have him dying. He hasn't even been set."[53]

Jaws: The Revenge opened in July 1987 and Scheider was quoted: "[I] turned down an offer to appear in the 'new' *Jaws* because 'we did *Jaws* once and did it right.' Set 15 years [later], this film focuses on ... the widow Brody. She blames the shark for [Martin's] fatal coronary and then her son [Sean] is killed."[54] Scheider's picture is shown prominently on the wall of the police station and his "early death" scene mentioned above was given to the actor who played his youngest grown-up son to get the film's revenge motif going. Roy further explained his nonappearance in *Jaws: The Revenge* in a 1989 interview for the opening of the film *Night Game*: "They wanted me in *Jaws IV*.... [That] would be asking for it. The shark would eat me."[55] Scheider told Nigel Andrews, "As it turned out, *Jaws 2* was passable. I absolutely refused to do *Jaws 3*. When I refused *Jaws 4*, I got myself in ... hot water. The studio thought I was being snooty, uppity, artistic. So for a long time I didn't do any Universal movies. They still may be angry."[56]

On January 8, 1987, Roy participated in "The Autumn of 1975," an ABC news program that dealt with the issue of segregation in Boston public schools. The debate, with Gerald Ford, Muhammad Ali, Chevy Chase, Harry Reasoner, Tom Wolfe, and Hubert Humphrey, among others, aired on the ABC news magazine, "Our World," hosted by Linda Ellerbee and Ray Gandolf.[57]

Roy Scheider offered one explanation for his lack of movie work at this time: he was getting divorced after 24 years. He narrated a seven-part series for Ted Turner, "Portrait of the Soviet Union," and a special for CBS called "Inside the Sexes." With Meryl Streep, he coproduced "Harold Clurman: A Portrait of Theater" for PBS.

On June 18, 1987, Roy was spotted at the American Film Institute's benefit premiere of Steve Martin's *Roxanne*. Scheider called the film "good-hearted." Mary Louise Oates noted, "Scheider is off to Moscow, to host and narrate ... Ted Turner's special on Russia ... starting July 5."[58] "Everyone I know wanted to come with me. It's because of Gorbachev. He's become a real Russian celebrity. He's stolen the president of the United States' thunder."[59]

On July 27, 1987, Roy was one of several celebrities who filmed anti-drug spots for theaters. "Clint Eastwood, Rosanna Arquette, Ally Sheedy, James Woods, Roy Scheider, Rae Dawn Chong, [and others] ... deliver a stark anti-crack message, "Don't even try it. The thrill can kill.' The spots ... run before all feature films produced by member studios, beginning with *Jaws—The Revenge*."[60]

Scheider returned to the movies with *Cohen and Tate*, a small feature with a novice director, Eric Red, who had specifically asked for him. *Cohen and Tate* was filmed on location in Texas in August 1987.[61] Scheider had barely arrived in Houston when he was asked to return to New York City to speak at a memorial service for Bob Fosse.

Scheider decided to tell a story at the service. He remembered when they were rehearsing the last number of *All That Jazz*, "Bye Bye Life," and how the Fosse character goes around saying goodbye to his wife, his mistresses, his producers, everyone in his life, and they all shake his hand and hug him. Fosse had asked Roy what that felt like. Roy said it felt terrific. So he told Fosse, "Why don't you try it?" So Fosse did. When he came back, he told Roy, "You know what, they all forgave me." Scheider replied, "Yeah, Bobby—we do."

When Roy wrote that out for his funeral speech, he started to cry. Scheider was seen briefly speaking at the memorial, telling this story in the PBS "Dance in America" series documentary "Bob Fosse: Steam Heat" which aired in 1990. *People* asked him for a quote for Fosse's obituary: "[Fosse] just wanted to provide the audience with as good a time as he possibly could. That's all he ever asked of himself."[62] Roy was left a bequest in Fosse's will of $378.79. Fosse set aside $25,000.00 for Scheider and 65 other friends. "I have made this provision so that when my friends receive this bequest they will go out and have dinner on me. They have all at one time or another been very kind to me. I thank them."[63] Martin Gottfried characterized the gesture as a way for Fosse to have a little sport after he was gone. Gottfried claimed in life that Fosse dreaded unoriginality, so he wanted something unique for his death.

Fosse's memorial service took place at the Palace Theater, the birthplace of *Sweet Charity*. Gwen Verdon arranged for everyone to come together on Halloween eve. This is where Roy gave his eulogy. The public memorial was announced in *the New York Times*, and about 15,000 Fosse fans queued up, filling the theater to standing room only.

Verdon took "dinner on me" literally and reserved the Crystal Room at Central Park's Tavern on the Green. The celebration began in the early afternoon. The guest list was everyone Fosse had named in his will. "It was as if Bob was orchestrating it," Roy said.[64] "If you thought you were Fosse's friend," says Graciela Daniele, "you would find out once and for all at the party. He only invited people he really liked."[65]

"Scheider signed up for *Cohen and Tate* just before shooting began. For Red ... getting an established star was quite a lift. 'I didn't write it with anyone in mind ... when I thought about it, I wanted Roy for Cohen. When he took the part, it was really exciting.'"[66]

Cohen is probably the meanest son of a bitch Roy ever played, a cold, professional hit man who's been in the business a long time. There is not much compassion left in him. The film is a psychological thriller and while there is action in it, the movie is more about psychological warfare. The kidnapped kid has enough savvy to recognize that these two men are not fond of each other, and he plays on that—to divide and conquer. There is nothing sympathetic about these two men except that they have human faults and human desires like everyone. These men do what they have to do, and they and the boy make this horrendous journey. The violence *should* be upsetting. Roy's character has a lot of integrity. He has his own code. He never lies to the kid or tells him he is in for a good time or that he'll be safe when they arrive in Houston. Cohen is not sympathetic and he is in a nasty business.

There are two biographical facets to Cohen. The first is his protection of the young hostage in every way he can, until the inevitable end. The other is a strange stop Cohen makes on the way to the final showdown. He stops the car at a mailbox, takes all the money he has, presumably what he has been paid for the job, and mails it to his estranged son.

Variety said, "Roy Scheider is excellent as the old pro Cohen, but perhaps a trifle too unmenacing."[67] Tim Pulliene added, "The film owes a more direct allegiance to the crime movie ... Siegel's *The Lineup* and *The Killers*. [These] echoes can also be discerned in the amoral professionalism which Cohen embodies.... the child's point of view is seldom adopted and ... the uneasy alliance ... remains unresolved."[68]

Scheider's next film, *White Train*, was scheduled to start in September 1987. It was about a rancher (Scheider) who objects

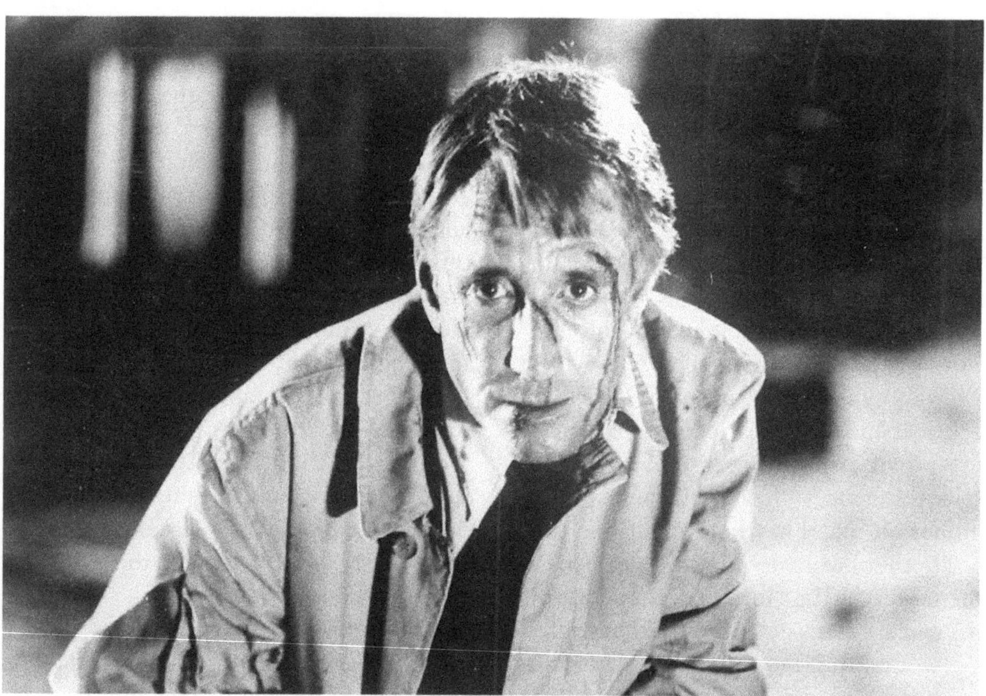

Cohen and Tate **(1988, Helmdale Entertainment). Cohen fights for his life against Tate.**

to a train moving nuclear warheads across his property. The *Los Angeles Times* announced this film,[69] but it never got made.

Scheider took part in an ABC three-hour special to celebrate the 200th anniversary of the Constitution called "The Blessings of Liberty." The *Christian Science Monitor* called it "a phenomenal birthday celebration [that] displays a fervent, almost fanatical dedication to the United States Constitution. Overflowing with a serious sense of history and a clear determination to find balanced perspective, it also manages to sneak in joy and celebration ... [a] satisfying combination of entertainment and information."[70] Roy played George Babbitt in a reconstruction of a landmark Supreme Court case. The program aired on Wednesday, September 16, 1987.

On January 24, 1988, the Miami PBS station, WPBT, aired a locally produced documentary called "Alabaster and Blue Nights." Bill Robertson of the *Miami Herald* said, "[It is] narrated by James Earl Jones, who is too solemn. Roy Scheider [is] the voice of Ernest Hemingway and Don Johnson [is] the ... narrator of Thomas McGuane's novel, *Ninety-two in the Shade.* Scheider and Johnson are indifferent readers.... why go outside the circle of Keys writers for ... voices?"[71] The (Fort Lauderdale) *Sun Sentinel*'s review stated, "The show's production quality is excellent with top talent ... James Earl Jones,... Oscar-winning [*sic*] actor Roy Scheider ... [and] Don Johnson. The biggest flaws ... arise from the oil and water mixing of hard literature with television. Quotations from ... novels with breathtaking Keys scenery ... simply falls flat."[72]

"Portrait of the Soviet Union" was broadcast in three segments on March 20, 21, and 22, 1998. The program was repeated on March 29 and April 10. Tom Shales wrote, "[It] tries to make the U.S.S.R. look as warm and inviting as Disney World, Busch Gardens and Grandma's

***Listen to Me* (1989, Columbia Pictures). Professor Nichols brings his freshman debaters to the Supreme Court. Charlie Nichols: Roy Scheider; Monica Tomansky: Jamie Gertz; Tucker Mulroney: Kirk Cameron.**

kitchen."[73] Martie Zad named it "[an] extensive look at the people [of] the world's largest nation. The documentary ... took nearly 2½ years to complete [and] cost ... 3.5 million. [Producer] Miskin ... made 28 trips to the U.S.S.R. and spent 11 months there. Actor Roy Scheider adds a top-of-the-line performance as host and narrator."[74] Clifford Terry thought the series was "well intentioned and ambitious ... but ultimately superficial and ingenuous. [It] is a seven-hour love letter to the USSR that is about as successful as the Goodwill Games. Crammed with cliches ... it is rarely critical or even analytical."[75] Janis Froelich called it "a gorgeous travelog [*sic*] that doesn't even try to be an interesting documentary.... the camera roams to nooks and crannies in the Soviet Union that Americans rarely see. The host is actor Roy Scheider. Mr. Cool Cat California, wearing shades and pastels, strolling among the Soviets."[76]

Leo Seligsohn was of the opinion: "[The program] ... is a feast for the eyes ... depth is not on the agenda. The tipoff ... for glossy glasnost is ... actor Roy Scheider as guide and narrator, instead of a qualified historian or journalist. Scheider ... comes across as America's junior-high school teacher of the year."[77] John Corry agreed the show was not to be taken seriously: "Portrait" is "similar to a production the United States Information Office would like to make about America but would be too embarrassed to release." Corry described Scheider as "the host and gee-whiz narrator."[78]

Roy was then cast in a new film called *Mismatch*, later renamed and released as *Listen to Me*. According to *People* magazine, "Now that James Garner has dropped out of *Mismatch* because of bypass heart surgery, Roy Scheider is ... stepping into the team coach's role in the Kirk Cameron comedy about, yes, college debating."[79]

In July 1998, *Still of the Night* was released on video.[80] Scheider's next movie project was a return to Texas to film the baseball serial-killer film *Night Game* beginning August 8, 1988.[81] Filming was disrupted by Hurricane Gilbert. "The crew ... including lead actor Roy Scheider, were among those to evacuate Galveston. The crew, rather than let the entire trip go to waste, returned to Houston ... and filmed ... at Grif's Shilleagh Bar. Stage hands boarded up Grif's windows ... to make it ... nighttime."[82] It was noticed by reporters that Scheider had a penchant for working in movies that involve baseball. Scheider said he worked out with the Astros in the Astrodome during filming breaks. His character in the film was named Seaver—after Tom Seaver? Scheider blamed Tony Palmer, who cowrote the film. Palmer was a Mets fan and can be seen in the film playing Mendoza, one of the detectives.

Scheider and Klaus Maria Brandauer were announced as the leads in a new film called *The Fourth War* in September 1988.[83] September was also when Roy decided to call Brenda King. "The moment they saw each other, Roy realized he was still in love with Brenda. Six months later they were married."[84]

On October 10, 1988, Roy Scheider appeared on stage in "*Sketches of War*, an evening of plays and readings on the subject of soldiers and veterans ... at Boston's Colonial Theater. The evening is to benefit the Boston-based Vietnam Veterans Workshop. The program ... included Don Ameche, Kevin Bacon, W. H. Macy, [and] Al Pacino."[85]

"Inside the Sexes" aired on November 21, 1988, and three CBS affiliates—Boston, Salt Lake City, and Louisville—refused to air the show, saying it was "inappropriate for us to air" and describing the beginning of the program as "extremely explicit." Tony Malara, president of CBS affiliate relations, said, "There's explicit foreplay and there is some breakthrough photography, some shots inside a vagina ... in the context of showing sexuality. We don't show the act."[86] The program was still banned in Boston.

People didn't understand the furor, calling the documentary, "Not much more than a harmless excuse for getting the word sex into the TV listings."[87] "The viewer discretion advisory [said], 'contains frank and realistic discussion of human sexuality.' It's the latest example of the relaxation of once hard and fast broadcast standards covering sex and nudity on network television. This hour uses state-of-the-art micro photography to actually watch what happens inside a body during sex."[88] Scheider's penchant for edge-pushing material continued. By the end of 1988, Roy Scheider had three films awaiting release and one of them needed to be a major hit.

— 11 —

Cold War Thaw

On January 9, 1989, a new film project for Roy Scheider was announced: "*The Crew*, a 22-million man-against-the-sea epic by an Italian production company. The film stars Roy Scheider ... and Matt Dillon ... and will be filmed [in Miami] in February."[1] "Yves Montand and Giancarlo Giannini round out the international crew headed by Roy Scheider, Matt Dillon and Greta Sacchi in Michelangelo Antonioni's *The Crew*, an Orion release to be filmed in Florida and Rome in March."[2] In June 1989, the production was still being touted: "Later this summer ... Roy Scheider [stars] ... as a [millionaire] tycoon living on a 120-foot sail boat. Scheider invites three bums on board the yacht, but conflicts ensue."[3] That was the last anyone said about *The Crew*, which never got made.

Cohen and Tate was released at the end of January. Shot in 45 days on location in Texas, the film cost $5.5 million. The director, Eric Red, said there were things that people don't deal with in their lives, dark undercurrents that exist beneath every personal relationship we have. *Cohen and Tate* dealt with that to some degree and concerned one of Red's favorite subjects: the American outlaw. Cohen, a seasoned hit man, was paired with a hotshot psycho named Tate. When they kidnap a mob stoolie's young son, the two men go on a dusk-to-dawn 600-mile car chase, from Muskogee to Houston, as law enforcement officials try to stop them. Red defined the genre he worked in as suspense with a psychological edge, and he named psychological terror as the nature of *Cohen and Tate*.

Steve Dollar stated, "Dub it a Psycho, a Sourpuss and a Brat. This [is a] lean, mean road movie. On this journey to the end of night, Mr. Scheider's prickly, sallow-faced Cohen is the performance that fuels the movie. The actor's sense of containment fits this frayed, jaded killer perfectly."[4] Juan Carlos Coto said, "Scheider and Baldwin are like a twisted version of ... Ralph Kramden and Ed Norton, slowly pushing each other to the boiling point. Scheider ... delivers an A-grade performance in a B-grade picture. Cohen has intriguing levels, and the veteran actor plays them with finesse."[5] Diana Aitchison informed us, "Roy Scheider does the best he can ... as

Cohen and Tate. **Roy Scheider as Cohen, Adam Baldwin as Tate, and Harley Cross as Travis Knight. Publicity still.**

a white collar killer who may have a heart after all. But it's sad to see someone with Scheider's considerable talents stoop to this substandard level of disgust."[6] *Cohen and Tate* was released on video on June 22, 1989.

Although this picture made very little money, Scheider was remembered: "He was perfect as the doomed hit man in Eric Red's forgotten *Cohen and Tate*, a movie that took in about $12 at the box office,"[7] declared Steve Dollar. Morgan Sheppard cited the film as the reason he did the "seaQuest" TV series. "I did the hologram because I wanted to work with Roy Scheider. He's a terrifically intelligent, stylish actor. Forget about *All That Jazz* and ... *Jaws*, for me ... the movie he made, *Mr. Cohen and Mr. Tate* [*sic*] was brilliant."[8]

Roy Scheider wanted to marry Brenda King before they went to Canada to film *The Fourth War*. "The ceremony was held on Valentine's Day 1989, one month after Scheider's divorce was final."[9] Brenda King referred to the movie as their honeymoon picture at a charity softball game in 1998. King is an uncredited extra. She dances at the Army wedding with a circle of children. Scheider's tendency to put his wife in his movies continued. The other biographical element is when Knowles gets drunk (on his birthday) to hide his pain of being alone and starts singing. He then crosses the border, captures the Russian sentries by blowing up their watchtower, and makes them kneel in the snow and sing him "Happy Birthday."

John Frankenheimer said:

> Wolf Schmidt, who owns Kodiak Film, had come to me with a script called *The Fourth War*. Roy Scheider said he would commit to it, if I would direct it. I liked the idea and I wanted to work with Roy again so I agreed to do it. Aside from the fact we were working in absolute bitter cold it went really well. Scheider was a joy after Don Johnson. [Frankenheimer is referring to his previous film, *Dead-Bang* (1989).] I have to say I loved doing the film. Schmidt made a distribution deal with Cannon that I was bitterly opposed to. But what determined the fate of the picture was that we made a movie about the Cold War and by the time it came out there was no Cold War. It became a historical picture and the reviews were mixed ... it left something to be desired. Not great material.[10]

Kenneth Chanko noted, "Scheider is working on *The Fourth War*, a distinctly antiwar film. He'll play an old-school trigger-happy US commander along the German-Czechoslovak border whose Russian counterpart is equally hawkish. Scheider says, 'Before you know it, these two guys are having their own little war.'"[11]

Stephen Schaefer wrote, "Only the 'war' isn't really a war. It's an escalation in Czech–American tensions along the Czechoslovakian border patrolled by the U.S. military. The 'tensions' which include bombings, defections, kidnaping, and espionage plots, are the result of a one man incendiary force, a demented Vietnam veteran."[12] Scheider didn't see Knowles as the hero. He had a bead on his character. Knowles was a burnt-out case when he was called for this job and had become neurotic, verging on the pathological. The colonel was the crackerjack soldier you want next to you in case of war. But in peacetime, his superiors have to put a muzzle on him. Knowles thought the way to solve problems was to go into combat. Catherine Hinman stated, "It is a story about the dangers of warring mentalities on the eve of the Cold War thaw. [Roy said], 'Jack Knowles is a trained, professional warrior, and when he doesn't have a battle to fight ... he is not ... doing what he does best.'"[13]

Gerald Pratley wrote:

> The film recalls Einstein's comment that he did not know what weapons would be employed in the next war, but if there was a fourth war it would probably be fought with stones. There's nothing conventional about this war film, if indeed, it can be called a war film. There is a feeling of futility in the routine activities of both Army camps, with their bored soldiers sullenly sitting out the Cold War. There is much symbolism in this often striking study of impressionism. What we are left with are the shadows of tanks and helicopters facing each other. They withdraw, and all goes quiet, with only the sound of the wind remaining. The film is full of haunting images such as this.[14]

***The Fourth War* (1990, New Age/Cannon). Col. Knowles checks out the Russian border.**

Scheider, who sometimes does his own stunts, found the location and weather on this shoot particularly daunting. For the climactic fight in the icy river, a hole was dug in the ice in subzero weather. They put a steel net underneath the actors to keep them from being washed down river. Scheider and Jurgen Prochnow could last about 15 seconds in the river in that temperature, even with wet suits on. It was 20 below outside. The water was as cold or colder. Scheider equated it to slowly freezing to death. The stars would film for 15 seconds and then get out to have their wet suits pumped full of hot water as stuntmen fought for the camera surrounded by the tanks and helicopters for the long shots. Then they'd go back in, all day long.

On "The Directors" series program about John Frankenheimer, Scheider added more detail: "The sequence took two days to shoot. We could not be in the water more than 10 seconds. We literally had someone counting to ten as we were trying to do what we had to do in that short time."[15] Jurgen Prochnow said, "In a way … it was almost unbearable to sit there, frozen, with the wind from the helicopter blowing around your head. It was something incredible to experience."[16] John Frankenheimer said, "Roy Scheider is … a wonderful actor and [an] equally … wonderful guy. Crews love Roy. He sets an example for everybody on the set. There are certain people you are privileged to know in life that are life givers. Roy is a life giver. He just makes you a better person by the very fact that you know him. He tries everything he can to make a picture better, to make the picture as good as it can be."[17] "He broke a rib during the shooting and tried to cover it up as not to delay us." "It was something very simple," Roy said, "an easy roll out of a moving car, I've done it dozens of times, but I fell on my own elbow."[18] "Mr. Prochnow … dislocated his knee in the same fight, which took two weeks to film, and which both actors insisted on completing without time out for recovery after their injuries. 'I cannot tell you the hardships these guys had to go through,' says Mr. Frankenheimer. 'It's been a very tough physical picture for both of them.'"[19]

John Frankenheimer commented:

> The script needed a Robert Rosen—I called him and he became involved … and we asked for Kenneth Ross who did *Black Sunday* for us, to rewrite the script. Stephen Peters, who wrote the novel, wrote the first draft. Wolf Schmidt [the producer] assumed we would go to Germany to shoot … but I knew that it would necessitate … bringing in an entire crew. Then Bob Rosen came up with … Calgary. I'd worked up there [on *Dead-Bang*] and we knew the facilities—so that's where we went. It was the coldest winter in … 30 years. We got all the snow we'd ever want, and with any other actor but Roy Scheider, we would have never finished the movie. We were out there in the snow almost the entire time. Dramatically … the snow was a third lead in the picture creating the bleak landscape of a terrible isolation; the story would not have worked in hot weather.[20]

Scheider said, "[The snow] … wasn't the ideal stuff to act in … but we had to damn well take advantage of it."[21] To make the most of the snow, Frankenheimer moved some of the larger-scale scenes to the very beginning of the 10-week schedule, using two or three cameras at a time, including one in a helicopter. Everyone feared a Chinook would arrive at any time and melt the snow. While the snow stayed, bitterly cold temperatures prevailed. At -40° Fahrenheit, the cold also created many problems besides film snapping in the camera. To move equipment and or personnel required four-by-four trucks, snowmobiles, and all kinds of winter gear.

Scheider said about Frankenheimer, "John's a very intelligent director and respects the intelligence of the people he works with. I think he expects the actor to expand, experiment, do more with the part than what's written on the page. Some directors don't encourage that, but John does."[22] Roy added that nobody is better than Frankenheimer in dealing with the military mind and that John understands politics, the drama of politics, and he understands movies. There is nothing vague about him, and his overall vision is always strong. He made Scheider feel secure when he worked with him. "I don't think there's an American director [with] more experience dealing with the military, and not just ... equipment, soldiers and special effects. I'm talking about the soul and the spirit as in *The Train* or *Seven Days in May* or *The Manchurian Candidate*."[23]

***The Fourth War*. Scheider confers with director John Frankenheimer. Outtake/publicity still.**

Frankenheimer and Scheider said they were looking for another Elmore Leonard novel to adapt, but that project never materialized. When Frankenheimer was casting *The Burning Season* in 1994, Roy Scheider was only too happy to recommend his former *Betrayal* cast mate Raul Julia for the job.[24]

Listen to Me was released in theaters in early May 1989, amid acute controversy from the religious right because the student debaters were discussing abortion. This furor killed whatever box office the film might have generated. As early as March 1989, Marilyn Beck had noted that the abortion issue would make the film "one of the year's most controversial."[25]

Elliott Stein declared, "For a while, *Listen to Me* lulls you pleasantly. Then, bit by bit, its real agenda emerges and in the final reels ... turns into a glibly demagogic anti-abortion diatribe ... the most manipulative sty of hogwash released by any major studio within memory."[26] Tim Pulliene thought the film was awful: "[It's] not ... that the debating scenes tend to stand apart from the rest [or] ... the outcome of the story is a foregone conclusion. The peremptory demise of Garson two-thirds of the way through ... leaves the action fatally broken-backed. The rout is completed by trite dialogue."[27]

Henry Mietkiewicz said, "According to coach Charlie Nichols, the scariest sport on the face of the planet is—believe it or not, debate. *Listen to Me* [is] one of the most inane, cliched, and ideologically devious entries in the current crop of drama/comedies about teenagers in search of themselves."[28] "Does *Listen to Me* strike you as manipulative?" Jay Boyar asked. "The script [is] a standard Rocky tale of underdogs vs. top dogs. The squad [of misfits] is led by Charlie Nichols (Roy Scheider) a dynamic and kindly man ... torn between his friendship [for debater] Garson and his responsibility to the team."[29] David Elliott warns us to "brace yourself for brat pack II" and then lists every cast member who is the son of someone famous: "Toss in ... Roy Scheider as a brilliant college debating coach and Anthony Zerbe as the egotistical father of Scheider's best pupil and you have the casting cream. Not since ... *A Chorus Line* ... have so many ... [hurled] lines that fall [as flat as] water balloons."[30]

Mike Clark said, "Roy Scheider, looking [like] he jogs two continents daily, plays the Bobby Knight (in performance, not temperament) of college debating. His top star publicly yearns to quit.... freshman blood, though, keeps the squad competitive. It's disconcerting when a movie full of sappy music ... takes on [such a] volatile issue."[31] The *New York Times* review did not critique Scheider's performance.[32]

Scheider inserted several biographical elements into the film. He feigns reading the *New York Times* to hide his watching of his debaters from his window. Since *Jaws*, Scheider has had daily delivery of this paper written into his contracts. Nichols also jogs. After an out-of-town debate, Charlie is seen dancing in the hotel with a blonde. He uses the dance as foreplay and they leave. He throws a barbeque for his debaters and cooks in an apron emblazoned "Dad."

Listen to Me. **Charlie Nichols introduces debate to his students.**

Roy was not afraid of the issue. "What was the last movie you remember that brought up the abortion issue? A lot of people have strong gut feelings about it, but when confronted with reasoned arguments or consequences from the other side, that makes them think. The movie's an entertainment, but you'll get caught up in the subject that's debated. It also takes a look at bright, goal-oriented and articulate kids. We don't get too many movies about them, either," Roy said on "Good Morning America," when he came to publicize the film. Host Charles Gibson noted the critics had already hammered the movie. Scheider was quick to say he wasn't getting savaged in the reviews, but the film certainly was.

Gibson asked Scheider if the outcry had caused the filmmakers to deviate from the original script and tone down the abortion issue. Scheider said no, the film reflected the stance of the director—"pro-choice, with responsibility"—and while the movie carried this message, it was an entertainment and that the reviewers were "remiss" in that they were focused on the abortion issue, instead of the performances. Scheider could tell "in the first paragraph or two" what side of the abortion issue the critic was on. The reviewers should have realized "how difficult it is to have a film about abortion made at a major studio." The critics should have noted the courage it took to make the movie instead.

Gibson noticed Roy had a bandage beside one eye and asked

about it. Scheider replied, "No, the critics didn't get to me. I had a lump removed from under my eye." Gibson then asked Scheider to handicap the upcoming Leonard-Hearns fight. Roy's pick was "Leonard, all the way."[33]

Showtime announced it had acquired the cable rights to *52 Pick-Up*—along with 16 other Cannon films—on May 11, 1989.[34] Roy Scheider was named as having the "right idea" at the Cannes Film Festival "by doing interviews in his shorts at the beach" in *USA Today* coverage on May 16, 1989.[35] There was no mention of which film he was promoting there. On June 21, Roy Scheider participated in a Pediatric AIDS Foundation fundraiser in Washington, D.C.[36]

"Broadway's Dreamers: The Legacy of the Group Theatre" aired as the first of three programs on June 26, 1989. This PBS "American Masters" series also included programs on Harold Clurman and Stella Adler.[37] Roy Scheider helped produce and was interviewed in the second program, called "Harold Clurman: A Portrait of Theater." "Meryl Streep narrates. Scheider ... reads from Clurman's lectures. Frank Langella narrates *Stella Adler: Awake and Dream!*"[38]

Clive Barnes said, "I knew [Clurman], I suppose only slightly, but I loved him much more. He was impossible, and he was fun. This documentary of his life and methods offers a well-rounded picture of Clurman in his later years. This intimate, loving portrait ... [celebrates his] spirit and vision."[39] John Stark stated, "You'll enjoy this portrait. Roy Scheider, Julie Harris are among the actors who reminisce about the nurturing experience of working with him."[40]

In August 1988, Roy Scheider had played in his first Artists and Writers Celebrity Softball Game. He was the catcher for his agent, Sam Cohn, who pitched for the Artists. Cohn had inherited a Long Island restaurant from Bob Fosse called the Laundry.[41] This restaurant was and continues to be the major sponsor and aftergame watering hole for this charity event. "Superman [Christopher Reeve, scored] the winning run with two outs in the ninth inning to give the Artists a 7–6 upset victory." Other Artists "included Paul Simon, Christie Brinkley and [boxer] Gerry Cooney." George Plimpton, first baseman for the Writers, said they were "gallery sweepers. You might call them ringers.... I remember Bella Abzug taking her swings. Those were the days."[42] Before this game, "In 25 years, the Artists have only won twice."[43]

Night Game was released in September 1989. Caryn James of the *New York Times* declared, "It is hard to see what could have been done to liven up *Night Game*, short of having someone run into the Galveston Police Station yelling, 'Shark!' Too bad no one does."[44] Steve Dollar stated, "Give the man a cigarette ... whiskey, a sex-starved gamin ... someone to punch and—presto—a Roy Scheider movie."[45] *Variety* wrote, "A solid cast, professional production and attractive locations help, but can't hide the threadbare plot of this limp thriller."[46]

Ralph Novak said, "Scheider is an irreverent Galveston police lieutenant who asks many questions beginning with, 'What the hell ...' and has a vendetta against a county sheriff he ... threatens every 10 minutes. He's also much older than [Karen] Young ... but they do snuggle ... [with] relatively convincing affection."[47]

There are biographical elements in *Night Game*. Seaver uses dancing as foreplay after proposing marriage to his girlfriend. Scheider again plays a loner cop with a checkered past trying to do the right thing. It is the first movie where Roy's character is married on screen. In an inside casting joke, Karen Young also played (in 1987) the wife of Michael Brody in *Jaws 3-D*. This is yet another film involving baseball.

Although none of his last three films were hits, Roy remained optimistic about his future. His current age was making it tough for him to find good parts, as movie roles were being written for actors under 30, the age of the audience. Roy wanted more interesting character parts, not the stereotypical good-guy cop, although Scheider admitted playing cops has its perks. If he's standing on a corner in New York, waiting for a cab, and a police car comes by, chances are he will be taken anywhere he wants to go.

Movie sequels are almost never as good as the originals, as they are usually made for the money, not artistic considerations. Scheider never did a TV series after 1972, although he had been offered several. He still has no intention of doing one, perhaps in 10 years. He'd rather work on fresh original stuff for feature films.

"In October of 1989, a new phenomenon in film releasing or more honestly, non–film releasing was noted. More films with short or nonexistent theater play ended up at the video rental store. *The Men's Club* was mentioned ... in this category."[48] This distribution trend continued in the 1990s and had a profound effect on the releasing of several theatrical films Scheider made in that decade. Scheider finished the year by filming *The Russia House* with Sean Connery in London.

In January 1990, eight weeks before *The Fourth War* opened, Roy's long-awaited son, Christian Ferrier Scheider, was born. On January 26, 1990, Scheider's first HBO film was announced as beginning production "in mid–March.[49] *All That Jazz* was released on video in England on February 8, 1990.

The Fourth War was released in March and did almost no business due to the fall of the Berlin Wall. John Frankenheimer said, "What we never could have foreseen—and if we [had], we'd have never made the movie—was ... that the border would disappear before the picture came out, so there was no [more] Iron Curtain. This hurt us severely, obviously. [The marketing was] up against it with a subject that was no longer pertinent. But it's a movie I'm proud of."[50] There were high hopes for *The Fourth War*, but the film's box office was hurt by the lack of marketing. Scheider was disappointed. It was one of his better roles.

Janet Maislin recorded, "*The Fourth War* takes some unusual risks. It attempts to understand the heroism of a man like Knowles by casting him in an extremely foolish light. The result is an idiosyncratic portrait. Scheider's performance is both steely and absurd, [which] befits the contradictions ... in the story."[51] Bill Hagen sympathized: "Not a great story, admittedly ... [but] with some good actors, crisp direction, eye-catching location ... and what happens? Communism collapses in Eastern Europe ... all the urgency and immediacy, vital to the story, is gone. You're done in by an outbreak of freedom."[52]

Tom Jacobs declared, "*The Hunt for Red October* is not the final cold war film after all. *The Fourth War* [is] a sincere but ultimately ludicrous military drama. Whether or not these two hotheads will accidentally set off World War III ... it all feels extremely dated [and] extremely implausible."[53] Hal Hinson concurred. "The premise is so surrealistically improbable that if Frankenheimer's approach wasn't so straight-faced it might be preposterously entertaining. And as Scheider ... signals the end by tossing aside yet another snowball, you wish you had invested in a nuclear arsenal of your very own."[54] David Quinlan said, "[It is] as dated as the militaristic dinosaurs it depicts, and ... overtaken by time and events. Any excuse for a fight is good enough for these disillusioned veterans, bleakly played by Roy Scheider and Jurgen Prochnow."[55]

Scheider went to Florida to film *Some-*

body Has to Shoot the Picture*, one of the first HBO original movies. "*Somebody* ... begins production [March 19] in Central Florida. Locations ... include Union Correctional Institute near Starke, Mount Dora and downtown Orlando. Producer Alan Barnette expects to wrap ... April 24."[56] One day into filming, the prison location was in jeopardy, after "somebody at some level of the state hierarchy read the script and didn't think Florida should support the picture." The producers initially requested some scenes from Florida State Prison, which is off-limits for security reasons. (They later decided the Starke Prison did not look menacing enough.) "All that is important, they say, is that it was resolved. And it was. Quite quickly, too. Californians and Floridians made a flurry of strategic phone calls. Producer Barnette flew to Tallahassee for meetings. Suddenly the problem evaporated as quickly as it had arisen."[57]

***Night Game* (1989, Trans World Entertainment). Lt. Mike Seaver investigates the murder of a third prostitute.**

"The filming caused a bit of a stir in some locations, but the folks in Seminole County were more than happy to have them film at Lake Jesup."[58] Mount Dora was another story. "Last week, they rocked this serene Lake County community for the last time. They spent a total of nine days here and Mount Dora will never forget it. The town wasn't painted pink [as it was for the film *Honky Tonk Freeway* in 1980, but] ... life as its residents knew it stopped."[59]

Scheider wanted to bring home to an audience what it was like to be on death row and let people decide for themselves the issue of capital punishment. Scheider's character was hard-nosed, but not quite the steely character he had become famous for. Paul Marish is a relentless investigator pursuing the truth, but he is also compassionate, demonstrating a sensitivity that is perhaps closer to the real Scheider than previous roles. Marish doesn't start out to save the death row inmate. He is given the shoot by his agent in a last-ditch attempt to rehabilitate Paul, who had crawled into a bottle after his fiancée was shot to death in front of him on a previous photo assignment. The quest for the truth gives Marish a reason to try. After some prodding

Somebody Has to Shoot the Picture **(1990, HBO). Paul Marish takes pictures at the scene of a policeman's suicide.**

from a crusading *Time* reporter looking for a scoop, the two men work together to find the truth. "I wanted to play this part," says Scheider. "I don't give a damn if they were doing it on local TV. These [HBO] television films reach millions more people than feature films do. It's always nice to make a film that has some profundity."[60]

"To prepare for his role, Scheider spent considerable time with screenwriter Doug Magee, a photo journalist.... The film ... [came from] his 1980 book, *Slow Coming Dark*. Scheider favors having convicted murderers serve life sentences without parole, 'with [a] work program to ... repay the victim, or the relatives.'[61] *The Magee Project* (working title) appealed to Scheider, "First, for the political statement, and second, for the character. I thought the subject matter was very, very powerful."[62]

The main biographical element in this film is drinking to hide his character's pain. Paul is in his cups when we first meet him and recovering from a hangover his first morning on the job. As Marish becomes involved in the case and with the widowed wife of the slain cop, his drinking stops. The character also has a dead girlfriend. Roy grew his "artist's" goatee and dresses in a slightly modified version of his usual: a photographer's vest instead of a safari jacket.

He looked so good that a still of him in costume was posted to a professional photographer's website as an example of how a photographer is supposed to look. In February 2001, Paul Gero wrote, "Scheider was convincing ... because someone ... (or Scheider) really did their homework. He was shooting with a Nikon F3. He was using a Vivitar strobe angled up, with a bounce card and he carried a Brown Domke bag."[63]

"Scheider's next role will be [Clarence] Darrow ... [and] focus on the killers Leopold and Loeb as 'maladjusted boys from a dysfunctional family.'"[64] I can find no record that this TV movie/miniseries was ever made. Susan Landau, Roy's producer from *Tiger Town*, told how the Loeb project was born: "Roy Scheider, an old friend ... never does TV, which makes him attractive. TV executives ... want what they can't have. At breakfast one morning,

[Roy said], 'I've always wanted to play Clarence Darrow; how do we do that?' We sold it [to NBC] as the Original Billionaires Boys Club."[65]

The Fourth War was released overseas the third week of June 1990.[66] Roy was asked his opinion of *Presumed Innocent* by Jeannie Williams of *USA Today* at the VIP screening, hosted by director Alan J. Pakula on Monday, July 9, 1990, at the New York Museum of Modern Art. "A swell job! It captured the essence of the book."[67] Roy also attended "the premiere of the HBO show called: *Men and Women: Stories of Seduction* on August 12, 1990."[68] "Produced by David Brown, the event was held at the East Hampton Cinema."[69]

***Somebody Has to Shoot the Picture*. Roy Scheider and Bonnie Bedelia. Publicity still.**

Somebody Has to Shoot the Picture was released on September 9, 1990, with much fanfare by HBO. It was part of the first-ever HBO Original Movie Weekend and showcased two films dealing with breakdowns in the criminal justice system, *Criminal Justice* and *Somebody Has to Shoot the Picture*. David Klinghoffer stated, "*Somebody* ... is propaganda, but not ... the fun, exuberant kind. Scheider ... plays the brilliant but disillusioned artist who achieves renewal when he discovers a new cause he ... can believe in. *Somebody* ... chooses a worst case scenario ... for what can go wrong in the American court-and-prison system."[70] *Variety* wrote, "Pierson, Magee and a fine cast communicate the weighty atmosphere of prison existence and the rural South, and the dark side of human nature that expresses itself as a thirst to severely punish lawbreakers."[71]

In the summer of 1990, Roy narrated 10 hours of a PBS series called "Race to Save the Planet." "An epic 10-part series, to air ... on five consecutive nights beginning [October 4] ... goes behind the headlines to uncover the hidden dramas taking place in the global environment. Hosted by Meryl Streep [and] narrated by Roy Scheider, the series examines critical environmental issues facing the world today."[72] "The big item in public TV's year long 'Operation Earth'—[it] offers a global view of our threatened environment, starting with a look back at man's former coexistence with nature and the disastrous shift since then."[73]

The *New York Post* declared, "The ...

"Race to Save the Planet" (1990, PBS). The host and narrator: Meryl Streep and Roy Scheider. Publicity still provided by Scheider's publicist.

dire thesis of [this] impressive documentary series in an already superlative PBS season is that we humans have about 10 years to clean up ... or else endure forever the results of what could be irreparable damage [to the Earth]. One of its strengths is its literally global scope."[74] Scott Williams said, "One of the best things about PBS' thoughtful new series ... it doesn't sugarcoat the bad news. [It] shows the state of the world's environment and the interconnection of the problems that threaten it. An antidote to despair ... sad and ... scary, but ... neither shrill or naive."[75]

Sorcerer was released on video on October 4, 1990. *The Fourth War* was released on October 18, 1990.[76] Roy was also interviewed on the cable program "A & E Revue."[77] In November, one of John Gotti's men recognized the actor in the Tutto Bene restaurant: "I like his movies. Tell him I want to pick up the tab. " Scheider gracefully declined, but Joey wasn't going to be denied his brush with stardom—he sent over a bottle of Barbaresco.[78] The date of the article made it very possible Scheider was out celebrating his birthday.

The Russia House was released on Christmas 1990. Roy attended "the black-tie benefit premiere ... at the Cineplex Odeon in Universal City ... to assist the Motion Picture and Television Fund's work in aiding industry retirees." Attendance was 1,100.[79]

The *San Francisco Examiner* declared, "The Americans [CIA], led by Roy Scheider, have a forced warmth, a crude energy, a scatological zing. The contrast is uproarious. Scheider and [James] Fox share an unexpected chemistry. These scenes perk the movie. *The Russia House* makes intelligence thrilling."[80] *Variety* said, "Most of the supporting roles are one-dimensional British or US Intelligence types, but such thesps as James Fox, Roy Scheider, John Mahoney and Michael Kitchen embody them solidly and with wit wherever possible."[81] Hal Hinson concurred: "Surrounding the leads is a gang of first-rate supporting performers. Both James Fox as Barley's British operator and Roy Schei-

The Russia House (1990, MGM). The CIA disagrees with British Intelligence. Russell: Roy Scheider; Ned: James Fox. Note the CIA issue bow tie.

der as his American counterpart are superb."[82]

"This is Connery as the Anti-Bond. The British spy chiefs, including James Fox and ... Ken Russell, are typically ninnyish and the American CIA chief, played by Roy Scheider, is true to cookie-cutter form, foulmouthed and unreasonable. Scheider's blustery performance doesn't help," was the opinion of Juan Carlos Coto.[83] David Denby weighed in: "The play of contrasting national types was part of the fun of Le Carre's book, and the movie picks up on this. Among the intelligence higher-ups, the Brits, (James Fox, Michael Kitchen) are saturnine but decent, the Americans (Roy Scheider, John Mahoney) intelligent, but hard-nosed."[84] Vincent Canby found the film too obtuse: "The supporting cast includes Roy Scheider ... all acting like actors trying very hard to find the interesting aspects of the characters who have none. The lines are not easily spoken. They are clumsy. Sometimes they are even overripe. The narrative structure is a mess."[85] "The measure of its up-to-dateness is the absurdity [of how] ... CIA and MI5 spymasters are depicted," said Jay Carr. "In the film's brave new world, people who trust their hearts have ... moved beyond the world of the grey men—who only trust their paranoia, leaving them mired in high-tech irrelevancy."[86]

These actors varied wildly in style and like most ensembles they all worked to get noticed. At one end there is the ultra-quiet, patient Fox and at the other is Scheider's impatient, almost manic Russell, who wants something, anything, to happen. During Barley's interrogation, Connery acts like a beleaguered bear surrounded by a pack of wild dogs, each nipping at him in his own way, and Scheider is the most persistent. They have an argument about Picasso that has to be heard to be believed.

There are no blatant biographical

The Russia House. **Russell briefs his team.**

elements. Roy's wardrobe does not consist of his usual choices. The clothing appears to have been picked to make him stand out among the assembled group. Scheider sports a garish yellow-and-black spotted bow tie with matching suspenders in one scene that all but screams "Look at me." (Robert Parker, whom Roy names one of his favorite authors, wrote in one of his novels how one always can tell a CIA agent from an FBI agent. The CIA agent is wearing the bow tie.) Roy ended 1990 by attending the New York premiere of *Havana*.[87]

In January 1991, Roy traveled to Toronto to film *Naked Lunch*, based on the cult classic book by William Burroughs. The catalyst for director David Cronenberg was British film producer Jeremy Thomas. On being introduced to Cronenberg at the Toronto Film Festival, Thomas said, "People tell me you are interested in making *Naked Lunch*. I really want to produce that film." Noted Cronenberg, "I still don't know where he heard of my interest."[88] Cronenberg continued, "What attracted me to this project is that it is impossible to do. A literal translation would cost 400 million and be banned in every country in the world. I'm taking some liberties with the book. The script [combines] the writing process [and Burroughs]."[89]

"Before the start of pre-production," Jody Duncan reported, "more than one actor expressed interest in the project. Peter Weller ... very early on wrote to [Cronenberg] and expressed his desire. Scheider, too, was enthusiastic. Ultimately, both actors were cast—Weller as Bill Lee [Burroughs] and Scheider as the manipulative Dr. Benway."[90]

Benway was described as "a perverted American doctor who, in prescribing an antidote drug for Bill Lee, further addicts Lee to the meat of the black centipede and Mugwump jissom." Scheider said, "Dr. Benway is probably the sleaziest scumbag in this movie. He's a manipulator, a drug user, drug seller, an autocrat and a dreadful person."[91] Benway also cross-dresses. Dr. Benway is "unforgettable ... callously flamboyant ... [and] approaches surgery the way matadors approach bullfights."[92]

Scheider had heard about the movie from Weller.[93] In the press kit, Scheider said, "The book [*Naked Lunch*] is about as bizarre, as perverse and as erotically aberrated as anything I can think of. Burroughs, who was thirty years ahead of his time, is capable of wild, flowing, vivid prose that is gorgeous in its horrendous descriptions." Knowing the book well, Scheider was avidly curious about how Cronenberg was going to deal with it. After reading the script, Roy said, "It's great. The movie is a white paper against drug abuse. It's one hallucinogenic nightmare and manages to offend almost everybody." "I was just delighted someone of his stature wanted to do it," remarked Cronenberg of his casting coup.[94]

Gary Kimber added, "Shooting [started] January 1991 and [they were to move to] Tangier, Morocco, in April. A week before [the filming of the Interzone exteriors] ... [the] Gulf War broke out."[95]

At the end of the film, Bill Lee's black meat supplier, the sensuous Fadela, is revealed to be the kindly Dr. Benway. In an extremely complicated latex makeup involving both actors, Benway's chest is first revealed by the actress playing Fadela, then the whole outer skin of Fadela rips in half to reveal Benway. James Isaac, the makeup man responsible, explained the transformation: "Scheider was ... in a total face and chest appliance. It took almost two hours to apply and he was totally blind. I had to walk him to the set. When it came off, he had to start acting. He got it ... on the first take."[96] Scheider was under pressure to get it as it took Isaac half a day to set up the complicated gag.

On January 28, there was a new project for Roy Scheider was announced, a TV movie called *Barr Sinister*.[97] "Roy Scheider and Sab Shimono head the cast of *Bar Sinister* [*sic*], a fantasy adventure that begins production in March in Malaysia, Thailand and London. Bar Sinister is a soldier-of-fortune comic-strip character."[98] "Shimono will soon head for Malaysia to co-star with Roy Scheider in a fantasy-drama called *Barr Sinister*. He plays the villain opposite Scheider's fantasy superhero."[99] Like *Leopold and Loeb*, there are no reports that this TV movie ever was made. Another TV movie with a psychotic judge who dressed as a cowboy to murder his victims did air. Fans of Scheider remember watching it and keep asking me for the title, but I can find no record of its existence.

The Scheiders threw a party for their second wedding anniversary. "Roy Scheider certainly knows how to make his guests happy. For last night's Valentine bash at R. J. Colors, erotic game prizes were given away.... [they] included edible underwear, large chocolate lips, heart patterned boxer shorts and banana flavored whipped cream."[100]

Roy Scheider was involved in the fight to save Joe Giarratano from being executed by the state of Virginia that same month—along with other celebrities, including Jack Lemmon, Arthur Ashe, politicians, authors, and musicians.[101] Giarratano was later released from death row and his sentence was commuted to life imprisonment.

In June 1991, Scheider pitched for one of the teams "in Central Park for the annual NY Women-in-Film Celebrity Softball Game.... the pitchers looked good."[102] Scheider was an easy recruit as the game took place almost on his doorstep and had predominantly female players.

Roy participated in a baseball documentary for HBO called "When It Was a Game." "Inspired by another HBO project ["Dear America: Letters Home from Viet-

Naked Lunch (1991, 20th Century–Fox). Scheider in his Fadela makeup.

nam"], [it] has James Earl Jones, Jason Robards ... [and] Roy Scheider ... waxing poetic. [The program] celebrates the personality of baseball when [the] game was played on grass, the Dodgers played in Brooklyn, a National League team played in Boston and an American league team played in Saint Louis."[103]

The program aired on July 9, 1991.[104] "This one hour special invokes ... the last era of innocence in ... sports: 1934–1957. What distinguishes ["Game"] ... is the pictures, enchanting silent color pictures shot on 8mm and 16mm by fans and ... ballplayers ... a remarkable array of images. Occasional dramatic readings ... mesh reasonably well."[105] "Actors James Earl Jones, Roy Scheider and Jason Robards chime in ... with ... The Old Fashioned Batter by George Phair [and] The Ballad of Dead Yankees by Donald Petersen."[106]

Roy played in his second Artists and Writers Celebrity Softball Game in August 1991. He pitched three innings in relief for his agent, Sam Cohn. Long Island's *Newday* described pitcher Scheider, "in deep tan, beard and sunglasses," and said, "The writers lost 10–3." Asked about the questionable Artists, Writer Ken Auletta said, "We tolerate it ... we let these people get away with murder. Their definition ... ranges from Sam Cohn, an agent, to Lori Singer, an actress. I hear they even have some house painters in there."[107] Also Roy narrated "Contact: The Yanomani Indians of Brazil" in 1991.

"20th Century–Fox opened *Naked Lunch* in December [1991] in New York and Los Angeles to be eligible for Oscar consideration. The film opened on January 10, 1992."[108] John Simon stated, "If ... you want ... elegant creepiness, baroque monsters, [and] drug fantasy crossed with facile romanticism of the artist's plight, you cannot do much better than this. *Naked Lunch* can be described as ... ugly and pointless and ... hypnotic and harrowing. It is also funny, obscene and sui generis."[109]

Brian Johnson concurred: "At once cerebral and visceral, the movie is a brilliantly, darkly comic exploration of the creative process. A fusion of two iconoclastic visions—[it] is exotic fare, a challenge to the palate of the mass audience. An acquired taste—but worth the risk."[110]

John Powers said, "Less an assault on star-spangled decency than an amusing gruesome fable. [Lee] is surrounded by schemers ... degenerates ... and the sexually ambivalent Dr. Benway, a dope dealing Machiavelli played by Roy Scheider (well served by his resemblance to a lizard skin handbag with teeth)."[111] Hillel Tryster observed, "Weller sets the ... deadpan tone. Around him flit Ian Holm's volatile Tom Frost, Judy Davis' decadent Joan and the darkly detached Roy Scheider as the doctor with a cure for everything, whatever the side effects."[112]

It is difficult to identify biographical elements in this film, as Scheider has almost no screen time as Benway. Roy wears small, gold, wire-rim glasses for the first time in his scene as the kindly doctor. Scheider donned glasses twice before when playing doctors, and this new frame style will show up many more times in this decade.

With an Oscar-nominated Kate Nelligan as his partner, Scheider joined a tour of *Love Letters,* playing the role of Andrew, in Boston "for an exclusive one week engagement ... the first week in March 1992."[113] In April 1992, Roy Scheider was a frequent courtside attendee at New York Knicks games at Madison Square Gardens.[114]

"When It Was a Game 2" aired on July 13, 1992. The sequel "was a montage of [new] 8mm and 16mm shot by fans and players from 1934 to 1960. The narrative is provided by players, writers and actors, including ... Roy Scheider and Billy Crystal. [Producer George Roy] really didn't want to do a sequel ... [for people would think it was] 'leftovers from the first show.'"[115] "With cameo narration by Jack Palance ... and Roy Scheider ... [the program] spans the years from 1925 to 1961. In all, it lasts an hour, the memories it recalls—and creates—are forever timeless."[116]

During the summer of 1992, the Scheiders rented a beach house in Bridgehampton surrounded by potato fields. They fell in love with the place and bought it.[117] In July, "Ann Reinking, Stephanie Zimbalist, [and] Roy Scheider ... will be featured along with other artists [in] the Musical Theater Project. Fifty musical theater apprentices will train in dance, voice, and theater from July 12 to Aug. 2, [1992]. The ... training will culminate in ... a musical revue."[118] Roy was a designated master teacher.[119]

On August 19, Roy played in his third Artists and Writers Celebrity Softball Game as a pitcher. In public access LTV coverage, a two-year-old tow-headed Christian was seen bouncing up and down in his mother's lap as he watched his father play.[120] The artists won 5–2 and raised $20,000 for the East Hampton day care center and the Retreat, the new 18-bed battered women's shelter.[121]

Roy didn't have time to enjoy the beach after he completed filming the miniseries "Wild Justice" in North Africa. In October 1992, the *Los Angeles Times* printed, "Steven Spielberg has reached an agreement with NBC to produce 22 episodes of a big-budget, underwater adventure series called, "Sea Quest" [*sic*]. Roy Scheider was ... being pursued to star in the series."[122]

— 12 —

Adventures in Television

In February 1993, the first Hamptons International Film Festival was organized. Roy Scheider was named as one of its local supporters and the Deauville (France) Film Festival agreed to become the event's sister festival.[1] Steven Spielberg had set up a meeting for Roy with his Amblin Entertainment television division as a possible star for his new underwater adventure TV series for NBC, "seaQuest DSV." Scheider flew to LA for the meeting and eventually signed for the series in March 1993.[2]

Army Archerd interviewed the principals in early April and was given a tour of the sets. "Roy Scheider stars in his first TV series. Spielberg [had him] meet with '12 Universal suits.' [Roy told Archerd], 'It's the best part offered ... me this year.'"[3]

In video promotional clips sent out by the NBC network, Scheider discussed his trip aboard a Navy submarine off Montauk, New York, with Dr. Robert Ballard. Scheider found the experience "Overwhelming, because it was such a big, big boat with very powerful engines and a nuclear reactor. I wasn't afraid because the engines made so much noise and were so powerful that I figured we were the biggest thing in the ocean." Scheider stopped short of being the Navy's newest recruit. "When they originally approached me to do this, the plan was for me to go to the Arctic Pole for two weeks. Wait a minute, hold on, let me go for a day and see whether or not I like it. I did like it, but two weeks would have been a little too much."[4] In the spring of 1993, Roy and his family moved to Los Angeles in preparation for Roy's new job. It was the second move for three-year-old Christian, who was now living the gypsy life his father loved.

NBC bought the UTV/Amblin show and committed to 22 segments without a script, but with Scheider. Scheider was overjoyed that Irvin Kershner was directing the premiere: "We are lucky to have him."[5] In May, Scheider and his wife, Brenda King (who also appeared in the two-hour series premiere), visited Dolphins Plus, a marine mammal and education center in Key Largo, Florida, to swim with dolphins as part of their preparation for the TV series.

Production began in June 1993. Roy

played the submarine's captain in what was planned to be a cross between an updated version of the 1960s TV show "Voyage to the Bottom of the Sea" and "Star Trek" underwater. No one—Universal, Amblin, or NBC—had a clear idea how to achieve this, but they forged ahead. Daniel Cerone stated, "Bridger is a former attack sub-commander who turned to ... science—after his son was killed following in his military footsteps. The maverick Bridger allows himself to be coaxed back ... seduced by the Navy's promises to ... use his submarine's vast capabilities for underwater research."[6]

The "Wild Justice" miniseries aired in syndication the week of May 23, 1993. Hoyt Hilsman wrote in *Variety*, "This pallid miniseries, based on a novel by Wilbur Smith, trots out all the ... cliches and stereotypes of the international thriller genre. Roy Scheider, in a wooden performance, adds little. This miniseries [makes] no point ... about the larger themes of international terrorism or ... the characters."[7] A second review said, "'Wild Justice' is the sort of high adventure, low intelligence miniseries that you thought they didn't make any more. Watching it should forestall any questions why. [It is] four hours of syndicated rot airing over two nights. Scheider looks haggard and pained throughout the whole ... mess."[8]

Robert Laurence stated, "The plot wanders down several dead ends, but the trip is most of the fun. 'Wild Justice' visits several exotic settings ... but if I want a travelogue, I'll find the travel channel."[9] "In Scheider's defense, the transparent and illogical script ... would dull the senses of any capable actor. The Stride character ... is expected to behave like a gullible fool throughout the two-part four-hour snorefest. The weariness sets in early," said Lou Grahnke.[10] *Entertainment Weekly* called it "a hodgepodge of romance and intrigue. Convoluted as this elaborate plot is, it still moves so arthritically that you'll have it figured out long before our hero."[11] *Newsday* wrote, "The first two-hour installment features ... a routine combination of foreign intrigue and sporadic violence. Part 2, however, ascends from the mundane to the ridiculous. Scheider ... trim in a dress uniform and debonair in evening wear [is] slightly long in the tooth for this ... action role."[12]

"Wild Justice." Roy Scheider as Col. Peter Stride. Publicity still.

Scheider's costar, Sam Wanamaker, said, Scheider was "dedicated to the project, a keen professional without any of the phony temperamental behavior you read about in the gossip columns. Roy came out of the theater and is much more disciplined in his attitude toward his work than many people you meet in TV."[13] The four-hour "Wild Justice" miniseries aired on HBO Asia. "Wild Justice" was edited down to two hours and released overseas

"Wild Justice" (1993, Tribune Entertainment). Magda and Peter realize they have been set up to kill each other by Caliph. Peter Stride: Roy Scheider; Magda Altmann: Patricia Millardet.

as a film entitled *Covert Assassin*. *Covert Assassin* was released on video in the United States on November 18, 1994, but never played on American cable at that time. *Covert Assassin* DVD was released January 2002.

The now familiar biographical elements are present in this miniseries. Stride cooks for his girlfriend. He hacks the sleeves off his long-sleeved shirt. Peter orders bourbon and drinks it to help his pain, after his best friend is killed. He has a good relationship with his teenage daughter. This was the first time Scheider rode a horse on film.

On July 10, 1993, Roy Scheider narrated "The Last African Flying Boat" on "ABC's World of Discovery." The program retraced the Imperial Airways route that linked five British colonies from Egypt to South Africa in the 1930s. The *Daily Variety* review did not mention Scheider.[14]

The "seaQuest DSV" TV show ran for three years and through too many producers to count. One month into filming, the first producer, Tommy Thompson, quit over "creative differences" with Roy Scheider. They could not come to a unified vision over what the show would be. Scheider had been promised that the show would do fact-based science/action adventure with an educational bent. Thompson wanted to do postapocalyptic, *Road Warrior,* underwater society-in-ruins stories. NBC thought it had bought a science fiction series, like "Star Trek," only the setting would be underwater on a sub, instead of in space on a starship.

Spielberg was in Poland filming *Schindler's List* and was the name on the masthead, until the Thompson crisis brought him back to the LA set to serve as mediator. Daniel Cerone cited "a poor relationship between ... Scheider and the executive producer, Tommy Thompson, [that] led to a creative meltdown. In May, after the pilot and two episodes were shot, Spielberg ... ordered the production ... shut down. A new executive producer was [named], script revisions were made, [and the show was] put back on course."[15] Filming resumed in August 1993.

"seaQuest DSV." Roy Scheider as Nathan Bridger.

Thompson was merely the first casualty in a two-year war over who controlled the content of the TV show: the NBC network, Universal/Amblin Entertainment, or the series star, Roy Scheider. Two new producers, David Burke and Robert Engels, were assigned to make fact-based science adventure stories. Two unfilmed scripts from the *Road Warrior* scenario were killed and the air dates of already filmed episodes were shuffled to put some characters' shows first. Several publicity shots were released of Spielberg's set visit. Bob Ballard, the science technical advisor, was included in this photo shoot. Ballard was sent out to promote the show in the schools. Mollified for the moment, Roy Scheider began plugging his new series in print and on television. Roy was not able to return to Long Island and play in the annual Hamptons charity softball game in 1993, as the TV show had resumed filming and he had to remain in LA.

Scheider made two television appearances to promote "seaQuest DSV." The first was "Larry King Live" on August 27, 1993, when King did a week of shows from Los Angeles. The second was "The Tonight Show with Jay Leno," on September 10, two days before the premiere. Scheider also appeared on the syndicated "This Is Your Life" in mid–September, which he knew nothing about, until he was surprised at the Los Angeles Joe Allen Restaurant. The set-up was orchestrated by his wife, Brenda, in cahoots with his restaurant business partner, Joe Allen. Scheider was affable and cooperative and at the end, a promo for the TV series was shown. This new version of "This Is Your Life" lasted all of four episodes in syndication before being canceled. It was widely stated on the first of three "seaQuest" usenet (internet) news groups (now defunct) that at the time Scheider's segment replaced the one planned for Angie Dickinson, who refused to be filmed and ran out of wherever she had been surprised.

"This Is Your Life" was Christian's first national TV appearance. Sporting a black satin "seaQuest DSV" logo jacket emblazoned Commander Christian, he waved at the studio audience when Roy took him from his mother into his arms—at least until the three-year-old turned shy and hid his face in his father's suede coat.[16] Roy's brother, Glenn, and his wife were on the show as well as Roy's grown daughter, Maximillia, and her husband, Scott Connolly, with Roy's grandchildren, Tanner and Sasha. Cynthia Bebout was conspicuously absent, as there was an ongoing court of appeals case over paying her alimony. A ruling on that would not be made until December 1994.

The "seaQuest DSV" series premiered with huge ratings, a 28 share. Nearly 67 million people watched the first show,[17] but as the season progressed, the ratings dropped. Richard Zoglin was amazed at the initial high numbers, having pegged the pilot as "a sea-going white elephant ... succeeding episodes have been better. They have emphasized the show's homespun attractions ... a talking dolphin ... and a 'Star-Trek' like combination of an imaginative sci-fi story and the cozy ethos of 'Wagon Train.'"[18]

There are many biographical elements in the "seaQuest DSV" pilot. Once again, Scheider plays a character with a dead wife, who is played by Scheider's real-life wife of four years, Brenda King. Bridger carries Carol's picture on board in a small blue book, one of the Yale Shakespeare series. Lucas wears a baseball jersey that proclaims the newly formed baseball expansion team, the Florida Marlins, as the World Series champions of 2010, a Scheider film reference. Roy considered Nathan Bridger a direct descendant of Dr. Heywood Floyd, and a picture of Scheider as Floyd illustrates Bridger's biography in the first-season writer's bible.[19] A running joke in the pilot episode about the talking dolphin telling everyone Bridger swam in the buff was deliberate. Scheider had a tendency to be filmed in his bathrobe throughout the series' run. There was a line in the pilot script that had Bridger saying, "It's showtime,"—the famous line from *All That Jazz*—when it came time to release the dolphin, but it was cut. Another line in the script where Bridger said, "We need a smaller boat," when the *seaQuest* left Pearl Harbor was also taken out. Bridger was supposed to wear a hat on his island with a New York Yankees logo. This didn't make the final print. Scheider is a self-proclaimed Mets fan.

Roy slipped his wife's picture into several episodes and talking to Carol Bridger's picture and hologram was a main plot element of the Halloween show, "Knight of Shadows." The three episodes that incorporated the hologram projection of Brenda King as Carol Bridger into their plots were "Whale Song," "Higher Power," and "To Be or Not to Be." A framed picture of Brenda as Carol sat on the desk in Bridger's cabin on the Los Angeles set and was carried to Orlando and placed as prominently on the desk in the second-season cabin set.

Whether or not Bridger's dead son, Robert, is named after Scheider's award-winning stage character from *Betrayal* was never stated. The character was written as Eric in early drafts of this pilot script, which also underwent a title change from "The Nathan Bridger Incident" to the more Shakespearean "To Be or Not to Be" before it aired.[20] The inside joke practice continued in Florida. A character named Lt. Brody, whose duty is basically that of a military policeman, was added to the second season crew in the opening episode, "Daggers." In the second episode, "Sympathy for the Deep," Scheider is deliberately filmed in front of the Universal Studios Florida *Jaws* ride, where the store sign Quint's Nautical Treasures can be seen prominently over his shoulder. In another second-season episode, "And Everything Nice," during a cabin pan, you see a framed black-and-white picture of Scheider at ten years old. More photos of Brenda

King and their son, Christian, make an appearance in Roy's first third-season episode, "Brave New World."

There were many other inside jokes on "seaQuest DSV," like the registration number of the *USS Enterprise* (1701) as part of guest star William Shatner's vidlink transmission code,[21] in the episode "Hide and Seek," and military policemen with name tags that read E. Ness and J. Webb in "Last Lap at Luxury," but the above were the ones that involved Scheider.

In October 1993, Roy was appointed to the honorary board of the newly formed Hamptons International Film Festival. The festival was "an attempt to turn the off-season on the East End of Long Island into a mini–Cannes, with fall foliage."[22] It would help business, as the current season ended Labor Day. The festival was scheduled from Thursday to Sunday, the third week in October. Scheider said, "I can't think of a better place for a film festival than East Hampton. There are film festivals all over the world now, but I think this one will be unique because of all the Hollywood people who have homes there."[23]

While the first-season Nielsen numbers for "seaQuest DSV" were respectable, they were not as high as NBC had hoped for. Scheider was on "Later with Bob Costas" on November 23. Dissatisfied with the scripts, Scheider asked that his part in "Nothing but the Truth" and "Greed for a Pirate's Dream" be minimized so he could play a Mafia don in the feature film *Romeo Is Bleeding*.

On March 13, 1994, Roy attended the Writers Guild of America Award banquet, where his friend Steven Spielberg won best Screenplay for *Schindler's List*.[24] His environmental activism came to the fore when Roy was asked to help stop the Navy from doing explosive ship-shock tests near a marine preserve off the California coast. Scheider appeared on the syndicated program "The Crusaders" during the week of March 24, 1994, saying, "Sea creatures should not be destroyed for war, as the tests would kill 10,000 animals."[25] E! Entertainment News" did a segment on this.[26]

The *Los Angeles Times* ran a story about how Roy Scheider was used as a fictional star of a movie in an FBI sting to catch corrupt teamsters. The film was called *The Convention* and was supposed to be filmed in Las Vegas. When asked why he floated Scheider's name for the project, the investigator hired to run the sting said, "You have to pay for stars."[27]

Romeo Is Bleeding was released into theaters in April 1994.[28] Reviewers found it too dark and too violent, and the public didn't go see it. Scheider's part wasn't large enough to include any biographical elements, unless you count him being filmed in a bathrobe and once again wearing his wire rim glasses to appear intelligent enough to quote famous writers. Kevin Jackson wrote, "[This is] a tale of carnal, bloody and unnatural acts so overblown and relentless as to verge on farce ... if so, it's not quite funny enough, even when the incongruously waspy Scheider quotes Robert Lowell. Scheider's mob boss is from the school of Sydney Greenstreet."[29] "Slam-bang in every sense of the word, this newfangled noir is one heady ride," David Noh stated. "The cops, led by the estimable Will Patton, are a good hard-bitten lot ... more than can be said for a somewhat melted-looking Roy Scheider, yawningly typecast as a malevolent mafioso."[30]

Joe Brown said, "Aside from formidable stars Gary Oldman, Lena Olin and Annabella Sciorra, the rest of *Romeo*'s wasted roster features Juliette Lewis, Ron Perlman, and Roy Scheider in colorfully trashy roles."[31] Jay Stone said, "[*Romeo*] is such a magnificent disaster ... you don't know whether to give it five stars or none. [Grimaldi] is caught [by] conflicting disloyalties, his wife ... his mistress ... [and]

***Romeo Is Bleeding* (1993, Gramercy Pictures). Roy Scheider as Don Falcone. Publicity still.**

Mafia Chieftain Roy Scheider ... dash to and fro with frenzied abandon, as if they are trying to get out of the story."[32]

Peter Travers classified Scheider as "sublime, as slime personified."[33] J. Hoberman called it a "... mordantly wacked-out extremely funny noir. *Romeo*'s cast ... includes Roy Scheider as a mafia don with the look and effect of smoked whitefish. The movie is a lovingly designed geek show."[34] Geoffrey Macnab declared, "Hilary Henkin's screenplay ... was ... 'one of the ten best unproduced scripts in Hollywood.' Unfortunately, the picture that was made never really clicks.... Roy Scheider, going through the motions ... seems relieved when Mona decides to bury him alive. A film ... as aimless as the Marie Celeste."[35] The same issue of *Sight and Sound* named *Romeo* "just one of a clutch of new pulps that are revisionist in spirit and occasionally in execution."[36]

Once again, Scheider was involved in a film that looked good in the production stage, but failed to find an audience that wanted to see it. *Romeo Is Bleeding* was the only film Scheider made during his TV series run.

Douglas Brode analyzed the film:

> *Romeo Is Bleeding* was the first major film to acknowledge that alliance, dramatizing the way in which the American and Russian Mafias symbolically began sleeping together by introducing two representative characters who do precisely that: Roy Scheider as Don Falcone, an aging American mobster, involved with Lena Olin as Mona Demarkova, deadly Soviet hit lady who immigrates and ... buys her American dreams of success with a gun. Near the end, a bound-and-gagged Falcone stands in a field, watching as another man digs the grave into which he will be shortly placed, still alive, then covered. Mona observed all this coolly.
>
> FALCONE: (nervously) We could have shared it all.
>
> MONA: (cynically) We did.
>
> It's impossible to feel much for Falcone, however, since he brought about his fate by soliciting the second man, Jack Grimaldi, to kill Mona before she could do precisely what she's doing: seize power. Like Falcone, grave-digger Jack fell under Mona's hypnotic spell. So it is Falcone who will be killed, though Jack eventually turns his gun on the delectable game. *Romeo* offers a modernization of film noirs from the 1940's, here endowed with a perestroika spin.
>
> Mona is merely representative of the future. "It's the fall of Rome out there," one of

Jack's fellow cops sighs. That is the vision of not only *Romeo Is Bleeding*, but of the modern crime movie: a world beyond repair, in which violence has become widespread and the once-dominant codes (even for criminals) have been tossed aside, into the gutter. It is not a pretty picture, yet it is one that the grim gangster films of the nineties insist upon."[37]

"Masters of Illusion" aired right before the season-ending cliffhanger of "seaQuest DSV" on May 22, 1994. This special, narrated by Roy and his costar Jonathan Brandis, was the final attempt at a cross-promotional effort to boost ratings that first season. They included a Halloween show, a Western theme show to tie in with the "Bonanza" TV movie airing the same night, and guest stars like Charlton Heston, David McCallum, and William Shatner. There also was a "seaQuest DSV" reference on Steven Spielberg's other TV show, a cartoon called "Animaniacs."

Scheider promoted this special on three different programs. The first one was on April 27 in Miami, Florida. Roy's interview focused more on the changes in the TV show and its renewal than on the fact that the special would be on soon.[38] On the second show, on WBZ in Boston on May 2, it was called, "a study of special effects over the last 20 or 30 years in motion pictures and on television." Roy said, "Scenes from *Jaws*, "seaQuest" and *Terminator* will be among those shown ... the best ["seaQuest DSV"] shows are coming up in May. A new season will begin in July."[39] On May 4, Roy was on "Late Night with Conan O'Brien." While he dutifully mentioned the special, more time was spent talking about a naked alien on a recently aired "seaQuest DSV" episode called "Such Great Patience." Conan showed a newspaper article entitled "Butt from Another Planet." O'Brien and Scheider discussed how silly it was when morality groups got upset about such things. Personally, "[Scheider] doesn't like to watch 'making of' specials. He doesn't particularly want to know [how] things are done in movies he hasn't seen yet. 'Masters of Illusion' was for people who want to know how special effects are done."[40]

The *Washington Post* said, "Roy Scheider and Jonathan Brandis host a tribute to those who helped bring ... imaginative films to life. 'Masters of Illusion: Wizards of Special Effects' will include behind the scenes footage [from] blockbuster films ... *The Abyss* ... *Aliens* ... *Ghost* ... [and] *Terminator 2*. Scheider and Brandis also visit Alterian studios."[41] Shawn McClellan wrote, "'Special effects are not an end in themselves; special effects are a tool,'" says filmmaker George Lucas. That's an ironic statement.... In this hour-long examination, special effects *are* an end in themselves. Roy Scheider hosts the first half. The narration [does not] talk down to the viewer."[42]

NBC remained disappointed with the ratings of "seaQuest DSV" at the end of the first year, despite all of the network's attempts to hype the show. Its solution was to revamp the series to emphasize science fiction. The producers added several younger and more scantily clad cast members to enhance the show's sex appeal to a younger male demographic—who were not watching. Five members of the first-season cast were let go, the rest were moved to Florida, the producers were juggled once again, and four were fired.

Several fantasy and or science fiction scripts were commissioned by the remaining producers for Orlando. The second-season episodes filmed that summer were full of mutants, alien encounters, and time travel. The crew now boasted two genetically engineered members, one with gills. Scheider was asked to grow a beard to make him look more wise. This was producer David Burke's idea and Roy complied.

Scheider had initially supported the move to Florida, thinking a change in the

"seaQuest DSV." Roy Scheider as a bearded Nathan Bridger. Publicity still.

venue would improve the writing. Roy outlined his hopes in an interview with Louis Chunovic, who wrote a book about the making of the TV series. This book was only published in England.

> Chunovic said, "It's obvious to me that you care passionately about the show."
>
> [Scheider replied], "Well, yeah, it's why I signed on. I don't want to be just a square-jawed captain of a submarine, a totally impenetrable guy. You know, a superman. I want my character to be vulnerable, I want him to be unsure of himself, I want him to be eccentric, I want him to be passionate. I feel I've tapped five percent of my capability."
>
> "What do you know about Captain Bridger?"
>
> "I know a lot about him. I know who his parents are. I know how he got through Annapolis. I know how he fell in love with his first wife; I know what happened. I know how he got interested in dolphins. I know what happened to his son. I know what kind of relationship he had with his son, what his son's loss meant to him. I know all of that and we haven't seen any of it. He had a very strong and disciplinary father, but his mother was a musician. She represents the softer, gentler, more nurturing, feminine side of Bridger and that enables him to be a scholar and a humanist, a political animal. He's not just in the Navy. I've talked about it to directors and ... to the people at Amblin and I keep waiting. This is my homework. This is what I've done to create the character I'm playing. If I put this much energy into it, I want to like it, I want to believe in it. If we go to Orlando ... I want to go down early, sit with all the writers, and really discuss the whole year, where we are going, what kind of stories we are going to tell and have some fun doing the show."[43]

"seaQuest DSV" moved to Florida in the summer of 1994. Scheider was given a house in the Orlando suburb of Ocoee owned by Universal Studios and once again moved his family across the country. Filming on the second-season sci-fi scripts began. They were 180 degrees from what Scheider wanted, but he gamely did publicity for the show. One press conference took place in the dolphin exhibition area during location shooting at Sea World for the episode "The Fear That Follows." Scheider was allowed into the restricted area with the trainer at the lowered pool edge to interact with the dolphins who performed, looking rather incongruous in his khaki uniform with nonregulation knee-high rubber boots on for the ankle-deep water. The dolphins were better trained than the reporters, who kept shouting questions about the show's move and its special effects as Scheider tried to pet a dolphin who had leaped up on the coaming at the trainer's signal for the photo op.

Roy and the trainer had obviously talked, as Scheider knew where to rub, and the dolphin rolled over at his touch like an affectionate dog. The attending press at least got their pictures, if not all the answers they wanted. One reporter verbalized the frustration of being kept behind the fence and seeing Scheider more interested in the dolphins than their questions, by prefacing his inquiry with, "Before you get too wet."[44]

In June, Roy attended an environmental fundraiser for the Group for the South Fork. *Newsday* noted, "[He] is a newcomer to the East End [and] ... building a house." Scheider commented on the current O. J. Simpson case, "Like O. J. was really thinking of the death penalty when he went over to that house. I don't think you can teach people not to kill by killing. Do they say, 'We don't dare do it to O. J.?'"[45] Roy returned to East Hampton to play in the Artists–Writers softball game in August 1994, pitched a low hitter, and was named the MVP of the game. Scheider quipped, "I'm *not* going to Disney World." (He was then employed at amusement park rival Universal Florida.) The Artists won 6–5.[46]

Scheider made five episodes in Florida before he was publicly asked his opinion of the new season by a local reporter in Orlando. Scheider, not being one to avoid the truth, told her exactly what he thought of the current time travel episode: "It's total, total childish trash. I'm ashamed of it. The other shows are Saturday afternoon 4 o'clock junk for children ... old, tired, time warp robot crap."[47] "I am very bitter about it. I feel betrayed. I feel I've not been told the truth. It's not real. It's not even good fantasy. 'Star Trek' does this stuff much better than we do." Scheider talked about the format changing, "from mostly fact-based programs to science fantasy."[48] "Everything is the same as it was last year, with the exception of opening the show up (i.e., getting off the sets and going on location). More water. Some ... interesting young people ... but they're loading it up with 'eye candy'—can you imagine?"[49]

Roy's negative comments were published right before the second-season premiere in September. This *Orlando Sentinel* article was quoted all over the country via the wire services, getting more publicity and air play than the series premiere episode. Producer Patrick Hasburgh responded: "I think Roy Scheider is wrong. I'm sorry he is such a sad and angry man. 'seaQuest' is ... a terrific and entertaining show for the whole family. He is lucky to be part of it." Hasburgh also said, "Scheider's comments were insulting to everyone involved in the production."[50] Roy's bitter comments did not sit well with Orlando crew members. Scheider apologized to the crew for his ill-timed criticism, but many did not forgive easily. It was the beginning of the end of Roy's association with the TV series. He spent less time in Florida as construction on his beach house continued. Roy was noted as involved when the small country store in his Hamptons neighborhood protested a rent hike in October. The store had been a local landmark since 1880.[51] The New York court rejected Scheider's divorce settlement appeal in December 1994. Roy was ordered to pay the five years of back alimony he owed to his ex-wife, Cynthia. This ruling was also appealed, and the fight continued for another two years.[52]

In January 1995, Roy Scheider traveled to Tampa to be part of "Crystals of Delight—an evening of baseball, ballet, beauty, stars and soul," that benefited three Pinellas County organizations that help people with HIV and AIDS.[53] In March, more charity reciprocity occurred. "Scheider will narrate *Aaron Copland's The Lincoln Portrait* ... in a free [Orlando Philharmonic] concert in Orlando's Loch Haven Park. Saturday's concert is part of the daylong commemoration of Orange County's 150th anniversary.... when [the] orchestra filmed a 'seaQuest DSV' scene [a 'Special Delivery' dream sequence where Scheider conducted part of Dvorak's *New World Symphony*] ... the group invited him to narrate."[54] In this dream sequence, Scheider and the orchestra wore their tuxedo suit jackets and no pants—only boxer undershorts—which may have been Scheider's inside joke, but the orchestra obviously didn't mind. Scheider was also seen attending Orlando Magic basketball games.

As the second-season scripts became more fantastic with giant crocodiles, Atlantis, and Greek gods appearing in the winter of 1995, Scheider grew more unhappy with the TV series and participated less. He asked to be written out of a supernatural script, "Something in the Air," and his part went to costar Don Franklin.[55] Finally, Roy asked to be let out of his series contract. "seaQuest DSV" had become something "he did not sign up for."[56] The second season cliffhanger took place on another planet, the cast was blown up, and the *seaQuest* sunk, so the producers and NBC could once again adjust cast and story lines, if they decided to renew the show for a third season. Roy announced his resignation, but by the time the news hit *TV Guide*, he had been coaxed back to make six guest appearances in the third season. There was a vigorous internet campaign during the latter half of the second season to "save seaQuest" and return it to its science fact–based adventures of the first season, but this hue and cry came from an older, mostly female demographic that NBC did not value, and the campaign was all but ignored by the show's producers and NBC executives. Scheider's announcement that he was leaving aggravated the situation. Roy was well liked across the fan base, from toddlers to senior citizens. At least two male babies born during the first season were named Nathan, after his character, according to postings on the internet news group alt.tv.seaquest.

Roy traveled to Los Angeles to participate in Steven Spielberg's American Film Institute tribute. Introduced as "the man who defeated the shark,"[57] Roy gave a short speech that was left out of the CBS network telecast: "For years, elders thought Steven's magic was too powerful—maybe even dangerous, since he viewed the world as a three-year-old."[58] Roy's AFI tribute speech was included in a later, longer version of the program broadcast on the A & E cable channel. Scheider said, "Picasso wrote, 'I once drew like Rafael, but it has taken me an entire lifetime to draw as a child.' Tonight, we honor you, at a very young age and for those of us who have made the journey with you know you are only halfway to wherever your Muse or goddess is guiding you. I wish for you that the rest of the voyage be only as tempestuous as need be, as fulfilling as you desire and that all its revelations and rewards continue to rain on us all."[59]

In the 20th anniversary laser disc documentary on the "Making of *Jaws*," Scheider spoke about the toll the ocean took on the mechanical shark and how that kept it from working—and about being left alone in the cabin while they sank the boat. His other stories were about the friends and family screening of *Jaws* at the Rivoli Theatre in New York City and the infamous food fight.[60]

The only bright spot during this whole spring was the birth of Molly Scheider in Boca Raton, Florida. After filming was completed on the second season, Scheider attended the final wrap party at the Hard Rock Cafe on the studio grounds.[61] Roy moved back to Bridgehampton into his newly completed beach house, leaving the acrimony in Orlando behind.

Renewed for a third season, the *seaQuest* and some of its crew—the ones with renewed contracts—had to be brought home from the planet Hyperion. Producers also had to write Scheider out of his lead role. Clifton Campbell, the only producer left Scheider would deal with, came up with the idea of using Bridger's dead son, Robert—a recurring plot element—as a reason for Bridger to leave. He gave Bridger a grandson whom he never knew he had when the crew returned 10 years after they had left.

The show found its new captain in June, in another NBC series. Michael Ironside was happy to leave "ER" and move up to the series lead of "seaQuest 2032." Roy returned to Orlando in late July to film his farewell episode. The grandson, Michael Bridger, was played by Roy's son, Christian Scheider, in his network television debut. He had no lines.

In a July promotion for the October Hamptons International Film Festival, Scheider and his wife attended a screening of the film *A Month by the Lake*.[62] Scheider pitched for the Artists in the 1995 Artists–Writers softball game on August 21. The *New York Daily News* said, "Beautiful people don't threaten any Yankee jobs but Roy Scheider is definitely a clutch performer."[63] The charity game was on "Entertainment Tonight" and "Showbiz Today."

Roy did voiceovers "in TV spots for the Mercury Villager and Mystique breaking [September 11], on ABC's 'Monday Night Football.' It was the start of a two-week blitz to clarify Mercury's muddy brand image and [carried] the new theme-line [sic], Imagine yourself in a Mercury."[64] Scheider hosted a one-hour sports special on TNT, "Joe Montana: The Fire Inside," that aired on September 12, 1995. Frank Ahrens called it " a fabulous highlight reel of Montana's greatest hits ... the best quarterback ever to play in the National Football League."[65]

Scheider did two additional episodes of "seaQuest 2032" in October. Universal booked a suite for Roy at the Peabody, a four-star hotel about a mile from the studio. A planned script where Bridger would find his dead son, Robert, was never written. Low ratings brought an end to the series by Thanksgiving. Roy wasn't originally in what became his final "seaQuest 2032" episode. The script was rewritten by Clifton Campbell at the last minute to fulfill Scheider's contract. Roy's last episode, "Good Soldiers," was filmed October 16–20, 1995.[66]

Roy left immediately afterward for Utah to play the romantic lead in the movie *Money Plays* with Sonia Braga which started filming on October 31.[67] The film was about a down-on-his-luck gambler and a hooker who score big in Las Vegas. The "seaQuest 2032" TV series was canceled four weeks later. Scheider never looked back.

—13—

New Markets

Roy Scheider began 1996 with his only (to date) interactive internet chat on Prodigy. Scheider stated he came to talk about acting and was "glad to be able to put aside this time to talk to people interested in film and any other forms of acting." Scheider said:

> Get yourself some place you can act. In the beginning it doesn't matter where you act as long as you get out and do it. Acting is about acting ... you can't talk about it, you just have to do it. You have to get yourself into acting companies. In the beginning it doesn't matter where it is. I think it's more important than most realize, for actors are really the interpreters of their time and they get what the poets have to say out to the people. What they are doing is portraying the lives of the people watching: it is a communication between the actor and the audience. It's all about living ... this is when it is working at its best, of course. The freest form of acting is still the theater because there is no censorship.

Unfortunately, the chat session was marred by technical problems and had to be cut short, but Scheider did field several questions about why he left the "seaQuest DSV" TV series. After this interview, the internet campaign against the show's producers subsided to a large extent, even though some fans continued to vent their anger at NBC for at least another year. Scheider replied, "The development sort of came to a standstill in the middle of the second year and it was never brought up to the level of the character it could have been. I became more of a combat commander than a scientific commander and I hadn't signed on to do that." Roy acknowledged the internet campaign when it was mentioned, but said their effort was outnumbered by the "fans who had stopped watching the program b/c [*sic*] it became too fantastic and childish."

Scheider stated that his character never was written up to potential, even in the first season, but he never was upstaged by the mechanical dolphin: "I always felt the humans would win out. I liked the character of Darwin ... for he really represented what the ocean was all about. We needed more of him and less flying creatures. The decision to phase myself out of the series was mine."[1]

Scheider talked briefly about *Jaws.* When asked if he needed to learn how to tie knots for the film, he admitted he did and that his grandchildren called him "Chiefy" and "Grandpa Big Fish." He named *All That Jazz* as his favorite role and *Paths of Glory* as his favorite film. Roy listed his hobbies as reading, listening to Dixieland jazz, and watching sports. He concluded with, "I enjoyed the past hour. It's always interesting to find out what I think. That's why I like doing these to see how my thoughts have changed over time. It's amazing how much I've changed since last year."[2]

In January 1996, a falling-out occurred at the Hampton Day private school and the disaffected group found itself in Roy Scheider's living room, planning a new school. "The Hayground experimental multi-cultural school was born. Their nursery was the Bridgehampton Methodist church for the first year of classes beginning on September 11, 1996, with 60 students, ages 3–13."[3]

The group included "nine of 19 ... school board members who had resigned after trustees disagreed about ... the [current] director and educational philosophy. [The group] included ... even Tinka Topping, the doyenne [who founded] the ... School, in 1966. Now, Topping is [on] the Hayground Board, drawn by the 'magical energy' ... [to] establish something altogether new."[4]

> Hayground has multi-age classes, basically divided into nursery (age 3–5), primary (ages 5–10) and middle school (ages 11–14). Students graduate after finishing ninth grade, but these are arbitrary dividing lines as there is constant movement between the classes and many of the older children teach the younger children in supervised activities. The curriculum is free form with a loose organization of reading and art in the morning and math and gym in the afternoon, with a "gathering" at the end of the day to discuss work done on group projects.
>
> The daily expectations of students are: Participating in sustained conversations, writing, reading, working with numbers, making things, investigating, thinking about aesthetics, collaborating, thinking about and from a multiplicity of perspectives, learning self-reliance and playing. Teachers meet each week to evaluate whether the students are: Learning things of importance, seriously engaged with interesting, rich and complex material, learning to think rigorously and adventurously, developing habits of self-restraint, learning to build community and learning how to become citizens capable of intelligent action. The school is governed by a council of 27: Scheider and his wife, other parents, teachers and interested members of the community. Hayground is the name of the area of Long Island where the school is located and one of the founders felt it was important to remember original names when naming the school.[5]

Scheider narrated "Spy in the Sky," an episode about the development of the U-2 spy plane for PBS on February 26, 1996, on the series "The American Experience." Tom Feran wrote, "The characteristically absorbing hour gives us an insider's view, a historian's perspective and a filmmaker's sense of history."[6]

On March 4, 1996, Roy attended a tribute for Robert Whitehead, the producer of *Betrayal.* The *New York Times* described the event as "a celebration of his 80th birthday and the 50th anniversary of his first Broadway show, *Medea.* The evening is [called] 'Mister Class.' Christopher Plummer will be the master of ceremonies. The tribute is a benefit for the Theater Development Fund at the Laura Pels Theater."[7]

Money Plays had a long wait for release. The market for theatrical films was changing rapidly and despite a screening at the Writer's Guild in March 1996,[8] the film did not find a buyer. *Money Plays* finally sold as a Movie Channel original film, one of the first six of an estimated 25, on January 27, 1997.[9] It went straight to cable, first airing in January 1998,[10] before being released on video in June 1999 and to other cable channels in 1999 and 2000. Scheider said, "It wasn't high-powered enough to go into theaters."[11]

Roy's next project took him to Canada to film *Word of Honor*, in which he played corrupt, embittered FBI agent John Taggart. Gary Busey was a psychotic serial killer vet named Dacy. Kristen Cloke, as the rookie FBI field agent sent out to apprehend him, in truth was put on the case by Taggart to find evidence against her new partner, agent Nick Travis (Lorenzo Lamas). Taggart wanted to fire Travis, as part of a long-standing feud over a previous incident (a fictionalized Waco Branch Davidian standoff), when Taggart was demoted.

This film also had a hard time finding a distributor. It was released first overseas under the titles *The Rage* and *The Final Conflict*. The film went straight to video in the United States as *The Rage* in June 1998. There was little opportunity for Scheider to invest his disagreeable, vindictive character with any biographical characteristics. Roy did find a distinctive way to wear his FBI-issue jumpsuit, standing out as the only agent with a turtleneck, with his badge on a very large chain around his neck.

Roy added the Mercury Mountaineer to his commercial voiceovers for Lincoln. There were six different television ads in a campaign that played for two years. In March 1996, Roy traveled to Bethel, Maine, to play a cold, unloving father in *The Myth of Fingerprints*.

Roy was spotted by the press at the *Twister* premiere on May 7. He claimed the film was, "*Jaws*, frame for frame. I saw it from the first take—the angles, the pacing. [It] is a depersonalized *Jaws* with computer effects. How much less personal can it get?? It's about the weather."[12] On May 11, Scheider was caught by the cameras of the entertainment show "Extra" at yet another premiere, when he took his children to see *Flipper*.[13] This film was produced by an old friend of Scheider, Sid Sheinberg, the ex-president of Universal, and directed by Alan Shapiro, who had done *Tiger Town*. On May 24, 1996, "Roy Scheider [was] the guest of honor at the ninth annual environmental benefit for the Group for the South Fork and

***The Rage* (1996, Norstar Entertainment). Taggart tells Travis his partner McCord is off the case. Nick Travis: Lorenzo Lamas; John Taggart: Roy Scheider.**

the Nature Conservancy's South Fork–Shelter Island chapter."[14]

Scheider's next project, *Plato's Run*, was filmed in Margate, Florida, in June 1996. Roy played a corrupt arms dealer who may have loved his dog but also enjoyed blowing up his enemies a bit too much. Both saw him undone. The film costarred Gary Busey and Tiani Warden from *Word of Honor* as well as Steven Bauer and Jeff Speakman. Roy did not bring much of himself to this film, besides his distinct way of dressing. As the owner of several dogs, working with the trained German shepherd in the film was easy for him. A picture of Scheider with one of the many dogs he has owned over the years appeared in the book *The Growling Gourmet*, published in 1976 by Simon and Schuster. This book is a collection of recipes that celebrities make for their dogs. Roy contributed a stew recipe for his Shih Tzu, appropriately named Willie Mays, after Roy's favorite ballplayer. Scheider stated that the stew recipe "will serve four adults and one dog."[15]

Plato's Run marked the beginning of Scheider's characters being driven around in large black limousines while talking on the phone.

The *Plato's Run* press kit described filming:

> "Cut," an authoritative voice rings out. Plato and Kathy (better known as Gary Busey and Maggie Myatt) ... retire to a conglomeration of director's chairs ... while, next to the van ... Roy Scheider ... confers with the director, Jim Becket. For the next thirty minutes, Busey, Myatt, Scheider do it again. And again. And again. "Things are going well," [James] Brooke says of the production, which has progressed into the fifth week of its seven shooting weeks. "The dailies have been terrific, the actors are all professionals, the locals have been great."[16]

"I took [the part] to be on the set with Roy Scheider," Jeff Speakman says with a smile. "I think maybe that was the main reason. This is a phenomenal location ... the weather's been difficult and there have been some snags along the way, but by and large this has been one of the better experiences I've had."[17]

Rick Clabaugh, who was the director of photography, said Roy Scheider "was really great to work with" and put up a picture on his website to prove it.[18] The exception to this happy set was Teamsters Local 390: "Union officials say the production tried to hire non-union drivers to avoid paying Teamsters rates. The Teamsters picketed a filming site in Miami on June 18, [and] the producers signed a contract with the union five hours later."[19]

Scheider returned to the Hamptons during the shoot to host a "kick off fundraiser for the Suffolk Theatre in Riverhead on Thursday, June 20, 1996."[20] In August, he pitched in the annual Artists and Writers Celebrity Softball Game. "The Artists lost in the last inning, 6–5,"[21] despite a record-breaking hit, out of the park and onto the tennis courts by football player Marty Lyons. Lyons' credentials as an Artist were protested by the Writers, even though they won.

In October 1996, the final settlement on the payment of alimony from Roy's divorce came when "[New York] State Judge Fern Fisher Brandveen [ruled] Scheider owes ex Cynthia $494,859.65, representing back alimony and upkeep for the Putnam Valley spread Cynthia won in the split."[22]

Scheider participated in the Hamptons Film Festival. "The biggest prize of the festival, the Golden Starfish Award, which will go to one of the new films in the festival's American Independents Showcase, will be chosen by a jury of four ... Roy Scheider, Ruth Charney ... Judith Klausner ... and David O. Russell."[23] "Those four judges—were always on time, and always together. 'We're bonding,'

Scheider said. The four sat through 10 movies in two and a half days ... [which] meant that the public could view the judges. 'We are not afraid to laugh [when] we find something funny.'"[24] *Puddle Cruiser* and *Mugshot* shared the award.[25]

Scheider went to Los Angeles in November 1996 to play the president in a film called *Flashpoint*. Later it was renamed *Speed Zone*. The chief executive is kidnapped by an ex-con, Nick James (Michael Madsen), whose wife is being held by the villain for his cooperation. Scheider's character is locked into the trunk of the getaway car and taken to a friend's house to save his life until Nick can work out a way to free his wife, Nadia (Kathy Christopherson), without sacrificing the president.

Biographical elements include Roy being the first president from New Jersey, being popular for his pro-environment, nonmilitary stance, and having a young blonde first lady. Roy also wears his gold wire-rim glasses and is driven around in a black limousine. Costar Kathy Christopherson wrote in her "Hot Starlet Diary," on the E-online web pages, how the cast waited for Roy's arrival on the set with much anticipation.

She stated how kind Scheider was, scrunching up into one corner of the ambulance to be out of camera for her close-ups. There was trouble with the side door of the ambulance, and she reported ruined takes where Roy was either locked in or locked out. Two pictures of Scheider adorned her website for months before they were taken down: one of everyone in the ambulance and a second of Kathy and Roy off-camera, with his arm around her.

Variety announced on November 21, 1996, that Roy was going to Toronto to film *Hellbent* with Dolph Lundgren.[26] Scheider plays the president again, with a southern accent. The president's "black bag" of launch codes and the war hero it was attached to are kidnapped by a deranged colonel. He had once served with the president, a former Army general. He stole the codes to launch missiles at Washington, D.C. The only way to stop the launch is for the president to kill himself on national television. There aren't any blatant biographical elements in this film, unless you count an extramarital affair, being filmed in a bathrobe, wearing the gold wire-rim glasses for the fourth time, and being driven around in the now-ubiquitous black limousine. Renamed *The Peacekeeper* for release in the United States, the movie aired as an HBO world premiere in November 1997 and continued to play on American cable into 2000. The film was released overseas as *The Red Zone*.

Scheider hosted his fifth annual Thanksgiving dinner for orphaned children at an inn in Connecticut. With Helen Hunt, Hank Azaria, and Roy's wife, Brenda, the gathering Scheider called "the Ritual" took place: "We do it because these kids don't have families to go to. It's very mysterious and fun. We don't know them before the dinner."[27]

January 1997 found *The Myth of Fingerprints* as one of the few films already sold—to Sony Pictures Classic—by the time it was shown at the Sundance film festival.[28] The film did well, getting coverage in *Variety* and almost winning the audience award. Roy did not attend the Sundance festival as he was in San Francisco filming a cameo as a high-powered insurance company CEO in Francis Ford Coppola's *John Grisham's The Rainmaker*.

On April 14, 1997, Roy Scheider participated in a celebrity fundraiser, Kids 4 Kids, that raised money for pediatric AIDS.[29] In the spring of 1997, Kathy Engel brought Roy Scheider and Danny Glover together after she heard Roy talking about the profound effect that mentors had on his life. "She arranged a breakfast meeting," Scheider recalled: "We swapped stories about mentors and immediately knew we had something. We will each talk about three mentors."[30]

On May 9–10, 1997, Scheider spoke for over an hour about the effect that Friend Avery, Darrell Larsen, and Harold Clurman had on his acting career. The benefit raised more than $50,000 for the Hayground building fund. Scheider's seven-year-old son, Christian, was a student at the school. Bob Herbert covered the event: "There are fewer than 60 pupils, ages five to 14, at Hayground. Some are white ... some are black. Some are Latinos and ... Shinnecock Indians. It is far too early to tell if Hayground will be a success.... Its splendid and courageous mission is tremendously important."[31]

Scheider was interviewed for a *Jaws* retrospective on the new entertainment show "Access Hollywood" on May 14, 1997. He retold the Christmas party story and how he "thought the movie premise was loony."[32] A film clip of Roy was used to promote the premiere of this show.

He gave a reading of *The Dead Boy*, a play by Joe Pintauro, at Mulford Barn in East Hampton on the weekend of June 21–22. "On June 28, the East Coast premiere of *Men in Black* further benefitted the building fund of the Hayground School."[33] The schoolhouse was built over the summer and made ready for the 1997-98 school year. The *East Hampton Star* gave Scheider credit for a last-minute paint job.[34]

Flashpoint—now renamed *Executive Target*—sold to HBO at the American Film Market in February. Paired with *Plato's Run*, the two films aired as an HBO double world premiere in July 1997. On July 12, Roy and Brenda attended a fundraiser for the Bay Street Theater at Long Wharf in Sag Harbor.[35] A new 35mm print of *Jaws* was shown as part of the 2nd Annual Radio City Film Festival on August 21.[36] Roy did an encore reading of *The Dead Boy* on August 24.

Scheider played in his seventh Artists and Writers Celebrity Softball Game on August 16 and pitched the entire game. Roy was filming *Evasive Action*, but managed to come home for the weekend to play. The Writers won. This was the first time I attended this charity event. The participants, showing more heart than skill, were very entertaining in their attempts to play "serious" softball. The *East End Independent* wrote, "[One] of the fans' favorite moments during the day [was] Roy Scheider serving up a turnip as a softball to Mort Zuckerman, [the opposing pitcher]. The publisher had apparently just fallen off the turnip truck, because he fell for the gag and smashed it to pieces."[37]

Another familiar player to Scheider was his director from *The Myth of Fingerprints*, Bart Freundlich, who grew up on the Long Island. Bart had returned to spend the summer. Scheider and Freundlich had become friends and Roy had Bart over for dinner during his time there.[38] Aware of this connection, the game announcer tried to plug their film, but kept mispronouncing the title as *The Myths of Fingerprinting*. Freundlich was up to bat the first time he mangled the title. Scheider, on the pitcher's mound, doubled over in laughter at the faux pas.[39] After a third botched attempt, I walked over to the booth and gave the man the correct film information. His fourth plug was much improved, with the proper title and new information about the Pier 17 free screening in five days. Talking to Scheider after the game, I mentioned I had done this and Roy thanked me.

Sony Classic Pictures was careful with *Myth*, previewing it at the Seattle film festival in May and running sneak previews in August 1997 in San Francisco, New York, Boston, and St. Louis. One of four films in a four-week series sponsored by Polo jeans, these previews were advertised in *Entertainment Weekly*. This outdoor movie series, shown on Pier 17 in New York on August 24, "are the urban dwellers' answer to the drive in. Polo Jeans executives were looking for 'what's right for Jeans?' Marian Schwindeman, Polo Ralph Lauren's vice president of global marketing, decided film was the perfect fit."[40]

The *Los Angeles Times* announced that "*Myth of Fingerprints* [was one] … of the 10 films in competition for a Grand Prize and a Jury prize … at the Deauville Festival of American Film."[41] *Myth* opened at the Deauville and Toronto film festivals prior to being released into American theaters. It won the audience award at Deauville. On September 12 at Deauville, Roy was "awarded the Piper-Heidsieck Award for his life's work. The prize is awarded each year to American actors who 'take risks' in shooting films that tackle difficult subjects or that have a small budget or to actors that take up directing."[42]

Scheider was asked if Steven Spielberg had seen the film. Roy answered, "Steven had attended the premiere in Los Angeles. He told me how much he liked the film and my performance. He acknowledged he had never seen me do anything quite like it. I wanted to answer him, Steven, that is what is called playing comedy. (laughter)"[43]

The Myth of Fingerprints **(1997, Sony Pictures Classics). Portrait of Roy Scheider as Hal. Publicity still.**

The Myth of Fingerprints was released by Sony Classic Pictures in September 1997. The marketing department built a campaign around Noah Wyle and the season premiere of "ER." Wyle, Michael Vartan, director Freundlich, and his new love, costar Julianne Moore, crisscrossed the country on a week-long promotion tour, appearing on MTV, TNT's "Rough Cut," and many other shows. Scheider promoted the film on "Live with Regis and Kathy Lee."

Roy related to the cold, distant father in *Myth*. Scheider commented:

> I approached Hal as a combination between the written father, my father and me. There is a lot of the dark side of me that is cynical and competitive, as there was with my own father. Not many people live up to their parents' expectations. Hal sees how frustrated his children are. He wants to tell them that it doesn't matter that much if they live up to his expectations. But he can't. He doesn't have the equipment or the tools to sit down and talk to his children. He realizes he is of no real use to them. He loves his children, but he has lost the capacity to tell them that. He's left that up to his wife for too many years.

Scheider's character "is eccentric and self-absorbed."[44]

Roy said he took the role "because of the story. Bart wrote characters you wanted to play. All of us know the film is unlikely to make money, but we are always looking for something this interesting … [for] characters that really grab you." Scheider wasn't worried about his young director. "Bart … knew enough [to do the job]."[45]

Bart Freundlich said, "It's like opening up a huge can of worms. [The children]

***The Myth of Fingerprints*. Hal and Lena discuss their children. Hal: Roy Scheider; Lena: Blythe Danner.**

feel this is a given—this is who their father is. They've grown up with him. And they are scared if they bring it up, they won't have a solution for it, that it will be more than they can handle. They've been taught denial in their family. That's the way to do things. You move away, you don't visit too much and you avoid dealing with your problems."

> And I think [Lena] sees him in a totally different way. I truly believe Hal loves Lena differently than he could ever love anyone else ... unconditionally. Roy Scheider and I did a lot of talking about his character, how even before the kids were home, he had all these rules: he wouldn't talk before 10:00 A.M. And Lena puts up with all his rules, his quirks and his insecurities. It's much easier for her ... because he gives something back to her. He actually communicates with her. He needs her—she is almost his link to the outside world. And I think she is a co-dependent person who's gotten used to be needed in that way. It's not that there is no true love between them, but ... their pathologies are very intertwined.[46]

"I think it's the best work Roy has done in years," Freundlich declared. "He said the movie was very important to him. Hal is his age, and has a very complex inner life."[47]

Modern Maturity named "*The Ice Storm* ... and another middle class family drama, *The Myth of Fingerprints*, [as a new trend in movies that] ... give sexy and stirring roles to parents of grown-up children."[48] In an interview done at Thanksgiving, Scheider elaborated on his role as the "emotionally inadequate" Hal. To play the character he drew on his own experiences with his father. "I loved [my father], but I didn't like him very much. Bart ... and I lunched ... and told ... our father stories. We both ended up crying, grieving for what we wanted from our fathers. I've learned ... the hurts of childhood stay with you. We all carry emotional wounds."[49] As previously stated, getting his father to admit he loved Roy was a major turning point in Scheider's life. Actually having the words said changed things between them. It wasn't perfect from then on, but at least his father valued Roy as an individual distinct from him.

During his prep for *Myth*, Scheider decided it was time to explore this because it was the richest vein he could tap. Yet Roy was reluctant to do so, because of the pain involved and the years of resentments that he had built up. Scheider stated that one of the greatest tragedies of adult life is that we become our parents. Knowing his father's difficulty in expressing his emotions was an enormous help to Roy in playing the father in *Myth*. They are a dysfunctional family where nobody really says what they're really thinking or feeling. It was a great opportunity to crawl into his father's skin and realize how difficult being distant was for his dad.

A few other biographical elements are evident. Hal's game is to ask everyone the time and insist that everyone be on time. Mia deliberately fails to do this on a regular basis. Scheider is a very prompt individual. He is well known for being on time and having no patience with people who aren't. Roy also sings in this film, without benefit of being drunk, and his song is on the movie soundtrack CD. Roy grew a beard (for his dark side) and is filmed in a bathrobe.

In DVD commentary released in May 2000, Freundlich further elaborated on Scheider's contributions to the film. He said Scheider came to watch some of the other actors film on his day off and told the director that the tree house used in the film needed to be painted yellow, to reflect the main house. There wasn't time to do this, but Freundlich marveled at how Roy was thinking about the film, even on his day off.

Bart sometimes found Roy a bit daunting, but appreciated the talks they had about how to best do some scenes. Freundlich remembered one discussion about how much crying he wanted in the basement scene and how Scheider used a cigarette to accomplish what was needed. Bart told a third story about Scheider pitching his bathrobe across the room, with appropriate swear words, when it hadn't been turned right side out again from being used previously.

Some of Scheider's work ended up on the cutting room floor after the film was shortened from 126 minutes to 93 and collapsed into three days instead of four. There was an elaborate gun-cleaning scene at the beginning, with overtones of suicide, that ended up being too grim. A dinner scene with only Warren from the first night and an expository bed scene with Blythe Danner were cut for telling too much too soon. A fantasy scene where Roy's character was the father he should have been and another Warren humiliation scene, where he was yelled at for being afraid to climb the tree house ladder, were edited out. Even with the cuts, director Bart Freundlich and cinematographer Steve Kazmierski agreed that it was Scheider's film, even though he only had eight or nine lines in the whole movie. Roy was so strong in his final scene that they had to end the movie with him.[50]

The critics were mixed on *Myth*. Some understood what Freundlich was trying to do and liked it, others thought Bart needed to show more than he did. Several did not care for the open ending. The *New York Times* critic, Stephen Holden, did not like the film, nor did he mention Scheider's performance. Jay Stone was of the opinion that "Freundlich ... has fashioned a sparse blueprint of the wounded family. The old battles and irreparable insults are only hinted at ... they are alluded to, figured out, supposed. The movie rests on the skillfully expressed power-tripping of Scheider's Hal, and the sullen bravery of Moore's Mia."[51]

Gene Siskel liked it. Roger Ebert did not, in their review on September 21, 1997. Jack Mathews said, "I hope I never see any of them again. Their father is such a strange, aloof character you'd think they would be united by shared experiences of surviving him. The story eventually settles on Warren and his scarred relationship with his father. [It is not strong enough] ... to engross us."[52] Eleanor Ringel stated, "The incomplete tone is set by Dad's behavior; he switches from being gruffly uncommunicative to out-and-out weird without any explanation. And it's never clear how we are supposed to take his weirdness. Sometimes, it is amusingly eccentric, other times, it is pretty ugly and threatening."[53]

Elizabeth Barr declared, "The wonderful characterizations couldn't have gotten a better cast. Hal ... is the father who has abdicated the duties of love and affection to his wife. Scheider's ... self-absorbed eccentric is brilliant. He says more with ... his face than most actors say with their voices."[54]

Paul Wunder's web movie review stated, "Black humor, the kind I find most entertaining, is dark and funny in this highly entertaining comedy about relationships among the members and friends of a dysfunctional family. While all the performances are quite good ... Roy Scheider demonstrates ... comedic flair as the father."[55]

Donna Adcock wrote, "Scheider is ... adept as the ... mean spirited and self-loathing father who is beginning to realize he is no longer of any use to his children. He loves his children but can't seem to tell them. At this point ... it may already be too late."[56] Frances Woods found the film too murky and obtuse, "but there are small evocative moments when this film ... gets under the skin of these people—the [mother's] ... story ... reveals a world about unconditional love. Warren does the same with a look. The childish father is a marvelously drawn character—odd in the way people are really odd."[57] Trevor Johnston agreed: "Dad ... is an aloof, preoccupied bear of a man. Brooding Scheider, whose ball bearing gaze has never seemed quite so unknowable [is] beautifully attuned to the material."[58]

"As the emotionally shut down father, Scheider freezes up the screen in every one of his scenes. Except his last, in which he seems to realize that withholding love from one's children is the greatest mistake a parent can make," said Kristin Tillotson.[59] Peter Matthews recounted, "The real [problem] is Mia's stern, uncommunicative father Hal—the kind of freeze-dried parent who invariably turns up in these family sagas of stifled emotions and autumnal regrets. Hal isn't ... the great castrating father ... [only] a dad whose inability is given a great deal of sympathy."[60] "And although the situation is classic, the characters are lively and fresh. Add to that top notch acting, especially from Mr. Wyle and Mr. Scheider, and you have the makings of a fine character study,"[61] declared Beth Pinsker. Laurie Stone opined: "Bart Freundlich misses the chance to turn his predictable family anatomy into a messy, intriguing tale. Meanwhile the disturbing father—Scheider doing Pinter in an episode of Relativity—is treated as a boilerplate depressive."[62] "It plays like a bitter combination of the Cheeveresque and the Pinteresque. The father is a monster (Roy Scheider is in the role), a Medea with testosterone whose rages haunt and embitter his children. The film has a true sense of WASP repressed horror,"[63] said Steven Hunter.

The critics were right about the Pinter connection. Bart Freundlich said that it helped him immensely that Scheider and Danner had a history of working together—*Myth* was their third project. They teased him, mostly about his tender age, by asking repeatedly, "Did he know Harold [Pinter]?" Casting snowballed after Freundlich signed Wyle. "Blythe Danner thought it would be great to play the mother of Wyle and Moore. Roy Scheider had worked in the theater with Danner and immediately agreed to work with her again."[64]

On the heels of *Myth*'s release, "The television show 'Chicago Hope' did homage to *All That Jazz* and Dennis Potter. Series regular neurosurgeon Aaron Shutt (Adam Arkin) hovered between life and death and hallucinated about his past life à la Joe Gideon in song during a brain aneurysm."[65] In November and December, preproduction location work was being done in Dallas for the independent film *Conspiracy of Weeds*. The *Dallas Morning Sun* wrote, "[The film] stars Roy Scheider, Sean Patrick Flanery (he was Powder), Judge Reinhold, Moira Kelly and Jeremy Sisto."[66] The production company may have found its barn to burn and its park to film in, but there is no record this movie was ever made by Allerton Films.

John Grisham's The Rainmaker was released into theaters in November 1997. The promotion campaign revolved around Matt Damon and Danny Devito. The ads for the film made little mention of Roy, who had 15th billing among an extensive cast of names. HBO ran a "making of" featurette, "HBO: First Look," on the film during the first two months of the theatrical release and while Roy is featured, the short concentrates on the Memphis shoot and only mentions San Francisco at the end, where Roy is shown briefly rehearsing his court scene.[67] Scheider was also in a "Hollywood One on One" promotional piece that aired on Starz cable on December 16, 1997. Scheider made brief appearances in some of the trailers and was featured in the production notes on the official website, with a short biography and four pictures from the film.

Roy said, "I read the script and I thought is the part really worth doing? Is it something I could feel I could do something with?" Toward the end of the shooting schedule, Scheider arrived at the Alameda location for his cameo appearance:

> Now I know the audience is going to see why I wanted to play the part. A lot of it has to do with Francis [Ford Coppola], because when he spoke to me, he said, "Don't worry, we'll have some fun, we'll improvise, we'll find ways of making this guy interesting," and I thought, well if anyone can do it, he can. So let's go. When Scheider first encountered his character, he [said], "I didn't realize how evil [Keeley] was. When I read the script I felt he was an executive put in a very uncomfortable position, but this particular guy really doesn't care. He doesn't seem to have much of a conscience or a soul, and business is business and that's it."
>
> Francis felt my attitude was so unemotional, it was almost devilish. He said, "You're the devil, that's who you are. You'd sell anything, you'd do anything, you are the devil incarnate." That's the way he talked to me for the rest of the movie.[68]

About working with Coppola, Scheider said, "There's a certain quality that I think really, really great directors have of making you feel very competent, of making you feel very good about yourself, about what you are contributing to the film, making you feel very valuable and constantly reassuring you. He does it well. He's very avuncular. He's very protective. He cares about each performance and he loves everybody in the film, because it's all part of his panoply of life, of what he sees, it's all part of his picture and he loves that picture."[69]

Scheider didn't insert any biographical elements, but his blue cardigan was probably selected for its ability to make him stand out amid the sea of lawyers in dark business suits, and it worked well enough for several of the reviewers to take notice. His wife is once again blonde.

Quentin Curtis wrote, "Francis Ford Coppola ... essays a genre piece. [Coppola] takes the dreary staples of a Grisham formula ... and makes ... them something witty and pointed, if never profound. Roy Scheider [is] conscienceless calm in a blue cardigan, as the head of the insurance firm."[70]

Brian Johnson stated, "And a gallery of rich supporting roles includes Jon Voight as the insurance company's high-priced lawyer, Roy Scheider as his reptilian boss and Danny Glover as the judge."[71] "Coppola also gets fine, sometimes startling performances from Mary Kay Place, Virginia Madsen, Dean Stockwell, Teresa Wright and Roy Scheider," Jay Boyar declared.[72]

Salon.com weighed in: "There's a bevy of highly enjoyable performances by aging male actors here—Jon Voight ... Dean Stockwell ... Roy Scheider in a powder blue suit as the insurance company's loathsome CEO ... a veritable catalog of white, middle-aged turpitude."[73] Janet Maslin noticed Roy "as the insurance company's slick CEO" but did not offer any further critique of his performance.[74]

Roy's contribution to the 1997 Hamptons International Film Festival (October 13–19, 1997) consisted of a review of the documentary *Moon over Broadway* by D. A. Pennabaker in the festival's Schedule and Celebrity Guide. Scheider thought it was a good documentary, but that they needed something better than "the embarrassing lame comedy" to document and that the amount of self-delusion about the worth of the play on display was "really painful to sit and watch."[75]

Roy filmed *Better Living* in New York in late November 1997. He played a neurotic father who came home to his family after a 15-year absence and proceeded to destroy their house in a deranged quest to "make it better." Roy described his character as bonkers, the worst in masculine energy, and grew the appropriate beard for the dark role. Other biographical elements include Tom being an ex-cop, who puts efficiency above all else, with dire results. This is the first time we see Scheider on a bicycle. Max Mayer, the director said, "When it came to casting Tom, Nora's absent husband,... Scheider's name came up. None of them had a personal connection, [but] they took a shot. We sent him the script, and two days later, he called back, 'This is wonderful. I'm in. When do we start?'"[76] In late November, Roy was spotted at the New Line *Wag the Dog* premiere in the Hamptons. Michael Fleming wrote, "It was well received by the most diverse [crowd] ever assembled for a post-Thanksgiving Hamptons movie screening."[77]

Money Plays finally aired as a Movie Channel original film on January 3, 1998.[78] A combination caper and love story, the film is about Johnny Tobin, a down-on-his-luck, recently widowed casino shill, and Irene, his once-a-month hooker. She suddenly comes into money when a mob courier drops dead in her bed. Johnny is the only man she trusts. They use Tobin's knowledge of the casino trade to double the money in a gambling scheme before giving the original sum back to the mob to escape retribution. Scheider plays a believable romantic lead. He has terrific chemistry with the volatile Sonia Braga, who keeps telling him off.

The biographical elements in this film are that Tobin has a dead wife and he is ex-military. Roy makes a point of reading the newspaper, which is folded in Scheider's own distinctive reading style. His character is a neat freak, so much so that it becomes a point of contention between the characters. In a final inside joke with many layers, Roy's son, Christian, is dressed as a cowboy and ambushes his father in the supermarket as an obnoxious child with fake six-shooters. In the background, we hear the mother calling his name, but I was unable to determine if it was Brenda King calling him. Christian was credited. She was not. Scheider did two things in this film he had never done before: wear a moustache as a disguise and dress up as a Texas cowboy. *Money Plays* continued airing on cable, even after its video release in 1999. I found one review that called it "a leisurely paced thriller."[79]

On January 9, 1998, *Variety* announced Scheider's nomination for an Independent Spirit Award in the category of best supporting actor for his role of Hal in *The Myth of Fingerprints*. Roy went to the premiere of *Ragtime* on January 18.[80] "He attended a special star-studded Valentine's Day performance of *The Vagina Monologues* with his wife on February 14."[81] A series of four commercials with Scheider voiceovers for Conseco Insurance began airing on CNN and The Discovery channel.

The Myth of Fingerprints was released on video on March 1, 1998,[82] and continued to air on the Independent Film channel, the Sundance channel, and Showtime through 2001. The Independent Spirit Awards were held on March 21, 1998, and aired on the Independent Film cable channel. Scheider did not win.[83]

In March, after a very bad winter, Roy was at the forefront of beachfront homeowners protesting a moratorium on bulkheads. He appeared on cable channel 12 in New York and in several newspapers on this issue. Scheider told the *Daily News*, "I've lost 300 feet of the dune that was protecting my home. I don't own the property behind my house, so I can't move." He said he would do whatever was necessary and take his chances in court. "My concerns are the same as anyone ... on the beach."[84] Scheider didn't have to go to court. The weather got better, the beach was rebuilt with leftover snow plow money, and bulkheads were not needed.

In the early spring of 1998, Roy helped out a fellow Artists–Writers softball team player and aspiring film producer, Sam Sokolow, by doing a cameo in his low-budget, but groundbreaking film, *The Definite Maybe*. Scheider plays Eddie Jacobson, a family friend who controls the trust fund of one of the young heroes. Rather than giving Eric (Josh Lucas) a loan against his fund to save his house, Eddie tells him to grow up and make something of himself.

Scheider's wardrobe is the only thing biographical about this cameo. They are his own clothes. He did the part as a favor for free. Studio Times On Line touted *The Definite Maybe* as "winner of the Best Feature Film award [at the] 1998 New York Independent Film Festival. Two 20-something ... guys ... escape ... to the swank Hamptons for a weekend ... [and confront] the adult rules of life: fraud, attempted murder, two-faced loyalty and well-catered cocktail parties."[85]

The four-hour "Seventh Scroll" miniseries was filmed in the late spring of 1998 and to date has only aired overseas. It debuted on Italian television on January 23, 2000. Scheider plays the villain, the very rich and nasty Grant Schiller, in a race with two archaeologists to recover valuable treasure from the tomb of the pharaoh Mamose. The miniseries stars Katrina Lombard, Jeff Fahey, and Art Malik. The program was adapted from the *River God* books by Wilbur Smith. Aside from the requisite safari jacket and blonde assistant, there appears to be nothing else biographical added to this role.

On May 9, Roy planted a tree at the Hayground school in memory of his mentor, Friend Avery, who had passed away. Glenn Scheider accepted the flag from Avery's casket for the school. Danny Glover also attended.[86] "At the memorial, Elizabeth Haile, a Shinnecock elder, led students in an Indian planting ceremony, Sam Yarabek, a student, read a letter to his grandfather [a mentor], and Tohanash Tarrant read poetry. Mr. Avery's wife, Rose, and his daughter, Sherry Santefer Rosenbaum, led a procession."[87]

On May 18, 1998, ABC aired "The World's Deadliest Sea Creatures," an hour of shark, octopus, and moray eel attacks, capped by Australian crocodiles going after humans. Scheider's nonsensational and educational narration helped offset the "in-your-face"[88] video of "spine tingling encounters between people and deadly denizens of the deep."[89] The program reran on August 27, 1998, and is in syndication on the USA cable channel.

Scheider's next film project, *Silver Wolf*, was announced on May 31. Roy was listed as a costar.[90] The movie, "filmed in Vancouver in late May and June of 1998,"[91] was a coproduction of Blue Rider Pictures, which released it as a film overseas in the fall of 1998, and the Fox Family channel, which debuted it as an original film on cable in January 1999.

Silver Wolf is a "suspenseful, yet heart-warming family adventure [about] young Jesse McLain and his love for a wounded wolf. After surviving a terrifying skiing accident that takes his father's life ... Jesse risks everything to protect his new friend from ... the town's most prominent rancher, Roy Scheider."[92]

John Grisham's The Rainmaker was released to video on May 31, 1998,[93] and ran almost nonstop on cable in 1999. On June 6, Roy and his wife attended the Planned Parenthood benefit at the home of artist Ross Bleckner.[94] *The Rage* was released to video on June 16, 1998. It played briefly on the pay-per-view channel Hot Choices, but has not had any other cable airings to date. Roy went home by way of Hawaii, where he received a second award from Piper-Heidsieck. *The Definite Maybe* was shown at the Nassau Independent Film Exposition on July 19, 1998.

The *New York Times* wrote, "Showcasing 17 feature films (including the World Premiere of *The Definite Maybe* with Bob Balaban, Teri Garr, and Roy Scheider) and 43 shorts ... the festival runs through Thursday at the Malverne Cinema 4."[95]

The Peacekeeper was released on video on July 23, 1998. "Dolph Lundgren stars here, as the one guy who can save the world from nuclear annihilation. The erstwhile action star is getting a little too old for all this stuff. Only Roy Scheider and Montel Williams ... save this disaster film from, well, disaster."[96] A second video review stated, "The plot's ludicrous, but this fast-paced Dolph Lundgren actioner's got outlandish stunts and Roy Scheider as a shady Prez."[97] A third review said, "A great all-around action flick ... despite a wooden performance by Roy Schneider [*sic*] as the President and Montel Williams trying to pass as a gung-ho military man."[98]

Artists against Abuse held its third annual plate auction on July 31 to benefit the Retreat, a shelter for victims of domestic violence. Roy was among the celebrities who donated one-of-a-kind painted plates.[99] The event raised $55,000 from 63 plates.[100] Roy was a guest speaker at the "Tuesdays in August" lecture series at the Bay Street Theater in Sag Harbor.

Scheider played in his eighth Artists and Writers Celebrity Softball Game on August 22. The 50th anniversary of the game was celebrated. The Artists won 16–7.[101] Roy did a victory dance for the news cameras after the game with his three-year-old daughter, Molly, up on his shoulders. This was the second time I attended this event. Scheider obligingly stayed after the game to sign autographs for his many fans and let several have their pictures taken with him.

Christian Scheider landed his second movie role in September 1998 as Max. His part was described as a "Dennis the Menace role involving slingshots and water pistols."[102] The film is called *Of Lies and Love*, and it may not be a coincidence that his character has the same name as his half sister. Retitled *Lies ... and Love*, the film was accepted into the 21st Independent Feature Film Market in New York

City. The film screened at the Long Island Film Festival on May 5, 2001. Christian's picture was displayed on the East End Pictures web page as "a pissed-off kid."[103] The festival "World Premiere" is the only release this film had.

In October 1998, an attempt to sell *Better Living* was made at the sixth Hamptons International Film Festival. "*Better Living* fit into the general New York theme [of the festival], as it was about a Queens family."[104] Roy had a full slate at the festival. He attended both screenings of his film and made himself available for questions afterward. Scheider was then the subject of the festival event "A Conversation with..." where "Scheider discussed his beginnings as a young actor, his numerous co-stars and his experiences in making *Jaws*.... Scheider's appearance proved to be a crowd pleaser, as he charmed his way through the hour-and-a-half discussion."[105] Roy also helped honor Blake Edwards with the festival's distinguished achievement award.[106] The entire Hayground school was taken to a special screening of Charlie Chaplin's *City Lights*.[107] Scheider even found time to attend the premiere of *Elizabeth*.[108]

The Hamptons Film Festival review of *Better Living* in *Variety* said, "[The] film focuses on a loony-bird mother and her three grown daughters. Tom, their father ... mysteriously disappeared 15 years ago ... [and is] inexplicably returning home again. He [displays] his faltering fatherly instinct ... by commandeering Nora's room digging project. Thesping is first-rate. Scheider plays rigid without being stiff."[109]

In November, Roy debuted as the host of "Legends, Icons and Superstars of the 20th Century." This ten-episode series, made for digital cable, premiered on November 16 with the episode "Five Who Made a Difference." Produced by David Wolper, the series devoted eight minutes to each icon. Scheider introduced each segment and then provided voiceover narration for the newsreel footage that followed. Filmed for the T-1 digital cable channel, the series also aired three episodes on the CBS Eye on People cable channel, before that channel became Discovery People cable channel, which aired four more episodes. When this channel became the Discovery Health channel, the "Legends" series was taken off the air with three episodes remaining to be shown.

Some of the icons profiled in the series were the century's world leaders: Hitler, Eisenhower, Roosevelt, Stalin, Mao; leading peace advocates: Martin Luther King, Jr., Nelson Mandela, Mother Teresa; sports figures: Babe Ruth, Muhammad Ali, Jackie Robinson, Michael Jordan; entertainers: Frank Sinatra, Marilyn Monroe, Lucille Ball, Louis Armstrong; and other influential people who weren't so easily categorized like Albert Einstein, Marie Curie, Helen Keller, and Pablo Picasso. "The 50 legends' choices were sometimes obvious—and sometimes less so. After much debate—the panel, made up of various Time Warner writers and editors, [made their selections.]"[110] I found no reviews of this series, which was released on video October 2, 2001.

Evasive Action was released on video in Finland and in Germany under the title of *Steel Train*. The plot involves several prison inmates being transferred by train after being involved in a knife fight. Roy received first billing on the German video jacket, but he is not the hero. Scheider plays the lead villain, Enzo, and had third billing.

Enzo stages the fight to get transferred so he can attempt a prison break from the train. His escape goes awry and the train becomes a runaway, headed into Los Angeles. The convict-hero, Sinclair, played by Dorian Harewood, manages to foil Enzo's plans at every turn. He receives parole for recapturing Enzo. Scheider didn't choose to add any blatant biographical characteristics to his villain. Roy once again has a beard, as expected, for his "dark" character. His weapon of choice for retribution after he was assaulted in the prison fight is, appropriately, a baseball bat. The only other information available on this film are video plot synopses written in German and Finnish. *Evasive Action* was also released on video in the Netherlands. R. Schatt contributed the following synopsis (in German) to the internet movie database: "Five criminals are to be [moved] by train to a high [security] prison in Los Angeles. The brakes fail [and the convicts] begin a merciless fight [of] life and death."[111]

On November 21, Roy cohosted a benefit dinner for the South Fork Groundwater Task Force. He attended a tribute to Paul Robeson on November 28.

Roy plays magazine publisher Tom Heath in *The White Raven*, which aired in December 1998. The film was his fifth straight-to-cable release and his fourth HBO world premiere movie. A reporter (played by Ron Silver) is called to the deathbed of a dying Nazi war criminal. Tully is to solve the riddle of a very large diamond that has been missing since World War II. He hopes that he doesn't get killed first by everyone else looking for the diamond. *The White Raven* was released to video on December 31, 1998.[112] Roy did not invest Tom Heath with any noticeable biographical characteristics other than being driven around in a large black limousine emblazoned with his magazine's name.

Silver Wolf premiered as a Fox Family Channel original on January 10, 1999, and was Scheider's sixth feature to become a cable channel original. The first review compared the film to the "made for TV wildlife stories that were the weekly mainstay of 'The Wonderful World of Disney' in the 1970s," but the reviewer acknowledged there are "certain story and visual elements [that] give the boy-and-wolf yarn a 90s spin. *Silver Wolf* is a pretty straightforward film, relatively free of sentiment."[113]

Vancouver Today wrote, "The chief villain is rancher John (Roy Scheider). Family films usually make their villains simple and Scheider's character is all gruffness and macho posturing. *Silver Wolf* won't be collecting any best-picture Oscars, but ... as family films go, you could do a lot worse."[114] Scheider wears a baseball cap instead of a Stetson and worries about his two children. He also cooks dinner for them, but that is the extent of the film's biographical elements.

A second screening of *Better Living* at the Director's Guild in Manhattan occurred during January 14–18, 1999.[115] Billed as the best of the 1998 Hamptons Film Festival, the event lasted four nights. Roy participated in a discussion led by actor Griffin Dunne on the night *Better Living* screened. Another screening was held at the 5th Annual Avignon/NY Film Festival on April 22, 1999. Neither event gained the film a distributor, however.

On March 8, The *Hollywood Reporter* announced that "Roy Scheider and Brenda Blethyn are the latest actors to be added to the cast of HBO's *RKO 281*."[116] *Variety* announced the film the same day and added that Roy Scheider plays "the role of George Schaefer."[117] *RKO 281* was filmed in London in the spring of 1999. While he was there, Roy appeared on the ribald channel 4 British chat show "So Graham Norton."

The HBO original film *RKO 281* is about the controversy over the making of the now-classic film *Citizen Kane*. Scheider plays the beleaguered head of RKO studios. "Based in part on an 'American Experience' PBS documentary ["The Battle over Citizen Kane"], this tele-movie tells the behind-the-scenes story ... and the reasons tycoon William Randolph Hearst fought so vehemently to quash Welles' movie debut."[118]

In an article on the Broadway opening of the 1999 Goodman Theater production of Arthur Miller's *Death of a Salesman*, which Scheider attended, Roy explained why this play doesn't leave an audience depressed: "They're free and clear, at the end of the play ... it's a communicative release. That's why the Greeks did it; that's why they wrote *Electra*."[119]

In the "*Jaws* never dies" category, Roy Scheider was featured in an April 26, 1999, David Letterman "Late Show" Top Ten List on "Ten Ways to Make Religious History More Entertaining. Number 5: At the end of Jonah and the Whale, Roy Scheider blows up the whale using a pressurized oxygen tank."[120] This was not the first *Jaws* reference and it won't be the last. Madison Avenue loves *Jaws* for commercials. The most recent examples using scenes from the film or the theme music include Hyundai Tiburon, Chevy Malibu, Trident chewing gum, and Red Lobster restaurants. Roy continued his commercial voiceover work as the first spokesperson for Acuvue 2 contact lenses, regular and bifocal.

I Know a Song, a documentary made by Brenda Siemer (Roy's wife), was featured in a segment about Alzheimer's disease on the "UPN Nine News" on May 23. The Group of the South Fork's annual benefit dinner-dance and auction was held on June 19. A shark-tagging expedition with Roy Scheider went for $6,000.[121]

Chain of Command was filmed in June 1999 in Los Angeles. The production company intended to sell it straight to HBO from the outset. Scheider plays the president of the United States for the third time, without his wire-rim glasses, but still being driven around in a black limousine.

Roy attended the Cedars-Sinai Sports Spectacular while he was in LA, "a gala sports event to honor Wayne Gretsky, Tommy Hearns, Jackie Joyner-Kersee and Randall Cunningham on Sunday, June 27, at the Century Plaza Hotel and Towers. The 14th annual event brings more than 1,500 ... to honor ... top sports stars while ... [combating] genetic birth defects."[122]

In June 1999, *Money Plays* was released on video. Roy was interviewed, but said very little about the film. When Glenn Lovell asked, "How [does] it feel, at 63, to play the romantic lead?" Roy insisted, "Oh, I'm older than that, I'm 66. I do push-ups and pull-ups and a lot of stretching. I'm not building anything: I'm maintaining."[123]

In July 1999, Roy taught at the Broadway Theater Project in Tampa, Florida. He believes acting is something true students of the profession never stop practicing. Acting is the study of the human body. It's how humans express ourselves, how we look when we walk, how we look when we stand, how we look in repose. These are the physical things that reveal the inner life of a person. Scheider not only watches movies and theater productions, but he is also an alert people watcher. "This is why we do what we do. We must do it. We have to communicate. We have to touch each other with our art."[124]

Brenda Siemer interviewed Reinking for her new documentary, *A Woman's Way*, while the Scheiders were in Tampa. "Christian and Molly enjoyed a visit to Busch Gardens' Edge of Africa attraction, where an AP reporter snapped Scheider feeding the resident hippo, Cleo."[125]

On July 31, Roy participated in a first reading of Joe Pintauro's *Karma Boomerang* at Mulford Barn in East Hampton.[126] His costars were Michael Nader and Marie Masters, who also directed the reading.[127] Scheider narrated the Children's Concert of the Bridgehampton Chamber Music Festival later that same week.[128]

Roy was on WOR-AM radio on August 13 to talk about his life in the Hamptons, his career, and *RKO 281*. Scheider played in his ninth Artists and Writers Celebrity Softball Game on August 21. This was the third time I attended this event and there was a possibility the game would be called, but the participants agreed to play in the mist. Everyone had fun. Scheider was awarded an MVP watch for his play in the seventh inning. "Most of the few hundred spectators assembled ... were there to glimpse celebrities like [Alec] Baldwin, Channel 11 weatherman, Mr. G. (Irv Gikofsky), actor Roy Scheider and writer Ken Auletta. Karine Benedicto [said], 'It's an ugly day out ... watching Baldwin was a good alternative to the beach.'"[129]

That weekend Roy also hosted, with his wife, Brenda, and Kathy Engel, a scholarship benefit for the Hayground school on August 22, called "When We Were Young." Many famous writers and performers came and talked about what books influenced them as a child. For Roy, it was Huckleberry Finn's friendship with the runaway slave, Jim. Scheider gave an inspired reading to a sold-out, appreciative audience of 300. "Other event performers were Alec Baldwin, Mercedes Ruehl, Edwidge Danticat, Susan Engel, Gwendolen Hardwick, Joan Alexander, Belvie Rooks, Susan L. Taylor, Khephra Burns, Chico Hamilton, Tiye Giraud, Safiya Henderson-Holmes, Christina Dobson, Jane Comfort, and Aleta Hayes."[130]

Roy Scheider wrote:

> Three years ago, some friends gathered in our home to talk about a dream: a new school that would combine true multi-culturism [*sic*] with intellectual depth and risk. Our dream became the Hayground school in September 1996. That evening we launched our scholarship program and planted the seeds of "Who's gonna be there?"—a fundraising event that took place the following year at the Bay Street Theater. When my first mentor, Friend Avery, died last year, I initiated a Hayground scholarship in his name. Today, August 22, we initiate a new Hayground tradition. "When We Were Young" brings together actors, dancers, musicians and writers to share favorite childhood stories and to celebrate work for and about children. To make a significant difference to Hayground children, we need new scholarship pledges. I invite you to join me, Camille and Bill Cosby, Susan Sarandon, Sallie and Robert Benton, HBO, Louise and Leonard Riggio and other good friends by investing in a child's education. Join the Hayground Circle. It could be the best investment you make this summer. Thanks for coming.[131]

Roy's brother, Glenn, was also at this event. Roy told Dan Rattiner, "We are doing this because we feel it also benefits the audience of children that come to see it. We believe education without the arts is not an education."[132]

Falling Through was announced on August 2,[133] and filmed in Luxembourg in late August 1999. Roy plays the head of security at the U.S. embassy in Paris, who assigns a young officer to find out who is selling black market passports. The film put up a website, held screenings at film markets, and actually managed to find a U.S. video distributor within the year.

On September 6, 1999, *Time* announced that filmmakers Sam Sokolow and Rob Lobl had made a deal with Amazon.com, "which had just begun a program to distribute indie films. Starting this week, people will be able to buy a videocassette ... [of *The Definite Maybe*] for 14.95.... Fully owned by Sokolow and Lobl, [they] will split the sale proceeds with Amazon. 'This is a whole new avenue for filmmakers,' [said Paul Capelli, an Amazon spokesman]."[134]

"It's exciting to be the first guys who try this," said Lobl. "What makes *The Definite Maybe* so unique is that it's a theatrical independent that has gone straight to video distribution. Now they [can] reach 10 million even though it's never been shown in broad-reach theaters," said Diane Zoi, manager at Amazon Advantage.[135]

The Definite Maybe became the first film to be released digitally over the internet. The mechanics of this were discussed in a segment of the "Nightly Business Report" on PBS on November 16, when Scheider was interviewed about appearing in independent films. Roy was again in the first film of a new genre.

Courted for *Mulligan Farm*, filmed on Long Island in November, "Roy turned down the role of the family lawyer in this tale about three brothers who inherit the family land, but can't sell it."[136] "Carrier: Cities of Steel" first aired on the Discovery Channel on November 14, 1999, and has been repeated several times. The show is about "how today's aircraft carriers are built and made ready for sea. Roy Scheider narrates the one-hour show, which brings viewers a sweeping look at the birth of a carrier [from] massive steel plates at a mill in Pennsylvania through ... construction at Newport News, Virginia."[137]

RKO 281 premiered as an HBO original film on November 20, 1999, making it Scheider's seventh movie to air on the channel. The telefilm won a Golden Globe for best made-for-TV movie in January 2000.

Laura Fries said, "The real protagonists of this story are Marion Davies, played by Melanie Griffith, and RKO Studio head George Schaefer (Roy Scheider), and both actors shine in their roles."[138] "Strong support is provided by John Malkovich, Melanie Griffith and Roy Scheider," said the *New York Daily News*.[139]

Hal Boedeker called it "Rosedud," but noted the film "boasts an outstanding cast. The film's jumble of fact, gossip, and Hollywood lore is distressing, but the performances compensate somewhat for the liberties taken. Roy Scheider takes a wisely understated approach to ... stressed RKO boss George Schaefer."[140]

Terry Jackson wrote, "Its theatrical shortcuts and weak dramatic inventions will undoubtedly irritate Kane buffs. Viewed as an allegorical tale between two obsessive men who shared many of the same traits—*RKO 281* ... is worth the effort. Although [Liev] Schreiber works hard ... Malkovich and Scheider steal ... their scenes."[141]

People wrote, "The most sympathetic characters are screenwriter Herman Mankiewicz (John Malkovich) and RKO Studio boss, George Schaefer, old hands trying to balance considerations of art, business and survival."[142] Lotta Reviews stated, "Roy Scheider does an admirable job as the conflicted studio head."[143] The movie aired in England on Christmas Day 1999 on the BBC2 channel.[144]

Roy's character spends too much time being aggravated by Welles to let any biographical characteristics creep in. The 1930s setting set the wardrobe choices.

And Roy made two more films before the year ended. *Daybreak* was filmed in the fall of 1999. *The Doorway* was made in Ireland in late 1999. In five short years, Roy Scheider had established himself as a marketable star for overseas films and the ever-expanding cable market. Cable was a very smart move on Scheider's part as it extended his movie career 15 years.

—14—

Into the New Millennium

In early January 2000, Roy Scheider was hard at work on another film. "*Angels Don't Sleep Here* was a detective thriller [about] a forensic scientist, Michael Daniels, who returned home [to find] his lost twin brother, Jessie. Roy played the mayor [and] father of his childhood friend, Kate Porter. Scheider's character [turned out] to be corrupt [and] was assassinated. Daniels' blood was found at the crime scene. Michael believed the blood [was from] his missing twin. Principal photography began January 31 and the film was completed in May of 2000."[1] The movie was offered for theatrical sale in October.

Once again Scheider grew a beard to show his dark side. He also had a death scene. Roy was once asked to picture how he might die in real life. Scheider replied he wanted something very fast when he was very old. In his late eighties he would step off a curb into the street without looking to follow a young girl on the other side with gorgeous legs and get hit by a truck.

In February 2000, right before the Super Tuesday primaries, Roy contributed his voice to an ad showing a toddler walking along a beach holding his father's hand, as part of, "A one million-dollar campaign ... the largest ... ever for conservation in California." Sponsored by "The Nature Conservancy, an international nonprofit conservation group," the ad aired February 2, 2000. Scheider narrated, "Californians don't stand separate from the land. Our parks, beaches and rivers and mountains are more than just places to visit."[2] The campaign was to benefit Proposition 12 and 13 on the March 7, 2000, ballot. Roy stated, "I like to keep a low profile in my participation in politics ... actors enjoy such popularity and adulation that they have to be careful what they say, because what they say has an effect on an enormous amount of people, and they are not political experts."[3]

On March 6, 2000, Roy Scheider was once again featured in a David Letterman top ten list. "When It Was a Game" was released on DVD April 19. *RKO 281* was released on DVD and videocassette, April 24, 2000. On April 26, *Variety* announced that Roy had been cast in "the four hour miniseries 'Diamond Hunters' that began shooting in South Africa, May 15. Scheider [is] the patriarch of a family-owned diamond dynasty. 'Hunters' [was] based on a bestseller by [novelist] Wilbur Smith. Alyssa Milano and Sean Patrick Flanery co-star. The miniseries aired on France's TF1 cable [channel]."[4]

Michael Easton co-starred in this miniseries. His web site stated, "Michael Easton portrays Benedict. In the Smith novel, Benedict is the son of Scheider's patriarch character, Josephus Van Der Byl. Alyssa Milano plays his daughter. She becomes romantically involved with his other son from his first marriage, Johnny Lance, played by Sean Patrick Flanery."[5]

Like "The Seventh Scroll" before it, this miniseries has not yet sold to the American Film Market. Some other projects of Scheider's that have sold in Europe, but are not yet available in America, include German only DVD releases of *Naked Lunch* on September 1, 1999, and *The White Raven* in 2001, as well as British only DVD releases of *Executive Target* on June 5, 2000, and *Better Living* on November 5, 2001.

On May 1, Roy attended the ribbon cutting ceremony of a new soundstage in Wainscott on Long Island, called Pinewood West.[6] Alec Baldwin volunteered that both he and Roy [who was in the crowd] would enjoy "never having to leave home to make movies in Los Angeles ... and Canada." The cavernous soundstage was so named "to stop people from calling it 'Hollywood East,'" said Frazer Dougherty, president of the facility. "Scheider has been interested since the beginning in working with us."[7] Roy added, "I've already talked to the other actors and we would love to make films here, there are so many talented people in the industry right here."[8]

The ABC television network showed a three-hour 25th anniversary version of the movie *Jaws* on May 6, complete with previously deleted scenes and interview footage from the 20th anniversary laser disc. The *Jaws* 25th anniversary DVD and an expanded VHS set (two tapes) were released on July 11. The new releases contained 75 minutes of deleted scenes, outtakes and cast interviews culled from the two hours of additional material on the 1995 laserdisc.

Roy then narrated a 5-hour PBS documentary series, "Secrets of the Dead," that aired on May 15, 16 and 17, 2000. The four shows were "Catastrophe!" "Lost Vikings of Greenland," "What Happened to the Hindenberg" and "Cannibalism in the Canyon." The *New York Times* compared the four specials to "hyperventilating documentaries on the Fox Channel" and stated, "in the end, the dead keep their secrets (from the investigative scientists) and PBS keeps its dignity, just barely." The narration was overly melodramatic, "augmented by X-files graphics plus music and sound effects lifted from a 1950s horror flick."[9]

The Hollywood Reporter announced in the summer of 2000 that Roy was in talks to play Janis Joplin's manager, Alfred Grossman, in *Joplin: The Movie*. This casting had previously been announced in *Variety* in November of 1999. The movie signed Laura Theodore, Meg Tilly and the wrestler, Steve Austin,[10] but the last web page update still had Scheider in negotiations,[11] and there was no start date for the project as of March 2002.

The Encore cable channel series, "The Directors," profiled Steven Spielberg on June 7. Roy Scheider was featured in three interview clips in the segment on *Jaws*. He mentioned the sinking of the "Balsa wood boat," how the shark not working made it a better movie and talked about Spielberg.[12] Marc Lichter wrote, "He gave the world *1941*. Yes, even Steven Spielberg isn't perfect. Of course, you can hardly tell that from this documentary, which is not ... a Spielberg biography but ... a toast (albeit an entertaining one) to his famous flicks."[13]

In the June 19 issue of *People* magazine, Roy was featured in an article called "*Jaws:* 25 Years Later." A large part of each feature was a current picture of the person from the film—Roy posed with his wife and dog. Scheider said about *Jaws*, "No one anticipated ... the universal fear of water," and that "Spielberg faced enormous odds" getting the movie made. Interviewed at his ocean front home on Long Island, Roy invited the reporter to "look at these vistas. And," he added, "I don't have ... sharks." Scheider's ten-year-old son, Christian, couldn't resist chiming in. "I knew [the movie] was fake. You [are] 55, 65 percent more likely to be hit by lightning." Roy also told reporter Maria Eftimiades with typical candor, "I do like to talk about other things."[14]

The 25th anniversary of *Jaws* was the subject of several more articles throughout the summer, including an essay in *Time* by Sarah Vowell that named "A Non-Swimmer's 25 Scariest Movies," with *Jaws* topping the list.

Falling Through screened at Cannes in May of 2000 and sold directly to Blockbuster Video in the United States. The film became available for rental in September of 2000 on both VHS and DVD. Billed third, Scheider spent most of the film dispensing fatherly advice to his younger colleague, the hero.

HBO announced the premiere of *Chain of Command* on June 25, 2000, and the trailer featured Scheider very prominently. The film began its run on HBO July 22, was featured on the HBO web page and aired continuously on HBO and HBO Plus through August of 2000. *Chain of Command* was released on DVD and video, January 23, 2001, and aired on pay-per-view in March, April and May of 2001, before moving to regular cable where it aired for the rest of 2001, and into 2002.

There were no reviews of Scheider's performance, only video web sites plot synopses. Scheider had first billing and played President Jack Cahill. Cahill was an unrepentant womanizer. His blatant infidelities led one of his secret service agents to seek a change of assignment to guard the president's nuclear command briefcase. When Cahill visited the president of Taiwan to broker a peace deal with China, he was kidnapped. The briefcase was used to fire missiles on China in an attempt to take over the Chinese government. This coup failed, at a terrible cost, as Washington and Beijing were destroyed by nuclear missiles.

There are a few biographical elements. Cahill's first infidelity is a blonde. The president is shown working out and is a former professor. Finally, Cahill smokes, a sure sign he is not heroic.

In DVD commentary released in January 2001, director John Terletsky and star Patrick Muldoon talked about their experience working with Scheider. Terletsky was well aware of Roy's career and it was a huge thrill for him to direct the actor. Roy was professional, incredibly easy to work with and his experience and camera savvy were invaluable to Terletsky. Roy knew all the moves. The director said he was very fortunate with his entire cast, they brought more to his "low budget action film," than he could have hoped for. With a two million dollar budget and only 18 shooting days, Terletsky was justifiably proud of what they did. He loved the way several of the actors—Roy, Susan Blakely, John Beck, and William Moses—were able to bring history and craft to the work he wanted for the film.

Muldoon was "thrilled" to be working with Scheider as he was a huge *Jaws* fan. Both men jokingly mentioned *Jaws* several times in their commentary. Terletsky noted Roy's favorite scene was the president having sex with a campaign contributor's young blonde wife up against the wall in the tennis club bathroom. Keeping the joke alive, Terletsky said Scheider's second favorite scene was having sex with the flight attendant on board the plane. It was hard to tell who was more pleased at all the "action" Roy was getting, Scheider or his co-workers. Muldoon's first scene was with Scheider and while Patrick was nervous, he got through it, only to have the presidential seal on the wall fall off in the middle of the scene and ruin that take. The director said most of his film's plot was taken from current news headlines.[15]

On July 27, *The French Connection* was shown in Los Angeles as part of the "AFI Associates Classic American Film series held at Arnie Morton's The Steakhouse. The evening raised money for the American Film Institute. Tickets were 100.00."[16]

Better Living was released to theaters on August 4 for one week in New York and Los Angeles. The *New York Times* said, "Everyone is a little crazy in a way that is intended to be ingratiating. Skin-deep quirkiness is not always adorable ... when everyone has been conceived as a 'character.' [The film] is jam packed with sarcasm. Any sense of reality is undermined by the shouting matches."[17]

The *Christian Science Monitor* stated, "Not even veteran talents like Dukakis and Scheider can surmount the artificial dialogue, arbitrary plots twists, and wan humor of this disappointing comedy-drama."[18] The *Bergen County Record* added, "[It's] a comedy that's too shrill to be much fun and too silly to be much of a drama. The characters are merely the sum of their quirks and the story depends too much on their dopey behavior."[19] Long Island *Newsday* wrote, "[Dukakis, Scheider and Herrman] struggle to out eccentric each other in a ghastly domestic comedy that is never as wacky or as profound as it wants us to think it is. [The film is] ill-served by director-screenwriter Max Mayer, who slides from cutesy to shrill in short order."[20]

Newhouse News Service in a capsule review stated, "Long gone reprobate dad (seedy-suave Roy Scheider) returns to recruit his dotty wife ... and three resentful daughters into a ... survivalist cult. Playwright George Walker's plodding satirical parable of patriarchy/nationalism /fascism never comes to life."[21] Elizabeth Weitzman said, "The only amusing thing ... [is that] it's billed as a comedy. It's not that the jokes aren't funny—you just can't find them. Scheider fares the best—simply because he is so far removed from the proceedings. There's got to be a better way to make a living."[22]

Also on August 4, "The Westhampton Beach Performing Arts Center [offered] *Karma Boomerang* [an encore reading of] Joe Pintauro's new work, starring Mercedes Ruehl and Roy Scheider."[23] *Dan's Papers* added "Michael Nader and Rebecca Roberts" to the cast list.[24] "After nine months of rewrites and working steadily with actors Roy Scheider, [and others, the playwright, said after the first reading], 'the blackness was there as well as the comedy, but poignancy and self-knowledge [had] failed to surface ... thank goodness for actors like these, who dig and claw, [and are] so doggedly committed.'"[25]

On Aug. 13, the 2nd annual Hayground Circle scholarship benefit, "When We Were Young," was held. "Roy was the host and read from Edgar Allan Poe's 'The Bells.' 'Nappy Hair' was read in tandem by Kate Capshaw and her daughter Jessica. Other performers [were] Chico Hamilton, Marsha Norman ... Daisy Mayer, Tiye Giraud ... Susan Engel, Latisha Ellis and Toukie Smith."[26] The *East Hampton Star* reported the benefit "drew a festive crowd of 200 ... [and] the event was reported to have taken in 70,000.00 for the school."[27]

On August 15, Scheider filmed *The Good War* in Bulgaria. Roy played Col. John Gartner, the commandant of the Hereford, Texas, Italian Prisoner of War camp. One prisoner, Luigi Marin, escaped, telling the outside world of the starvation rations the prisoners are being forced to endure. Recaptured, Marin was returned to the camp, but all the prisoners have been transferred. Only the Colonel remained. "As the rest of the world celebrates peace, Luigi and Gartner are trapped in the middle of nowhere ... and forced to spend the night alone in the abandoned camp. For them, the war continues."[28] Camp Hereford was the place, "where most of the non cooperator [Italian] officers were gathered"[29] and put on starvation rations by the United States government. Filming ended on September 16, 2000. The film was shown at Cannes in May of 2001 and has representation to market the film in the U.S. *The Good War* has sold to several overseas markets, was screened at the Venice Film Festival in August of 2001 and had an Italian premiere, January 16, 2002.

"Fox News Live" ran a piece called "The Hollywood Shuffle" on September 12 about film release delays because of post production problems or a sudden current event (a bombing, a hostage situation or the World Trade Center) that would damage the box office receipts of a movie about that particular subject if it came out at that time. After a clip of *Better Living* was shown, Roy said, "It gets confusing, because you forget what movie you just did and what wasn't released."[30] *Good War* was offered for sale at the American Film Market February 18–24, 2002.

On October 24, *The Doorway* was released on video. "The film ... boasts a fairly long cameo by Roy Scheider, he plays a professor who is an expert of the occult. *The Doorway* at times seems lost between a horror film and ... *Scary Movie*. As a B film, it is what it is and does not pretend to be something else."[31] Ed Hulse wrote, "Another strictly by-the-numbers low budget genre film ... [it] has ... enough gore and sex [for] undiscriminating renters. Scheider fans, however will be disappointed, since the movie is almost half over before he appears and he barely gets 20 minutes of screen time. That doesn't warrant top billing."[32] The director, Michael Druxman, admitted the film was made primarily to capitalize on the popularity of *The Blair Witch Project*. Playing a professor and his wardrobe are the biographical bents in Scheider's character.

Roy narrated the first of three episodes for the PBS Series "Nova," on October 24. The first program detailed the salvage of the Civil War armored combat vessel, *The Monitor*, and was called, "Lincoln's Secret Weapon." There were no reviews of this program. The second program Scheider narrated was "Hitler's Lost Sub." It aired on November 14, 2000, and was a two-hour special on John Chatterton's six year quest to identify the sunken U-boat he found off the coast of New Jersey. The one review I found did not mention Scheider. The third program was "Nazi Prison Escape," about Allied prisoners held in Colditz Castle. This program aired February 6, 2001. It received an excellent review. Hal Boedeker applauded the film makers for their use of surviving Colditz inmates and their perfect blend of history and science. Many of the methods the prisoners used are demonstrated in recreations, including a glider. "Nazi Prison Escape will impress fans of World War II films ... *Stalag 17* and *The Great Escape*."[33]

Scheider was also interviewed for a "Bravo Profile," on Gene Hackman. The program began airing on the Bravo cable channel in December 2000 and was rerun in January 2001 with another showing in July. Roy finished 2000 by assisting the Hayground students in staging "A Midsummer's Night's Dream" on December 15 and 16, 2000. *The East Hampton Star* wrote, "There will be [two] performances at the Bay Street Theater in Sag Harbor. The performances are open to the public."[34]

Roy was the special guest of the playwright in residence, Joe Pintauro, at St. Mary's College in Indiana on February 13, 2001. *All That Jazz* was screened and there was a question and answer with the students after the screening. 20th Century Fox may release a restored version of the film on DVD and sent a film crew to tape Scheider's session as a possibility for an extra.[35]

Roy became the "poster boy" for "a fitness regime based on the Stanislavsky (acting) method" in March. He told the *London Times*, "Ten years ago ... we were going to have a baby. I created a new character for myself ... and I literally gave up smoking overnight. I told myself, 'He wouldn't be that dumb,' and it worked."[36] Scheider is working with teachers at the Stella Adler School to bring the program to the masses. Dr. Alexander Shaknovich is overseeing the clinical trials in New York and Dr. Ronald Marsden will do the trials in St. Petersburg, Russia. Anchor International came out with a book on this technique, written by Marshall Yeager, that was published in October of 2001. Roy is quoted in the book several times and is pictured on the front cover.

Roy began filming *King of Texas* for Turner Network Television on April 19, 2001.[37] This TNT original film transplants the story of King Lear to 1840 Texas. "John Lear, a wealthy, megalomaniacal rancher, challenges his three daughters to prove their loyalty ... to claim their inheritance. When the youngest daughter refuses ... Lear disowns her, unwittingly causing his own downfall." The film stars Patrick Stewart as Lear, Marcia Gay Harden, Lauren Holly and Julie Cox as the daughters and Patrick Bergin as Rebecca's (Holly's role) brutal husband, Hightower. Roy Scheider plays Westover, "a neighboring rancher who tries to save Lear from himself." Matt Lescher plays Emmett, Scheider's ruthless son, and David Alan Grier is Rip, a "razor-tongued ranch hand."[38] TNT first aired the film on June 2, 2002, and heavily promoted it beforehand on their Rough cut website (www.roughcut.com/Movies/KingofTexas) and on the Hallmark Entertainment Website (www.hallmarkent.com). Scheider spoke to polo.com magazine about his role in *King of Texas* in December of 2001. "I've just completed a project filmed in Mexico. The stories and the characters are exactly parallel to [King Lear], the only thing we don't have is the glorious Shakespearean language. The story is set in 1842 in Texas, about a year after The Alamo. The clothes don't look like the Westerns we are accustomed to; they look Spanish. Patrick Stewart and I are the patriarchs of these families. It's a very good cast. They sent me the script. At first, I thought it was rather bold ... but then I read and realized it still kept the integrity of the play. There was no attempt to soften what is basically a very dark story and a very deep, deep tragedy."[39]

Angels Don't Sleep Here was offered at the American Film Market, February 22, 2001 and released on DVD, May 8, 2001. Roy played Harry S. Porter, a third generation mayor with ties to the mafia. Porter paid a policeman to protect him and they share a dark secret. This secret cost Harry the love of his terminally ill wife and has estranged him from his grown daughter. When Michael Daniels' return and the death of Mrs. Porter revealed the secret, Mayor Porter was killed to stop his daughter from exposing the conspiracy and incriminate both men in the murder. Roy did not have enough screen time to add many biographical elements to his dapper villain, but it's clear his character still loved his invalid wife and daughter, even if he can't give up his corrupt ambitions. Once again he had a blonde secretary who went everywhere with him in a large black limousine. The autopsy report of Porter, per Roy's usual, stated his age as three years younger and had him six feet tall. I could not find any reviews of this DVD.

"When It Was a Game 2" was released on DVD, May 1, 2001. *Jaws 2* was released on DVD, May 22. The second *Jaws* DVD included a "making of" featurette, a documentary, deleted scenes, production notes, talent bios, the trailer, story boards and shark facts.[40] The commentary was mostly from director Jeannot Szwarc, Joe Alves, the production designer and producers Richard Zanuck and David Brown. A special feature by Keith Gordon told of the "teen" experience. Scheider was mentioned, but he did not contribute to this DVD.

Roy was featured as one of the commentators on the third American Film Institute special, "100 years, 100 Thrills" that aired on CBS, June 12, 2001. He talked about three films, two of his own, *The French Connection* (#8) and *Jaws* (#2), and *The Maltese Falcon* (#26). Another one of Roy's films, *Marathon Man*, was #50 on the list. Clips of Scheider's famous "you need a bigger boat," scene from *Jaws* and the hot dog vendor from *The French Connection* were shown.

On June 30, Scheider and his wife Brenda attended a benefit for Phoenix House. Roy made an appearance on the Joan Hamburg Show (WOR 710 AM) on July 27. The Hayground students put on *The Duke, the Bard and You* as their third fund-raising effort for the Scholarship Fund on August 5. They started with cocktails at 5:00 P.M., then did excerpts from a *Midsummers Night's Dream* at 6:00 with Roy as master of ceremonies. The sold out night ended with dinner and dance music from Art Baron and the Duke's Men.[41]

Mishima: A Life in Four Parts was released on DVD August 7, 2001, without Roy's narration track. On August 10, Roy narrated a profile of author Jules Verne on the Learning Channel's "Great Books" series. Scheider pitched at the 52nd annual Artists and Writers Celebrity Softball Game in East Hampton on August 18. *People* magazine gave Alec Baldwin the loss when he missed a fly ball in the bottom of the eighth inning. "I blew it," he told *People*'s Marianne V. Stochmal. "That hurt," teammate Roy Scheider ... agreed. "We love to beat those writers," he said, "even though we didn't today." The Writers ... [defeated] the Artists 10–7.[42] After the game, Scheider attended a benefit for the Hamptons Shakespeare Festival in Montauk.

The movie *Daybreak* was released straight to DVD on August 21. Starring most American TV stars for the European film market—Adam Wylie ("Picket Fences"), Jamie Bergman ("Son of the Beach") and Ken Olandt ("Superforce")—the film is about passengers on board an L.A. subway train wrecked in an earthquake. They must find a way out before the tunnels fill with water. The DVD included a gallery of production stills, cast/crew biographies and a trailer.

A review on the Internet Movie Data Base said, "Roy Scheider is the head of the transit authority, and deserves better. He makes the most of what he has to work with. Mix equal parts of *The Poseidon Adventure* and *Daylight*, mix in really bad dialogue and acting, [and you have] *Daybreak*."[43] Buzz McClain wrote, "This amusing low-budget disaster movie recalls the great disaster flick of the '70's. Given the budget limitations, the dangers the survivors encounter are ... well-rendered and clever. With just enough thrills ... *Daybreak* is for those who fondly remember ... Charlton Heston dangling from a 747."[44]

Scheider's supporting role is mostly giving pep talks to his trapped maintenance scheduler (Ted McGinley) and trying to rescue the trapped passengers. The deputy mayor (Olandt) is the villain and keeps thwarting Scheider's efforts. There are several confrontations between Scheider and the deputy mayor and believable chemistry between Scheider and McGinley, who previously worked together in *Wild Justice*. The film can't make up its mind whether or not it wants to be an action thriller or a character study. The trapped passengers all have major issues that they have to work out: McGinley's child was killed, the nurse was raped, etc. This makes the film overly histrionic between the action scenes of escaping from fire, flood, downed power lines and explosive toxic waste. One of the passengers (Mark Kiely) is such an obnoxious, macho jerk that his demise is a blessing. I did not find any biographical elements slipped into Scheider's role.

The *Marathon Man* DVD was released August 28. Peter Bracke wrote in his DVD review about the added features that the documentary "The Magic of Hollywood, the Magic of People" was "pretty funny and self-congratulatory, [with] rare [and] interesting behind-the-scenes footage. [A] rather bizarre look at the acting process ... plays [more] like a PSA for SAG."

Bracke also reviewed the second documentary, "Going the Distance: Remembering Marathon Man" favorably, saying "it is Keller's, Scheider and ... Hoffman's recollections on working together ... and moving remembrances [of] the late Laurence Olivier that fascinate." About the rehearsal footage, Bracke said, "I love this stuff ... but some may find it boring ... comments are cut in with Scheider and Keller discussing their process and offering additional perspective."[45] To date, this is most participation Scheider has filmed for DVD special features.

The Encore cable channel showed all four *Jaws* films in succession all day long on Labor Day from 5:00 A.M. September 3 to 2:00 September 4 with the tag-line, Jaws 4–People 0. *Silver Wolf* was released on DVD, September 4.

20th Century–Fox released two versions of *The French Connection* on DVD for the film's 30th anniversary on September 25, 2001. The first is a two-disc Five Star Collection set that includes two documentaries, "Making the Connection: The Untold Stories of *The French Connection*" and the BBC's "Poughkeepsie Shuffle." There are also seven deleted scenes with commentary from director William Friedkin, a still gallery and an audio commentary track that included Friedkin, Gene Hackman and Roy Scheider. The other DVD release is a set of both films, *The French Connection* and *French Connection II*, without any special features.

Roy was interviewed by the *Houston Chronicle* and the *Philadelphia Inquirer* for comments on the 25th anniversary DVD release and to recall his filming experience. He told Bruce Westbrook (*Houston Chronicle)* the film had "a gritty street-level reality ... it was guerrilla filmmaking. Friedkin was impatient. He couldn't wait for permits and paperwork, so we stole shots, sometimes filming illegally. The Situation caused ... traffic jams, yet New Yorks' finest helped out. Plus the real cops [Sonny Grosso and Eddie Egan] were on the set daily."[46] Scheider also mentioned that he had watched the DVD of *The French Connection* and was pleased to see that it had held up, but he didn't know himself, mostly because he was so young when he did it.

"It was the first picture that dealt seriously with ... drugs. No one had dramatized a story like that. The film was done in a documentary, hard-hitting style. The cops were human and understandable, and they were as tough as the crooks,"[47] Scheider said to Desmond Ryan (*Philadelphia Inquirer)*. Ryan wrote that the pairing of Hackman and the feisty Scheider—who once considered making his living in baseball or boxing—was the template for the modern cop/buddy film. Scheider's participation in the documentary was an interview from a program filmed in the early eighties and the stories he related have already been told in an earlier chapter.

The first 30th Anniversary showing of *The French Connection* occurred on the Fox Movie Channel on September 30, 2001. The channel started with *The Seven Ups*, which is apparently considered a sequel by Fox, then debuted the documentary, showed the movie and concluded the evening with *French Connection II.* Fox showed the documentary and film again in December.

The channel touted their "complete" *French Connection* series on their web page for the entire month of September, with flash pictures of Scheider's interview from the "Making the Connection: The Untold Stories of *The French Connection*" documentary. A new 35mm print of *The French Connection* was also screened as part of an eight-week Film Forum series on the NYPD on Oct. 4 in New York City.

The 2001 Hamptons International Film Festival was held October 17–21 and a special memorial was held for Jeff Salaway, the East Hampton restaurant owner and community activist who was one of the key founders of the Festival. Salaway was killed in an automobile accident and will be sorely missed, not only by the festival, but by the Hayground School, which he also helped found. A memorial scholarship in Salaway's name was established at the school in his memory and all memorial donations tendered at his funeral were given to this fund.[48]

Roy was announced as having a role in the independent film, *Love Thy Neighbor.* Directed by Nicholas Gregory, the son of Andre Gregory (*My Dinner with Andre*), Nicholas is making his directorial debut. Roy's penchant for working with first time director's continues. Reuters reported Scheider had a supporting role in the story about "two couples who are [enduring] domestic monotony. When one of the husbands has an affair with the wife of the other man, his dangerous game unravels the couple's world and introduces the possibilities of AIDS."[49] Updates can be found at lovethyneighborthemovie.com.

The Fox Movie Channel aired *The Seven Ups* as a birthday tribute to Roy on November 10 at midnight. Not to be outdone, the Thrillermax channel showed *Chain of Command.*

On November 27, the movie *Time Lapse* was released straight to DVD by Lion's Gate Films. The only publicity for this film came from the Blockbuster web site. Scheider had first billing above the title and played special agent Quinton La Nova of the NSA who is caught in an illegal arms sale by one of his best agents, Clayton Pierce (William McNamara).

Pierce refused to complete the sale after he found he was transferring a nuclear trigger. He is wounded after he is notified via his wire that his cover is blown. During Pierce's recovery, he was given the drug Oblivion and lost his memory of the last three years. He is forced to recover the trigger and beat a murder charge before La Nova eliminates everyone who can clear him of the frame, including his supposedly dead partner Simon, his ex-wife Kate and his doctor.

Roy was quite ruthless as the villain, killing the doctor at point blank range and directly ordering the deaths of several others. Pierce is able to piece together the chess clues to gain the antidote to the drug and stop La Nova from completing the sale in the fiery checkmate finale.

The first web review called the film "the first *Memento* clone to appear in the grade-b world." The review also stated while there is an antidote to the drug "Oblivion," there isn't one for the film's plot, calling it "confusing and barely watchable."[50] Ed Hulse wrote, "Worth's thriller is technically proficient but lacks scope and originality. Scheider plainly walks through his role and even the least astute viewer will peg him for the heavy within minutes of his first appearance on the screen."[51]

On December 19, 2001, Librarian of Congress James Billington announced the 2001 addition of 25 new films to the National Film Registry. Two films of Scheider's (*Jaws* and *All That Jazz*) made the list. The National Film Registry was established by the Library of Congress in 1988 to "preservation film deemed culturally, historically or esthetically important. Each year the National Film Preservation Board selects 25 films to add. Public nominations are welcome." The only other criteria is the film must be 10 years old.[52]

The wide-screen DVD of *Russia House* was released on December 26, 2001, but contained no special features. Scheider narrated the first of two shows of the documentary series "The Feds: U.S. Postal Inspectors" on January 4, 2002. The series is an "inside look at Federal Postal Inspectors from the front lines of the war on crime."[53] *Klute* was released on wide-screen DVD on February 5, 2002. Roy guest starred on the TV series "Third Watch" February 25 and March 4. He was signed for the film *Bulls Night Out* in March of 2002. He is also in one of the sequels to *Dracula 2000* due in theaters in early 2003.

Scheider loves acting. He continues to work on the stage, screen and in television. He is an active member of the Hayground Council, has served on the Advisory Board of the Hamptons International Film festival and often attends Hamptons movie premieres and charity benefits. Roy's career has been long and varied. He was named one of the "50 Greatest Movie Heroes of All Time," in the March 2001 issue of *Total Film* magazine. His other contributions to the movies in the last 35 years have been well documented.

Variety stated that seven of his films, *The French Connection, Klute, Jaws, Jaws 2, The Seven-Ups, Marathon Man* and *All That Jazz*, have grossed over half a billion dollars. *Jaws* was the first motion picture to make one hundred million dollars. Roy is happy with his career and considers himself lucky, having made a great adventure film, *Jaws*, a ground-breaking police film, *The French Connection*, and an offbeat and courageous musical, *All That Jazz*. In a December 2001 interview, Roy said, "You have to consider my age. They are not writing many parts for 60- to 68-year-old guys. So I have more or less become a character man. My work now is mostly supporting roles. Occasionally, a film comes along like ... *The Good War*. I was one of the co-leads in it. That will become rarer and rarer as I age. My relationship to the business is a bit different than it used to be."[54]

So is anything left undone? Roy has never considered acting work ... although he works very hard at it. Roy believes his job is to act, period. The actor is important to society. When Scheider began, he didn't see movie-making in his future, but was content to earn a modest living in the theater. Scheider never had a formal acting lesson. He learned to act by going to the movies. He imitated everybody he saw—Cary Grant, James Stewart, Fred MacMurray. He never has a line memorized until he has the physical motion to go with it. When he gets his body going the right way, the line is his. The "as if" is the most important direction he can get. Finding the right "as if" for the moment is crucial, because then the child in him will make him do it right.

A person isn't interesting if they don't keep in contact with life. With maturity, one gets richer, deeper, more expansive. Scheider realized he was unique, but it took years. The minute an actor starts believing how wonderful he is, he stops learning. "If ... you're doing it for awards, you're in a lot of trouble. You have to be doing it because you love it, and it's your way of communicating and making contact with your fellow human being. It's very nice to receive awards because they are tokens of appreciation. But if you need to be rewarded from the outside to satisfy your inside, then you are not functioning properly ... the satisfaction that I get out doing the work myself is the most paramount thing. That doesn't mean I wouldn't accept any award given to me."[55]

"People constantly amaze me, they're full of surprises ... they ... have a great desire for dignity. They want to be loved ... and praised and they don't want to hear any criticism. People laughing, people loving, people ... passionate about something—I don't care what it is. That's what makes us special ... our passion ... when you sit with someone who's really, really excited about something—it's infectious ... you can't help but get involved in it." "[I don't like] cynicism, self-pity, mean-spiritedness, poverty, lack of opportunity, fighting [and] war."[56]

Roy says, "The Theater lies like the truth. That's Harold Clurman's phrase. The Theater lies because it expands the truth. And by expanding and dramatizing the truth, it makes it more than just the facts. That's what writers do. That's what actors do. That's what I do."[57]

Filmography

Curse of the Living Corpse (20th Century–Fox, 1964); *Producers:* Del Tenney and Alan V. Iselin; *Director and Writer:* Del Tenney; *Photography:* Richard Hilliard; *Editors:* Jack Hirschfield and Gary Youngman; *Music:* Bill Holmes. 84 minutes.

CAST: Helen Waren (Abigail Sinclair), Roy R. Scheider (Phillip Sinclair), Margot Hartman (Vivian Sinclair), Robert Milli (Hugh Sinclair), Hugh Franklin (James Benson), Candace Hilligoss (Deborah Benson), William J. Blood (Minister), Jane Brice (The Cook), George Cotton (Constable Winters), Linda Donovan (Letty Crews), Paul Haney (Constable Barnes), J. Frank Lucas (Seth Lucas), Dino Narizzano (Robert Harrington).

Paper Lion (United Artists, 1968); *Producer:* Stuart Millar; *Director:* Alex March; *Screenplay:* Lawrence Roman, based on the book by George Plimpton; *Photography:* Morris Hartzband; *Editor:* Louis San Andres; *Music:* Roger Kellaway. 107 minutes.

CAST: Alan Alda (George Plimpton), Lauren Hutton (Kate), Alex Karras (Himself), David Doyle (Oscar), Ann Turkel (Susan), Frank Gifford (Himself), Vince Lombardi (Himself), John Gordy (Himself), Sugar Ray Robinson (Himself). The entire 1967 season Detroit Lions football team play themselves. Roy Scheider received no credit for his role as a magazine writer.

Star! (20th Century–Fox, 1968); *Producer:* Saul Chapin; *Director:* Robert Wise; *Screenplay:* William Fairchild; *Photography:* Ernest Laszlo; *Editor:* William Reynolds; *Music:* Lennie Hayton. 175 minutes.

CAST: Julie Andrews (Gertrude Lawrence), Richard Crenna (Richard Aldrich), Michael Craig (Sir Anthony Spencer), Daniel Massey (Noel Coward), Robert Reed (Charles Fraser), Bruce Forsyth (Arthur Lawrence), Beryl Reid (Rose), John Collin (Jack Roper), Alan Oppenheimer (Andre Charlot), Richard Karlan (David Holtzmann), Lynley Laurence (Billie Carleton), Garrett Lewis (Jack Buchanan), Elizabeth St. Clair (Jeannie Banks), Jenny Agutter (Pamela Roper), Anthony Eisley (Ben Mitchell), Jock Livingston (Alexander Woolcott), J. Pat O'Malley (Dan), Harvey Jason (Bert), Damian London (Jerry Paul), Richard Angarola (Cesare), Mathilda Calnan (Dorothy). Roy Scheider received no credit for his summer stock theater director. Others who received no credit: Ian Abercrombie (Cockney singer), Conrad Bain (Salesman at Cartiers), Ballard Berkeley, Eric Brotherson, Peter Church (Newsreel Narrator), Cathleen Cordell (Fashion Show Vendeuse), Don Crighton (Limehouse

Blues Dance Partner), Linda Dano, Bernard Fox (Assistant to Lord Chamberlain), Jan Gernat (Stage Manager), Shelah Hackett, Ann Hubbell (Beryl), Robin Hughes (Hyde Park Speaker), Pamela Kosh (Woman on Bus), Jeanette Landis (Eph), Anna Lee (Hostess), Lester Mack, Murray Matheson (Bankruptcy Judge), Lester Matthews (Lord Chamberlain), Ellen Plasschaert (Moo), Dinah Ann Rogers (Molly), Barbara Sandland (Mavis). Edited Version: ***Those Were the Happy Times***. 120 minutes.

Stiletto (Avco Embassy, 1969); *Producer:* Norman Rosemont; *Director:* Bernard Kowalski; *Screenplay:* A. J. Russell, based on the novel by Harold Robbins; *Photography:* Jack Priestly; *Executive Producer:* Joseph E. Levine; *Editors:* Frank Mazzola and Stuart Chasmar; *Music:* Sid Ramin. 98 minutes.

CAST: Alex Cord (Cesare), Britt Ekland (Illeana), Patrick O'Neal (Baker), Joseph Wiseman (Matteo), Barbara McNair (Ahn Dessie), John Dehner (Simpson), Titos Vandis (Tonio), Edwardo Ciannelli (Don Andrea), Roy Scheider (Bennett), Lincoln Kilpatrick (Hannibal Smith), Luke Andreas (Macy), Dominic Barto (Franchini), James Tolkan (Edwards), Louis Elias (Mann). Amaru (Rosa), Leonardo Cimono (Allie Fargo), Michelina Martel (Blonde At Casino), Luis Antonio Martinez (John Vanicola), Charles Durning, M. Emmett Walsh, Raul Julia, Olympia Dukakis and Ken Tilles received no credit for their roles.

Loving (Columbia Pictures, 1969); *Producer:* Don Devlin; *Director:* Irving Kershner; *Screenplay:* Don Devlin, based on the novel by J. M. Ryan; *Photography:* Gordon Willis; *Executive Producer:* Raymond Wagner; *Editor:* Robert Lawrence; *Music:* Bernardo Segall. 90 minutes.

CAST: George Segal (Brooks), Eva Marie Saint (Selma), Sterling Hayden (Lepridon), Kennan Wynn (Edward), Nancie Phillips (Nelly), Janis Young (Grace), David Doyle (Will), Paul Sparer (Marve), Andrew Duncan (Willy), Sherry Lansing (Susan), Roland Winters (Plommie), Edgar Stehli (Mr. Kramm), Calvin Holt (Danny), Mina Kolb (Diane), Mrs. Shavelson (Diana Douglas), David Ford (Al), James Manis (Charles), Martin Hulsewit (Ted), John Fink (Brad), William Duffy (Jay), Irving Selbst (Renny), Martin Friedburg (Roger), Lorraine Cullen (Lizzie), Cheryl Bucher (Hannah), Ed Crowley (Mr. Shavelson), Roy Scheider (Skip), Sab Shimono (Bryon), Eileen O'Neill (Cindy), Diane Davies (Barbie).

Puzzle of a Downfall Child (Universal, 1970); *Producer:* John Foreman; *Director:* Jerry Schatzberg; *Screenplay:* Carole Eastman from her story (as Adrien Joyce); *Photography:* Adam Holender; *Editor:* Evan A. Lottman; *Music:* Michael Small. 104 minutes.

CAST: Faye Dunaway (Lou Andreas Sand), Barry Primus (Aaron Reinhardt), Viveca Lindfors (Paula Galba), Barry Morse (Dr. Galba), Roy Scheider (Mark), Ruth Jackson (Barbara Casey), John Heffernan (Dr. Sherman), Sydney Walker (Psychiatrist), Clark Burke Holder (Davy Bright), Shirley Rich (Peggy McCavage), Emerick Bronson (Fallo), Joe George (Man in Bar), John Eames (Doctor), Harry Lee (Mr. Wong), Jane Halloren (Joan), Susan Willis (Neighbor), Barbara Carrera (T. J. Brady), Sam Schacht (George). This film was unavailable for preview.

Klute (Warner Brothers, 1971); *Producer and Director:* Alan J. Pakula; *Writers:* Andy and Dave Lewis; *Photography:* Gordon Willis; *Editor:* Carl Lerner; *Music:* Michael Small. 114 minutes.

CAST: Jane Fonda (Bree Daniels), Donald Sutherland (John Klute), Charles Cioffi (Peter Cable), Roy Scheider (Frank Ligourin), Dorothy Tristan (Arlyn Page), Rita Gam (Trina), Vivian Nathan (Psychiatrist), Nathan George (Lt. Trask), Shirley Stoller (Mama Reese), Jane White (Janey Dale), Morris Strassberg (Mr. Goldfarb), Barry Snider (Berger), Anthony Holland (Actor's Agent), Richard Shull (Sugarman), Betty Murray (Holly Gruneman), Fred Burrell (Man in Chicago Hotel), Jean Stapleton (Goldfarb's Secretary), Robert Milli, (Tom Gruneman), Robert Ronan (Off-Broadway Director), Richard Ramos (Stage Manager), Antonia Ray (Mrs. Vasek, Landlady), Jan Fielding (Psychiatrist's Secretary). Margaret Linn (Evie), Rosalind Cash (Pat), Lee Wallace (Nate Goldfarb), Mary Louise Wilson

(Ad Agency Secretary), Joe Silver (Dr. Spangler), Tony Major (Bill Azure), Kevin Dobson, Veronica Hamel and Sylvester Stallone received no credit.

The French Connection (20th Century–Fox, 1971); *Producer:* Philip D'Antoni; *Director:* William Friedkin; *Screenplay:* Ernest Tidyman, based on the book by Robin Moore; *Photography:* Owen Roizman; *Executive Producer:* G. David Schine; *Editor:* Jerry Greenburg; *Music:* Don Ellis. 104 minutes.

CAST: Gene Hackman (Jimmy "Popeye" Doyle), Fernando Rey (Alain Charnier), Roy Scheider (Buddy "Cloudy" Russo), Tony Lo Bianco (Sal Boca), Marcel Bozzuffi (Pierre Nicoli), Frederic De Pasquale (Devereaux), Bill Hickman (Mulderig), Anne Rebbot (Marie Charnier), Harold Gary (Joel Weinstock), Arlene Farber (Angie Boca), Eddie Egan (Lt. Walt Simonson), Andre Ernotte (Maurice La Valle), Sonny Grosso (Officer Klein), Benny Marino (Lou Boca), Pat McDermott (Howard, Chemist), Allan Weeks (Drug Pusher), Al Fann (Undercover Agent), Irving Abrahams (Police Mechanic), Robert Weil, (Auctioneer), Randy Jurgensen (Police Sergeant), William Coke (Motorman), The Three Degrees (Sheila Ferguson, Fayette Pinkney and Valerie Holiday). Sarina C. Grant (Hooker on the Street), Eric Jones (Little Boy), Lora Mitchell (Woman with Baby Carriage), Maureen Mooney (Bicycle Girl), Silvano Nolemi (Dock Worker), Darby Lloyd Rains (Stripper), Burt Richards (Auction Bidder), Robert Weil (Auctioneer) and Melba Tolliver (Reporter) received no credit.

The French Conspiracy aka ***L'Attendat*** aka ***Plot*** (Cine Globe, 1973); *Producers:* Guiliani G. De Negri and Tullio Odevaine; Yvon Guebel; *Director:* Yves Biosset; *Screenplay:* Ben Barzman, Basilio Franchina and Jorge Semprun; *Photography:* Ricardo Aronovich; *Editor:* Albert Jurgenson; *Music:* Ennio Morricone. 125 minutes.

CAST: Jean-Louis Trintignant (Francois Darien), Michel Piccoli (Kassar), Jean Seberg (Edith Lemoine), Gian Maria Volante (Sadiel), Michel Bouquet (Lempereur), Bruno Cremer (Vigneau), Daniel Ivernel (Antoine Acconeti), Philippe Noiret (Garcin), Roy Scheider (Michael Howard). Jacques Francois, Jean Bouise, Denis Manuel, Marc Mazza, Jacques Richard, Karin Shubert (Sabine), Nigel Davenport and Karl Otto Alberty received no credit.

The Outside Man aka ***Funerale à Los Angeles*** aka ***Un Homme Est Mort*** (United Artists, 1973); *Producer:* Jacques Bar; *Director:* Jacques Deray; *Screenplay:* Jean-Claude Carriere and Ian McLellan Hunter; *Photography:* Silvano Ippoliti and Terry K. Meade; *Editors:* Henri Lanoe and William Chulack; *Music:* Michel Legrand. 104 minutes.

CAST: Jean Louis Trintignant (Lucien Bellon), Ann-Margret (Nancy Robson), Roy Scheider (Lenny), Angie Dickinson (Jackie Kovacs), Georgia Engle (Mrs. Jane Barnes), Felice Orlandi (Anderson), Carlo De Mejo (Karl), Michael Constantin (Antoine), Umberto Orsini (Alex), Ted De Corsica (Victor), Jackie Earle Haley (Eric), Carmen Argenziano (Second Hawk), Rico Cattani (Butler), Edward Greenburg (Hitchhiker), Phillipa Harris (Sales Girl), John Korkes (First Hawk), Connie Kreski (Rosie), Ben Piazza (Desk Clerk), Lionel Vitrant (Paul), John Hillerman (Department Store Manager), Alex Rocco (Miller), Talia Shire (Make-up Girl).

The Seven Ups (20th Century–Fox, 1973); *Producer and Director:* Philip D'Antoni; *Screenplay:* Albert Rubin and Alexander Jacobs, based on a story by Sonny Grosso; *Photographer:* Urs Furrer; *Executive Producers:* Kenneth Utt and Barry J. Weitz; *Editord:* John C. Horger and Stephen A. Rotter; *Assistant Editor:* Cynthia Scheider; *Music:* Don Ellis. 109 minutes.

CAST: Roy Scheider (Buddy Manucci), Victor Arnold (Barilli), Jerry Leon (Mingo), Ken Kercheval (Ansel), Tony Lo Bianco (Vito Lucia), Larry Haines (Max Kalish), Richard Lynch (Moon), Bill Hickman (Bo), Ed Jordan (Bruno), David Wilson (Bobby), Robert Burr (Lt. Hanes), Lou Polan (Carmine Coltello), Matt Russo (Festa), Joe Spinell (Toredano), Rex Everhart (Inspector Gilson), Mary Multari (Mrs. Pugliese), Frank Macetta (Barber), Frances Chaney (Sarah Kalish), Mike Treanor (Policeman), Benny Marino (Festa's son), Bill Funaro (Big Bill), Billy Longo (Mobster 1),

Ace Alagn (Mobster 2), Sheldon Adler (Doctor), Adeline Leonard (Nurse), Edward F. Carey (Police Commissioner). John Aprea received no credit for his role as a killer.

Sheila Levine Is Dead and Living in New York (Paramount, 1974); *Producer:* Harry Korshak; *Director:* Sidney J. Furie; *Screenplay:* Kenny Solms, from the novel by Gail Parent; *Photography:* Donald M. Morgan; *Editor:* Argyle Nelson; *Music:* Michel Legrand. 112 minutes.

CAST: Jeannie Berlin (Sheila Levine), Roy Scheider (Dr. Sam Stoneman), Rebecca Diana Smith (Kate), Janet Brandt (Bernice), Sid Melton (Manny), Charles Woolf (Wally), Leda Rogers (Agatha), Jack Bernardi (Uncle Herm), Allen Secher (Rabbi), Tally Parker (Rochelle), Jon Miller (Norman), Noble Willingham (Principal), Evelyn Russell (Miss Burke), Richard Rasof (Attendant), Don Carrera (Harold), Sharon Martin Goldman (Melissa), Karin Anders (Aunt Min), Craig Littler (Steve), Sandy Helberg (Artist), John Morgan Edwards (Conductor), Charles Walker (Engineer), Charles Arthur (Clerk), Cecilia McBride (Typist), Erin Fleming (Girl), Lyle Moraine (Pianist), Sandra Golden (Performer), Victor Rafael (Performer).

Jaws (Universal, 1975); *Producers:* Richard D. Zanuck and David Brown; *Director:* Steven Spielberg; *Screenplay:* Peter Benchley and Carl Gottlieb, based on the book by Peter Benchley; *Photography:* William Butler; *Editor:* Verna Fields; *Music:* John Williams. 124 minutes.

CAST: Roy Scheider (Police Chief Martin Brody), Robert Shaw (Quint), Richard Dreyfuss (Matt Hooper), Lorraine Gary (Ellen Brody), Murray Hamilton (Mayor Vaughn), Carl Gottlieb (Meadows), Jeffrey C. Kramer (Deputy Len Hendricks), Susan Backlinie (Chrissie Watkins), Jonathan Filley (Cassidy), Ted Grossman (Estuary Victim), Chris Rebello (Michael Brody), Jay Mello (Sean Brody), Lee Fierro (Mrs. Kintner), Jeffrey Voorhees (Alex Kintner), Craig Kingsbury (Ben Gardner), Dr. Robert Nevin (Medical Examiner), Peter Benchley (TV Interviewer), Robert Chambers (Charlie), Edward Chalmers, Jr. (Denherder), Cyprien P. R. Dube (Posner), Robert Caroll (Polk), Donald Poole (Harbormaster), Alfred Wilde (Iteisel/Mr. Wiseman). Chris Anastasio, Fritzi Jane Courtney and Belle McDonald received no credit. Steven Spielberg had a cameo as an Amity Point Life Station Worker.

Marathon Man (Paramount, 1976); *Producers:* Robert Evans and Sidney Beckerman; *Director:* John Schlesinger; *Screenplay:* William Goldman, based on his novel; *Photography:* Conrad (L.) Hall; *Editor:* Jim Clark; *Music:* Michael Small. 125 minutes.

CAST: Dustin Hoffman (Babe), Lawrence Olivier (Dr. Szell), Roy Scheider (Doc Levy), William Devane (Commander Janeway), Marthe Keller (Elsa), Fritz Weaver (Professor Biesenthal), Richard Bright (Karl), Marc Lawrence (Erhard), Allen Joseph (Babe's Father), Tito Goya (Melendez), Ben Dova (Szell's Brother), Lou Gilbert (Rosenbaum), Jacques Marin (LeClerk), James Wing Woo (Chen), Nicole Deslauriers (Nicole), Lotta Andor-Palfi (Old Lady in Street), Lina Pina (Street Gang), Church Trioche (Street Gang), Jaime Tirelli (Street Gang), Wilfredo Hernandez (Street Gang), Harry Goz (Jewelry Salesman), Michael Vale, Fred Stuthman, Lee Steele, William Martel (Bank Guard), Glenn Robards, Ric Carrott (Plainclothesman), Alma Beltran (Laundress), Daniel Nunez (Guard in Uruguay), Tony Pena (Guard in Uruguay), Chuy Franco (Guard in Uruguay), Billy Kearns, Sally Wilson (Tourists), Tom Ellis (TV announcer), Bryant Fraser (Young Photographer), George Dega (Hotel Valet), Gene Bori (French Doctor), Annette Claudier (Nurse), Roger Etienne (Headwaiter), Ray Serra (Truck Driver), John Garson (Bystander), Charlott Thyssen (Bystander), Estelle Omens (Bystander), Madge Kennedy (Lady in Bank), Jeff Palladini (Young Babe), Scott Price (Young Doc). S. C. Dacy, Shaun McAllister and Louis Tanno received no credit.

Sorcerer aka ***Wages of Fear*** (Paramount/Universal, 1977); *Producer and Director:* William Friedkin; *Screenplay:* Walon Green, based on the book by Georges Arnaud; *Photography:* John M. Stephens and Dick Bush; *Editor and Associate Producer:* Bud Smith; *Editor:* Robert

K. Lambert; *Assistant Editor:* Cynthia Scheider; *Music:* Tangerine Dream. 121 minutes.

CAST: Roy Scheider (Scanlon/Dominguez), Bruno Cremer (Victor Manzon/ "Serrano"), Francisco Rabal (Nilo), Amidou (Kassem "Martinez"), Ramon Bieri (Corlette), Peter Capell (Latique), Karl John ("Marquez"), Frederick Ledebur ("Carlos"), Chico Martinez (Bobby Del Rios), Joe Spinell (Spider), Rosario Almontes (Agrippa), Richard Holley (Billy White), Anne Marie Deschott (Blanche), Jean-Luc Bideau (Pascal), Jacques Francois (Lefavre), Andre Falcon (Guillot), Gerard E. Murphy (Donnelly), Desmond Crofton (Boyle), Henry Diamond (Murray), Ray Dittrich (Ben), Frank Gio (Marty), Randy Jurgensen (Vinnie), Gus Allegretti (Carlo Ricci), Nick Discenzo (Father Ricci). Frank Pesce and Tom Signorelli received no credit.

Jaws 2 (Universal, 1978); *Producers:* Richard D. Zanuck and David Brown; *Director:* Jeannot Szwarc; *Screenplay:* Carl Gottlieb and Howard Sackler; *Photography:* Michael Butler; *Editors:* Neil Travis, Steve Potter and Arthur Schmidt; *Music:* John Williams. 123 minutes.

CAST: Roy Scheider (Chief Martin Brody), Lorraine Gary (Ellen Brody), Murray Hamilton (Mayor Larry Vaughan), Joseph Mascolo (Len Peterson), Jeffrey Kramer (Deputy Leonard 'Jeff' Hendricks), Collin Wilcox (Dr. Lureen Elkins), Ann Dusenberry (Tina Wilcox), Mark Gruner (Mike Brody), Barry Coe (Andrews), Susan French (Old Lady), Gary Springer (Andy), Donna Wilkes (Jackie), Gary Dubin (Ed), Keith Gordon (Doug), John Dukakis (Polo), G. Thomas Dunlop (Timmy), David Elliott (Larry), Marc Gilpin (Sean Brody), Cynthia Grover (Lucy), Ben Marley (Patrick), Martha Swatek (Marge), Billy Van Zandt (Bob Burnside), Gigi Vorgan (Brooke Peters), Jerry M. Baxter (Helicopter pilot), Jeanne Coulter, (Ski Boat Driver), Daphne Dibble, (Swimmer #1), Christine Freeman (Water Skier), April Gilpin (Renee), William Griffith (Lifeguard), Greg Harris, (Diver #2), Coll Red McLean (Red), Susan O. Macmillan (Denise), David Owsley (Donnie), Allan L. Paddack (Crosby), Oneida Rollins (Ambulance Driver), Frank Sparks (Diver #1), Thomas A. Stewart (Assistant Dive Master), David A. Tintle, (Swimmer #2), Jim Wilson (Swimmer with child), Kathy Wilson (Mrs. Bryant), Herb Muller (Phil Fogarty), Jane Courtney, Alfred Wilde, Cyprian "Phil" Dube, Mary A. Gaffney, William "Bill" Green (Irate Man), George Buck.

Last Embrace (MGM-UA, 1979); *Producers:* Michael Taylor and Dan Wigutow; *Director:* Jonathan Demme; *Screenplay:* David Shaber, based on the book 13th Man by Murry Teigh Bloom; *Photography:* Tak Fujimoto; *Editor:* Barry Malkin; *Music:* Miklos Rozsa. 102 minutes.

CAST: Roy Scheider (Harry Hannan), Janet Margolin (Ellie Fabian), John Glover (Richard Peabody), Sam Levene (Sam Urdell), Charles Napier (Dave Quittle), Christopher Walken (Eckart), Jacqueline Brookes (Dr. Coopersmith), David Margulies (Rabbi Drexel), Andrew Duncan (Bernie Meckler), Marcia Rodd (Adrian), Gary Goetzmann (Tour Guide), Lou Gilbert (Rabbi Jacobs), Mandy Patinkin (First Commuter), Max Wright (Second Commuter), Sandy McLeod (Dorothy Hannan), Burt Santos, Joe Spinell, Jim McBride (Men in Cantina), Cynthia Scheider (Adrian's Friend), Sasha Von Scherler (Shopper), George Hillman (Ukelele Player), Gary Gunter (Newscaster). Jonathan Demme has a cameo as a man on the train.

All That Jazz (Columbia/20th Century–Fox, 1979); *Producer:* Robert Alan Aurthur; *Director and Choreographer:* Bob Fosse; *Screenplay:* Robert Alan Aurthur and Bob Fosse; *Photography:* Guiseppe Rotunno; *Executive Producer:* Daniel Melnick; *Editor:* Alan Heim; *Music:* Ralph Burns. 123 minutes.

CAST: Roy Scheider (Joe Gideon), Jessica Lange (Angelique), Ann Reinking (Kate Jagger), Leland Palmer (Audrey Paris), Ben Vereen (O'Connor Flood), Cliff Gorman (Davis Newman), Erzabet Foldi (Michelle), Michael Tolan (Dr. Ballinger), Max Wright (Joshua Penn), William LeMassena (Jonesy Hecht), Chris Chase (Leslie Perry), Deborah Geffner (Victoria), Kathryn Doby (Kathryn), Anthony Holland (Paul Dann), Robert Hitt (Ted Christopher), David Marguilies (Larry Goldie), Sue Paul (Stacy), Keith Gordon (Young Joe), Frankie Man (Comic), Alan

Heim (Eddie Lerner), John Lithgow (Lucas Sargeant), Sandahl Bergman (Dancer), Bruce Davis (Dancer), Jennifer Nairn-Smith (Dancer), Sloan Shelton (Mother), Ben Masters (Dr. Garry), Stephen Strimpell, Leonard Drum, Eugene Toobnick, Jules Fisher, Kathryn Shirriff, Joanna Merlin, Leah Ayres, Nancy Beth Bird, Harry Agress, C.C.H. Pounder, Tito Goya, Tiger Haynes, Lotta Palfi-Andor, K. C. Townsend, Melanie Hunter, Rita Bennett, Gary Bayer, Wayne Carson, Kerry Casserly, Judy Passletiner, Steve Ellmore, Vicki Frederick, P. J. Mann, Minnie Gaster, Michael Green, Bruce MacCallum, Joyce Ellen Hill, I. M. Hobson, Edith Kramer, Barbara McKinley, Mary McCarty, Theresa Merritt, Gavin Moses, Mary Mon Toy, Wallace Shawn, Jacqueline Solotar, Sloan Shelton, Sammy Smith, Arnold Gross, Eileen Casey, Gary Flannery, Danny Ruvolo, Leland Schwantes, John Sowinski, Candace Tovar, Rima Vetter, Trudy Carson, Mary Sue Finnerty, Lesley Kingsley, Cathy Rice, Terry Treas, Sonja Stuart, Ralph E. Burntsen, Jan Flato, John Paul Fetta, Andy Schwartz, Robert Levine. Nicole Fosse plays an rejected dancer.

Still of the Night (MGM-UA, 1982); *Producer:* Arlene Donovan; *Director:* Robert Benton; *Screenplay:* David Newman and Robert Benton; *Photography:* Nestor Almendrios; *Editors:* Jerry Greenburg and Bill Pankow; *Music:* John Kander. 91 minutes.

CAST: Roy Scheider (Dr. Sam Rice), Meryl Streep (Brooke Reynolds), Jessica Tandy (Grace Rice), Joe Grifasi (Joseph Vitucci), Sara Botsford (Gail Phillips), Josef Sommers (George Bynum), Rikke Borge (Heather Wilson), Irving Metzman (Murray Gordon), Larry Joshua (Mugger), Tom Norton (Auctioneer), Richmond Hoxie (Mr. Harris), Hyon Cho (Mr. Chang), Danielle Cusson (Girl), John Bentley (Night Watchman), George A. Tooks (Elevator Operator), Sigrunn Omark (Receptionist), Randy Jurgenson (Car Thief), Palmer Deane (Auction Spotter), William Major (Auction Spotter), Joseph Priestly (Auction Spotter), Will Rose (Auction Spotter), Arnold Glimcher (Bidder), Jeffery Hoffeld (Bidder), Linda Leroy Janklow (Bidder), Elinor Klein (Bidder), Susan Patricof (Bidder), Mike Tremont (Bidder). Cynthia Scheider received no credit as an Auction bidder.

Blue Thunder (Columbia, 1982); *Producer:* Gordon Carroll; *Director:* John Badham; *Writers:* Dan O'Bannon and Don Jacoby; *Photography:* John Alonzo; *Executive Producers:* Phil Feldman and Andrew Fogelson; *Editors:* Frank Morriss and Edward Abroms; *Music:* Arthur B. Rubinstein. 108 minutes.

CAST: Roy Scheider (Frank Murphy), Malcolm McDowell (Cochrane), Warren Oates (Braddock), Candy Clark (Kate), Daniel Stern (Lymangood), Paul Roebling (Icelan), David S. Scheiner (Fletcher), Joe Santos (Montoya), Ed Bernard (Sgt. Short), Jason Bernard (Mayor), Mario Machado (Himself), James Murtaugh (Alf Hewitt), Pat McNamara (Matusek), Jack Murdock (Kress), Clifford A. Pellow (Allen), Paul Lambert (Holmes), Phil Feldman (Colonel Coe), John Garber (Tough Mechanic), Anthony James (Grundeltus), Robin Brantos (Diana McNeely), Anna Forest (Nude Lucy), Ricky Slyter (Timmy), Reid Cruickshanks (Chief of Police), Billy Ray Sharkey (Air Controller), Fred Slyter (Air Controller), John Gladstein (Fighter Pilot), Ross Reynolds (Helicopter Pilot), Karl A. Wickman (Helicopter Pilot), James W. Gavin (Helicopter Pilot), Tom Friedkin (Helicopter Pilot), James Read (Policeman at Bridge), Mickey Gilbert (Policeman), Bill Lane (Policeman), Lolly Boroff, Patti Clifton (Hooker), Ernest Harada (John), Frances E. Nealy (Mayor's Aide), Jose Pepe R. Gonzales (Drive-In Custodian), Jerry Ziesmer (Pilot), Tom Lawrence (Observer), John Ashby (Thief), Tony Brubaker (Thief), Norman Alexander Gibbs (Man in Beanie), Bill Ryusaki (Vietcong Soldier), Gary Davis (Motorcycle Cop), Tom Rosales (Thug), Larry Randles (Thug), Kevin P. Donnelly (Double Pilot), Peter Miller (Detective), Mike McGaughy (Observer), Calvin Bronx, Lucinda Crosby (Bel-Air Woman).

Tiger Town (Disney Channel, 1983); *Producer:* Susan B. Landau; *Screenplay and Director:* Alan Shapiro; *Photography:* Robert Elswit; *Editors:* John Link and Richard A. Harris; *Music:* Eddy Manson. 76 minutes.

CAST: Roy Scheider (Buddy Young), Justin

Henry (Alex), Ron McLarty (Buddy, Alex's Father), Bethany Carpenter (Nancy, Alex's Mother), Noah Moazezi (Eddie), Mary Wilson (Soloist), Lindsay Barr (Peanut Vendor), Dave Bokas (Crusty Man), Chris Bremmer (Loud Kid), Katie Delozier (Little Girl), Jack Fish (Stadium Guard), Gerald L. Monford (Lunch Room Kid), Leon Smith (Druggist), Whit Vernon (Mister Cullen), Von Washington (Souvenir Vendor), Larry Williams (Bus Driver), Sparky Anderson (Himself), Ernie Harwell (Himself), Al Ackerman (Himself), Ray Lane (Himself).

2010: The Year We Make Contact (MGM-UA, 1984); *Producer and Director:* Peter Hyams; *Screenplay:* Peter Hyams, based on the book by Arthur C. Clarke; *Photography:* Peter Hyams; *Editor:* James Mitchell; *Music:* David Shire. 117 minutes.

CAST: Roy Scheider (Dr. Heywood Floyd), John Lithgow (Walter Curnow), Helen Mirren (Tanya Kirbuk), Bob Balaban (Dr. R. Chandra), Keir Dullea (Dave Bowman), Douglas Rain (Hal 9000), Madolyn Smith (Caroline Floyd), Dana Elcar (Dmitri Moisevitch), Taliesin Jaffe (Christopher Floyd), James McEachin (Victor Milson), Mary Jo Deschanel (Betty Fernandez), Elya Baskin (Max Brailovsky), Savely Kramarov (Vladimir Rudenko), Oleg Rudnik (Vasali Orlov), Natasha Shneider (Irina Yakunina), Vladimir Skomarovsky (Yuri Svetlanov), Victor Steinbach (Mikolai Ternovsky), Jan Triska (Alexander Kovalev), Larry Carroll (Anchorman), Herta Ware (Jessie Bowman), Cheryl Carter (Nurse), Ron Recasner (Hospital Neurosurgeon), Robert Lesser (Dr. Hirsch), Olga Mallsnerd (Sal 9000), Delana Michaels (Commercial Announcer), Gene McGarr (Commercial Announcer). Arthur C. Clarke plays a man on a park bench. Candice Bergen is the voice of Sal 9000 (see fake credit above).

Mishima: A Life in Four Chapters (Warner Brothers, 1985); *Producers:* Mata Yamamoto and Tom Luddy; *Director:* Paul Schrader; *Writers:* Paul Schrader and Leonard Schrader; *Japanese Screenplay:* Cheiko Schrader; *Photography:* John Bailey; *Executive Producers:* George Lucas and Francis Ford Coppola; *Editor:* Michael Chandler; *Music:* Philip Glass. 121 minutes.

CAST: Ken Ogata (Yukio Mishima), Masayuki Shionoya (Morita), Hiroshi Mikami (Cadet 1), Junya Fukada, (Cadet 2), Shigeto Tachihara (Cadet 3), Go Riju (Mishima 18-19), Yuki Nagahara (Mishima—Age 5), Kyuzo Kobayashi (Literary Friend), Junkicki Orimoto (General Mashita), Yuki Kitazume (Dancing Friend), Haruko Kato (Grandmother), Yasoku Bando (Mizoguchi), Hisako Manda (Mariko), Naomi Oki (First Girl), Miki Takakura (Second Girl), Imari Isujikoichi Cato, Kenji Sawada (Osamu), Reisen Lee (Kiyomi), Setsuko Karasuma (Mitsuko), Tanadori Yokoo, Yakuari Kurata (Takei), Mitsuru Hirata (Thug), Toshiyuki Nagashima (Isao), Hiroshi Katsuno (Lieutenant Hori), Naoyo Makoto (Kendo Instructor), Hiroki Ada (Izutsu), Jun Negami (Kurahara), Ryo Ikebe (Interrogator), Toshio Hosokawa, Hideo Fukahara (Military Doctor), Yosuke Mizuno (Yokuku Producer), Eimei Ezumi (Ichigaya Colonel), Shoichiro Sakata, (Isao's Classmate), Alan Mark Poul (American Reporter), Ren Ebata (Reporter no. 1), Yasuhiro Arai (Reporter no. 2), Fumio Mizuhima (Reporter no. 3), Shinji Miura (Pavilion Acolyte), Yuichi Sato, Sachiko Akagi (Thug's Girl Friend), Tsutomu Harada (Romeo), Mami Okamato (Juliet), Atsushi Takayama, Kimiko Ito (Grandmother's Nurse), Kojiro Oka (MP), Tatsuya Hiragaki (Actor), Shinichi Nosaka (Policeman), Sachiko Hidari (Osamu's Mother). English Narration by Roy Scheider.

Men's Club (Atlantic Entertainment, 1986); *Producer:* Howard Gottfried; *Director:* Peter Medek; *Screenplay:* Leonard Michaels, based on his book; *Photography:* John Fleckenstein; *Executive Producers:* Thomas Coleman, John Harada and Michael Rosenblatt; *Editors:* Cynthia Scheider, David Dresher and Bill Butler; *Music:* Lee Holdridge. 100 minutes.

CAST: David Dukes (Phillip), Richard Jordan (Kramer), Harvey Keitel (Solly Berliner), Frank Langella (Howard Canterbury), Roy Scheider (Cavanaugh), Treat Williams (Terry), Craig Wasson (Paul), Stockard Channing (Nancy), Gina Gallegos (Felicia), Cindy Pickett (Hannah), Gwen Welles (Redhead), Penny Baker (Lake), Rebeccah Bush (Stella), Claudia

Cron (Stacey), Ann Dusenberry (Page), Marilyn Jones (Allison), Mannette La Chance (Billy), Jennifer Jason Leigh (Teensy), Ann Wedgeworth (Jo), Laurie Ambert (Waitress), Joan Foley (Nurse), Kelly Haverhur (Phoebe), Karen Trott (Maid). Helen Shaver received no credit for playing Cavanaugh's wife Sarah; nor did Cynthia Scheider as a cafe customer.

52 Pick-Up (Cannon, 1986); *Producers:* Yoram Globus and Menachem Golan; *Director:* John Frankenheimer; *Screenplay:* Jon Steppling, based on the book by Elmore Leonard; *Photography:* Jost Vacano; *Executive Producer:* Henry T. Weinstein; *Editor:* Robert F. Shugrue; *Music:* Gary Chang. 111 minutes.

CAST: Roy Scheider (Harry Mitchell), Ann Margret (Barbara Mitchell), Vanity (Doreen), John Glover (Alan Raimy), Robert Trebor (Leo Franks), Lonny Chapman (Jim O'Boyle), Kelly Preston (Cinnie), Doug McClure (Mark Averson), Clarence Williams the III (Bobby Shy), Alex Hentleloff (Dan Lowenthal), Michelle Walker (Counter Girl), Philip Bartko (Test Site Worker), Robin Bronfman (Injured Driver), Debra Berger (O'Boyle's Wife), Laisa Carrie (Janet), Tom Bryon (Party Goer), Harvey Cowen (Party Goer), Ron Jeremy Hyatt (Party Goer), Amber Lynn (Party Goer), Sharon Mitchell (Party Goer), Ines Ochoa (Party Goer), Allison Palmeter (Party Goer), Katherine Poland (Party Goer), Debra Satell (Party Goer), Amy White (Party Goer), Charles Bowen (Factory Worker), Marc Castanada (Factory Worker), Mike Caruso (Factory Worker), Steven Clawsen (Factory Worker), Christopher Cory (Factory Worker), Maurice Jenkins (Factory Worker), John Kahnen (Factory Worker), Bobby Ponce (Factory Worker), Ray Vela (Factory Worker), Blackie Dammett (Drug Dealer), Barbara Ferris (Lisa), John Francis (Policeman), Conroy Gedeon (James Boyer), Bill Gratton (Ed Salvon), Jai. M. Jefferson (Patron), Lenora Logan (Lady in Hall), Mark M. Mayuga (Passerby), Lorrie Lovett (Nude Model), Barbara Summers (Nude Model), William J. Murphy (Grady), Anthony Palmer (Tom), Frank Sivero (Vendor), Arlin Miller (Celebrity voice Impersonation), Richard Bright.

Cohen and Tate (Hemdale Entertainment, 1988); *Producers:* Antony Rufus Isaacs and Jeff Young; *Writer and Director:* Eric Red; *Photography:* Victor J. Kemper; *Editor:* Edward Abroms; *Music:* Bill Conti. 86 minutes.

CAST: Roy Scheider (Cohen), Adam Baldwin (Tate), Harley Cross (Travis Knight), Cooper Huckabee (Jeff Knight), Suzanne Savoy (Martha Knight), Marco Perella (FBI George), Tom Campitelli (FBI Fred), Andrew R. Gill (FBI Roy), Frank Bates (Highway Patrolman), James Jeter (Trooper #1), Jeff Bennett (Trooper #2), Ron Jackson (Trooper #3), Ted Baader (Trooper #4), Kenneth McCabe (Gas Station Attendant), Ina B. Bott (Fat Woman), Craig Busch (Farmer).

Listen to Me (Columbia Pictures, 1989); *Producer:* Mary Kay Powell; *Writer and Director:* Douglas Day Stewart; *Photography:* Fred J. Koenekamp; *Editors:* Anne V. Coates, Daniel Craven and Bud S. Smith; *Music:* David Foster. 107 minutes.

CAST: Kirk Cameron (Tucker Muldoney), Jami Gertz (Monica Tomanski), Roy Scheider (Charlie Nichols), Amanda Peterson (Donna Lumis), Tim Quill (Garson MacKellar), George Wyner (Dean Schwimmer), Anthony Zerbe (Senator MacKellar), Christopher Atkins (Bruce Arlington), Quinn Cummings (Susan Hooper), Timothy Dang (Bobby Chin), Peter DeLuise (Cameron Sweet), Jason Gould (Hinkelstein), Jon Matthews (Braithwaite), Christopher Rydell (Tom Lloynd), Dan Schneider (Nathan Gore), Yeardley Smith (Cootz), Moon Zappa (Longnecker), Ron Masak (Monica's Father), Dottie Archibald (Monica's Mother), Jamie Kantrowitz (Monica's Little Sister), Barbara Pilavin (Monica's Aunt), Francine Selkirk (Monica's Aunt), Rance Howard (Tucker's Father), Sean Stewart (Reform School Boy at Fence), Stephanie Copeland (Kenmore Cheerleader), Jodi Engleman (Kenmore Cheerleader), Francine L. Julius (Kenmore Cheerleader), Alison Morgan (Kenmore Cheerleader), Traci L. Murray (Kenmore Cheerleader), Tammi Urner (Kenmore Cheerleader), Nancy Valen (Mia), Dorrie Krum (Tasha), Dylan Stewart (Chess Player), Julie Dretzin (Sloan), Lynn Fischer (Bobby Chin's Girlfriend), Mark Christopher Laurence (Attila), Robert A. Chumbrook

(Horny), Lilyan Chauvin (French Professor), Julie Simone (Fountain Girl), Annette Sinclair (Fountain Girl), Dianne Turley Travis (Garson's Mother), Anna Lee (Garson's Grandmother), Kenneth G. Patterson (Garson's Grandfather), Thomas Heinkel Miller (Columbia Debate Official), Priscilla Kovary (Charlie's Dancing Partner), Rick A. Lundin (Hansom Cab Driver), Jon Lindstrom (Television Reporter), David Downing (Officer of the Court), Don Galloway (Harvard Coach), Ed Wright (Justice Patterson), Norwood Smith (Justice Goodman), Dave Gilbert (Justice Tarlton), Mary Gregory (Justice Brooderworth), Martin West (Justice Blyleven).

Night Game (Trans World Entertainment, 1989); *Producer:* George Litto; *Director:* Peter Masterson; *Screenplay:* Spencer Eastman and Anthony Palmer, based on a story by Spencer Eastman; *Photography:* Fred Murphy; Executive *Producers:* Moshe Diamant and Eduard Sarlui; *Editors:* Robert Barrere and King Wilder; *Music:* Pino Donaggio; 95 minutes.

CAST: Roy Scheider (Mike Seaver), Karen Young (Roxie Bennett), Lane Smith (Lamar Witty), Richard Bradford (Nelson), Paul Gleason (Broussard), Carlin Glynn (Alma), Anthony Palmer (Mendoza), Matthew James Carlson (Bibbee), Rex Linn (Floyd Epps), Alex Garcia (Silvio Baretto), Michelle Cochrane (Cindy Baretto), Bob Allen (Baseball Announcer), Marco Parella (Color Man), Lisa Hart Caroll (Blonde #1—Loretta Akers), Sarah Chattin (Eva Lyons), John Martin (Nick Finley), Tony Frank (Alex Lynch), Teresa Dell (Shirl), James Monroe (Dale), Matt Posey (Donnie), Renee O'Connor (Lorraine Beasley), Dee Hennigan (Beverly), Kevin Cooney (Essicks), Michael Marich (Pizza Man), Everett Sifuentes (Norman), Joel Anderson (Steve), Ron Jackson (Sportscaster), Howard French (Guy), Ken Page (Andy), Mark Mitchell (Fat Boy), Bethany Wright (Barefoot Blonde), Paul James Vasquez (Foreman), Sharon Dunn (Sales Lady), Brandon Smith (Barman), Sebastian White (Patrolman #1), Rick Ramirez (Patrolman #2), Chris Kinkade (House of Mirrors Attendant). Peter Masterson (the Director) played Davy.

Fourth War (Cannon/New Age, 1990); *Producers:* Wolf Schmidt and Robert L. Rosen; *Director:* John Frankenheimer; *Screenplay:* Stephen Peters and Kenneth Ross, from a story by Stephen Peters; *Photography:* Gerry Fisher; *Executive Producers:* Sam Perlmutter and William Stuart; *Editor:* Robert F. Shugrue; *Music:* Bill Conti. 91 minutes.

CAST: Roy Scheider (Col. Jack Knowles), Jurgen Prochnow (Col. N. A. Valachev), Tim Reid (Lt. Col. Timothy Clark), Lara Harris (Elena Novotna), Harry Dean Stanton (Gen. Roger Hackworth), Dale Dye (Sergeant Major), Bill MacDonald (MP Corporal), David Palffy (Gawky Soldier), Neil Grahn (Needle Nosed Soldier), Ernie Jackson (Knowles' Driver), Ron Campbell (Young U.S. Soldier), John Dodds (Defector), Harold Hecht, Jr. (Dwayne), Alice Pesta (Hannalore), Gregory A. Gale (Communications Corporal), Henry Kope (Mayor), Guy Buller (Czech Guard), Gary Lazinsky (Red Private 1), Ed Siobelman (Red Private 2), Gary Spivak (Red Private 3), Yefim Korduner (Red Army Major 1), Brent Woolsey (Red Army Major 2), Kent McNeill (U.S. Private 1), Brian Warren (MP and Wide soldier), Roman Podhora (Czech Guard 1), Joseph Vrba (Czech Guard 2), George Scholl (Innkeeper), Gordon Signer (Bavarian Farmer), Lilo Bahr (Innkeeper's Wife), Claus Diedrich (Frontier Police Captain), Kyle Maschmeyer (Villager 1), Kurt Darmohray (Villager 2), Igor Burstyn (Czech Guard Tower), Matus Ginzburg (Puppeteer), Boris Novogrudsky (Aide to Valachev), Tom Kelly (Sports Announcer). Brenda King (Mrs. Roy Scheider) received no credit as a wedding dancer.

Somebody Has to Shoot the Picture (HBO 1990); *Producer:* Alan Barnette; *Director:* Frank Pierson; *Screenplay:* Doug Magee, from his book; *Photography:* Bojan Bazelli; *Executive Producer:* William Sackheim; *Editor:* Peter Zinner; *Music:* James Newton Howard. 104 minutes.

CAST: Roy Scheider (Paul Marish), Bonnie Bedelia (Hannah McGrath), Robert Carradine (Sgt. Jerry Brown), Andre Braugher (Dan Weston), Arliss Howard (Raymind Eames), Bob Barnes (Governor Dean), Rex Benson (Buddy Eames), Harold Bergman (Judge Landis), Ginger Burgett (Jean Watley), Traber Burns (Ron

Felders), Patrick Cherry (Donnie), Antoni Corone (Mike Knighton), Jay Glick (Prison Chaplin), Marietta Haley (TV Reporter), Danny Haneman (Doug McGrath), John Glenn Harding (Waiter), Tom Kouchalakos (Burke), Ann Kimberlie (Clerk), Shane Le Mar (Gospel Singer), Michael Leopard (Guard 1), Mark McCauley (Superintendent Stanton), Shawn McAllister (Dr. Milliken), Mark McCracken (Nathanson), Greg Paul Myers (Jackie McGrath), Kathy Neff (Doreen Rusher), Tom Nowicki (Steve March, Prosecuting Attorney), Michael O'Smith (Police Chief), John Polce (Executioner), Kevin Quigley (Floyd Tatum), James Lea Raupp (Electrician), Ric Reitz (Aide #1), Tracy Roberts (Betty), Tom Schuster (Jake Rusher), Robert Small (Aide #2), Lou Walke (Blohm), Mattie Wolf (Mrs. Landers), Steve Zurk (Guard in Charge).

Russia House (MGM, 1990); *Producers:* Paul Malansky and Fred Schepisi; *Director:* Fred Schepisi; *Screenplay:* Tom Stoppard, based on the book by John Le Carre; *Photography:* Ian Baker; *Editor:* Peter Honess; *Music:* Jerry Goldsmith. 126 minutes.

CAST: Sean Connery (Barley Blair), Michelle Pfieffer (Katya Orlova), Roy Scheider (Russell), James Fox (Ned), John Mahoney (Brady), Michael Kitchen (Clive), J. T. Walsh (Quinn), Ken Russell (Walter), David Threlfall (Wicklow), Klaus Maria Brandauer (Dante), Mac McDonald (Bob), Nicholas Woodeson (Niki Landau), Martin Clunes (Brock), Ian McNiece (Merrydew), Colin Stinton (Henzinger), Denys Hawthorne (Paddy), George Roth (Cy), Peter Mariner (U.S. Scientist), Ellen Hurst (Anna), Peter Knupffer (Sergey), Nicolai Pastukhov (Uncle Matvey), Jason Salkey (Johnny), Eric Anzumonyin (Nasayan), Daniel Wozniak (Zapadny), Georgi Andzhaparidze (Yuri), Vladek Nikiforov (Tout), Christopher Lawford (Larry), Marc La Mura (Todd), Blu Mankuma (Merv), Tuck Milligan (Stanley), Jay Benedict (Spikey), David Timson (George), Yelena Stroyeva (Anastasia), Fyodor Smirnov (Watcher), Pavel Sirotin (Watcher), Paul Jutkevitch (Misha), David Henry (Minister Whitehall), Martin Wenner (Scientist Whitehall), Paul Rattee (Army Officer Whitehall), Simon Templeman (Psychoanalyst Whitehall), Gina Nikiforov (Russian Guest), Raisa Ryazanov (Russian Guest), Kate Lock (Jacky), Charlotte Cornwell (Charlotte), Craig Crosbie (Technician), Keith Edwards (Hoover), Michael Fitzpatrick (Hoover), Rob Freeman (Hoover), Gennadi Venov (Katya's Father), Sasha Yatsko (Russian Writer), Vladimir Zunetov (Dan), Jack Raymond (Lev), David Ryall (Colonial Type), Alexei Jawdokimov (Arkady), Constantine Gregory (KGB Man), Sergei Reusenko (KGB Man), Yegushe Tsturvan (Flute Player).

Naked Lunch (20th Century–Fox, 1991); *Producer:* Jeremy Thomas; *Director:* David Cronenberg; *Screenplay:* David Cronenberg, based on the book by William Burroughs; *Photography:* Peter Suschitzky; *Editor:* Ronald Sanders; *Music:* Howard Shore. 115 Minutes.

CAST: Peter Weller (Bill Lee), Judy Davis (Joan Frost and Joan Lee), Ian Holm (Tom Frost), Julian Sands (Yves Cloquet), Roy Scheider (Dr. Benway), Monique Mercure (Fadela), Nicholas Campbell (Hank), Martin Zelniker (Martin), Robert A. Silverman (Hans), Joseph Scorsiani (Kiki), Peter Boreski (Creature Voices/Exterminator 2), Yuval Daniel (Hafid), John Friesen (Hauser), Sean McCann (O'Brien), Howard Jerome (A. J. Cohen), Michael Caruana (Pawnbroker), Kurt Reis (Exterminator 1), Justin Louis (Exterminator 3), Julian Richings (Exterminator 4), Jim Yip (The Chink), Claude Aflalo (Forgeman), Laurent Hazout (Interzone Boy), Joe Dimambro (Interzone Boy), Denardo Coleman, Ornette Coleman and Perry Phillips (The Ornette Coleman Trio).

Covert Assassin (Tribune Entertainment, 1993); *Producers:* Andrea Piazzesi and Paul Madigan; *Director:* Tony Wharmby; *Screenplay:* J. H. Carrington, based on the book *Wild Justice* by Wilbur Smith; *Photography:* Brian West; *Editor:* John Shirley; *Music:* Alan Parker. 120 minutes.

CAST: Roy Scheider (Col. Peter Stride), Patricia Millardet (Magda Altman), Christopher Bucholtz (Colin Noble), Ted McGinley (Aubrey Billings), Clive Francis (Sir Steven), Sam Wanamaker (Kingston Parker), Kelly Marcel (Melissa Stride), Richard Ridings (Carl), Constantine Gregory (Serge Bulov), David Yip (Wong), Kevork Malikyan (Ali Hassan), Rita

Wolf (Vritra), Emma Healey (Ililda), Billy J. Mitchell (General Anders), Sandra Chelbi (Fara), Charmaine Parsons (Dorothy), Mark Longhurst (Eddy), Iain Rattray (Inspector Richards), James Hayes (Doctor), Bob Sessions (Newscaster), Ruby Snape (Peter's Assistant), Earlene Bentley (Female Army Sergeant), Benson Wong (Rebel Commander), Paul Sharma (Ali Hassan Assistant), David Taylor (Atlas Technician), Zoubeir Bornaze (Customs Official), Mohktar Mesrigui (Customs Official), Mark Zuber (Customs Official), Sean McCabe (Customs Official), Andrew Readman (Dispatcher), Ahmed Khalil (Arab Major), Ian Kelsey (Narmco Clerk), Roy Jewers (Admiral), Amanda Weston (Atlas Secretary), Raymond Johnson (Bartender), Knight Mantell (Butler), Fiona Mollison (Sylvia), Terry Wale (Male Passenger), Leon Tanner (Airport Official), June Page (Policewoman), Adel Saidi (Native Boy). Also released as a syndicated 4 hour miniseries, ***Wild Justice***.

Romeo Is Bleeding (Gramercy, 1993); *Producers:* Hilary Henkin and Paul Webster; *Director:* Peter Medak; *Screenplay:* Hilary Henkin; *Executive Producers:* Tim Bevan and Eric Fellner; *Photography:* Dariusz Wolski; *Editor:* Walter Murch; *Music:* Mark Isham. 110 minutes.

CAST: Gary Oldman (Sgt. Jack Grimaldi), Lena Olin (Mona Demarkov), Juliette Lewis (Sheri), Roy Scheider (Don Falcone), Annabella Sciorra (Natalie Grimaldi), David Proval (Scully), Will Patton (Martie), Larry Joshua (Joey), Paul Butler (Skouras), James Cromwell (Cage), Michael Wincott (Sal), Gene Canfield (John), Ron Perlman (Jack's Attorney), Wallace Wood (Waiter), William Duff-Griffin (Paddy), Tony Sirico (Malacci), Victoria Bastel (Girl #1), Katrina Rae (Girl #2), Joe Paperone (Ginny), Owen Hollander (Stan), Neal Jones (Clerk), James Murtaugh (Priest), Gary Hope (Driver), Americo and James Mongiello (Men), Dennis Farina (Nick).

Money Plays (Hallmark Entertainment, 1996); *Producer:* William Tannen; *Writer and Director:* Frank D. Gilroy; *Photography:* Ric Waite; *Executive Producers:* Wayne Rogers and Henry S. Schlieff; *Editor:* Bill Johnson; *Music:* Philip Marshall. 92 minutes.

CAST: Roy Scheider (Johnny Tobin), Sonia Braga (Irene), Jon Polito (Lou Spano), Carmine Ciardi (Victor), Seth Jaffe (Carmine), Elisabeth Lund (Stacey), John Durren (Jester), John Buchanan (Dealer #1), Ken Coleman (Boxman), Michael Kelsey (Dealer #2), Steve May (Casino Executive), Vince Del'Ostia (Casino Manager), Michael Flynn (The Shylock), Nancy Gentry (Cashier), Rick Bugg (Motel Clerk), Donre Sampson (Hood #1), Zane Parker (Hood #2) Fenton Quinn (Hood #3), Josephine Thaut (Woman Tourist), David Jensen (Cab Driver), Laura Rogers (Kitty), Michelle Wilson (Alice), Ivan Crosland (Maitre'd), Geoffrey Bennett (Young Man), Christian Scheider [Roy's son] (Gilly), Jeff Olson (Photographer), Dennis Saylor (Coroner), Michael Scott (Minister), Rita Bankhead (Mrs. Williams), Daniel Dudley (Stickman), Teddy Constanzo (Dealer 3).

The Rage aka ***Final Conflict*** (Norstar Entertainment, 1996); *Producers:* Daniel Grodnik and Robert Snukal; *Director:* Sidney J. Furie; *Screenplay:* Greg Mellot and Sidney J. Furie; *Executive Producer:* Peter R. Simpson; *Photography:* Donald M. Morgan; *Editor:* Nick Rotundo; *Music:* Paul Zara. 93 minutes.

CAST: Lorenzo Lamas (Nick Travis), Kristen Cloke (Kelly McCord), Gary Busey (Art Dacy), David Carradine (Lucas), Roy Scheider (John Taggart), Brandon Smith (Len), Tiana Warden (Dacy's Girlfriend), Dell Yount (Bobby Joe), David Jensen (Agent Green), Russ McGinn (Coroner), Dick Kyker (Militia Leader), Ashlee Nicole (Sergeant Greta), Terra Allen (Sheila Cramer), Kaye Wade (Lucille Dacy), Jeff Doucette (Dr. Arnold), Mark Allen (Mechanic), Richard Mitchell (Club President), Jim Platt (Speaker), Lynn Peterson (Driver), Gary Gingold (Deputy Gray), Shannon Lavender (Mother), Jennifer Miller (Mother of Killed Boy).

Plato's Run aka ***The Cuba Connection*** (Nu Image, 1996); *Producers:* Mitchell Blumberg and James Brooke; *Writer and Director:* James Becket; *Photography:* Richard Clabaugh; *Executive Producers:* Avi Lerner, Danny Dimbort and Trevor Short; *Editor:* Alain Jakubowicz; *Music:* Robert O. Ragland. 96 minutes.

CAST: Gary Busey (Plato Smith), Roy Scheider (Alexander Senarkian), Steven Bauer (Sam), Jeff Speakman (Dominick), Tiani Warden (Marta), Mia Myatt (Kathy), Horacio Le Don (Felix), Doug DeLuca (Buddy), Deborah Magdalena (Constancia), Melanie Chartoff (Stephanie), Salvador Levy (Gomez), Mark Macauley (Baker), Julie Upton (Julie), Chris Hinton, (Cueball), Mario Ernesto Sanchez (Flaco), Chick Bernhardt (Gordo), Steve Wise (Fed), Marcos Casanova (Gaunt Man), Mitchell Carey (Rotund Man), Steve Greenburg (Fearful Man), Victoria Bass (Matty), Antoni Corone (Barnes), Neil DeGroot (Millhouse), Bob Kranz (Prescott), Mitchell G. Blumberg (Governor's Aide), Tom Wahl (Technician), Gustavo Laborie (Jose), George Tapia (Cuban Commander), Dana Mark (Cuban Soldier), Suzanne Coker (Cuban Soldier), Rand McClain (Guard/Thug), Tony Perez (Guard/Thug), Tom Turvey (Guard/Thug/Mercenary), Ralph Gonzales (Guard/Thug), Tom Shirley, Jr. (Mercenary), Bruno Ramos (Mercenary), Artie Malesci (Mercenary), Steve Filmore (Mercenary), Bill Orsini (Mercenary), Jeff Moldovan (Mercenary), Jim Vickers (Mercenary), James M. Churchman (Mercenary), Mike Christopher (Mercenary), Paul Barth (Helicopter Pilot), Al Guthery (Helicopter Pilot). Sevy Di Cione (Security Guard) and Phil Hoelcher (Mercenary) received no credit.

Executive Target (PM Entertainment, 1996); *Producers:* Joseph Mehri and Richard Pepin; *Director:* Joseph Merhi; *Screenplay:* Dayton Callie and Jacobson Hart; *Photography:* Ken Blakey: *Editors:* John Gilbert and David Kern; *Executive Producer:* Anthony Esposito; *Music:* John Sponsler. 100 minutes.

CAST: Michael Madsen (Nick James), Roy Scheider (President Carlton), Angie Everhart (Lacey), Keith David (Lamar), Dayton Callie (Bela), Kathy Christopherson (Nadia), Gareth Williams (Clay Ripple), Robert Miano (Jack), Mathias Hues (Vic), Mike Genovese (Smoke), Jacobsen Hart (Ray), Jessica Cushman (Det. Green), Jana Robbins (Dorothy), Sal Landi (Luther), Lance LeGault (Gen. Moore), Peter Allas (Smith), Dan Martin (Carter), David 'Shark' Fralick (Simpson), Michele Colucci (The First Lady), Robert Carter (Lead Agent), Ray Laska (Guard), Frank Stager (Inmate), Buck Flower (Window Washer), Carolyn Renee Smith (Dancer), Kevin La Rosa (Pilot), Wayne Richardson (Pilot), Rick Shuster (Pilot).

The Peacekeeper aka ***Red Zone*** (Millennium Films, 1996); *Producer:* Nicholas Clermont; *Director:* Frederick Forestier; *Screenplay:* Robert Geoffrion and James H. Stewart; *Photography:* John Berrie; *Executive Producers:* Avi Lerner and Elie Samaha; *Editor:* Yves Langlois; *Music:* Francois Forestier. 96 minutes.

CAST: Dolph Lundgren (Major Frank Cross), Roy Scheider (President Robert Baker), Michael Sarrazin (Col. Douglas Murphy), Montel Williams (Col. Bernard Northrop), Ken Rush (Troy), Christopher Heyerdahl (Hettinger), Allen Altman (McGarry), Martin Neufeld (Decker), Monika Schnarre (Jane), Tim Post (Nelson), Carl Alacchi (Holbrook), Roc LaFortune (Abbott), Phil Chiu (Kong), Serge Houde (Secretary of Defense), David Francis (Major General Harding), Larry Day (Maxwell), Alan Fawcett (Samuels), Philip Pretten (Clark), Andy Bradshaw (Johnson), Dave Nichols (Air Force Chief of Staff), Frank Fontaine (Chairman Joint Chiefs Greensfield), Viastra Vrana (General Douglas), Michael Caloz (Billy), Michel Perron (Space Command), David Siscoe (Launch Command Controller), Mark Camacho (Presidential Aide 1), Susan Glover (Presidential Aide 2), Rod Charlebois (NNN Reporter), Al Dubois (NNN Reporter), Gwen Tolbart (Reporter), Eramelinda Boquer (Reporter), D'Arcy Kieran Butler (Reporter), John Dunn-Hill (Homeless Man), Nathalie Sanchagrin (Heat Wave). Barry Bellamy, Jeff Bottoms, Kevin Coyle, Michael Cullin, Michael Jaye, Allen Nebelthau and Steve Routman received no credit for their roles.

The Myth of Fingerprints (Sony Pictures Classics, 1997); *Producers:* Mary Jane Skalski and Tim Perell, Bart Freundlich; *Director and Writer:* Bart Freundlich; *Photography:* Stephen Kamierski; *Executive Producers:* James Schamus and Ted Hope; *Associate Producer:* Noah Wyle; *Editors:* Kate Williams and Ken J. Sackheim; *Music:* David Bridie and John Phillips. 93 minutes.

CAST: Arija Bareikis (Daphne), Blythe Danner (Lena), Hope Davis (Margaret), Laurel

Hollman (Leigh), Brian Kerwin (Elliot), James Legros (Cezanne), Julianne Moore (Mia), Roy Scheider (Hal), Michael Vartan (Jake), Noah Wyle (Warren), Randee Allen (Waitress), Justin Barretto (Young Jake), Chris Bauer (Jerry), Nicholas Bourgeois (Young Warren), Tom Cumler (Man at Train Station), Christopher Duva (Tom), Kelsey Gunn (Young Leigh), Polly Pelletier (Young Mia), Pamela Polhemus (Bookstore Woman), Michael Rupert (Warren's Psychiatrist).

John Grisham's The Rainmaker (Paramount, 1997); *Producers:* Michael Douglas, Steven Reuther and Fred Fuchs; *Director and Writer:* Francis Ford Coppola; *Photography:* John Toll; *Editor:* Barry Malkin; *Music:* Elmer Bernstein. 135 minutes.

CAST: Matt Damon (Rudy Baylor), Danny Devito (Deck Schifflet), Claire Danes (Kelly Riker), Jon Voight (Leo F. Drummond), Mary Kay Place, (Dot Black), Dean Stockwell (Harvey Hale), Teresa Wright (Ms. Birdie), Virginia Madsen, (Jackie Lemanczyk), Mickey Rouke (Lyman "Bruiser" Stone), Andrew Shue (Cliff Riker), Red West (Buddy Black), Johnny Whitworth (Donnie Ray Black), Wayne Emmons (Prince Thomas), Adrian Roberts (Butch), Roy Scheider (Wilfred Keeley), Danny Glover (Tyrone Kipler-Uncredited), Randy Travis (Billy Porter), Michael Girardin (Everett Lufkin), Randall King (Jack Underhall), Justin Ashforth (F. Franklin Donaldson), Michael Keys Hall (B. Bobby Shaw), James Cunningham (J. Michael Floquet), Frank Clem (Mr. Van Landel), Alan Woolf (Kermit Aldy), Sonny Shroyer (Delbert Birdsong), Pamela Tice Chapman (Vera Birdsong), Trula Marcus (Jewelry Saleswoman), Tony Dingman (Bruiser's Driver), Daniel O'Callaghan (Carl), Tom Kagy, John Yancey (Homicide Detectives), Chris Gray (Jailer), Verda Davenport (Jury Foreman), Johnetta Shearer (Courtroom Clerk), Tammy Wendel (Court Reporter), Nate Bynum (Mr. McKenzie), James W. Redmond (CNN Reporter), John Gray (Hospital Volunteer), Sherry Sanford (Nurse), Billy Ray Reynolds, Mary Lester (Murder Scene Bystanders), Deborah Frasier (St. Peter's Receptionist), Vernon Newman (Great Benefit Salesman), Lynn Carthane (Newscaster), Rodney Peck (Rehab Center Desk Clerk), Bill Lunn (Himself), Terrance Stewart (Boy with Broken Arm), Bridget Brunner (Bruiser's Receptionist), Mike Cody (Tinley Britt Lawyer), Donald Polden (Legal Commentator), Eloise Dukes (Court Clerk), Katherine Morrow (Deposition Court Reporter), Alex Harvey (Bar Exam Proctor), Melissa Hurst (Waitress at Bar), Anasa Briggs-Graves, Ronnie Dee Blaire (Bailiffs). Narration by Michael Herr.

Evasive Action aka ***Steel Train*** (Royal Oaks Entertainment, 1998); *Producers:* Ashok Amritraj and Andrew Stevens; *Director:* Jerry P. Jacobs; *Screenplay:* Tripp Reed; *Photography:* Ken Blakey; *Executive Producer:* Alan B. Burstein; *Film Editor:* Lewis Schoenbrun; *Music:* David and Eric Wurst. 90 minutes.

CAST: Dorian Harewood (Luke Sinclair), Ray Wise (Wes Blaldek), Roy Scheider (Enzo), Delane Matthews (Zoe Clark), Ed O'Ross (Jack Kramer), John Toles-Bey (Tommy Zimmer), Clint Howard (Hector), Don Swayze (Ian), Richard Foronjy (Vince), Steven Barr (Joe Manetti), Michael Tucci (Judge), Dick Van Patten (Parole Officer), Blake Gibbons (Ralph Kantor), Mallory Farrow (Alex), Chick Vennera (Edward), Keith Coogan (Anthony Tait), Bill McGee (Matt Baker), Heidi Epper (Marney), Tom Poster (Dave Danner), Toby Holguin (Devin Campbell), Sam I. Jones (Inmate). As of March 2002, this film had only been released on video in Europe.

White Raven (Royal Oaks Entertainment, 1998); *Producers:* Ashok Amritraj and Andrew Stevens; *Director:* Andrew Stevens; *Screenplay:* Michael Blodgett; *Executive Producers:* Jorg Hermes and Alan B. Burstein; *Photography:* Michael Slovis; *Editor:* Brett Helund; *Music:* David and Eric Wurst; Norman Greenstein. 92 minutes.

CAST: Ron Silver (Tully Windsor), Joanna Pakula (Julia Konnemann), Roy Scheider (Tom Heath) Hannes Jaenicke (Dockmonish), Elizabeth Sheppard (Hannah Rothschild), Jan Rubes (Markus Stroud), Jack Recknitz (Inspector Zielinski), Doug Lennox (General Dodd), Larry Poindexter (Lt. Kreisler), Agnieszka Wagner (Zofia), Monikz Switaj (Wanda), Jerzy Zydkiewicz, (Uncle Boy),

Joanna Kasperska (Mildred), Wladyslaw Byrdy (Lou), Jerry Flynn (Alain Levon), S. Brejdygant (Major Rothschild), A. Zarnecki (Judge Janusz B. Czech), D. Paul Thomas (Ambassador Kennedy), Peter Snider (Sgt. Paul), Jacfk Samojlowicz (Standard), Anais Granofsky (Jill), Michael Clark (Jake), Ann Holloway (Ruth), Jack Newman (Cliff), Andrzej Zielinski, (Sgt. of the Guards), Joanna Samojlowicz (Zofia's Model), Ireneuz Dydlinski, (Police Captain), Andrzej Bednarski (Policeman), M. Budny (Marine Lt.), Wenanty Nosul (Waiter), Ali Rizvi (Bartender), Katarzyna Jamroz (Young Hannah), Jacek Burcuch (Young Erwin), Julian Mere (Guard), Zofia Saretok (Charlotte), John Stocker (Dr. Cohen), Alice Poon, Rhea Akler, Yaov Dekelbaum, Doug Murray (Reporters).

Silver Wolf (Blue Rider Pictures, 1998); *Producers:* Deboragh Gabler and Gary Howsam; *Director:* Peter Svatek; *Screenplay:* Michael Amo; *Photography:* Curtis Petersen; *Executive Producers:* Jeff Geoffray and Walter Josten; *Editors:* Denis Papillon and David LeGault; *Music:* Robert Carli. 96 minutes.

CAST: Michael Biehn (Roy McLain), Roy Scheider (John Rockwell), Shane Meier (Jesse McLain), Kimberley Warnat (Lucinda Rockwell), Shaun Johnston (Frank McLean), Jade Pawluk (Clay Rockwell), Lynda Boyd (Anna McLain), Don MacKay (Sonny LaFrambois), Christine Willes (Mrs. Cates), Ron Suave (Sheriff Lawrence), Samaya Jardey (Mary Clifton), Reg Tupper (Investor #1), A. J. Bond (Chaz), John Hawkes (Randy), Trevor Roberts (Dale).

Better Living (Goldheart Productions, 1998); *Producers:* Ron Kastner and Lemore Syvan; *Director:* Max Mayer; *Screenplay:* Max Mayer, based on a play by George F. Walker; *Editor:* Steve Silkensen; *Photography:* Kurt Lennig; *Music:* John M. Davis. 95 minutes.

CAST: Olympia Dukakis (Nora), Roy Scheider (Tom), Edward Herrman (Jack), Catherine Corpeny (Maryann), Deborah Hedwall (Elizabeth), Wendy Hoopes (Gail), James Villemaire (Junior), Phyliss Somerville (Nellie), Scott Cohen (Larry), Jamie Gonzalez (Pock), Dan Moran (Dan), Brian Tarantina (Danny), Myra Lucretia Taylor (Waitress), Jessy Terrero (Biker #1), Gary Zazulka (Biker #2).

The Definite Maybe (Latent Image, 1999); *Produced, Directed and Written by:* Rob Rollins Lobl and Sam Sokolow; *Photography:* Elia Lyssy; *Executive Producers:* Bob Balaban and Patrick Sheedy; *Editor:* Claire Larson; *Music:* Adam Hirsh and Billy Jay Stein. 102 minutes.

CAST: Bob Balaban (Wolfe Rollins), Josh Lucas (Eric Traber), Jeffrey Buehl (Ziggy Sinclair), Claudia Rocafort (Sasha Rollins), Teri Garr (Dionne Waters), Roy Scheider (Eddie Jacobson), Al Franken (Vagabond), Dan Patrick (as Himself), Alex English (The Premiere), Ally Sheedy (Joanne), Mark Swinson, (Basil), Larc Spies (Henry), Julia Fowler (Jane), Sig Liebowitz (Billy Bad Boy), Mary Gilbert (Lee McGregor), Harvey Miller (Arthur), Jerry Della Famina (Jerry Hampton), Michelle Madison (Mrs. Hampton), Matthew Ballard (Larry Love), Richard T. Lobl (Irv Schlossberg), Robert Bogue (Ted), Amelia Campbell (Toby), Melissa Marsala (Liz), Darren Matthias (Big Pete), Dave Potischman (Joey D.), Manny Marianakis (Bouncer), Jason B. Testa (Duke), Amanda Talbot (Stacy), Julie Ann Beres (Guy's Little Sister), Stephanie Borgas (Jan), Matt Ogens (Valet Parker), Kristy Hinchcliffe (Amanda), Goli Samii (Kelly), Holly Schenck (Model at Bar), Iveta Vittola (Billy's Model), Brenda Price (Larry's Model), Maylin Pultar (French Model), Wendy Waring (Party Girl), Colby Diddle (Billy's Other Model), Etienne Yansomwe (DJ), Sheila Hawkins (Jerry's Daughter), Josh Wolf (Waiter), Sheila Villivicencio (Waitress), Big Frank (Limo Driver), Dan Ingram (Chet), Hope Adams (Golf Model), Kim O'Mara (Model).

RKO 281 (HBO Pictures, 1999); *Producer:* Su Armstrong; *Director:* Benjamin Ross; *Screenplay:* John Logan; *Photography:* Mike Southon; *Executive Producers:* Ridley Scott, Tony Scott; *Editor:* Alex Mackie; *Music:* John Altman. 87 minutes.

CAST: Liev Schreiber (Orson Welles), John Malkovitch (Herman Mankiewicz), James Cromwell (William Randolph Hearst), Melanie Griffith (Marion Davies), Brenda Bethyn (Louella Parsons), Roy Scheider (George Schaefer), Liam Cunningham (Greg Toland), Fiona Shaw (Hedda Hopper), Anastasia Hille (Carole Lombard), David Suchet (Louis B. Mayer), Simeon Andrews (John Houseman), Lucy Cohu (Dolores Del Rio), Angus Wright (Joseph Cotton), Kerry Shale (Bernard Herrmann), Tim Woodward (Jack Warner), Ron Berglas (Selznick), Geoffrey Hutchings (Cohn), Roger Allam (Disney), Jay Benedict (Zanuck), Paul Burchard (Top Brass 2), Neil Conrich (Mr. Thomson), Michael Cronin (Joe Willicombe), Sarah Franzi (Dorothy Comingore), Briony Glassco (Script Girl), Louis Hammond (Flunkie #2), Aaron Keeling (Young Orson Welles), Geoffrey Hutchings (Harry Cohn), Gareth Marks (Top Brass #1), Olivier Pierre (Sam Goldwyn), Roger Rose (Newsreader), Rolf Saxon (Flunkie #1), Adrian Schiller (Paul Stewart), Cyril Shaps (Jeweller), Tusse Silberg, (Welles' Mother), Toby Whitehouse (Sound Technician).

Chain of Command (Cinetel Films, 2000); *Producers:* Paul Hertzberg and John Paul Pettinato; *Director:* John Terletsky; *Screenplay:* Roger Wade; *Photography:* Maximo Munzi; *Executive Producer:* Lisa Hansen; *Editor:* Daniel Duncan; *Music:* Joseph Stanley Williams. 94 minutes.

CAST: Roy Scheider (President Jack Cahill), Patrick Muldoon (Connelly), Maria Conchita Alonso (Vice-President Grace Valdez), Michael Biehn (Thornton), Ric Young (Fung), Sung Hi Lee (Iris), William R. Moses, (Phillips), Tom Wright (Burke), Philip Tan (Wu), Michael Mantell (Lehman), Byron Field (Lt. Southern), John Putch (Agent Lambert), Pat Skipper (Elroy), Frank Maikai (Ting), Herb Mitchell, (Harrington), Michael Yama (Chairman Tzu), Susan Blakely (Danforth), John Capodice (Ellis), Kim Roberts (Stephanie), Joey Piziali (Technician), Jason Lesater (Young Journalist), Richard Yniguez (Michael Valdez), Giana LaMonica (Flight Attendant), Jayne Brock (Connelly's Ex-Wife).

Falling Through (Le Monde Entertainment, 2000); *Producers:* Louis B. Chestler, Jean-Claude Marchant, George Campana; *Director:* Colin Bucksey; *Writers:* Ian Corson and Nick Villiers; *Photography:* Peter Sinclair; *Executive Producers:* Mark Forby, Patrice Theroux, Alain Bordeic, David M. Perlmutter; *Editor:* George Roulson; *Music:* Mark Korven. 90 minutes.

CAST: Gordan Currie (Peter Connelly), Ekaterina Rednikova (Kateryna), Peter Weller (Lou Fairchild), Roy Scheider (Earl Miller), Nadia Cameron (Linda), Vernon Dobtcheff (Father), Steve Nicholson (Dimitri), Eric Connor (Polatch), Helena Sarah Coomes (Nina), Sophie Knuff (Olga), James West (Groom), Marjo Baayen (Bride), Judy Parfitt (Ambassador), Carrie O'Brien (Ambassador's Assistant), Lee Danner (Sally), Patrick Dean (Business Man), Chris Anthony (Immigration Officer #1), Robert Hall (Filing Room Clerk), Valerie Scheil (Lou's Secretary), Herve Sogne (Ponytail), Jean-Luc Rustic (Cop), Patrick Hastert (Bartender), George Arrendell (Agent), Radica Yujicin (Flight Attendant), Frederic De Brabant (Immigration Officer #2), R. J. Adams (Embassy Agent).

The Doorway (Concorde Pictures, 2000); *Producer:* Marta M. Mobley-Anderson; *Director and Writer:* Michael B. Druxman; *Photography:* Yoram Astrachan; *Executive Producer:* Roger Corman; *Editor:* Brian J. Cavanaugh; *Music:* Derek Gleeson. 91 min.

CAST: Roy Scheider (Professor Robert Lamont), Suzanne Bridgham (Susan), Christian Harmony (Rick), Don Maloney (Owen), Teresa De Priest (Lydia/Evelyn), Lauren Woodland (Tammy), Ricco Se (Hoskins), Brendan Murray (Abbott), Joe Moylan (Charlie), Christopher Burdett, Daniel McNamara, (Mirror Demons), Hoda Saoup (Demon #1), Ruter Ainer (Demon #2) John Cullen (Demon #3), Robert G. Hall (Walter Van Buren). Michael Druxman received no credit as the college dean.

Angels Don't Sleep Here (Silverline Pictures, 2000); *Producers:* Leman Cetiner and Axel Munch; *Writer and Director:* Paul Cade; *Photography:* George Mooradian; *Executive Producers:* Gunter Heinlein, Uwe Boll; *Editor:* Kristopher Lease; *Music:* William V. Malpede. 90 minutes.

CAST: Dana Ashbrook (Michael/Jessie Daniels), Kelly Rutherford (Kate Porter), Roy Scheider (Mayor Harry S. Porter), Robert Patrick (Russell Stark), Kari Wuhrer (April Williams), Gary Farmer (Lou Washington), Christina Pickles (Angela Porter), Channon Roe (Jay Stanton), Birgit Steen (Maggie), Cee Cee Harshaw (Ravin), Trevor Gruhot (Young Jesse), Travis Gruhot (Young Michael), Drew Fuller (Teenage Jesse), Jordi Vilasuso (Teenage Michael), Michelle Durham (Teen Kate), Frank Jones (Richard), David Doumeng (Detective), David St. James (Charlie), Stefan Umstead (Cop), Susan Allison (Mary Daniels), Geraldine Kerns (Arlene Gray Eagle), Richard Saxon (Reporter 1), Amy Powell (Reporter 2), Boots Sutherland (Bartender), Sam Ayers (David Roy), Steve Lambert (Big Daddy), Lisa Hoyle (Hooker), Cinda James (Harry's Secretary).

Daybreak aka ***Rapid Transit*** (Paramount, 2000); *Producers:* Kenneth Olandt, Jeffrey Beach, Phillip Roth and Melanie J. Elin; *Director:* Jean Pellerin; *Screenplay:* Jonathan Raymond from a story by Geri Cudia Barger and Phillip Roth; *Photography:* Patrick Rousseau; *Executive Producers:* James Hollinsteiner, Thomas J. Niedermeyer, Jr. and Richard Smith; *Editor:* Randy Carter; *Music:* Daniel J. Neilsen. 93 minutes.

CAST: Ted McGinley (Dillon), Roy Scheider (Stan Marshall), Ken Olandt (Deputy Mayor), Ursula Brookes (Savanna), Adam Wylie (Nathan Warner), Mark Kiely (Griffin), Jaime Bergman (Suzy), Ann Lockhart (Mrs. Warner), Troy Evans (Repo Man), Duane Davis (Ford), Marc McClure (Samuel White), Julie Brown (Connie Spheres), Pepe Serna (Herman Ortiz), Alison Dunbar (Reporter #3), William O'Leary (Lead Security Man), Kyle Olandt (Kid #1), Taylor Olandt (Kid #2).

Time Lapse aka ***Past Tense*** (Lions Gate, 2001); *Producer:* Paul Hertzberg; *Director and Photographer:* David Worth; *Writers:* David Keith Miller and Karen Kelly; *Executive Producer:* Jean Paul Pettinato; *Editor:* Daniel Duncan; *Music:* Deddy Tzur. 88 Minutes.

CAST: Roy Scheider (Agent Quinton La Nova), Dina Meyer (Kate), William McNamara (Clayton Pierce), Henry Rollins (Gaines), Barry Lynch (Simon), Adoni Maropis (Iraqi Leader), Endre Hules (Rossovitch), Cassandra Hitti (Sool Lee), Gabriella Born (Ann), Brian Simpson (Finn), Tod Barba (Agent Elman), Brian Christensen (Agent Duff), Haskell Vaughan Anderson III (Doctor Warren), Brent Jones (Agent Strom), Daniel Nathan Spector (Doctor), Adam Gordon (Security Guard), William B. Johnson (Gas Station Manager), Carol Kiernan (Restaurant Manager), Bob Kirsh (Detective), William Dixon (Policeman), Diana Morgan (TV Reporter).

The Good War aka ***Texas 46*** (Orango Film, 2001); *Producers:* Alessandro Verdecchi and Giuseppe Pedersoli; *Writer and Director:* Giorgio Serafini; *Photography:* Adolfo Troiani; *Executive Producers:* Vincenzo Verdecchi and Philippe Martinez; *Editor:* Rinaldo Marsili; *Music:* Carlo Siliotto. 90 minutes.

CAST: Roy Scheider (Colonel John Gartner), Luca Zingaretti (Luigi Manin), Charles Fathy (Luca), Sue Cremin (Betty), Vince Ricotta (Manuel), Nicholas M. Loeb (Lieutenant Trench), Mario Opinato (Carlo), Luciano Miele (Italo), Robert Farrior (Lt. Donovan). Giorgio Serafini has a cameo as Paolo. This film had not been released in the United States as of March 2002.

King of Texas (Turner Network Television, 2002) *Director:* Uli Edel; *Screenplay:* Stephen Harrigan; *Executive Producers:* Robert Halmi, Sr., Patrick and Wendy Stewart; *Music:* John Altman. 120 minutes.

Cast: Patrick Stewart (John Lear), Marcia Gay Harden (Susannah), Lauren Holly (Rebecca), Roy Scheider (Westover), David Alan Grier (Rip), Colm Meaney (Tumlinson), Patrick Bergin (Highsmith), Matt Letscher, (Emmett), Liam Waite (Thomas), Stephen Bauer (Menchaca), Julie Cox (Claudia), Richard Lineback (Warnell), Lynne Goulet (Dancer), Meno Escebedo (Cowboy), Anna Doddrige (Dancer), Clint Allen (Cowboy).

Love Thy Neighbor (2002); *Director and Writer:* Nicholas Gregory; *Photography:* Dejan Georgevich; *Executive Producer:* Marshall Persinger; *Editor:* Eric Albertson. 85 minutes.

CAST: Jennifer Bransford (Tammy), John Enos (Chuck), Jack Gwaltney (Jack), Kellie Overbey (Molly), Roy Scheider (Fred), Wallace Shawn (Doctor), Scott Wolf (Kenny), Jake

Weber (Bondage Man), Harry O'Reilly (Cop #2), Greg Zola (Car Salesman).

Joplin: The Movie (Cinnamon Productions, 2002); *Producer:* Joel L. Freedman; *Director:* Steve Austin; *Music:* Janis Joplin.

CAST: Laura Theodore (Janis Joplin), Roy Scheider (Albert Grossman), Jennifer Tilly (Drug Dealer), Sam Andrew (Joplin's Guitarist), Steve Austin (Hell's Angel Motorcyclist).

Dracula: Resurrection*; *Dracula: Ascension (2003)

CAST: Rutger Hauer, Roy Scheider, Jason Scott Lee, Jason London, Craig Sheffer, Brande Roderick, John Light, Alex Westcourt, Stephen Billington, Diane Neal and Khary Peyton. In post-production with 2003 release planned. Films are sequels to ***Dracula 2000.***

Bulls Night Out (2003)

CAST: Danny Aiello, Armand Assante, Lou Gossett, Roy Scheider. In Production March 2002.

Films That Never Got Made

Lightstone **(1976)**

1940s detective drama.

Perfect Strangers **(1977)**

Romantic drama co-starring Romy Schneider and Oskar Werner. Directed by Michael Cimino.

Everything's Jake **(1983)**

Romantic comedy written by Anthony Palmer. Directed by Peter Medak.

Across the River and Into the Trees **(1985)**

An adaption of the Hemingway book. Directed by Robert Altman.

White Train **(1987)**

A rancher objects to nuclear warheads crossing his land.

The Crew **(1990)**

A millionaire yacht owner (Roy) with an unruly crew. With Matt Dillon and Greta Sacchi. Directed by Michangelo Antonioni.

Palisades Park **(1991)**

A killer stalks the amusement park.

Leopold and Loeb **(1991)**

Roy was to play Clarence Darrow in this NBC TV movie. I can find no record of this telefilm. There is one reference in a Scheider biography for a 1994 miniseries of the same name that didn't get released either.

Barr Sinister **(1992)**

TV movie based on a popular comic book was announced three times but never made.

Conspiracy of Weeds **(1996)**

Co-starring Moira Kelly, Judge Reinhold and Sean Patrick Flanery.

The Harp **(1998)**

Announced at the 1998 Cannes Film Festival. A true story of loyalty, conflict and brotherhood. Co-starring Tony LoBianco and John Armstead. Directed by Gianni Bozzacchi.

The Bunker Hill Boys **(1998)**

A French film in the vein of *The French Connection*, only set in Boston.

Men's Lives **(1999)**

Fishermen on the South Fork of Long Island. Announced once.

Near Misses

Roy was under consideration for *The Exorcist* (1973), until Scheider introduced William Friedkin to Jason Miller.

Roy had the Robert DeNiro part in *The Deer Hunter* (1978) but left before filming began. He had a contract to do *Jaws 2* and he didn't like the ending of this film.

Roy considered taking a role in *Fort Apache: The Bronx* (1980).

Roy was announced as playing Houdini in ***Ragtime*** (1981) but is not in the film.

Roy called David Brown and asked for the lead role in ***The Verdict*** (1982). Brown wanted Robert Redford. The part went to Paul Newman when Redford wouldn't sign.

Bob Fosse wanted Roy to play Hugh Hefner in ***Star 80*** (1983). Scheider didn't want to do a cameo.

Roy was considered for the lead in ***The Name of the Rose*** (1986).

Roy turned down the part of the basketball coach in ***Hoosiers*** (1986).

Roy turned down a part as a lawyer in ***Mulligan Farm*** (1999).

Credits, Awards, Nominations

Television Credits

"U.S. Steel Hour," 1955
"Studio One," 1959
"Camera Three," Ben Jonson: The Alchemist, 1964, [Face]
"Love of Life" (serial), 1965, [Jonas Falk]
"Search for Tomorrow" (serial), 1965, [Dr. Wheeler]
"The Defenders"
"Hallmark Hall of Fame" Lamp at Midnight, 4/27/66, [Francesco Barberini]
"Coronet Blue" A Charade for Murder, 7/24/67
"Secret Storm" (serial), 1967, [Bob Hill]
"N.Y.P.D." Cry Brute, 2/6/68, [Paul Jason]
"Hidden Faces" (serial), Dec. 30, 1968–June 30, 1969, [series regular]
"Where the Heart Is" (serial), 1969, [series regular]
"N.E.T. Playhouse" Father Uxbridge Wants to Marry, 1970, [Father Ongar]
"Cannon" No Pockets in a Shroud, 11/23/71, [Daniel Bowen]
"Cop Talk," 1971
"N.E.T. Playhouse" To Be Young, Gifted and Black, 1/22/72, [Sidney]
"44th Academy Awards" Best Supporting Actor nominee, 4/10/72
"Assignment: Munich," 4/30/72, [Jake Webster]
"Theatre in America" (Encore of) To Be Young, Gifted and Black, 5/1/74
"The Dinah Shore Show," 10/6/75, Interview subject
"Peoples Choice Awards," 2/19/76
"48th Academy Awards" Presenter—Best Sound, 3/29/76
"Golden Globe Awards," 1/77, Accepted an award for Lawrence Olivier
"49th Academy Awards" Presenter—Special Visual Effects Award, 3/29/77
"American Theatre Wing Antoinette Perry Awards" Presenter, 6/4/78
"Mike Douglas Show," 12/29/78, Interview subject
"The Today Show," 5/2/79, Interview subject
"The Today Show," 1/80, Interview subject
"Golden Globe Awards," 1/80, Nominee
"34th Annual Emmy Awards," 9/19/82, Tribute to Edward Morrow
"The Tonight Show," 5/20/83, Interview subject
"Jacobo Timerman: Prisoner Without a Name, Cell Without a Number," 5/22/83, [Jacobo Timerman]
"Tiger Town," 10/9/83, [Billy Young]
"Good Morning America," 1/85, Interview subject
"Saturday Night Live," 1/19/85, Host

"Good Morning America," 4/26/85, Interview subject
"Starring the Actors" Roy Scheider, 1985, Interview subject
"Great Performances" Follies in Concert, 3/14/86, narrator
"Today," 11/8/86, Interview subject
"Our World" The Autumn of 1975, 1/8/87, panelist
"The Blessings of Liberty," 9/16/87, [George Babbitt]
"Alabaster and Blue Nights," 1/24/88, [voice of Ernest Hemingway]
"Portrait of the Soviet Union," 3/20–22/88, 7-part series Host/narrator
"Inside the Sexes," 11/21/88, narrator
"Good Morning America," 5/89, Interview subject
"American Masters" Harold Clurman: A Portrait of Theater, 7/3/89, passage narrator
"Dance in America" Bob Fosse: Steam Heat, 2/23/90
"Howard Stern," 7/21/90
"Race to Save the Planet," 10/4–10/9, 1990, narrator
A & E Revue, 1990, Interview subject
"Somebody Has to Shoot the Picture," 1990, [Paul Marish]
"When It Was a Game," 7/9/91, passage narrator
"Dick Smith: Master of Makeup," 1991, Interview subject
"13th Annual Cable ACE Awards," 1992
"When It Was a Game 2," 7/13/92, passage narrator
"Wild Justice" (4 hr. syndicated miniseries), May–June 1993, [Col. Peter Stride]
"ABC'S World of Discovery" The Last African Flying Boat, 7/10/93, narrator
"The Tonight Show with Jay Leno," 9/10/93, Interview subject
"This Is Your Life," 9/93, (syndicated) Interview subject
"seaQuest DSV," 9/12/93–12/20/95, aka "seaQuest 2032" [Captain Nathan Hale Bridger]
"The Crusaders," 1993, Interview subject
"Movie Magic," 1993, Interview subject
"Later with Bob Costas," 11/23/93, Interview subject
"News 4 at Noon" WTVJ Miami, FL, 4/27/94, Interview subject
"WBZ News 4 at 12:00" WBZ, Boston, 5/2/94, Interview subject
"Late Night w/ Conan O' Brien," 5/04/94, Interview subject
"Masters of Illusion: The Wizards of Special Effects," 5/22/94, Host/narrator
"AFI Salute to Steven Spielberg," 3/95, Speaker
"The Films of John Frankenheimer," 1995, Interview Subject
"Joe Montana: The Fire Inside," 9/12/95, narrator
"Before They Were Stars," 11/4/95
"American Experience: Spy in the Sky," 2/26/96, narrator
"E! Chicago Premiere," 11/16/96
"Access Hollywood," 5/14/97, Interview subject
"Live with Regis and Kathy Lee," 9/97, Interview subject
"Nova: Coma," 10/7/97, narrator
"World's Deadliest Sea Creatures," 5/18/98, narrator
"AFI: 100 years… 100 movies," 8/18/98
"Life and Times" Guy Lombardo: When We Danced, 1998, narrator
"Legends, Icons and Superstars of the 20th Century," 11/16/98, 12/7/98, 1/4/99, 2/8/99, 3/8/99, 5/3/99, 6/7/99, Host/narrator
"Bob Fosse: The True Hollywood Story," 1/3/99, Interview Subject
"So Graham Norton," 3/19/99, Interview Subject
"Biography: Bob Fosse: Dancing on the Edge," 8/24/99, Interview Subject
"Carrier: Cities of Steel," 11/14/99, narrator
"Nightly Business Report," 11/16/99, Interview subject
"Secrets of the Dead," 5/15, 5/16, 5/17/00, narrator
"The Films of Steven Spielberg," 6/7/00, Interview subject
"Nova: Lincoln's Secret Weapon," 10/24/00, narrator
"Nova: Hitler's Lost Sub,"11/14/00, narrator
"Bravo Profiles: Gene Hackman," 12/28/00, Interview subject
"Nova: Nazi Prison Escape," 2/7/01, narrator

"AFI: 100 years ...100 Thrills," 6/12/01, Interview subject
"Great Books" Twenty Thousand Leagues Under the Sea, 8/10/01, narrator
"The Feds: U. S. Postal Inspectors," 1/4/02, narrator
"Third Watch" The Superheroes Part 1, 2/25/02; Part 2, 3/4/02, [Fyodor Chevchenko]

UNAIRED IN THE USA AS OF 2/2002:

"Seventh Scroll" 4 hour miniseries, 1998, [Grant Schiller], Aired on Italian TV in January 2000
3 episodes of "Legends Icons and Superstars of the 20th Century," Host/narrator
"Diamond Hunters" 4 hour miniseries, [Jacobus Van Der Byl], Sold to French TV

Awards

Theresa Helburn/John Opdycke Acting Award, 1954 and 1955
Village Voice OBIE, Distinguished Performance *Stephen D.*, 1968
Peoples Choice Award, *Jaws,* 1975
Palm D'or (shared), *All That Jazz,* 1980
Drama League of NY Delia Austrian Award, *Betrayal,* 1980
Career Achievement Special Award (ShoWest), 1986
23rd Deauville Festival of American Film Audience Award: *Myth of Fingerprints,* 9/12/97
Deauville Piper-Heidsieck Award (Career), 9/12/97

Nominations

Best Supporting Actor Oscar Nomination, *French Connection,* 1971
Golden Globe Nomination, *Marathon Man,* 1976
Best Actor Oscar Nomination, *All That Jazz,* 1980
Golden Globe Nomination, *All That Jazz,* 1980
BAFTA (British Academy Award), *All That Jazz,* 1980
Independent Spirit Best Supporting Actor Nomination, *Myth of Fingerprints,* 1998

Theatre Credits

1955, Pocono Playhouse
1959, Legion Star Playhouse, Ephrata, PA
Richard the Third, March 3–12, 1960, [Richard III] Green Room Theatre, Lancaster, PA
Boston Arts Festival
The Gazebo
Kiss Me, Kate
Romeo and Juliet Feb.–May, 1961, [Mercutio] (Pro debut)
The Skin of Our Teeth, The Glass Menagerie, The Miracle Worker, 1961, State Department Tour of South America
Duchess of Malfi, March–April, 1962, [Ferdinand] McCarter Theater, Princeton, NJ
The Tragedy of King Richard the Second [Sir Henry Green]; *Henry the IV, Part 1,* [Edmund Mortimer, Earl of March], Jun. 12–Sep. 16, 1962, Shakespeare Festival, Stratford, CN
Once in a Lifetime, Oct. 23–Nov. 21, 1962 [Jerry Hyland], *Volpone,* December 18–Jan. 15, 1963 [Mosca], *12 Angry Men,* January 15, 1963–Feb. 12, 1963 [The Ad Man], *The Hostage,* Feb. 12–March 10, 1963, [IRA officer] Arena Stage, Washington, DC, 1962–1963.
Chinese Prime Minister, Jan. 2–Apr. 4, 1964, [Tarver] Royale Theater
The Alchemist, September 14–October 24, 1964, [Face] Gate Theatre
Tartuffe, January 14–May 22, 1965, [Clerk, Sergeant] Washington Square Theatre at Lincoln Center
Incident at Vichy, [A Major] 1965, Los Angeles
Long Day's Journey into Night, [Jamie Tyrone] 1965, State Department Tour—Tokyo
Serjeant Musgrave's Dance, Mar. 8–June, 1966, [Private Hurst] Theatre De Lys
Incident at Vichy, June 1966, Playhouse in the Park, Philadelphia
Stephen D., August 1966, [Cranly] Olney Theater, Olney, NJ
Cyrano De Bergerac, October 6–29, 1966, [Christian] Studio Arena Theatre, Buffalo, NY

What Do You Really Know About Your Husband? Mar. 9–11, 1967, [Donald Wallace, Jr.] Shubert Theatre, New Haven, CT

Stephen D., Sept. 24–Nov. 12, 1967, [Cranly] E. 74th Street Theater

Nobody Hears a Broken Drum, March 19–22, 1969, [uncredited] Fortune Theater

The Year Boston Won the Pennant, May 22–June 22, 1969, [Marcus Sykowski] Forum Theater, Lincoln Center

The Nuns, June 1, 1970, [Sister Angela] Cherry Lane Theater

Henry IV, Spring 1974, [King Henry] Fulton Opera House, Lancaster PA

Betrayal, Jan. 5–Jun. 1980, [Robert] Trafalgar Theatre

Remembering Harold Clurman, May 15, 1983, Hunter Playhouse, Hunter College

Sketches of War, October 10, 1988, Colonial Theater, Boston

Love Letters, March 8–15, 1992, [Andrew Makepeace Ladd III] Wilbur Theatre, Boston

Who's Gonna Be There? May 10–11, 1997, Old Whaler's Church, Sag Harbor, NY

The Dead Boy, August 24, 1997, Mulford Barn, East Hampton, NY.

Peter and the Wolf, [date unknown]

Karma Boomerang, July 31, 1999, Mulford Barn, East Hampton, NY; Westhampton Beach Performing Arts Center, Aug. 4, 2000.

When We Were Young..., August 22, 1999, Madoo Conservatory, Sagaponack, NY

When We Were Young ... II, August 13, 2000, Madoo Conservatory, Sagaponack, NY

A Midsummers' Nights Dream, December 15–16, 2000, Bay Street Theater Sag Harbor, NY.

The Duke, the Bard and You, August 5, 2001, Madoo Conservatory, Sagaponack, NY.

Chapter Notes

1. Early Influences

1. Cunningham, Laura, "Roy Scheider: In the Raw," *Cosmopolitan*, May 1976, pp. 98, 102.

2. Burke, Tom, "Roy Scheider: Hollywood's Hot Leading Man," *Cosmopolitan*, June 1978, p. 76.

3. Freedman, Richard, "Choosy Actor Finds Success in L.A. with a Little Help from Spencer Tracy," *Newark Star-Ledger*, November 16, 1986, n.p.

4. Anderson, Nancy, "I'll Never Forget What It's Like to Be Weak and Unwanted," *Motion Picture*, November 1975, p. 18.

5. Tornabene, Lyn, "Star with a Cutting Edge," *Cosmopolitan*, May 1983, p. 193.

6. Shewey, *Caught in the Act*, p. 124.

7. "The Mike Douglas Show," December 29, 1978.

8. Flatley, Guy, "Roy Scheider, *Sorcerer* Star, Talks of Thrillers," *New York Times*, January 21, 1977, section 3, p. 6.

9. Sarno, *Academy Award Oscar 1980 Annual*, p. 43.

10. Merrill, Sam, "Roy Scheider: A Candid Conversation," *Playboy*, September 1980, p. 66.

11. Plutzik, Roberta, "Roy Scheider: Tough and Tender," *Moviegoer*, November 1982, p. 17.

12. Katz, Carissa, "Performers Accent a School's Mission," *East Hampton Star*, August 19, 1999, section III, p. 3.

13. Tornabene, "Star with a Cutting Edge," p. 193.

14. Columbia High School web page, http://www.localsource.com/maplewood/.

15. Merrill, "A Candid Conversation," p. 66.

16. Snowden, Lynn, "Neighbors: Roy Scheider," *New York Woman*, Dec./Jan. 1992, p. 35.

17. Tornabene, "Star with a Cutting Edge," p. 225.

18. Ebert, Alan, "Roy Scheider No Longer Fears Jaws, Trucks—or His Own Marriage," *Us*, August 23, 1977, p. 43.

19. Marshall, Arthur G., "Tell Me That You Love Me," *Independent* (London), December 2, 1997, p. 19.

20. Plutzik, "Roy Scheider: Tough and Tender," pp. 18–19.

21. "Roy Scheider," Hollywood Foreign Press Association interview, August 13, 1983, p. 1.

22. Katz, Carissa, *East Hampton Star*, May 15, 1998, section III, p. 3, captioned photo.

23. Heilbrun, Lisa, and David Rattray, "They Got Where They Were Going," *East Hampton Star*, May 15, 1997, section III, p. 4.

24. "This Is Your Life," syndicated, 1993.

25. Green Room Club program, *The Tragedy of Coriolanus*, p. 7.

26. "The Tonight Show with Jay Leno," September 10, 1993.

27. Green Room Club program: *Knight of the Burning Pestle*, p. 4.

28. Ibid., p. 10.

29. Shewey, *Caught in the Act,* p. 124.

30. Walker, Kevin, "Roy Scheider Jaws about Acting," *Tampa Tribune*, July 27, 1999, p. 6.

31. "Roy Scheider," Hollywood Foreign Press Association interview, August 13, 1983, p. 8.

32. Stoop, Norma McClain, "Roy Scheider: Three Seasons, Two Presidents and What Did and Didn't Lead Up to *Jaws*," *After Dark*, July 1975, p. 48.

33. Green Room Club programs, 1953-1955.

34. Psi Kappa Psi Fraternity web page, http://www.phikappapsi.com/fraternity/famous.html.

35. Shewey, *Caught in the Act,* p. 124.

36. Green Room Club program, *Darkness at Noon*, p. 8.

37. Green Room Club program, *My Three Angels*, p. 6.]

38. Franklin and Marshall College press release, Spring 1980, no p.

39. Hunt, Gordon, "Starring the Actors: Roy Scheider," Worldvision Video, 1985.

40. Shewey, *Caught in the Act*, p. 124.

41. Hutchison, Curtis, "Roy Scheider," *Film Review*, April 1985, p. 17.

42. "This Is Your Life," syndicated, 1993.

43. Sarno, *Academy Award Oscar 1980 Annual*, p. 43.

44. [No author], "All About Roy Scheider and *All That Jazz*," *Movie News*, June/July 1980, pp. 29–30.

2. Delayed Ambition

1. Shulman and Youman, *How Sweet It Was,* p. 206.

2. Ibid., p. 198.

3. Franklin and Marshall College press release, Spring 1980, n.p.

4. Ibid.

5. *Theatre World*, 1959–60, p. 224.

6. Shewey, *Caught in the Act,* p. 124.

7. "This Is Your Life," syndicated, 1993.

8. Wells, Jeffery, "Roy Scheider," *Us,* December 7, 1982, p. 15.

9. Green Room Club program, *Richard III*, p. 15.

10. Green Room Club program, *Mr. Roberts*, p. 11.

11. Taylor, Sam, "Scheider 'Great' in Richard 3rd role," *Lancaster New Era*, March 4, 1960, p. 3.

12. *Franklin and Marshall Alumnus* magazine, May 1960, p. 13.

13. Franklin and Marshall press release, Spring 1980, n.p.

14. Shewey, *Caught in the Act,* p. 124.

15. Kronenberger, *Best Plays of 1960–1961*, p. 46.

16. Taubman, Howard, "Papp Offers 'Romeo' at Hughes High," *New York Times Theatre Reviews,* February 24, 1961.

17. Barrow, *Helen Hayes,* p. 178.

18. Shewey, *Caught in the Act,* p. 124.

19. Barrow, *Helen Hayes,* p. 207.

20. Hayes and Hatch, *My Life in Three Acts*, p. 223.

21. "Rona's Tell and Tell," *Rona Barrett's Hollywood*, December 1975, p. 82.

22. Thomas, Bob, "This Isn't Just Another Typical Cop Movie," *New Bedford Standard Times*, May 1983, n.p.

23. Ross, Marilyn T., "Fights Make Their Love Life Sizzle," *Photoplay*, October 1978, p. 72.

24. Drew, Bernard, "Life As a Long Rehearsal," *American Film*, November 1979, p. 75.

25. Taubman, Howard, "'Duchess of Malfi' Opens Princeton Season," *New York Times Theatre Reviews,* March 5, 1962.

26. Hewes, *Best Plays of 1962–63*, pp. 348–349.

27. Gelb, Arthur, "Stratford, Conn., Opens with Richard II," *New York Times Theatre Reviews*, June 18, 1962.

28. "American Shakespeare Festival," *Theatre World* (1962–63), p. 212.

29. Gelb, "Stratford, Conn., Opens with Richard II," June 18, 1962.

30. Gelb, Arthur, "Stratford Scorecard:

One Hit, One Miss at Connecticut Theatre," *New York Times Theatre Reviews*, June 24, 1962.

31. Stevenson, Laura H., "*Jaws*' Roy Scheider," *People*, August 25, 1975, p. 22.

32. Ross, "Fights Make Their Love Life Sizzle," p. 73.

33. Hewes, *Best Plays of 1962–63*, pp. 43–44.

34. Taubman, Howard, "Troupe in Capital Gives 'Once in a Lifetime'," *New York Times Theatre Reviews*, October 30, 1962.

35. Hewes, *Best Plays of 1962–63*, pp. 43–44.

36. *Playbill*, "The Chinese Prime Minister," March 1964, p. 17.

37. Ross, "Fights Make Their Love Life Sizzle," p. 72.

38. *Who's Who in Entertainment*, p. 565.

39. "Centerfold Interview," *Rona Barrett's Gossip*, February 1976, p. 79.

40. "This Is Your Life," syndicated, 1993.

41. Barrett, Rona, *Rona Barrett's Hollywood*, January 1977, n.p.

42. "Centerfold Interview," p. 78.

43. Winn, *Murder Ink*, p. 413.

44. Archer, Eugene, "Horror of Party Beach/Curse of the Living Corpse," *New York Times Film Reviews*, April 30, 1964, p. 3463.

45. Jones, *Monster Movie Guide*, p. 93.

46. The Bad Movie Report 11/15/98, http://www.stomptokyo.com/badmoviereport/livingcorpse.html.

47. The Astounding B Monster No. 9, http://www.bmonster.com/scifi1.9.html.

3. Off Broadway

1. Hewes, *Best Plays of 1963–64*, p. 11.

2. Ibid., p. 318.

3. "The Chinese Prime Minister," *Theatre World*, 1963–64, p. 69.

4. Taubman, Howard, "Enid Bagnold Comedy Opens at the Royale," *New York Times Theatre Reviews*, January 3, 1964.

5. Battelle, Phyllis, "Roy Scheider, Not Your Average Everyday Movie Tough Guy," *Good Housekeeping*, August 1978, p. 90.

6. Loynd, *Jaws 2 Log*, p. 49.

7. "The Alchemist," *Theatre World*, 1964–65, p. 148.

8. Taubman, Howard, "Revival of 'Alchemist' Staged at Gate," *New York Times Theatre Reviews*, September 15, 1964.

9. Hunt, Gordon, "Starring the Actors: Roy Scheider," Worldvision Video, 1985.

10. "Tartuffe," *Theatre World*, 1964–65, p. 129.

11. Taubman, Howard, "'Tartuffe' Moliere's Play Staged by Lincoln Theater," *New York Times Theatre Reviews*, January 15, 1965.

12. "Closing the Record Book on 1964-65," *New York Times Theatre Reviews*, June 27, 1965.

13. Hinman, Catherine, "Big-Money Productions Have Eluded Scheider," *Orlando Sentinel*, April 17, 1990, n.p.

14. Copeland, *Soap Opera History*, p. 178.

15. [No author], "Centerfold Interview," *Rona Barrett's Gossip*, February 1976, p. 27.

16. Barrow, *Helen Hayes*, p. 178.

17. Ibid.

18. *Serjeant Musgrave* showcard.

19. Clurman, *All People Are Famous*, p. 193.

20. *New York Times*, "Harold Clurman Dies at 78," September 10, 1980, section 4, pp. 1, 23.

21. "American Masters: Harold Clurman: A Portrait of Theatre," PBS, 1989.

22. Ibid.

23. Viewed at the Museum of Television and Radio, New York, August 18, 1997.

24. Copeland, *Soap Opera History*, p. 307.

25. Guernsey, *Best Plays of 1965–1966*, p. 33.

26. Ibid., p. 432.

27. Arden, John, "*Serjeant Musgrave's Dance*," Arena Stage program, March 17–April 17, 1966, p. 7.

28. "Serjeant Musgrave's Dance," *Theatre World*, 1965–66, p. 156.

29. Rotter, Clara, "Closing the Record Book on 1966–67," *New York Times Theatre Reviews*, June 25, 1967.

30. Kauffman, Stanley, "Colicos in Title Role of John Arden's Play," *New York Times Theatre Reviews*, March 9, 1966.

31. Kauffman, Stanley, "The Art of John Arden," *New York Times Theatre Reviews*, March 20, 1966.

32. "Roy Scheider," *Theatre World*, 1966–67, p. 248.

33. Guernsey, Otis L., Jr., ed., *The Best Plays of 1965-1966*, p. 67.

34. Kaufmann, Stanley, "The Cast," *New York Times Theatre Reviews,* August 5, 1966.

35. "Studio Arena Theatre," *Theatre World*, 1966–67, p. 209.

36. *"What Do You Really Know about Your Husband?" Theatre World*, 1966–67, p. 184.

37. "The Secret Storm," *Who's Who in Daytime TV #1*, 1967, p. 61.

38. Martin, Helen, "Where Are They Now?" *TV Picture Life*, January 1968, p. 35.

39. Wetzsteon, *Obie Winners*, p. 797.

40. *"Stephen D.," Theatre World*, 1967–68, p. 105.

41. Barnes, Clive, "Hugh Leonard Adapts Novel by Joyce," *New York Times Theatre Reviews,* September 25, 1967.

42. Kerr, Walter, [untitled], *New York Times Theatre Reviews,* October 8, 1967.

43. Rotter, Clara, "Closing the Record Book on 1967–68," *New York Times Theatre Reviews,* May 28, 1968.

44. Anderson, Dave, [untitled], *New York Times Film Reviews,* October 24, 1968, pp. 3798–99.

45. *Paper Lion*, United Artists, 1968.

46. Bier., "Paper Lion," *Variety*, October 2, 1968, n.p.

47. Anderson, Dave, [untitled], *New York Times Film Reviews,* October 24, 1968, p. 3799.

48. Adler, Renata, "Paper Lion," *New York Times Film Reviews,* October 24, 1968, p. 3798.

49. Adler, Renata, *"Star!" New York Times Film Reviews,* October 24, 1968, p. 3798.

50. Copeland, *Soap Opera History*, p. 269.

51. Ibid.

52. *"Nobody Hears a Broken Drum," Theatre World*, 1969–70, p. 125.

53. Rotter, Clare, "Closing the Record Book on 1969–70, *New York Times Theatre Reviews,* June 28, 1970.

54. Guernsey, *Best Plays of 1968–1969,* p. 25.

55. [No author], "All About Roy Scheider and *All That Jazz*," *Movie News*, June/July 1980, p. 30.

56. Gilroy, Harry, "The Cast," *New York Times Theatre Reviews,* May 23, 1969.

57. [Untitled], *New York Times Theatre Reviews,* June 8, 1969.

58. Copeland, *Soap Opera History*, pp. 246–247.

59. Terrace, *Complete Encyclopedia of Television Programs,* p. 432.

60. Copeland, *Soap Opera History*, p. 246.

61. Thompson, Howard, "A Mafia Melodrama," *New York Times Film Reviews*, August 7, 1969, p. 61.

62. Whit., *"Stiletto," Variety*, July 30, 1969, p. 6.

63. Kael, *Deeper into Movies*, p. 119 (originally run in the *New Yorker*, March 7, 1970).

64. Monaco, *American Film Now,* p. 289.

65. Greenspun, Roger, "George Segal Stars in Kershner's *Loving*," *New York Times Film Reviews*, March 5, 1970, pp. 138–139.

66. Greenspun, Roger, "'Puzzle of Downfall Child' with Faye Dunaway Here," *New York Times Film Reviews,* February 8, 1971, pp. 17–18.

67. Hunter, *Faye Dunaway*, p. 85.

68. Ibid., pp. 85–86.

69. Dunaway and Sharkey, *Looking for Gatsby,* p. 200.

70. Ibid.

71. Ibid., pp. 212–213.

72. Kael, *Deeper into Movies*, pp. 250–251. (originally run in the *New Yorker*, February 13, 1971).

73. Greenspun, Roger, "*'Puzzle of a Downfall Child,'" New York Times Film Reviews,* February 8, 1971, pp. 17–18.

74. Cocks, Jay, "Cinema," *Time*, February 15, 1971, p. 64.

75. Hunter, *Faye Dunaway*, p. 86.

76. Dunaway and Sharkey, *Looking for Gatsby*, p. 203.

77. Battelle, "Roy Scheider," p. 86.

78. *"The Nuns," Theatre World*, 1970–71, p. 108.

79. Barnes, Clive, "Hit in Europe Doesn't Survive the Crossing," *New York Times Theatre Reviews,* June 2, 1970.

80. "This Is Your Life," syndicated, 1993.

4. 1971: Break-Out Year

1. Young, *Let Me Entertain You,* p. 29.
2. *Klute*, Warner Brothers, 1971.
3. Ibid.

4. Cohen, Larry, "Warner's 'Klute' Looms as a Box Office Go," *Hollywood Reporter*, June 24, 1971, p. 3.

5. Thomas, *International Dictionary of Film and Filmmakers*, p. 887.

6. Monaco, *American Film Now*, pp. 108, 290.

7. Brady, James, "In Step with Roy Scheider," *Parade*, January 31, 1999, p. 14.

8. Shewey, *Caught in the Act*, p. 125.

9. Shirkani, K. D., "Klute Lands NY Honor," *Variety* web page, article no longer available.

10. Clagett, *William Friedkin*, p. 90.

11. Emery, *The Directors—Take Two*, p. 247.

12. Segaloff, *Hurricane Billy*, p. 112.

13. Emery, *The Directors—Take Two*, p. 247.

14. Burkhart and Stuart, *Hollywood's First Choices*, pp. 107–108.

15. 20th Century Film Corporation, "No Life but an Actor's Life," *The French Connection* press kit, 1971.

16. Reed, *Valentines and Vitriol*, p. 231.

17. Robe., "*The French Connection*," *Variety*, October 4, 1971, p. 16.

18. Sarris, Andrew, "Films in Focus," *Village Voice*, October 21, 1971, p. 77.

19. Cocks, Jay, "Chasing Frog One," *Time*, November 1, 1971, p. 109.

20. Darrach, Brad, "Parting Shots: Now at Your Theater a New Kind of Shoot 'Em Up," *Life*, November 5, 1971, p. 83.

21. Schickel, Richard, "A Real Look at a Tough Cop," *Life*, November 19, 1971, p. 13.

22. [No author], "Your Own Scoreboard for the Big TV Show," *Life*, April 7, 1972, p. 48.

23. Martin, Helen, "Where Are They Now?" *Daytime TV*, June 1972, p. 16.

24. [No author], "Catching Up with Roy Scheider," *TV Dusk to Dawn*, November 1972, p. 24.

25. "This Is Your Life," syndicated, 1993.

26. Sirkin, Elliott, "A Long Leap from Jaws," *New York Times*, March 9, 1980, section 2, p. 3.

27. Shedlin, Michael, "Police Oscar: *The French Connection*," *Film Quarterly*, Summer 1972, p. 5.

28. Biskind, *Easy Riders*, pp. 205–206.

29. Levy, *And the Winner Is*, p. 168.

30. Monaco, *American Film Now*, p. 147.

31. Thomas, *International Dictionary of Film and Filmmakers*, pp. 887–88.

32. Zinman, *Fifty Grand Movies*, p. 218.

33. Lev, *American Films of the 70s*, pp. 27–28.

34. Segaloff, *Hurricane Billy*, p. 113.

35. Ibid., p. 117.

36. Ibid., pp. 110–111.

37. Brady, James, "In Step with Roy Scheider," *Parade*, May 20, 1990, p. 22.

38. Segaloff, *Hurricane Billy*, p. 109.

39. Clagett, *William Friedkin*, p. 94.

40. Segaloff, *Hurricane Billy*, p. 114.

41. Druxman, *One Good Film*, pp. 140–141.

42. Clagett, *William Friedkin*, p. 87.

43. Osborne, *60 Years of the Oscar*, p. 218.

44. Wiley and Bona, *Inside Oscar*, p. 582.

45. Snowden, Lynn, "Neighbors: Roy Scheider," *New York Woman*, Dec./Jan. 1992, p. 35.

5. Rocky Road to Stardom

1. Battelle, Phyllis, "Roy Scheider: Not Your Average Everyday Movie Tough Guy," *Good Housekeeping*, August 1978, p. 90.

2. Brennan, Oliver L., "TV Week," *Boston Sunday Globe*, April 30, 1972, p. TV9.

3. "Assignment: Munich" press kit.

4. Kearney, Patricia, "You Can See Them in the Movies," *Daytime TV*, September 1972, p. 14.

5. Brooks and Marsh, *Complete Directory*, p. 60.

6. Reed, *Valentines and Vitriol*, pp. 231–232.

7. Canby, Vincent, "*The French Conspiracy*," *New York Times Film Reviews*, November 15, 1973, p. 132.

8. Moskowitz, G., "*Un Homme Est Mort*," *Variety*, February 14, 1973, p. 18.

9. Canby, "*The French Conspiracy*," p. 132.

10. Canby, Vincent, "A Shabby Fiction about JFK," *New York Times Film Reviews*, p. 137.

11. Haskell, Molly, "Barka up the Wrong Tree," *Village Voice*, November 22, 1973, p. 81.

12. Moskowitz, G., "*The French Conspiracy*," *Daily Variety*, October 18, 1972, p. 24.

13. Kael, *Reeling*, p. 209 (originally run in the *New Yorker*, November 19, 1973).

14. Westerbeck, Colin L., Jr., "The Screen: Stranger Than Truth," *Commonweal*, December 28, 1973, p. 344.

15. Tarratt, Margaret, "Plot," *Films and Filming*, August 1973, p. 50.

16. "Roy Scheider," Hollywood Press Association interview, August 13, 1983, p. 10.

17. Moskowitz, G., "*Un Homme est Mort*," *Variety*, February 14, 1973, pp. 18, 92.

18. American Cinematheque's Tribute to Jean Melville and the French Crime Film, www.americancinematheque.com/pressreleases/prfrench.htm.

19. Murphy, Mary, "Karen Black to Play Daisy," *Los Angeles Times*, January 19, 1973, section IV, p. 13.

20. D'Antoni, Philip, "*The Seven Ups*," *Action*, September/October 1973, p. 26.

21. [No author], "Roy Scheider: The Way They Were," *Rona Barrett's Gossip*, January 1976, p. 35.

22. *The Seven Ups*, 20th Century–Fox, 1973.

23. "A Leading Man in the Style of Men Who Lead," *The Seven Ups* press book, 20th Century–Fox, 1973.

24. Ibid.

25. *The Seven Ups* press book.

26. Campbell, Mary, "The *Connection* Spawns Twins," *Chicago Tribune*, April 1, 1973, section 6, p. 22.

27. Ibid.

28. Canby, Vincent, "*The Seven Ups*," *New York Times Film Reviews*, December 22, 1973, p. 146.

29. Stuart, Alexander, "*The Seven Ups*," *Films and Filming*, April 1974, pp. 44–45.

30. [No author], "*The Seven Ups*," *Independent Film Journal*, January 7, 1974, p. 10.

31. Frumkes, Roy, "*The Seven Ups*," *Films in Review*, February 1974, p. 121.

32. Denby, David, "Movie Cops, Pure and Corrupt," *Film 73/74*, p. 226.

33. Cocks, Jay, "Cinema: 2173 and All That," *Time*, January 7, 1974, p. 63.

34. Zimmerman, Paul D., "Misconnection," *Newsweek*, January 14, 1974, p. 73.

35. Reed, *Valentines and Vitriol*, p. 232.

36. [No author] "Roy Scheider: The Way They Were," *Rona Barrett's Gossip*, January 1976, p. 69.

37. Press book and merchandising manual, *Sheila Levine Is Dead and Living in New York*, Paramount Pictures, 1974, p. 2.

38. Canby, Vincent, "*Sheila Levine Is Dead and Living in New York*," *New York Times Film Reviews*, May 17, 1975, p. 43.

39. Herrmann, Rick, "*Sheila Levine Is Dead and Living in New York*," *Movietone News*, April 1975, pp. 39–40.

40. Haskell, Molly, "A Terminal Case of Singles," *Village Voice*, May 26, 1975, pp. 82–83.

41. Farber, Stephen, "The Hausfrau, the Ugly Duckling, and the Funny Lady," *Hudson Review*, Autumn 1975, pp. 416–417.

42. Kael, *Reeling*, p. 429 (originally run in the *New Yorker*, February 3, 1975).

43. Crist, Judith, "That's Why the Lady Has a Cramp," *New York*, February 10, 1975, pp. 52–53.

44. Monaco, *American Film Now*, pp. 117, 233.

45. Everson, William K., "*Sheila Levine Is Dead and Living in New York*," *Films in Review*, March 1975, p. 181.

46. Champlin, Charles, "*Sheila* Sugarcoated from Book to Screen," *Los Angeles Times*, March 27, 1975, part IV, p. 12.

47. Murf., "*Sheila Levine Is Dead and Living in New York*," *Variety*, February 5, 1975, p. 20.

48. Kearney, Patricia, "You Can See Them in the Movies," *Daytime TV*, May 1975, p. 16.

6. A Shark Eats a Boat

1. Perry, *Steven Spielberg*, p. 26.

2. [No author], "Jaws Now Ranking in All-Time Top Ten," *Boxoffice*, August 11, 1975, p. 4.

3. Osborne, *Academy Awards 1976 Oscar* Annual, n.p.

4. Gottlieb, *The Jaws Log*, p. 69.

5. Brown, *Let Me Entertain You*, p. 146.

6. Gottlieb, *The Jaws Log*, p. 70.

7. Andrews, *Nigel Andrews on Jaws*, p. 50.

8. Griffin, Nancy, "In the Grip of *Jaws*," *Premiere*, October 1995, p. 92.
9. Andrews, *Nigel Andrews on Jaws*, p. 51.
10. Ibid., p. 157.
11. Gottlieb, *The Jaws Log*, p. 70.
12. Andrews, *Nigel Andrews on Jaws*, p. 51.
13. Gans, Herbert J., "*Jaws*: Urban Hero," *Social Policy*, January/February 1976, p. 52.
14. Andrews, *Nigel Andrews on Jaws*, pp. 51–53.
15. Ibid., p. 159.
16. Reed, *Valentines and Vitriol*, pp. 232–233.
17. Andrews, *Nigel Andrews on Jaws*, p. 56.
18. Griffin, "In the Grip of *Jaws*," p. 98.
19. Andrews, *Nigel Andrews on Jaws*, p. 52.
20. Dalbey, Diane, "*Jaws*: The Behind the Scenes Story," *Rona Barrett's Hollywood*, December 1975, p. 47.
21. Reed, *Valentines and Vitriol*, p. 233.
22. Gottlieb, *The Jaws Log*, p. 45.
23. Taylor, *Steven Spielberg*, pp. 85–86.
24. Johns, Therese, "The Terror of Making *Jaws*," *Screen Stars*, December 1975, p. 31.
25. Reed, *Valentines and Vitriol*, pp. 234–235.
26. [No author], "Summer of the Shark," *Time*, June 23, 1975, p. 49.
27. Culhane, *Special Effects in the Movies*, p. 22.
28. Biskind, *Easy Riders*, p. 266.
29. 20th anniversary special edition laser disc *Jaws*, Universal, 1995.
30. *Rona Barrett's Gossip*, "Centerfold Interview," February 1976, p. 79.
31. Gottlieb, *The Jaws Log*, p. 201.
32. Reed, *Valentines and Vitriol*, p. 233.
33. 20th anniversary special edition laser disc *Jaws*, Universal, 1995.
34. Ibid.
35. Blake, *The Making of the Movie Jaws*, p. 115.
36. Ibid., p. 114.
37. Gottlieb, *The Jaws Log*, pp. 199–200.
38. Brown, *Let Me Entertain You*, p. 146.
39. Andrews, *Nigel Andrews on Jaws*, p. 159.
40. 20th anniversary special edition laser disc *Jaws*, Universal, 1995.
41. *Jaws* press book, "Publicity."
42. Gottlieb, *The Jaws Log*, pp. 189–192.
43. Hunt, Gordon, "Starring the Actors: Roy Scheider," Worldvision Video, 1985.
44. Reed, *Valentines and Vitriol*, pp. 233–234.
45. Dalbey, "*Jaws*: The Behind the Scenes Story," pp. 29, 47.
46. Blake, *Making of the Movie Jaws*, pp. 149–151.
47. Reed, *Valentines and Vitriol*, p. 234.
48. Cribben, Mik, "On Location with *Jaws*," *American Cinematographer*, March 1975, p. 351.
49. "The New Classics: *Jaws*," TNT, 1998.
50. [No author], "One Minute Interview with Roy Scheider," *Rona Barrett's Gossip*, December 1975, p. 60.
51. Reed, *Valentines and Vitriol*, p. 234.
52. "The Late Show with Conan O'Brien," May 1994.
53. 20th anniversary special edition laser disc *Jaws*, Universal, 1995.
54. Bookbinder, *Films of the Seventies*, p. 123.
55. Hunt, "Starring the Actors: Roy Scheider."
56. TNT presentation of *Jaws*, 1998.
57. Retherford, Bill, "*Jaws*: Feeding Frenzy," *Remember Magazine*, October 1995, p. 41.
58. TNT presentation of *Jaws*, 1998.
59. "The New Classics: *Jaws*," TNT, 1998.
60. 20th anniversary special edition laser disc *Jaws*, Universal, 1995.
61. "The New Classics: *Jaws*," TNT, 1998.
62. Walker, Kevin, "*Jaws* No Pain for Scheider," *Tampa Tribune*, July 27, 1999, p. 1.
63. Culhane, *Special Effects in the* Movies, p. 22.
64. Canby, Vincent, "Entrapped by 'Jaws' of Fear," *New York Times Film Reviews*, June 21, 1975, p. 58.
65. Canby, Vincent, "Sci-Fi: From Sports to Sharks," *New York Times Film Reviews*, June 29, 1975, pp. 62–63.
66. Farber, Stephen, "*Jaws* and *Bug*—The Only Difference Is the Hype," *New York Times Film Reviews*, p. 80.
67. Castell, David, "Background: *Jaws*," *Films Illustrated*, January 1976, p. 165.

68. Champlin, Charles, "Don't Go Near the Water," *Los Angeles Times*, June 20, 1975, section IV, p. 1.

69. Turan, Kenneth, "A Success and a Lead Balloon," *Progressive*, July 25, 1975, p. 38.

70. Pechter, William S., "Man Bites Shark (and Other Curiosities)," *Commentary*, November 1975, p. 68.

71. Siskel, Gene, "*Jaws*: A Fish Tale That's Tops in Scare Tactics," *Chicago Tribune*, June 20, 1975, section 3, p. 3.

72. Rice, Susan, "The Movies: Broken Cookies," *Media and Methods*, October 1975, pp, 21, 54.

73. Andrews, *Nigel Andrews on Jaws*, p. 158.

74. Monaco, *American Film Now*, p. 71.

75. [No author], "*Jaws* Named Best Film in People's Choice Poll," *Box Office*, March 1, 1976, p. 9.

76. Osborne, *Academy Award's 1976 Oscar Annual*, n.p.

77. Ibid.

78. [No author], "Profit Sharing," *Variety*, July 16, 1975, p. 6.

7. Olivier and Beyond

1. *Marathon Man* press book, Paramount Pictures, 1976, n.p.

2. [No author] "Sneak Preview: The *Marathon Man*," *Preview*, November 1976, p. 29.

3. Hunt, Gordon, "Starring the Actors: Roy Scheider," Worldvision Video, 1985.

4. Goldman, *Adventures in the Screen Trade*, p. 251.

5. Ibid., pp. 20–21.

6. Brode, *Films of Dustin Hoffman*, p. 182.

7. Steranko [*sic*], "Devane," *Prevue*, April/May 1982, p. 37.

8. Hunt, "Starring the Actors: Roy Scheider."

9. Ebert, Alan, "Roy Scheider: He's Learned How to Destroy Terrors More Frightening than 'Jaws,'" *US* , January 1976, p. 60.

10. Brode, *Films of Dustin Hoffman*, pp. 178–179; 182.

11. Young, George M., Jr., "Unlikely Hero, Guaranteed Villain," *National Review*, May 13, 1977, p. 555.

12. Canby, Vincent, "*Marathon Man*," *New York Times Film Reviews*, October 7, 1976, p. 268.

13. [Murf.], "*Marathon Man*," *Variety*, September 29, 1976, p. 30.

14. Crist, Judith, "Sherlock Meets Sigmund," *Saturday Review*, October 10, 1976, p. 54.

15. Monaco, *American Film Now*, p. 285.

16. Archerd, Army, "Just for Variety," *Daily Variety*, December 2, 1997, p. 4.

17. [No author], "Genre Gems," *York Daily Record*, August 9, 1999, p. D01.

18. Graham, Lee, "Pathos, Suspense and Glamour at the 34th Golden Globes," *Hollywood Studio Magazine*, March 1977, p. 7.

19. Scott, Vernon, "Scheider: At His Wife's Mercy," *UPI Newswire*, October 26, 1986.

20. Biskind, *Uneasy Riders*, p. 309.

21. Clagett, *William Friedkin*, p. 141.

22. Ibid., pp. 142, 166–167.

23. *Sorcerer* press book, Paramount Pictures, 1977, pp. 14–15.

24. Flatley, Guy, "Roy Scheider, *Sorcerer* Star, Talks of Thrillers," *New York Times*, January 21, 1977, section 3, pp. 6.

25. [No author], "*Sorcerer*," *Sack Theatre Show Guide*, July 1977, pp. 4.

26. Biskind, *Uneasy Riders*, pp. 310–311.

27. [No author], "Roy Scheider Plays It Not So Safe, for Real," *Gossip World*, November 1977, p. 45.

28. Clagett, *William Friedkin*, p. 141.

29. Ibid., p. 154.

30. Siskel, Gene, "*Jaws* of Success Puts the Bite on Roy Scheider," *Chicago Tribune*, 1980, p. 2.

31. Eisenberg, Lawrence, "Talking with Roy Scheider," *Redbook*, November 1982, p. 12.

32. Biskind, *Uneasy Riders*, pp. 337–338.

33. Monaco, *American Film Now*, p. 150.

34. Canby, Vincent, "*Sorcerer*," *New York Times Film Reviews*, June 25, 1977, p. 73.

35. Canby, Vincent, "Let's Call It the Accountant's Theory of Filmmaking," *New York Times Film Reviews*, July 10, 1977, p. 78.

36. *Sorcerer* press book, p. 15.

37. Badder, David, "Wages of Fear," *Monthly Film Bulletin*, January 1978, p. 57.

38. Turan, Kenneth, "Remakes," *Progressive*, September 1997, pp. 38–39.

39. Monaco, *American Film Now*, p. 73.

40. [No author], "Background," *Films Illustrated*, March 1978, p. 246.

41. Smith, Michael, "How Roy Scheider Ended Up Doing *Jaws 2*," *Jaws* home page, http://www.winternet.com/~tandj04/jaws/roydoes2.html.

42. Johnston, Laurie, "no title," *New York Times*, October 16, 1975, p. 26.

43. *Modern Screen*, January 1976, captioned photo, p. 68.

44. [No author], "MGM Puts the Bite on Roy Scheider for 120,000.00," *Rona Barrett's Gossip*, April 1976, p. 14.

45. [No author], "Bad News," *Movie TV Gossip*, July 1977, n.p.

46. Cummings, Julie, "Scheider Calls TV a Wonderful Graveyard for Actors," *New York Times*, August 4, 1980, section 2, p. 4.

47. Ebert, Alan, "Roy Scheider No Longer Fears Jaws," p. 44.

48. *Jaws* home page.

49. Goldberg, *Science Fiction Filmmaking*, p. 251.

50. [No author], "On the Set: *Jaws II*," *Rona Barrett's Hollywood*, February 1978, p. 63.

51. Kirk, Christina, "Problems Plague *Jaws 2*," *Star*, August 9, 1997, p. 45.

52. Loynd, *Jaws 2 Log*, pp. 54–55, 57.

53. Ibid., pp. 57–59.

54. Barrett, Rona, [no title], *Rona Barrett's Gossip*, November 1978, n.p.

55. Flippo, Chet, "Roy Lets Fly at Critics, Reagan and *All That Jazz*," *People*, May 23, 1983, p. 74.

56. Brown, *Let Me Entertain You*, p. 155.

57. Loynd, *Jaws 2 Log*, pp. 51–53.

58. Ibid., p. 46.

59. Brown, *Let Me Entertain You*, pp. 154–155.

60. *Jaws 2* press book, "Publicity: Roy Scheider Recalls the Awesome Ocean," n.p.

61. [No author], "Jaws 2," *Photoplay: Film and TV Scene*, January 1979, p. 19

62. *Jaws 2* press book, "Shorts," n.p.

63. Loynd, *Jaws 2 Log*, p. 50.

64. Ibid., pp. 50–51.

65. Ibid., p. 57.

66. [No author], "Winners and Losers," *Rona Barrett's Hollywood*, February 1978, p. 17.

67. Smith, Liz, "Hero-Worship Is Strong in the Land," *New York Daily News*, August 19, 1977, p. 6C.

68. Kirk, "Problems Plague *Jaws 2*," p. 45.

69. [No author], "*Jaws 2* Gets a Fishy Ending," *Star*, October 18, 1977, p. 42.

70. Cocchi, John, "Actor David Elliott Declares *Jaws 2* Is Good 'Artistically, Technically'," *Box Office*, February 13, 1978, p. 8.

71. Jones, Jerry, "*Jaws* Principals Meet the Press to Describe Production of the Sequel," *Box Office*, March 27, 1978, p. 15.

72. Kent, Leticia, "Back in the Grip of *Jaws*," *New York Times*, July 31, 1978, section 2, p. 16.

73. Shaw, Russell, "Fishmongers Get Sequel Time," *Crawdaddy*, May 1978, p. 14.

74. Biskind, *Uneasy Riders*, p. 330.

75. "*Jaws* Team Enjoys a Jaws Session," *Star*, May 2, 1978, p. 23.

76. Playbill, "32nd Annual Antoinette Perry Awards," June 4, 1978, n.p.

77. Kaminsky, Ralph, "Universal Pictures Media Luncheon Is Hosted by the Director of *Jaws 2*," *Box Office*, June 18, 1978, p. 4.

78. *Jaws 2* press book, "Promotion," n.p.

79. "The Mike Douglas Show," December 29, 1978.

80. Haskell, Molly, "Say Ahhhh," *New York*, July 3, 1978, p. 67.

81. Canby, Vincent, "The Great White Redux," *New York Times Film Reviews*, July 16, 1978, p. 221.

82. Jackson, Martin A., "*Jaws 2*," *USA Today* magazine, September 1978, p. 64.

83. Gow, Gordon, "*Jaws 2*," *Films and Filming*, December 1978, p. 31.

84. Bookbinder, *Films of the Seventies*, pp. 208–209.

85. *Jaws* home page.

86. [No author], "They Say," *Photoplay*, September 1977, p. 58.

87. "Roy Scheider," Hollywood Foreign Press interview, August 13, 1983, p. 7.

88. *Last Embrace* press book, United Artists, 1979, pp. 2.

89. Scott, David, "Roy Scheider," *Club*, July 1979, pp. 19–20.

90. Sragow, Michael, "Jonathan Demme on the Line," *American Film*, January–February 1984, p. 47.

91. Bliss, *What Goes Around Comes Around*, pp. 46–48.

92. [No author], "Join the Fun," *Movie Stars*, November 1979, p. 43.

93. Sarris, Andrew, "Captains Courageous," *Village Voice*, May 7, 1979, p. 49.

94. Charlton, Leigh, "Demme Fondly Embraces Hitchcock," *Feature*, May 1979, p. 17.

95. Barrett, Rona, "*The Last Embrace*," *Rona Barrett's Hollywood*, October 1979, n.p.

96. Minsky, Terri, "The Bitter Taste in Roy Scheider's Mouth," *New York Daily News*, November 5, 1986, n.p.

97. Musto, Michael, "A Tough Guise: Roy Scheider Faces Up to Stardom," *GQ*, April 1983, p. 161.

8. Dancing for Fosse

1. Sarno, *Academy Award Oscar 1980 Annual*, p. 29.

2. Ibid.

3. [No author], "All about Roy Scheider and *All That Jazz*," *Movie News*, June/July 1980, p. 29.

4. Gottfried, *All His Jazz*, pp. 377–378.

5. Ibid., p. 379.

6. Grubb, *Razzle Dazzle*, p. 224.

7. Brady, James, "In Step with Roy Scheider," *Parade*, January 30, 1999, p. 14.

8. Beddow, *Bob Fosse's Broadway*, p. ix.

9. Drew, Bernard, "Life as a Long Rehearsal," *American Film*, November 1979, p. 75.

10. Tomlinson, *Actors on Acting*, p. 499.

11. Scott, David, "Roy Scheider," *Club*, July 1979, p. 20.

12. Williamson, Bruce, "All That Fosse," *Playboy*, March 1980, p. 176.

13. "Roy Scheider," Hollywood Press Association interview, August 13, 1983, p. 6.

14. [No author], "Gotta Dance: Broadway Legend Gwen Verdon Shares Her Passion for Theater with Students at USF," *Tampa Tribune*, July 30, 1999, p. 1.

15. Barrett, Rona "Rona Looks at the 1980 Oscars," *Rona Barrett's Hollywood*, June/July 1980, p. 19.

16. Gluckman, Ron, "Scheider's Intensity Is Key to Appeal," *Anchorage Times*, April 11, 1985, n.p.

17. Gray, Marianne, "I Lead a Very Routine Life," *Photoplay: Film, TV, Video*, December 1980, p. 42.

18. "This Is Your Life," syndicated, 1993.

19. Persall, Steve, "Inspiration at Center Stage," *St. Petersburg Times*, July 28, 1999, p. 1D.

20. "This Is Your Life," syndicated, 1993.

21. "Bob Fosse: The True Hollywood Story," E! Entertainment channel, 1999.

22. Hunt, Gordon, "Starring the Actors: Roy Scheider," Worldvision Video, 1985.

23. [No author], "Fathers and Daughters: Roy Scheider and Maximillia," *Seventeen*, December 1978, p. 108.

24. Sarno, *Academy Award Oscar 1980 Annual*, p. 29.

25. Gottfried, *All His Jazz*, p. 397.

26. Ibid., p. 390.

27. Ibid., p. 394.

28. [No author], "Tribute: Life Was a Cabaret," *People*, October 12, 1987, p. 87.

29. Sarno, *Academy Award Oscar 1980 Annual*, p. 28.

30. Ibid., p. 43.

31. Ibid., p. 28.

32. Siskel, Gene, "'Jaws' of Success Puts the Bite on Roy Scheider," *Chicago Tribune*, April 27, 1980, p. 2.

33. Slater, Douglas, "Let's Do the Show Right Here in the Intensive Care Unit," *Films Illustrated*, December 1980, p. 111.

34. Wells, Jeffrey, "*All That Jazz*: Two Views," *Films in Review*, February 1980, p. 113.

35. Edelman, Rob, "*All That Jazz*: Two Views," *Films in Review*, February 1980, pp. 113–114.

36. [No author], "Capsules," *Films in Review*, February 1980, p. 128.

37. Canby, Vincent, "Roy Scheider Stars in *All That Jazz*," *New York Times*, December 20, 1979, section 3, p. 13.

38. Canby, Vincent, "Film View: Robert Duvall," *New York Times*, July 20, 1980, section 2, p. 13.

39. Rich, Frank, "Fan Dance," *Time*, December 31, 1979, p. 45.

40. Sarris, Andrew, "Autobiographical Portraits as Reel Life," *Village Voice*, January 7, 1980, p. 35.

41. Summers, Jimmy, "*All That Jazz*," *Box Office*, January 28, 1980, p. 13.

42. Reed, Rex, "Movies: *All That Jazz*," *Vogue*, January 1980, p. 24.

43. Crawley, Tony, "Roy as Fosse?" *Photoplay: Film and TV Scene*, July 1980, p. 28.

44. Crist, Judith, "To Tell the Truth—More or Less," *50 Plus*, February 1980, p. 64.

45. [No author], "Clips," *Boston Magazine*, March 1980, p. 192.

46. Rottenberg, Dan, "Film Clips," *Washingtonian*, July 1980, p. 49.

47. Arnold, Gary, "Mostly Fosse and Feathers," *Washington Post*, February 15, 1980, p. C1.

48. Mariani, John, "Roy Scheider," *Playboy Guide to Electronic Entertainment*, Fall-Winter 1982, p. 22.

49. Gottfried, *All His Jazz*, p. 403.

50. Harmetz, Aljean, [no title], *New York Times*, February 26, 1980, Section 3, p. 5.

51. *AP Newswire*, March 27, 1980.

52. Wiley and Bona, *Inside Oscar*, pp. 578, 582.

53. [No author], "Star Wars: 20 Actors Rate Their Chances in the Battle for Oscar," *Us*, April 15, 1980, p. 57.

54. Mariani, "Roy Scheider," p. 22.

55. "Premieres: *All That Jazz*," *Season Pass*, National Subscription Television, February 1981, p. 6.

56. Mr. Showbiz web page, http://mrshowbiz.go.com/movies/reviews/AllThatJazz_1979/review.html.

57. Cobb, *How They Met*, pp. 88–89.

9. High-Flying Eighties

1. "*Betrayal*," *Curtain Time*, Fireside Theatre Book Club, December 1980, n.p.

2. Vincent, Mal, "Scheider: Part-Time Tough Guy," *Norfolk Virginian-Pilot*, May 15, 1983, n.p.

3. Cantwell, Mary, "Men and Women: Love & Sex and Roy Scheider," *Mademoiselle*, July 1980, pp. 161, 163.

4. Kakutani, Michiko, "The Pauses in Pinter Give Three Actors Pause," *New York Times*, January 16, 1980, p. C19.

5. Clurman, Harold, "Theater," *Nation*, January 26, 1980, p. 93.

6. Kerr, Walter, "*Betrayal*," *New York Times Theatre Reviews*, January 7, 1980, p. 236.

7. Sirkin, Elliott, "Long Leap from Jaws," *New York Times*, March 9, 1980, section 2, page 3.

8. "*Betrayal*," *Curtain Time*, n.p.

9. Brustein, Robert, "Robert Brustein on Theater," *New Republic*, February 9, 1980, p. 26.

10. [No author], "Scheider Wins Drama Award," *New York Times*, May 9, 1980, section 3, p. 7.

11. Franklin and Marshall press release, June 1980, n.p.

12. Biskind, *Easy Riders*, p. 16.

13. "Saturday Night Live," January 19, 1985.

14. [No author], "Star Tracks: Scheider Protests," *People*, March 24, 1980, p. 86.

15. Scheider, Roy, "Letters to the Editor," *New York Times*, July 27, 1980, section 2, p. 26.

16. Battita, Mary, "Roy Scheider's est for Life," *Washington Post*, April 6, 1981, p. C1.

17. Dutka, Elaine, "Talking with Meryl Streep," *Redbook*, September 1982, p. 14.

18. *Still of the Night* press kit, "Roy Scheider Talks about His Role, His Leading Lady and Director," n.p.

19. Smurthwaite, *Meryl Streep*, pp. 69–76.

20. Collins, Glenn, "Robert Benton Brews Thrills after *Kramer*," *New York Times*, November 14, 1982, section 2, p. 17.

21. Pfaff and Emerson, *Meryl Streep*, p. 69.

22. Ibid.

23. [No author], "The Vasari Diary: Whodunnit? Whosinnit?" *ARTnews*, May 1983, p. 22.

24. Lane, Christopher, "Conch Republic Salutes Island Living with Festival," *Miami Herald*, January 28, 1983, p. 1C.

25. Bellido, Susan, "Key West's Checkered Past a Boon to Homeowners," *Miami Herald*, July 21, 1996, p. 3B.

26. Eisenberg, Lawrence, "Talking with Roy Scheider," *Redbook*, November 1982, p. 12.

27. Viewed at the Museum of Television and Radio, New York City, August 18, 2000.

28. Maychick, *Meryl Streep*, pp. 125–126.

29. Ibid.

30. Ansen, David, "This Shrink for Hire," *Newsweek*, November 22, 1982, p. 118.

31. Smurthwaite, *Meryl Streep*, p. 76.

32. Canby, Vincent, "Lady of Mystery," *New York Times Film Reviews*, November 19, 1982, pp. 191–192, 321

33. Schickel, Richard, "Hitchhiking the Mean Streets," *Time*, November 22, 1982, p. 108.

34. Wilmington, Michael, "Home Tech: Video News and Reviews," *Los Angeles Times*, July 22, 1988, part 6, p. 23.

35. Asahina, Robert, "Holiday Turkeys," *New Leader*, December 27, 1982, p. 20.

36. Haller, Scot, "Psychoed Out," *Boston Magazine*, December 1982, pp. 136, 138–139.

37. Sarris, Andrew, "High Life and Low Life in Gotham," *Village Voice*, November 30, 1982, p. 59.

38. Wells, Jeffrey, "*Still of the Night*," *Film Journal*, November 19, 1983, p. 51.

39. O'Toole, Lawrence, "Borrowed Personalities," *Maclean's*, November 29, 1982, p. 60.

40. Williamson, Bruce, "Movies," *Playboy*, December 1982, p. 48.

41. [No author], "Picks and Pans: *Still of the Night*," *People*, December 13, 1982, p. 30.

42. Crist, Judith, "Triple Suspense," *50 Plus*, November 1982, p. 66.

43. [No author], "Movie: The Winner's Circle," *Washingtonian*, February 1983, p. 48.

44. Summers, Jimmy, "Reviews," *Boxoffice*, January 1983, p. 53.

45. *Herald* Staff, "Q & A," *Miami Herald Tropic Magazine*, July 10, 1983, p. 6.

46. "Roy Scheider," Hollywood Press Association interview, August 13, 1983, p. 1.

47. Base and Haslam, *Movies of the Eighties*, pp. 78, 82.

48. Cobb, *How They Met*, p. 89.

49. Ibid., p. 90.

50. Mann, Roderick, "Batting Three for Three, Scheider Seeking Another Homer," *Los Angeles Times*, April 19, 1983, p. 4.

51. "Roy Scheider," Hollywood Press Association interview, August 13, 1983, p. 10.

52. Ryan, Desmond, "He's in His Element as an Airborne Cop," *Philadelphia Inquirer*, May 15, 1983, n.p.

53. Glauberman, Naomi, "Dialogue on Film: John Badham," *American Film*, May 1983, p. 65.

54. Randy and Jean-Marc Lofficier, "Roy Scheider Piloting *Blue Thunder*," *Starlog*, August 1983, p. 28.

55. Goldberg, *Science Fiction Filmmaking*, p. 70.

56. Emery, *The Directors—Take Two*, p. 341.

57. "The Tonight Show," May 1983.

58. Hackett, Pat, "John Badham," *Interview*, July 1983, p. 39.

59. Ticket stub from Filmex premiere.

60. Vincent, "Scheider: Part-Time Tough Guy," n.p.

61. "Roy Scheider," Hollywood Press Association interview, August 13, 1983, p. 2.

62. Canby, Vincent, "Spying from Above," *New York Times Film Reviews*, May 13, 1983, p. 56.

63. Canby, Vincent, "Are Video Games about to Zap the Action Movie?" *New York Times Film Reviews*, May 15, 1983, p. 57.

64. [No author], "Not Another (Pow!) 'Message' (Bam!) Movie!" *Los Angeles*, May 1983, p. 34.

65. Von Buchau, Stephanie, "*Blue Thunder*," *San Francisco*, August 1983, p. 147.

66. Dowell, Pat, "Get Out Your Funny Glasses," *Washingtonian*, June 1983, p. 59.

67. Kehr, Dave, "Movies: Wide Open on the Wide Screen," *Chicago*, June 1983, pp. 111–112.

68. Fuller, Richard, "Films: Summer Scorecard," *Philadelphia*, August 1983, p. 57.

69. Haller, Scot, "Meat Chopper," *Boston Magazine*, May 1983, p. 108.

70. Petley, Julian, "*Blue Thunder*," *Films and Filming*, July 1983, p. 38.

71. Ansen, David, "High-Tech Paranoia," *Newsweek*, May 30, 1983, p. 96.

72. Asahina, Robert, "Stale Popcorn," *New Leader*, May 30, 1983, p. 20.

73. [No author], "Picks and Pans: *Blue Thunder*," *People*, May 30, 1983, p. 10.

74. Flatley, Guy, "Cosmo Goes to the Movies," *Cosmopolitan*, May 1983, p. 28.

75. Bricker, Rebecca, "Take One," *People*, August 1, 1983, p. 21.

76. Zorn, Eric, "Nice Picture of Roy Scheider, Huh?" *Chicago Tribune*, May 14, 1983, p. 1C.

77. *AP Newswire*, February 14, 1983.

78. Buck, Jerry, "TV Talk: Linda Yellen and 'Prisoner without a Name' on NBC," *AP Newswire*, May 19, 1983.

79. *AP Newswire*, February 14, 1983.

80. [No author], "Keep Your Eye on Roy Scheider in *Blue Thunder*," *Harper's Bazaar*, May 1983, p. 92.

81. "Roy Scheider," Hollywood Press Association interview, August 13, 1983, p. 1.

82. Ibid., p. 3.

83. Lane, "Conch Republic Salutes Island Living with Festival," p. 1C.

84. *Herald* Staff, "Last Home and Garden Tour Includes Roy Scheider's House," *Miami Herald*, May 4, 1983, p. 1C.

85. Carmody, John, "Now Here's the News," *Washington Post*, April 1, 1983, p. D8.

86. Flippo, Chet, "*Blue Thunder*'s Roy Scheider Lets Fly at Critics, Reagan and *All That Jazz*," *People*, May 23, 1983, p. 76.

87. Lawson, Carol, [no title], *New York Times*, May 6, 1983, section 3, p. 2.

88. Buck, "TV Talk: Linda Yellen and 'Prisoner without a Name' on NBC."

89. "Roy Scheider," Hollywood Press Association interview, August 13, 1983, p. 2.

90. Ibid., p. 4.

91. Mansfield, Stephanie, "NBC's Torturous Timerman," *Washington Post*, May 21, 1983, p. D11.

92. Earley, Sandra, "*Prisoner* Is Cynical Television," *Miami Herald*, May 22, 1983, p. 7L.

93. "Roy Scheider," Hollywood Press Association interview, August 13, 1983, p. 5.

94. Ibid., p. 9.

95. Scheider, Roy, "The Method vs. the Fast Ball," *Playboy*, April 1984, p. 178.

96. Garcia, Guy D., "People," *Time*, August 29, 1983, p. 63.

97. *UPI Newswire*, June 22, 1983.

98. [No author], "Dynamic Baseball?" *New York Times*, July 1, 1983, section A, p. 18.

99. [No author], "Star Tracks," *People*, August 8, 1983, p. 61.

100. [No author], "Roy Scheider in *Tiger Town*," *Disney Channel Magazine*, October 1985, p. 4.

101. [No author], "Roy Scheider Becomes a Baseball Star in *Tiger Town* for the Disney Channel," *Tiger Town* Press Kit, Disney, 1983, p. 1.

102. *AP Newswire*, October 7, 1983.

103. Shales, Tom, "Trading in Rabbit Ears for Mickey Mouse Ears," *Miami Herald*, December 22, 1983, p. 6B.

104. [No author], *Daily Variety*, October 23, 1983, n.p., http://www.primenet.com/~shabrino/tt3C.html.

105. Shapiro, Alan, Lake Walloon Productions web page, *Tiger Town* Tour, http://www.primenet.com/~shabrino/ttA4A.html.

106. Ibid., http://www.primenet.com/~shabrino/ttX.html.

107. Ibid., http://www.primenet.com/~shabrino/tt3.html.

108. Ibid.

109. Landau, Susan B., "Confessions of a Woman Producer," *Cosmopolitan*, March 1990, p. 222.

110. Roy Scheider," Hollywood Press Association interview, August 13, 1983, p. 7.

111. Clarke and Hyams, *Odyssey File*, pp. 3, 112.

112. Ibid., p. 47.

113. Ibid., p. 55.

114. Ibid., pp. 60–62.

115. Ibid., p. 65.

116. Ibid., pp. 75–76.

117. Ibid., p. 77.

118. McMurran, Kristin, "*Scarface* Premiere," *People*, December 19, 1983, p. 55.

119. Clarke and Hyams, *Odyssey File*, p. 102.

120. Ibid., pp. 13–15.

121. Elliott, David, "A Bold Leap into *2010*," *San Diego Times Union*, November 25, 1984, p. E1.

122. Hollis, Richard, "*2010*," *Starburst*, April 1985, pp. 13–15.

123. Williams, George, "Scheider Keeps It Simple in *2010*," *Sacramento Bee*, December 2, 1984, n.p.

124. Siskel, Gene, "Roy Scheider: *2010*'s Everyman Adventure Hero," *Chicago Tribune*, November 25, 1984, section 13, pp. 5–6.

125. Goldberg, *Science Fiction Filmmaking*, p. 246.

126. Ibid., pp. 247–248.

127. Goldberg, Lee, "Elya Baskin," *Starlog*, February 1985, p. 18.

128. "The Tonight Show," September 10, 1993.

129. McAleer, *Arthur C. Clarke*, p. 321.

130. Carmody, John, "Now Here's the News," *Washington Post*, May 24, 1984, p. D13.

131. Ibid.

132. George Hackett, "Newsmakers," *Newsweek*, April 30, 1984, p. 57.

133. *AP Newswire*, April 17, 1983.

134. Childress, Deidre M., "Prince Admires Chopper," *UPI Newswire*, April 17, 1983.

135. Oney, Steve, "Hollywood Left Helps Sandinistas," *Miami Herald*, August 6, 1984, p. 1G.

136. [No author], "Scheider Roots on Tigers," *San Diego Union-Tribune*, June 8, 1994, p. C4.

137. Shapiro, Alan, Lake Walloon Productions web page, http://www.primenet.com/~shabrino/tt4.html.

138. *Disney Channel Magazine*, October 1985, p. 5.

139. Canby, Vincent, "*2010*," *New York Times Film Reviews*, December 7, 1984, p. 330.

140. MacKay, Gillian, "Voyage of the Bland," *Maclean's*, December 19, 1984, p. 69.

141. Attanasio, Paul, "*2010*: The Long Awaited Sequel Gets Lost in Space," *Washington Post*, December 7, 1984, p. D1.

142. Sublett, Scott, "2010: Human Drama Eclipses Technology," *Washington Times*, December 7, 1984, n.p.

143. Ribischon, Noah, "Smart Man, Stupid Questions," *Entertainment Weekly*, January 7, 2000, p. 32.

144. Har., "*2010*," *Variety Weekly*, December 12, 1984, p. 19.

145. [No author or title], *Us*, November 19, 1984, [no page number given].

146. "Scheider vs. Scheider," *New York Law Journal*, October 15, 1991, p. 31

10. Choices and Changes

1. [Video], "The Making of *2010*," Zaloom Productions, 1984.

2. [No author], "Hyams Sets Precedent in *2010* by Wearing Four Hats in a Major Pic," *Variety*, November 14, 1984, p. 18.

3. "Good Morning America," January 1985.

4. Laufer, Aliza, "John Hill, Chuck Berry Jam for VW, DDB," *Back Stage*, February 8, 1985, p. 8.

5. Gluckman, Ron, "Scheider's Intensity is Key," *Anchorage Times*, April 11, 1985, n.p.

6. Scott, Vernon, "Scheider: At His Wife's Mercy," *UPI Newswire*, October 26, 1986.

7. Hasen, Jeff, "Fight Notebook," *UPI Newswire*, April 16, 1985.

8. "Good Morning America," April 16, 1985.

9. Sonsky, Steve, "Altman Takes the Plunge to Cable," *Miami Herald*, April 1, 1985, p. 1C.

10. Heningburg, Maria Morrison, "CHS Hall of Fame," Maplewood Matters web page, http://www.maplewoodonline.com/matters/fame.

11. Attanasio, Paul, "Mishima Impossible," *Washington Post*, October 15, 1985, p. E3.

12. Tomasson, Robert E., "Social Events: Indoors and Out," *New York Times*, June 9, 1985, section 1, part 2, p. 68.

13. *Rona Barrett's Gossip*, November 1985, n.p.

14. Cobb, *How They Met*, p. 90.

15. Wallach, Allen, "PBS' Follies," *Newsday*, March 14, 1986, n.p.

16. "Follies: In Concert," PBS, March 14, 1986.

17. Kuchwara, Michael, "A Documentary Celebrating Stephen Sondheim's 'Follies' on PBS," *AP Newswire*, May 13, 1986.

18. Mills, Bart, "Some Good Ol' Boys Take a Serious Look at Love," *San Francisco Examiner and Chronicle*, September 28, 1986, n.p.

19. Turnquist, Kris, "*The Men's Club*," *Box Office*, December 1986, p. R136.

20. Maislin, Janet, "That's Life! Has Fun with Morality," *New York Times Film Reviews*, September 26, 1986, p. 346.

21. Williamson, Bruce, "Movies," *Playboy*, October 1986, p. 25.

22. Stone, Laurie, "Bad Boys on the Loose," *Ms.*, September 1986, p. 14.

23. Joyner, Will, "Film Goes an Orgy Too Far," (Bergen County) *Record*, September 22, 1986, p. B6.

24. Turnquist, "*The Men's Club*," p. R136.

25. [No author], "Japanese Firm Gives

Boy George the Gong," *Miami Herald*, August 31, 1986, p. 3K.

26. Thomas, Bob, "Star Watch: Roy Scheider Is on the Run Again," *AP Newswire*, November 28, 1986.

27. Siskel, Gene, "Roy Scheider: *2010*'s Everyman Hero," *Chicago Tribune*, November 25, 1984, section 13, p. 7.

28. Champlin, *John Frankenheimer*, p. 171.

29. "Sneak Previews: The Making of *52 Pick-Up*," syndicated cable, 1986.

30. *PR Newswire*, February 14, 1986.

31. Champlin, *John Frankenheimer*, pp. 171–172.

32. Pratley, *Films of Frankenheimer*, p. 194.

33. Roberts and Graydos, *Movie Talk from the Front Lines*, pp. 281–285.

34. Emery, Robert, "The Directors: John Frankenheimer," Media Entertainment, 1997.

35. "Roy Scheider," Hollywood Foreign Press Association interview, August 13, 1983, p. 4.

36. McGilligan, Patrick, "Get Dutch," *Film Comment*, March–April 1998, p. 51.

37. Champlin, *John Frankenheimer*, p. 174.

38. Pratley, *Films of Frankenheimer*, p. 195.

39. *Business Wire*, October 28, 1986.

40. "Today," November 1986.

41. "The Making of *52 Pick-Up*," Trudeau/Cummings Productions, 1985.

42. Maislin, Janet, "Vicious Moments," *New York Times Film Reviews*, 1985-1986, November 7, 1986, p. 365.

43. Kelleher, Ed, "*52 Pick-Up*," *Film Journal*, December 1986, p. 43.

44. Hoberman, J., "Career Moves," *Village Voice*, November 18, 1986, p. 58.

45. Williamson, Bruce, "Movies," *Playboy*, February 1987, pp. 15–16.

46. Kempley, Rita, "*52 Pick-Up*: Same Old Game," *Washington Post*, November 7, 1986, p. N27.

47. Salem, Rob, "Good Cards Need Better Shuffle," *Toronto Star*, November 7, 1986, p. D9.

48. Hagen, Bill, "Just the Same Vigilante Theme in *52 Pick-Up*," *San Diego Union-Tribune*, November 12, 1986, p. C11.

49. Hurlburt, Roger, "When Art Imitates a Violent World," *Sun-Sentinel*, November 7, 1986, p. 3.

50. Cosford, Bill, "*52*: It's a Winner," *Miami Herald*, November 7, 1986, p. 2D.

51. King, Susan, "Actor Prizes Role in a Movie with a Message," *Sun-Sentinel*, September 9, 1990, p. 3G.

52. Burden, Michael, "A Ballpark Figure," *New York Post*, September 12, 1989, n.p.

53. Mulcahy, Susan, "Inside New York," *Newsday*, December 26, 1986, n.p.

54. Rosenthal, Donna, "The Shark That Won't Go Away," *Newsday*, March 22, 1987, n.p.

55. Burden, "A Ballpark Figure," n.p.

56. Andrews, *Nigel Andrews on Jaws*, p. 163.

57. Brooks, *Complete Directory*, p. 677.

58. Oates, Mary Louise, "*Roxanne* AFI Benefit Nets Whopping Profit," *Los Angeles Times*, June 20, 1987, View, p. 1.

59. Barringer, Felicity, "Soviet Union Is the 'In' Place to Be This Year," *New York Times*, August 17, 1987, p. 1A.

60. Crain Communications, "Anti-Drug Spots Hit Theaters," *Advertising Age*, July 27, 1987, p. 64.

61. Westbrook, Bruce, "Scheider Aims for the Real Thing," *Houston Chronicle*, December 10, 1987, n.p.

62. [No author], "Tribute: Life Was a Cabaret to Bob Fosse," *People*, October 12, 1987, p. 87.

63. Grubb, *Razzle Dazzle*, p. 273.

64. Gottfried, *All His Jazz*, p. 457.

65. Grubb, *Razzle Dazzle*, p. 282.

66. Westbrook, "Scheider Aims for the Real Thing," n.p.

67. Besa., "*Cohen and Tate*," *Variety*, October 19, 1988, p. 14.

68. Pulliene, Tim, "*Cohen and Tate*," *Monthly Film Bulletin*, June 1989, p. 176.

69. Modderno, Craig, "Outtakes: The Sequel, Casting Around," *Los Angeles Times*, June 21, 1987, p. 84.

70. Unger, Arthur, "Blessings of Liberty Blends Entertainment and Information," *Christian Science Monitor*, September 15, 1987, p. 21.

71. Robertson, Bill, "Keys Make Pretty

Pictures, but More Talk Would Be Nice," *Miami Herald Tropic*, January 24, 1988, p. 4.

72. Mabe, Chauncey, "Key West: Where the Writers Go," *Sun Sentinel TV Book*, p. 4.

73. Shales, Tom, "The U.S.S.R., on the Bright Side," *Washington Post*, March 19, 1988, p. C1.

74. Zad, Martie, "On Russia, with Love," *Washington Post*, March 20, 1988, p. Y7.

75. Terry, Clifford, "Turner's Look at Soviets Ambitious but Superficial," *Chicago Tribune*, March 19, 1998, p. 7C.

76. Froelich, Janis D., "U.S.S.R. Portrait Short on Substance," *St. Petersburg Times*, March 20, 1988, p. 1F.

77. Seligsohn, Leo, "Turner's Polite Soviet Union Travelogue," *Newsday*, March 19, 1988, n.p.

78. Corry, John, "Russia, through Rose-Colored Lenses," *New York Times*, March 20, 1988, section 2, p. 29.

79. Lansden, Pamela, "Take One," *People*, May 8, 1998, p. 35.

80. Wilmington, Michael, "Home Tech: Video News and Reviews," *Los Angeles Times*, July 22, 1988, part 6, p. 23.

81. Klady, Leonard, "Cinefile," *Los Angeles Times*, July 17, 1988, p. 29.

82. "Quirks of a Natural Disaster," *UPI Newswire*, September 17, 1988.

83. [No author], "Are You Ready for One More Planet of the Apes?" *Los Angeles Times*, September 8, 1988, p. 8C.

84. Cobb, *How They Met*, p. 90.

85. "Vietnam Veterans Workshop Benefit," *PR Newswire*, August 10, 1998.

86. McCabe, Bruce, "Channel 7 Won't Run 'Inside the Sexes'," *Boston Globe*, November 17, 1988, p. 90.

87. [No author], "Inside the Sexes," *People*, November 21, 1988, p. 15.

88. Burlingame, John, "Prime-Time Pick," *St. Petersburg Times*, November 21, 1988, p. 7D.

11. Cold War Thaw

1. Tasker, Fred, "Despite All, Southerland's Still Truckin'," *Miami Herald*, January 9, 1989, p. 1C.

2. Los Angeles Times, "Antonioni International Crew," *Toronto Star*, January 23, 1989, p. B9.

3. Hinman, Catherine, "Film Shoots: Miami, Fort Myers, St. Pete," *Orlando Sentinel*, June 8, 1989, p. E2.

4. Dollar, Steve, "Violent *Cohen and Tate* a Screeching Psycho Trip," *Atlanta Journal*, February 1, 1989, n.p.

5. Coto, Juan Carlos, "Red's *Cohen* Is Auspicious Film Debut," *Miami Herald*, January 31, 1989, p. 5C.

6. Aitchison, Diana, "List of Annoyances Long in Gory *Cohen and Tate*," *Sun Sentinel*, January 31, 1989, p. 7E.

7. Dollar, Steve, "Roy Scheider Is Key Player in Simple Minded Game," *Atlanta Constitution*, October 10, 1989, p. 3B.

8. Nazzaro, Joe, "The Hologram Interviews: seaQuest's W. Morgan Sheppard," *Starburst*, September 1994, p. 19.

9. Stasi, Linda, "Inside New York: The Wildest?" *Newsday*, February 15, 1991, n.p.

10. Champlin, *John Frankenheimer*, p. 179.

11. Chanko, Kenneth M. "Them's Fightin' Words, Roy," *New York Daily News*, May 3, 1989, n.p.

12. Schaefer, Stephen, "Scheider Plays Bad Guy in Film," *Boston Herald*, March 21, 1990, n.p.

13. Hinman, Catherine, "Big Money Productions Have Eluded Scheider," *Orlando Sentinel*, April 17, 1990, n.p.

14. Pratley, *Films of Frankenheimer*, pp. 204–205.

15. Emery, Robert, "The Directors: John Frankenheimer," Media Entertainment, 1997.

16. Quinlan, David, "*The Fourth War*," *Film Monthly*, July 1990, p. 20.

17. Emery, *The Directors—Take One*, p. 264.

18. Pollack, Joe, "John Frankenheimer's *War*," *St. Louis Post-Dispatch*, March 23, 1990, p. 1F.

19. Brennan, Brian, "Cold War Relics Fight On," *New York Times*, April 30, 1989, section 2, p. 22.

20. Pratley, *Films of Frankenheimer*, p. 205.

21. Brennan, "Cold War Relics Fight On," p. 22.

22. Emery, *The Directors—Take One*, p. 264.

23. Riley, Wendy, "Scheider's *War*," *Film Monthly*, July 1990, p. 34.

24. Emery, Robert, "The Directors: John Frankenheimer," Media Entertainment, 1997.

25. Beck, Marilyn, "*Mismatch* to Tackle Abortion Controversy," *Louisville Courier-Journal*, March 27, 1989, p. 3C.

26. Stein, Elliott, "Roe vs. Cameron," *Village Voice*, May 16, 1989, p. 73.

27. Pulliene, Tim, "*Listen to Me*," *Monthly Film Bulletin*, August 1990, p. 229.

28. Mietkiewicz, Henry, "Feeble Movie Debate Conceals Pro-life Agenda," *Toronto Star*, May 5, 1989, p. D12.

29. Boyar, Jay, "You Can't Help Hearing Hyperbole in *Listen*," *Orlando Sentinel*, May 6, 1989, p. E1.

30. Elliott, David, "*Listen to Me* Loses the Debate," *San Diego Union Tribune*, May 9, 1989, p. C6.

31. Clark, Mike, "*Listen to Me*: A Debatable Topic," *USA Today*, May 5, 1989, p. 6D.

32. James, Caryn, "This Campus Has Debaters as Its Heroes," *New York Times*, May 5, 1989, section C, p. 10.

33. "Good Morning America," May 1989.

34. *Business Wire*, May 11, 1989.

35. Williams, Jeannie, "Actors in Role of Promoters," *USA Today*, May 16, 1989, p. 2D.

36. Trott, William C., "Helping AIDS Kids," *UPI Wire*, June 20, 1989.

37. Sweeney, Louise, "Recalling a Theatrical Revolution," *Christian Science Monitor*, June 23, 1989, p. 11.

38. *AP Wire*, June 26, 1989.

39. Barnes, Clive, "Harold Clurman: A Life of Theatre," *Video Review*, April 1989, p. 86.

40. Stark, John, "Harold Clurman: A Life of Theatre," *People*, July 3, 1989, p. 10.

41. Grubb, *Razzle Dazzle*, p. 274.

42. Fleming, Michael, "Writers Succumb 7–6 in East Hampton Classic," *Newsday*, August 28, 1989, n.p.

43. Fleming, Michael, "Take Greenburg out to the Bawl Game," *Newsday*, August 25, 1989, n.p.

44. James, Caryn, "Waiting to Be Murdered While Police Talk and Sigh," *New York Times*, September 16, 1989, section 1, p. 15.

45. Dollar, "Roy Scheider Is Key Player in Simple Minded Game," p. 3B.

46. Rens., "*Night Game*," *Variety*, September 20, 1989, p. 29.

47. Novak, Ralph, "Picks and Pans," *People*, October 2, 1989, p. 11.

48. Rizzo, Frank, "Big Screen By-pass: More Major Movies Go Straight to Video," *Hartford Courant*, October 26, 1989, p. E1.

49. [No author], "Coming Soon,"*Orlando Sentinel*, January 26, 1990, p. A2.

50. Pratley, *Films of Frankenheimer*, p. 205.

51. Maislin, Janet, "Roy Scheider in a Parable of the Cold War," *New York Times*, March 24, 1990, section 1, p. 16.

52. Hagen, Bill, "Global Events Undermine 'War'," *San Diego Union Tribune*, April 4, 1990, p. D5.

53. Jacobs, Tom, "*The Fourth War*," *Courier Journal* (Hartford), March 24, 1990, p. 23S.

54. Hinson, Hal, "'Fourth': Snowball Warfare," *Washington Post*, March 26, 1990, p. B2.

55. Quinlan, David, "*The Fourth War*," *Film Monthly*, July 1990, pp. 20–21.

56. [No author], "Names and Faces," *Orlando Sentinel*, March 19, 1990, p. A2.

57. [No author], "Prison Fracas Shows State Is Still Learning," *Orlando Sentinel*, March 20, 1990, p. E1.

58. [No author],"A Bit of Hollywood Comes to Seminole," *Orlando Sentinel*, March 29, 1990, p. 2.

59. Hinman, Catherine, "Why Some Townsfolk Wanted to Shout Cut," *Orlando Sentinel*, April 17, 1990, p. E1.

60. King, Susan, "Actor Prizes Role in Film with Message," *Sun-Sentinel*, September 9, 1990, p. 3G.

61. Arar, Yardena, "Cable-Network Films," (Los Angeles) *Daily News*, September 7, 1980, n.p.

62. Groves, Bob, "Somebody Had to Do It," (Bergen County) *Record*, September 9, 1990, p. O36.

63. Quoted in: Deni, Elliott, "Media Ethics Goes to the Movies: What Photojournalism Films Can Teach Us about Our profession," *News Photographer*, February 2001, p. 15.

64. Groves, "Somebody Had to Do It," p. O36.

65. Landau, Susan B, "Confessions of a Woman Producer," *Cosmopolitan*, March 1990, p. 222.

66. [No author], "Film: New Releases," *Independent* (London), June 22, 1990, p. 27.

67. Williams, Jeannie, "The Verdict on 'Innocent' Is Unanimous Approval," *USA Today*, July 11, 1990, p. 2D.

68. Poster, Roura, "The Big Stars Come Out at Long Island Premiere," *San Francisco Chronicle*, August 14, 1990, p. E1.

69. Suzy, "Brando's Girls Tell It All," *Miami Herald*, July 30, 1990, p. 1C.

70. Klinghoffer, David, "When HBO Is Good ... and When It's Rotten," *Washington Times*, September 7, 1990, p. E1.

71. Bier., "Somebody Has to Shoot the Picture," *Variety*, September 3, 1990, n.p.

72. "Meryl Streep Hosts Spectacular 'Race to Save the Planet,'" *PR Newswire*, September 18, 1990.

73. Bunce, Alan, "Worth Noting on TV," *Christian Science Monitor*, October 3, 1990, p. 10.

74. [No author], "Have We Lost the Race?" *New York Post*, October 4, 1990, n.p.

75. Williams, Scott, "PBS Rattles the Planet," *Los Angeles Times*, October 7, 1990, p. 79.

76. [No Author], "Autumn Video List Starts at Miami," *Washington Times*, October 18, 1990, p. M2.

77. Lomartire, Paul, "Untouted A & E, HBO Shows Shine," *Palm Beach Post*, April 12, 1991, p. 11D.

78. Stasi, Linda, "Inside New York," *Newsday*, November 14, 1990, n.p.

79. Higgins, Bill, "Into the Night: Film Czars Spied at 'Russia' Premiere," *Los Angeles Times*, December 7, 1990, part F, p. 8.

80. Sragrow, Michael, "Melting the Cold War," *San Francisco Examiner*, December 21, 1990, n.p.

81. Cart., "*The Russia House*," *Variety*, December 19, 1990, p. 43.

82. Hinson, Hal, "*Russia House*: Into the Maze," *Washington Post*, December 21, 1990, p. D4.

83. Coto, Juan Carlos, "Stars Rise above *Russia House*," *Miami Herald*, December 21, 1990, p. 5G.

84. Denby, David, "Movies," *New York*, December 17, 1990, p. 71.

85. Canby, Vincent, "Connery and Pfeiffer in *The Russia House*," *New York Times*, December 19, 1990, section C, p. 21.

86. Carr, Jay, "The Spy Movie That Came in from the Cold," *Boston Globe*, December 21, 1990, Arts & Film, p. 49.

87. [No author], "Hors D'oeuvres across America," *People*, December 24, 1990, p. 90.

88. Kimber, Gary, "Cronenberg Naked Lunch," *Cinefantastique*, April 1992, p. 8.

89. Shapiro, Marc, "*Naked Lunch*," *Fangoria #94*, July 1990, p. 11.

90. Duncan, Jody, "Borrowed Flesh," *Cinefex 49*, p. 25.

91. *Naked Lunch* press kit 20th Century–Fox, 1991, p. 30.

92. Palmer, Robert, "The Novelist, the Director and the Mugwumps," *American Film*, January/February 1992, pp. 34–35.

93. Silverberg, *Everything Is Permitted*, p. 68.

94. *Naked Lunch* press kit. 20th Century–Fox, 1991, p. 8.

95. Kimber, Gary, "The *Naked Lunch*," *Cinefantastique*, February 1992, p. 12.

96. French, Lawrence, "Special Effects *Naked Lunch*," *Cinefantastique*, April 1992, pp. 16–17.

97. Roberts and Gaydos, *Movie Talk from the Front Lines*, p. 277.

98. [No Author], "Turner to Star in House of Cards," *Miami Herald*, January 28, 1991, p. 3C.

99. Buck, Jerry, "Drama Recalls Immigrant Lives and Hard Times," *Sun-Sentinel*, May 22, 1991, p. 3E.

100. Stasi, Linda, "Inside New York," *Newday*, February 15, 1991, n.p.

101. Woffinden, Bob, "Joe Giarratano Should Not Go to the Chair," *Independent* (London), February 15, 1991, p. 19.

102. Scaduto, Anthony, et al., "Inside New York," *Newsday*, June 19, 1991, n.p.

103. Chi, Victor, "Colorful Heroes of Baseball Get Fresh Look on TV," *Detroit Free Press*, July 8, 1991, n.p.

104. MacMinn, Arlene, "Morning Report," *Los Angeles Times*, May 31, 1991, part F, p. 2.

105. Mink, Eric, "Required Viewing for Baseball Fans," *St. Louis Post-Dispatch*, July 8, 1991, p. 7D.

106. Wulf, Steve, "When It Was a Game," *Sports Illustrated*, July 1, 1991, p. 51.

107. Weidenkeller, Pat, "Game Is Celebrity Poor, Quip Rich," *Newday*, August 19, 1991, n.p.

108. *Naked Lunch* press kit insert. 20th Century-Fox, 1991.

109. Simon, John, "*Naked Lunch*," *National Review*, March 2, 1992, p. 56.

110. Johnson, Brian D., "*Naked Lunch*," *Maclean's*, January 20, 1992, p. 49.

111. Powers, John, "Buggy," *New York*, January 20, 1992, p. 56.

112. Tryster, Hillel, "Unclothed, Unappetizing,"*Jerusalem Post*, November 11, 1992, n.p.

113. Smith, Liz, "Oscar's Prize Moments," *Newday*, February 6, 1992, n.p.

114. Glauber, Bob, "Starry Nights," *Newday*, April 5, 1992, n.p.

115. Cahill, Dan, "Thankfully, More of the Same for 'When It Was a Game,'" *Chicago Sun-Times*, July 3, 1992, p. 85.

116. Freeman, John, "HBO's Game II Is in an All-Star League by Itself," *San Diego Union Tribune*, July 10, 1992, p. C13.

117. Tyler, Jan, "Private Lives: A Rambling Classic," *Newsday*, September 15, 1996, n.p.

118. Jones, Michelle, "Musical Theater Project Planned for Summer," *St. Petersburg Times*, December 6, 1991, p. 5.

119. Maupin, Elizabeth, "Reinking Comes Home to Dance and Teach," *Orlando Sentinel*, October 27, 1991, p. F1.

120. "Artists-Writers Softball Game," LTV, 1992.

121. Rabin, Roni, "Hits in a Starry Field," *Newday*, August 24, 1992, n.p.

122. Cerone, Daniel, "NBC Said to Be Undertaking Spielberg's Sea Quest," *Los Angeles Times*, October 5, 1992, p. F1

12. Adventures in Television

1. Pener, Degen, "Egos and Ids; Film Festival Is Planned for the Hamptons," *New York Times*, February 21, 1993, section 9, p. 4.

2. [No author], "Spielberg at Work on TV Series," *Montreal Gazette*, March 11, 1993, p. D6.

3. Archerd, Army, "Just for Variety," *Daily Variety*, April 5, 1993, n.p.

4. "seaQuest" video press kit, NBC/Amblin, 1993.

5. Archerd, "Just for Variety," n.p.

6. Cerone, Daniel, "NBC Takes Risky Plunge," *Los Angeles Times*, August 15, 1993, n.p.

7. Hilsman, Hoyt, "Wild Justice," *Variety*, May 23, 1993, n.p.

8. Carman, John, "Miniseries All Over the Map," *San Francisco Chronicle*, May 27, 1993, p. E1.

9. Laurence, Robert P., "Random Violence Supports Thin Plot," *San Diego Union-Tribune*, May 27, 1993, p. 42.

10. Grahnke, Lou, "Better Luck Next Time," *Chicago Sun-Times*, June 9, 1993, section 2, p. 47.

11. Sauter, Michael, "*Covert Assassin*," *Entertainment Weekly*, November 18, 1994, p. 114.

12. Kelleher, Terry, "Archvillains, Assassinations and Absurdity," *Newsday*, May 30, 1993, n.p.

13. Stanley, John, "An Affinity for Espionage," *San Francisco Chronicle*, May 23, 1993, TV Commentary, p. 3.

14. Scott, Tony, "Review," *Daily Variety*, July 8, 1993, n.p.

15. Cerone, "NBC Takes Risky Plunge," n.p.

16. "This Is Your Life," syndicated, 1993.

17. [No author], "67,000,000 Viewers Took the Plunge," *Daily Variety*, September 16, 1993, pp. 8–9.

18. Zoglin, Richard, "seaQuest DSV," *Time*, October 11, 1993, p. 82.

19. Universal Studios/Amblin Entertainment, *seaQuest DSV*: Operations Manual Introduction and Overview: *The Captain*, n.p.

20. "The Nathan Bridger Incident," Universal/Amblin, "seaQuest DSV" script, March 1993.

21. Van Heerden, *Film and Television In-Jokes*, p. 209.

22. Lipson, Karen, "The Hamptons as Cannes West," (Bergen County) *Record*, October 20, 1993, p. E11.

23. Wick, Steve, "East Hampton Lures the Stars, New Film Fest," *Newsday*, October 29, 1993, Showtime, p. 16.

24. "Fox News Sunday," KTTV, Los Angeles, March 13, 1994.

25. "The Crusaders," syndicated, 1993.

26. "E! News Daily," March 24, 1994.

27. Lieberman, Paul, "FBI's Venture into Film Business Less than Boffo," *Los Angeles Times*, November 23, 1994, p. A1.

28. Dargis, Manohla, "Pulp Fictions," *Sight and Sound*, May 1994, p. 8.

29. Jackson, Kevin, "Film," *Independent* (London), April 29, 1994, p. 25.

30. Noh, David, "*Romeo Is Bleeding*," *Film Journal*, March 1994, p. 62.

31. Brown, Joe, "Wherefore Art Thou Bleeding?" *Washington Post*, February 4, 1994, p. N43.

32. Stone, Jay, "Comedy Hurts All Over," *Ottawa Citizen*, March 4, 1994, p. E6.

33. Travers, Peter, "Movies—*Romeo Is Bleeding*," *Rolling Stone*, February 10, 1994, p. 51.

34. Hoberman, J., "Desperate Characters," *Village Voice*, February 8, 1994, p. 53.

35. Macnab, Geoffrey, "*Romeo Is Bleeding*," *Sight and Sound*, May 1994, pp. 53–54.

36. Dargis, "Pulp Fictions," p. 8.

37. Brode, *Money, Women and Guns*, pp. 231, 234.

38. "News 4 at Noon," WTVJ, Miami, April 27, 1994.

39. "WBZ News at Noon," WBZ, Boston, May 2, 1994.

40. "Late Night with Conan O'Brien," May 3, 1994.

41. [No author], "This Week's Picks: Special Effects and Angels," *Washington Post*, May 22, 1994, p. Y3.

42. McClellan, Shawn, "Grand 'Illusion'," *Times-Picayune* (New Orleans), May 22, 1994, p. T3.

43. Chunovic, *seaQuest DSV*, pp. 47–48, 50, 53.

44. NBC video publicity clip, 1994.

45. Whitehouse, Beth, "Life, Death and Roy Scheider," *Newsday*, June 21, 1994, n.p.

46. Whitehouse, Beth, "Where Have You Gone, Paul Simon," *Newsday*, August 23, 1994, n.p.

47. Lorando, Mark, "Shock Cousteau Scheider Makes More Waves," *Times-Picayune* (New Orleans), September 19, 1994, n.p.

48. Hinman, Catherine, "'seaQuest' Star Calls Series 'Total Trash,'" *Orlando Sentinel*, September 15, 1994, quoted in *Denver Post*, September 29, 1994, p. E8.

49. Werts, Diane, "'seaQuest' Swims Out of Its Goldfish Bowl," *Newsday*, September 13, 1994, n.p..

50. [No author], "Producers Miffed by "seaQuest DSV" Star's Criticism," *Orlando Sentinel*, September 15, 1994, quoted in *Montreal Gazette*, September 15, 1994, p. C10.

51. Moritsugu, Ken, "Hamptons Cause: Save the Deli," *Newsday*, October 24, 1994, n.p.

52. [No author], "Names and Faces," *Orlando Sentinel*, December 24, 1994, p. A2.

53. Fleming, John, "A Night for Star Gazing," *St. Petersburg Times*, January 20, 1995, p. 8C.

54. Brown, Steve, "Roy Scheider in Narrator Role at Orlando Event," *Orlando Sentinel*, March 9, 1995, p. A2.

55. "seaQuest DSV" shooting script, "Something in the Air," 1st rev. draft, January 13, 1995; 3rd rev. draft, January 23, 1995.

56. Internet chat, Prodigy, January 18, 1996.

57. "AFI Tribute to Steven Spielberg," A & E, August 1995.

58. Dutka, Elaine, "On Filmdom's A-List of a Lifetime," *Los Angeles Times*, March 4, 1995, p. F1.

59. "AFI Tribute to Steven Spielberg," A & E, August 1995.

60. *Jaws* 25th anniversary laser disc, "The Making of *Jaws*," Universal Studios, 1995.

61. [No author], "Names and Faces," *Orlando Sentinel*, March 17, 1995, p. A2.

62. Shain, Michael, "Inside New York," *Newsday*, July 13, 1995, n.p.

63. [No author], "Caught on Camera," *New York Daily News*, August 21, 1995, p. 14.

64. [No author], "Roy Scheider Becomes the Voice of Mercury," *Adweek*, September 11, 1995, p. 37.

65. Ahrens, Frank, "No Ordinary Joe: Montana's Amazing Skill," *Washington Post*, September 12, 1995, p. B4.

66. "Good Soldiers" filming schedule, October 16–20, 1995, Universal/Amblin.

67. [No author], "Future Films," *Weekly Variety*, October 30–November 5, 1995, p. 16

13. New Markets

1. Prodigy interactive chat, January 18, 1996.
2. Ibid.
3. Hayground school brochure, 1999, n.p.
4. Haberstroh, Joe, "School's First Bell," *Newsday*, September 12, 1996, p. A23.
5. Hayground school brochure, 1999, n.p.
6. Feran, Tom, "Spy in the Sky Recalls Glory Days of U-2," *Plain Dealer*, February 26, 1996, p. 7D.
7. Brozan, Nadine, "Chronicle," *New York Times*, March 4, 1996, section B, p. 4.
8. Granger Entertainment invitation to screening.
9. Brown, Rick, "Cable Takes Wraps off New Projects," *Broadcasting and Cable*, January 27, 1997, p. 58.
10. McWilliams, Michael, "TV Fights the Winter Doldrums," *Detroit News*, January 2, 1998, p. C1.
11. Lovell, Glenn, "Scheider Still Plays It Straight,"*Akron Beacon Journal*, June 18, 1999, http://www.ohio.com/bj/fun/movie/reviews/0699/032176.htm.
12. Rush, George, and Joanna Malloy, "New Project Warms Schlesinger's Heart," *New York Daily News*, May 10, 1996, p. 14.
13. "Extra," *Radio TV Reports*, May 13, 1996.
14. Gay, Verne, "CBS Shakes Up the Line-up," *Newsday*, May 23, 1996, n.p.
15. Graham, *Growling Gourmet*, p. 133.
16. Ibid., p. 1.
17. *Plato's Run* production notes, p. 3.
18. Clabaugh, Rick, "*Plato's Run*," http://www.rclabaugh.com/plato.html.
19. Duran, Gil Jose, "*Plato's Run* Helps Fill Cash Register," *Miami Herald*, July 26, 1996, p. 1BR.
20. *Suffolk Theatre* web page. This URL is no longer available.
21. Graves, Jack, "Artists and Writers Girding," *East Hampton Star*, August 14, 1997, http://www.archive.easthamptonstar.com/ehquery/970814/news4.html.
22. Rush, George, and Joanna Molloy, "Did Heidi Get High?" *New York Daily News*, October 3, 1996, p. 14.
23. Mermelstein, Susan, and Carissa Katz, "Film Fest Fever on the East End," *East Hampton Star*, October 17, 1996, http://www.archive.easthamptonstar.com/ehquery/961017/feat1.htm.
24. Ketchum, Diane, "Long Island Journal," *New York Times*, October 27, 1996, section 13, p. 3.
25. Indiewire internet newsletter, http://www.filmmag.com/hypermail/0071. html. No longer available.
26. Yahoo News! n.d.
27. Rush, George, and Joanna Molloy, "Two Star Thanksgiving Dinner," *New York Daily News*, November 18, 1996, p. 14.
28. Caryn, James, "Hollywood Breathes in the Spirit of Sundance," *New York Times*, February 2, 1997, n.p.
29. "NY-1 Cable Channel Hourly News," April 19, 1997.
30. Brozan, Nadine, "Chronicle," *New York Times*, May 8, 1997, section B, p. 10.
31. Herbert, Bob, "Break Down the Barriers," *New York Times*, May 19, 1997. n.p.
32. "Access Hollywood," *Video Monitoring Services of America*, May 14, 1997.
33. *East Hampton Star*, July 3, 1997, captioned photo.
34. Haberstroh, "School's First Bell," p. A23.
35. Jedell, Joan, "Hamptons," *Newsday*, July 14, 1997, p. A10.
36. Variety, "Flash!: The Latest Entertainment News," *Newsday*, July 29, 1997, n.p.
37. Boyle, Adam, "Star Gazing at Herrick," *East End Independent*, August 20, 1997, http://www.indyeastend.com/sports/08209710.htm.
38. Brady, James, "In Step with Julianne Moore," *Parade*, September 14, 1997, p. 22.
39. "1997 Writers-Artists Softball Game," LTV, 1997.
40. Hoban, Phoebe, "Drive-In Shootout on Pier 17," *New York Times*, August 17, 1997, section 1, p. 47.
41. Covington, Richard, "Lowering French Resistance to U.S. Films," *Los Angeles Times*, September 4, 1997, CAL, p. 43.
42. "*Jaws* Star Scheider Gets French

Cinema Award," *Agence France Presse*, September 12, 1997, n.p.

43. De Groot, Lawrence, "Discussion with Roy Scheider," Cinemanics web page, http://www.cinemaniacs.be/cgi/fimfr.asp?id=3521. Translated from French.

44. *The Myth of Fingerprints* press kit, Sony Classic Pictures, 1997, p. 6.

45. Gladstone, Valerie, "Film Maker Tied to Ocean, Any Ocean," *New York Times*, September 7, 1997, section 13LI, p. 31.

46. *The Myth of Fingerprints* press kit, p. 10.

47. Sheffield, Skip, "At a Turning Point," *Boca Raton News*, October 17, 1997, p. 15C.

48. "Star Power: The 50 Most Powerful Actors over Age 50," *Modern Maturity*, March–April, 1998, p. 36.

49. Oliver, Victor, "Star Interview," Total Entertainment website. URL no longer available.

50. *The Myth of Fingerprints* DVD, Columbia Tristar Home Video, 2000.

51. Stone, Jay, "Hinting at Hidden Secrets is Not Enough to Carry Film," *Ottawa Citizen*, December 5, 1997, p. D3.

52. Mathews, Jack, "Angst for Thanksgiving," *Newsday*, September 17, 1997, http://www.newsday.com/movies/mmxz07g.htm.

53. Ringel, Eleanor, "Movies," *Atlanta Journal and Constitution*, November 21, 1997, p. 11P.

54. Barr, Elizabeth, "Reprints: A Family Gathers to Learn from the Sins of the Father," *Buffalo News*, October 3, 1997, p. 33G.

55. Paul Wunder's Movie Review web page, http://www.pwunder.com/reviews/myth_finger.html. No longer available.

56. Adcock, Donna, "*The Myth of Fingerprints* ... It's Still a Mystery," Launch Online Movie Review. http://www.2launch.com/myth_fingerprints.html. No longer available.

57. Wood, Frances, "*The Myth of Fingerprints*," Film.com web page, http://www.film.com/backlot/filmfests/siff97/myth.htm.

58. Johnston, Trevor, "A Sophisticated New Release at Christmas?" *Scotsman*, December 18, 1997, p. 17.

59. Tillotson, Kristin, "*Fingerprints* Rewards Patience with Subtlety, Acting, Reality," *Minneapolis Star Tribune*, March 1, 1998, p. 15F.

60. Matthews, Peter, "*The Myth of Fingerprints*," *Sight and Sound*, December 1997, p. 48.

61. Pinsker, Beth, "Wyle Leaves His Mark on 'Fingerprints,'" *Dallas Morning News*, October 17, 1997, p. 5C.

62. Stone, Laurie, "*The Myth of Fingerprints*," *Village Voice*, September 23, 1997, p. 96.

63. Hunter, Stephen, "The Dirty Rotten Basters," *Washington Post*, November 23, 1997, p. G1.

64. Lester, Barbara, "The Making of a Myth," *City Link*, October 15, 1997, p. 51.

65. Pennington, Gail, "A Musical Interlude on TV's 'Chicago Hope,'" *St. Louis Post-Dispatch*, October 15, 1997, p. 6E.

66. Sumner, June, "Doing Arlington by Way of Houston," *Dallas Morning Sun*, December 5, 1997, p. 5C.

67. "HBO First Look: *The Rainmaker*," HBO, 1997.

68. *The Rainmaker* web page, Paramount, 1997, http://www.therainmaker.com. No longer available.

69. Ibid.

70. Curtis, Quentin, "Coppola Polishes Up the Old Grisham Formula," *Daily Telegraph*, April 24, 1998, p. 24.

71. Johnson, Brian, "Films: Godfather in Court," *Maclean's*, November 24, 1997, p. 133.

72. Boyar, Jay, "Rainmaker Is Understated Gem," *Orlando Sentinel*, June 5, 1998, p. 30.

73. "Patches of Sunlight," Salon.com, http://www:://salon.com/ent/movies/1997/11/21rainmaker.html.

74. Maislin, Janet, "A Young Legal Eagle Flies with Vultures," *New York Times*, November 21, 1997, n.p.

75. Scheider, Roy, "*Moon over Broadway*," Hamptons International Film Festival 1997 Film Schedule and Celebrity Guide, *East Hampton Star* (insert), October 15, 1997, p. 17.

76. Towle, Angela Phipps, "Not the Same Old Story," *Back Stage West*, August 2000, p. 9.

77. Fleming, Michael, "Dish," *Variety*, December 2, 1997, *Variety.com* web page. No longer available.

78. McWilliams, Michael, "TV Fights the Winter Doldrums," *Detroit News*, January 2, 1998, p. C1.

79. Levine, Alan, "Next Week," *Arizona Republic*, May 28, 1999, p. D10.

80. "CNN Showbiz Today," January 19, 1998.

81. McPhee, Michelle, "A Stage of Stars," *New York Daily News*, February 16, 1998, p. 24.

82. Tillotson, Kristin, "Video Watch," *Star Tribune*, March 1, 1998, p. 15F.

83. "1998 Independent Spirit Awards—Best Supporting Male," http://www.ifctv.com.events/98isa/supmale.html.

84. Gearty, Robert, "Bulkhead Moratorium Splits Southhampton," *New York Daily News*, March 22, 1998, p. 11.

85. Studio Times OnLine, Kaufman Astoria Studios, Astoria, http://www.kaufman-astoria.com/studtime/win982.htm.

86. [No author], "Hayground," *East Hampton Star*, May 7, 1998, section 1, p. 7.

87. Katz, Carissa, "Memorial at Hayground," *East Hampton Star*, May 14, 1998, section 1, p. 8.

88. Thompson, Kevin D., "TV Today," *Palm Beach Post*, May 18, 1998, p. 5D.

89. Currie, Jan, "It's Still Not Safe to Go in the Water," *Des Moines Register*, May 18, 1998, p. 4.

90. Graham, Renee, "Newport Holding Its First Film Festival," *Boston Globe*, May 31, 1998, p. E11.

91. [No author], "Film Notes," (Bergen County) *Record*, May 26, 1998, p. Y8.

92. Blue Rider Pictures web page, http://www.blueriderpictures.com/silvwolf.htm.

93. [No author], "New on Video," (Raleigh) *News and Observer*, May 28, 1998, p. E10.

94. *East Hampton Star*, June 11, 1998, captioned photo.

95. Delatiner, Barbara, "Long Island Guide," *New York Times*, section 14LI, p. 15.

96. Blowen, Michael, "*The Peacekeeper* Needs Saving," *Boston Globe*, July 26, 1998, p. E3.

97. *Herald Staff*, "Direct to Video Movies," *Miami Herald*, February 6, 1999, p. 3E.

98. The Definitive Dolph Lundgren Guide web page. http://www.darkseid.com.dolph/films/peacekeeper.html.

99. [No author], "Artists against Abuse," *East Hampton Star*, July 23, 1998, section 3, p. 3.

100. Sansegundo, Sheridan, "Sixty Three Plates," *East Hampton Star*, August 6, 1998, captioned photo.

101. Williams, Jeannie, "Artists Ride Billy Ball to Win Over Writers," *USA Today*, August 25, 1998, p. 2D.

102. Harris, Chris, "Telling Lies in Sag Harbor," *East Hampton Star*, September 24, 1998, section III, p. 4.

103. East End Pictures web page, http://www.eastendpictures.com/HTM/synopsis.htm.

104. O'Haire, Patricia "News Beat," *Daily News*, October 14, 1998, p. 38.

105. Whitehouse, Beth, "Scheider's Hometown Gig: Actor Speaks at Hampton Fest," *Newsday*, October 17, 1998, p. A8.

106. Roman, Monica, "Hamptons Fest Fetes Blake," *Weekly Variety*, October 19–25, 1998, p. 36.

107. Katz, Carissa, "Festival," *East Hampton Star*, October 21, 1998, section III, p. 1.

108. "NY-1 News All Weekend," October 17, 1998.

109. Jones, Oliver, "*Better Living*," *Weekly Variety*, November 16–22, 1998, pp. 36–38.

110. Rubin, Sylvia, "50 Who Counted," *San Francisco Chronicle*, November 14, 1999, p. E1.

111. Schatt, R., internet movie database, *Evasive Action*, http://www.imdb.com.

112. [No author], "Phantom of the Movies," *Washington Times*, December 31, 1998, p. M18.

113. Punter, Jeannie, "The Wild Comes Calling Again," *Toronto Star*, December 10, 1999, n.p.

114. Andrews, Mark, "*Silver* Keeps Things Simple," Vancouver Today web page, http://vancouvertoday.com/city_guide/movies/reviews/silver_wolf.html.

115. Katz, Carissa, "Film Directors Look at the Craft," *East Hampton Star*, January 14, 1999, section 3, p. 3.

116. Hollywood Reporter, "HBO Set to Shoot 'RKO 281,'" *Cincinnati Post*, March 8, 1998, p. 4C.

117. [No author], "Channel Surfing," *Variety*, March 8, 1999, p. 51.

118. Biancuilli, David, "TV," *New York Daily News*, November 20, 1999, p. 35.

119. Hahn, Lucinda, "Miller Time," *Chicago*, April 1999, p. 28.

120. "Late Night with David Letterman," April 26, 1999.

121. Berry, Conor, "Huge Turnout for Environmental Benefit," *East Hampton Star*, June 24, 1999, section 1, p. 8.

122. Yahoo! Business Wire, June 26, 1999.

123. Lovell, "Scheider Still Plays It Straight," *Akron Beacon Journal*, June 18, 1999.

124. Persall, Steve, "Inspiration at Center Stage," p. ID.

125. "*Jaws* Star Pays Visit to Tampa Zoo," *AP Newswire*, July 25, 1999.

126. [No author], "Pintauro's Karma," *East Hampton Star*, July 29, 1999, section 3, p. 3.

127. *East Hampton Star*, August 8, 1999, section 3, p. 5 (captioned photo.)

128. Delatiner, Barbara, "Music Festivals Mix Business with Friendship," *New York Times*, July 4, 1999, section 14LI, p. 14.

129. Thomas, Katie, "Celebrities Swing into Action," *Newsday*, August 22, 1999, p. A8.

130. "When We Were Young" program.

131. Ibid.

132. Rattiner, Dan, "For the Kids," *Dan's Papers*, August 20, 1999.

133. Yahoo! Business Wire, n.d.

134. Quittner, Joshua, "Amazon Goes to the Movies," *Time*, September 6, 1999, p. 53.

135. Lieberman, Alison, "Indie Filmmakers Making OnLine Market Premiere," *New York Post*, http://promotions.nypost.com/082699/13175.htm.

136. Katz, Carissa, "Filmmaking 101: *Mulligan Farm*," *East Hampton Star*, November 19, 1999, Section 3, p. 2.

137. Zad, Martie, "Carriers: Assembling a City of Steel," *Washington Post*, November 14, 1999, p. Y4.

138. Fries, Laura, "*RKO 281*," November 15, 1999, Variety web page, http://www.variety.com/search/review.asp.

139. Biancuilli, "TV," p. 35.

140. Boedeker, Hal, "Rosedud—HBO Weakly Tells Story of 'Citizen Kane'," *Orlando Sentinel*, November 20, 1999, p. E1.

141. Jackson, Terry, "'Kane' Story Traces Behind-Scenes Feud," *Miami Herald*, November 20, 1999, p. 2E.

142. Kelleher, Terry, "Tube: Picks and Pans," *People*, November 22, 1999, p. 29.]

143. Lotta Reviews, http//www.lottareviews/com/tv/rko281.html.

144. Buss, Robin, "TV Choice," *Independent* (London), December 19, 1999, p. 53.

14. Into the New Millennium

1. Silverline Pictures New Releases [on-line]. Available: http://www.silverlinepic tures. com/index.html.

2. La Rue, Steve, "TV Ads Set Stage for Open-space Measures," *San Diego Union-Tribune*, February 3, 2000, p. B1.

3. "Roy Scheider," Hollywood Foreign Press Association Interview, August 13, 1983, p. 8.

4. Feiwell, Jill, "Cast Set for Diamond Mini," *Variety*, April 26, 2000 [on-line]. No longer available.

5. Valjean, "Diamond Hunters," Synchronicity: The Official Michael Easton Web Page [on-line]. Available: http://www.michael easton.com/synchronicity/body.html.

6. Katz, Carissa, "Fanfare Greets LTV Sound stage," *East Hampton Star*, May 3, 2000, Section II, p. 7.

7. Tuma, Debbie, "LI Sound Stage Premieres," *New York Daily News*, May 2, 2000, p. 8.

8. Curran-Kopell, Janice, "Hollywood East!" *New York Review* [on-line]. Available: http://new yorkreview.com/ENTERTAINMENT_3NEWS.html.

9. Wertheimer, Ron, "A Seance in Four Parts, with Narration," *New York Times*, May 15, 2000, Section E, p. 8.

10. Joplin: The Movie web page [on-line]. Available: http://www.Joplinthemovie.com/janis22.html.

11. Ibid.

12. Emery, Robert, "The Films of Steven Spielberg," Encore, 2000.

13. Lichter, Marc, "The Directors: Steven Spielberg," *See*, June 2000, p. A310.

14. Eftimiades, Maria, "Jaws: 25 Years Later," *People*, June 19, 2000, pp. 65–67.

15. *Chain of Command* DVD Commentary, Studio Line, 2001.

16. [No author], "Best Bets Thursday 7/27," *Los Angeles Times*, July 27, 2000, p. F2.

17. Mitchell, Elvis, "A Dysfunctional Welcome for Not-So-Dear-Old-Dad," *New York Times*, August 4, 2000, Section B, p. 16.

18. "The Monitor Movie Guide," *Christian Science Monitor*, August 4, 2000, p. 14.

19. Ivry, Bob, "Quirky, Quirkier, Quirkiest," *Record* (Bergen County, NJ), August 4, 2000, p. 12.

20. Stuart, Jan, "Loopy Family Is Gone with the Whim," Long Island *Newsday*, August 4, 2000, p. B10.

21. Campbell, Bob, "Capsule Reviews of Current Films," *Newhouse News Service*, September 4, 2000.

22. Weitzmann, Elizabeth, "Better Not," *New York Daily News*, August 4, 2000 [on-line]. Available: http://www.nydailynews.com/2000-08-04/New York Now/Movies/a-75464.asp.

23. Delatiner, Barbara, "The Guide," *New York Times*, July 30, 2000, Section 14LI, p. 14.

24. Rattiner, Dan, "Plan the Weekend," *Dan's Papers Web Page* [on-line]. Available: http://www.danspapers.com.plan.html.

25. "Karma Boomerangs," *East Hampton Star*, August 3, 2000, Section 3, p. 3.

26. "When We Were Young Benefits the Hayground School," *Dan's Papers*, August 18, 2000, p. 69.

27. Zimmerman, Iris, "Benefits Parties," *East Hampton Star*, August 17, 2000, Section III, p. 20.

28. *The Good War*, Bauer Martinez Studio Press Release, 2000.

29. Keefer, Louis E., *Italian Prisoners of War*, p. 133.

30. *Fox News Live*, September 12, 2000.

31. Wehner, Christopher, "Screenwriter/Director Michael B. Druxman," Screenwriters Utopia Web Site [on-line]. Available: http://www.screenwritersutopia.com/interviews/the_doorway.html.

32. Hulse, Ed, "The Doorway," *Video Business*, October 2, 2000, p. 16.

33. Boedeker, Hal, "Great Escapes 'Nova'," *Orlando Sentinel*, February 6, 2001, p. E1.

34. "Hayground," *East Hampton Star*, December 14, 2000, Section 1, p. 6.

35. Coppens, Julie York, "*All That Jazz* Still Says Something to Scheider," *South Bend Tribune*, February 11, 2001, p. E1.

36. McKee, Victoria, "Acting the Part of a Thinner Person Changes Your Life," *London Times*, March 10, 2001 [no page number].

37. "Stewart Beams Lear to 1840's Texas," *Variety*, March 16, 2001 [on-line]. Available: http://library.northernlight.com/HA20010316230000010.html.

38. *PR Newswire*, March 15, 2001.

39. Polo.com Online Magazine, "Roy Scheider: An American Classic," December 2001 [on-line]. Available: http://www.polo.com/editorial/static/roy_scheider.asp.

40. DVDFile.com, "Press Release Archive" [on-line]. Available: http://www.dvdfile.com/news.web_wire/press_release/titles/jaws2.html.

41. *East Hampton Star*, "The Duke, the Bard and You," August 2, 2001, Section 3, p. 9.

42. People.com, "Hamptons: Batter Up!" [on-line]. http://people.aol.com/people/news/now/0,10958.120114,00.html. No longer available.

43. Internet Movie Database, "*Daybreak*" [on-line]. Available: http://www.imdb.com/title?0219640.

44. McClain, Buzz, "Daybreak," *Video Business Tipsheet*, July 16, 2001.

45. DVDFile.com, "Marathon Man Review" [on-line]. Available: http://www.dvdfile.com/software/review/dvd-video_4/marathonman.html.

46. Westbrook, Bruce, "Making a 'Connection,'" *Houston Chronicle*, September 27, 2001, Preview, p. 13.

47. Ryan, Desmond, "'French Connection' put Roy Scheider on Fast Track," *Philadelphia Inquirer*, October 10, 2001.

48. "Many Are Touched by One Man's Life," *East Hampton Star*, September 6, 2001, Section 1, p. 1 [on-line]. Available: http://archive.easthamptonstar.com/ehquery/20010906/news1.html.

49. Reuters/Variety, "Gregory Greets 'Neighbor'" [on-line]. Available: http://dailynews.yahoo.com/h/nm/20010809/en/film-gregory_1.html.

50. "Time Lapse from Johnny Web" [on-line]. Available: http://www.scoopy.com/timelapse.com.

51. "Time Lapse," *Cahners Business Information Tipsheet*, October 22, 2001.

52. U. S. National Film Registry, "Titles" [on-line]. Available: http://www-2.cs.cmu.edu/unofficial/movies/NFR-titles.html.

53. *PR Newswire*, "Heintz Media Productions Announces the Feds: U.S. Postal Inspectors Series Debut," December 17, 2001 [on-line.] Available: http://www.prnewswire.com.

54. Polo.com Online Magazine.

55. "Roy Scheider," Hollywood Foreign Press Association Interview, August 13, 1983, p. 8.

56. Ibid., p. 10.

57. Hamill, Pete, "Recognizing Roy Scheider," p. 60.

Bibliography

Alvarez, Max Joseph, *Index to Motion Pictures Reviewed by* Variety, *1907–1980*, Metuchen, NJ: Scarecrow Press, 1982.

Andrews, Nigel, *Nigel Andrews on* Jaws, New York: Bloomsbury Publications, 1999.

Barrow, Kenneth, *Helen Hayes: First Lady of the American Theatre*, New York: Doubleday, 1985.

Base, Ron, and David Haslam, *The Movies of the Eighties*, New York: Portland House, 1990.

Beddow, Margery, *Bob Fosse's Hollywood*, New York: Heinemann, 1996.

Best Plays of 1960–1961, New York: Dodd, Mead, 1961. Edited by Louis Kronenberger.

Best Plays of 1962–1963, New York: Dodd, Mead, 1963. Edited by Henry Hewes.

Best Plays of 1963–1964, New York: Dodd, Mead, 1964. Edited by Henry Hewes.

Best Plays of 1964–1965, New York: Dodd, Mead, 1965. Edited by Henry Hewes.

Best Plays of 1965–1966, New York: Dodd, Mead, 1966. Edited by Otis L. Guernsey, Jr.

Best Plays of 1966–1967, New York: Dodd, Mead, 1967. Edited by Otis L. Guernsey, Jr.

Best Plays of 1967–1968, New York: Dodd, Mead, 1968. Edited by Otis L. Guernsey, Jr.

Best Plays of 1968–1969, New York: Dodd, Mead, 1969. Edited by Otis L. Guernsey, Jr.

Best Plays of 1969–1970, New York: Dodd, Mead, 1970. Edited by Otis L. Guernsey, Jr.

Best Plays of 1979–80, New York: Dodd, Mead, 1980. Edited by Otis L. Guernsey, Jr.

Biskind, Peter, *Easy Riders and Raging Bulls*, New York: Simon and Schuster, 1998.

Blake, Edith, *The Making of the Movie Jaws*, New York: Ballantine Books, 1975.

Bliss, Michael, *What Goes Around Comes Around: The Films of Jonathan Demme*, Carbondale, IL: Southern Illinois University Press, 1996.

Bookbinder, Robert, *Films of the Seventies*, Secaucus, NJ: Carol Publishing, 1982.

Brode, Douglas, *The Films of Dustin Hoffman*, New York: Citadel Press, 1983.

_____, *The Films of Steven Spielberg*, New York: Citadel Press, 1995.

_____, *Money, Women and Guns: Crime Movies from Bonnie and Clyde to the Present*, Secaucus, NJ: Carol Publishing, 1997.

Brooks, Tim, and Earle Marsh, *The Complete Directory to Prime Time Network and Cable TV Shows, 1946–Present*, New York: Ballantine Books, 2000.

Brown, David, *Let Me Entertain You*, New York: Warner Books, 1990.

Brownstone, David, *People in the News*, New York: Macmillan, 1991.

Burkhart, Jeff, and Bruce Stuart, *Hollywood's First Choices: How the Greatest Casting

Decisions Were Made, New York: Crown, 1994.

Champlin, Charles, *John Frankenheimer: A Conversation with Charles Champlin*, Burbank, CA: Riverwood Press, 1995.

Chunovic, Louis, *seaQuest DSV: The Official Publication of the Series*, London: Boxtree Limited, 1994.

Clagett, Thomas, *William Friedkin: Films of Aberration, Obsession and Reality*, Jefferson, NC: McFarland, 1990.

Clarke, Arthur C., and Peter Hyams, *The Odyssey File*, New York: Ballantine/Del Rey Books, 1984.

Clurman, Harold, *All People Are Famous*, New York: Harcourt Brace, 1974.

Cobb, Nancy, *How They Met*, New York: Turtle Bay Books, 1992.

Cocks, Jay, and David Denby, *Film 73/74: An Anthology by the National Society of Film Critics*, New York: Bobbs, Merrill and Company, 1974.

Copeland, Mary, *Soap Opera History*, New York: Mallard Books, 1991.

Culhane, John, *Special Effects in the Movies: How They Do It*, New York: Ballantine Books, 1981.

Daniel Blum's Theatre World, New York: Chilton, 1959–60, 1961–62, 1962–63, 1963–64, 1964–65.

Derry, Charles, *The Suspense Thriller: Films in the Shadow of Alfred Hitchcock*, Jefferson, NC: McFarland, 1988.

Druxman, Michael, *One Good Film Deserves Another*, New York: A. S. Barnes, 1977.

Dunaway, Faye, *Looking for Gatsby: My Life*, New York: Simon and Schuster, 1995.

Emery, Robert, *The Directors—Take One: In Their Own Words*, New York: TV Books, 1999.

_____, *The Directors—Take Two: In Their Own Words*, New York: TV Books, 2000.

Film Literature Index, Albany, NY: Film and Television Documentation Center, 1973–1981, 1983–1995.

Goldberg, Lee, et al., *Science Fiction Filmmaking in the 1980s*, Jefferson, NC: McFarland, 1995.

Goldman, William, *Adventures in the Screen Trade*, New York: Warner Books, 1983.

Gottfried, Martin, *All His Jazz*, New York: Bantam Books, 1990.

Gottlieb, Carl, *The Jaws Log*, New York: Dell Books, 1975.

Graham, Ellen, *The Growling Gourmet*, New York: Simon and Schuster, 1976.

Grubb, Kevin Boyd, *Razzle Dazzle: The Life and Work of Bob Fosse*, New York: St. Martin's Press, 1989.

Hanson, Patricia King, and Stephen L. Hanson, *Film Review Index, Vol. 2: 1950–1985*, Phoenix, AZ: Oryx Press, 1987.

Hayes, Helen, with Katherine Hatch, *My Life in Three Acts*, New York: Harcourt Brace Jovanovich, 1990.

Hunter, Allan, *Faye Dunaway*, New York: St. Martin's Press, 1986.

John Willis' Screen World, New York: Crown, 1972, 1973, 1974, 1976, 1977, 1978, 1979, 1980, 1983, 1984, 1985, 1987, 1990, 1991, 1992, 1995, 1998.

John Willis' Theatre World, New York: Crown, 1965–66, 1966–67, 1967–68, 1968–69, 1969–70, 1970–71, 1981.

Jones, Stephen, *The Essential Monster Movie Guide: A Century of Creature Features on Film, TV and Video*, New York: Billboard Books, 2000.

Kael, Pauline, *Deeper Into Movies*, New York: Little, Brown, 1969.

_____, *Reeling*, New York: Little, Brown, 1972.

_____, *Taking It All In*, New York: Holt, Rinehart and Winston, 1984.

Kay, Eddie, *Box Office Champs: The Most Popular Movies of the Last 50 Years*, New York: M & M Books, 1990.

Keefer, Louis E., *Italian Prisoners of War in America, 1942–1946: Captives or Allies?* New York: Praeger, 1992.

Lev, Peter, *American Films of the 70's: Conflicting Visions*, Austin: University of Texas Press, 2000.

Levy, Emanuel, *And the Winner Is... The History and Politics of the Oscar Awards*, New York: Ungar, 1987.

Loeb, Anthony, *Filmmakers in Conversation*, New York: Columbia College, 1982.

Loynd, Ray, *The Jaws 2 Log*, New York: Dell, 1978.

McAleer, Neil, *Arthur C. Clarke: The Authorized Biography*, Lincolnwood, IL: NTC Contemporary Publishing, 1992.

Marquis' Who's Who, *Who's Who in Entertainment*, 1989–1990, Wilmette, IL: Macmillan Directory Division, 1988.

Maychick, Diana, *Meryl Streep, The Reluctant Superstar*, New York: St. Martin's Press, 1992.

Monaco, James, *American Film Now: The People, the Power, the Money, the Movies*, New York: Oxford University Press, 1979.

Mott, Donald, *Steven Spielberg*, New York: Twayne, 1986.

New York Times Film Reviews, Volume 5, 1959–1968, New York: New York Times and Arno Press, 1970.

New York Times Film Reviews, 1969–1970, New York: New York Times and Arno Press, 1971.

New York Times Film Reviews, 1971–1972, New York: New York Times and Arno Press, 1973.

New York Times Film Reviews, 1973–1974, New York: New York Times and Arno Press, 1975.

New York Times Film Reviews, 1975–1976, New York: New York Times and Arno Press, 1977.

New York Times Film Reviews, 1977–1978, New York: New York Times and Arno Press, 1979.

New York Times Film Reviews, 1979–1980, New York: New York Times and Arno Press, 1981.

New York Times Film Reviews, 1981–1982, New York: New York Times and Arno Press, 1984.

New York Times Film Reviews, 1983–1984, New York: New York Times and Arno Press, 1988.

New York Times Film Reviews, 1985–1986, New York: New York Times and Arno Press, 1988.

New York Times Theatre Reviews, 1920–1970; Volume 7, 1960–66, Volume 8, 1967–70, Volume 9, Appendix-Index, New York: New York Times and Arno Press, 1971.

New York Times Theatre Reviews, 1979–1980, New York: New York Times and Arno Press, 1981.

Nowlan, Robert A., *Films of the Eighties*, Jefferson, NC: McFarland, 1991.

Osborne, Robert, *Academy Awards 1976 Oscar Annual*, La Habra, CA: ESE California, 1976.

_____, *60 Years of the Oscar: The Official History of the Academy Awards*, New York: Abbeville Press, 1989.

Perry, George, *Steven Spielberg: The Making of His Movies*, New York: Thunders Mouth Press, 1998.

Pfaff, Eugene, *Meryl Streep: A Critical Biography*, Jefferson, NC: McFarland, 1987.

Pratley, Gerald, *The Films of Frankenheimer: Forty Years in Film*, Cranbury, NJ: Lehigh University Press, 1998.

Reed, Rex, *Valentines and Vitriol*, New York: Dell, 1977.

Roberts, Jerry, and Stephen Gaydos, *Movie Talk from the Front Lines*, Jefferson, NC: McFarland, 1995.

Sarno, Art, *Academy Award Oscar 1980 Annual*, La Habra, CA: ESE California, 1980.

Segaloff, Nat, *Hurricane Billy: The Stormy Life and Films of William Friedkin*, New York: William Morrow, 1990.

Shewey, Don, *Caught in the Act: New York Actors Face to Face*, New York: New American Library, 1986.

Shulman, Arthur, and Roger Youman, *How Sweet It Was: Television a Pictorial Commentary*, New York: Bonanza Books, 1966.

Silver, Alain, *Film Noir*, New York: Overlook Press, 1979.

Silverberg, Ira, *Everything Is Permitted: The Making of Naked Lunch*, New York: Grove Weidenfield, 1992.

Smurthwaite, Nick, *The Meryl Streep Story*, New York: Beaufort Books, 1984.

Stewart, Joseph, *Viewers Guide to the Academy Awards, 1964–1994: Volume 2*, Santa Monica, CA: Santa Monica Press, 1995.

Taylor, Phillip, *Steven Spielberg: The Man, His Movies and Their Meaning*, New York: Continuum Publishing, 1994.

_____, *Steven Spielberg, The Man, His Movies and Their Meaning*, New York: Continuum Books, 1999. Expanded 3rd edition.

Terrace, Vincent, *The Complete Encyclopedia of Television Programs, Volume 2, L–Z*, New York: A. S. Barnes and Company, 1976.

Thomas, Nicholas, *International Dictionary of Film and Filmmakers: Volume 3: Actors and Actresses*, Detroit, MI: St. James Press, 1990.

Tomlinson, Doug, *Actors on Acting for the Screen: Roles and Collaborations*, New York: Garland Publishing, 1994.

Van Heerden, Bill, *Film and Television In-Jokes*, Jefferson, NC: McFarland, 1998.

[Variety], *Variety Action Movies*, New York: Mallard Press, 1992.

Wetzsteon, Ross, ed., *The Obie Winners: The Best of Off Broadway*, New York: Doubleday, 1980.

Wiley, Mason, and Damien Bona, *Inside Oscar: The Unofficial History of the Academy Awards*, New York: Ballantine Books, 1987.

Winn, Dilys, *Murder Ink: The Mystery Reader's Companion*, New York: Workman Press, 1977.

Young, Jordan, *Let Me Entertain You: Conversations with Show People*, Beverly Hills, CA: Moonstone Press, 1988.

Zinman, David, *50 Grand Movies of the 60's and 70's*, New York: Crown, 1986.

Index

Page numbers in *italics* have photographs.